D0322313

The Fenland Project, Number 11: The Wissey Embayment: Evidence for Pre-Iron Age Occupation Accumulated Prior to the Fenland Project

by Frances Healy

with contributions by
C. Balyuzi, M. Chapman, A. Hibbert, R.A. Housley,
P. Lawrance, R. H. Lennon, A.J. Legge, W. McIsaac,
G. Jones, P. Murphy, J.I. McKinley, D. Pert and R.E. Sims

illustrated by
Denise Derbyshire
with Steven Ashley, Frances Healy, John Hostler,
Margaret Mathews, Hoste Spalding, Jean Stokes and
Susan White

photographs by
David Wicks, Frank Curtis, the Cambridge University
Committee for Aerial Photography and the
British Tourist Authority

East Anglian Archaeology
Report No. 78, 1996

Fenland Project Committee
Field Archaeology Division, Norfolk Museums Service

EAST ANGLIAN ARCHAEOLOGY
REPORT NO. 78

Published by
Field Archaeology Division
Norfolk Museums Service
Union House
Gressenhall
Dereham
Norfolk NR20 4DR

in conjunction with
The Scole Archaeological Committee

Editor: David Buckley
Managing Editor: Jenny Glazebrook

Scole Editorial Sub-committee:
David Buckley, County Archaeologist, Essex Planning Department
Keith Wade, County Archaeological Officer, Suffolk Planning Department
Peter Wade-Martins, County Field Archaeologist, Norfolk Museums Service
Stanley West

Set in Times Roman by Joan Daniells using ®Ventura Publisher
Printed by Geerings of Ashford Ltd., Ashford, Kent

© FIELD ARCHAEOLOGY DIVISION, NORFOLK MUSEUMS SERVICE

ISBN 0 905594 20 7

For details of *East Anglian Archaeology*, see inside front cover

This volume is published with the aid of a grant from English Heritage

Cover:
Frank Curtis with a small part of his collection and a plan of burials in
Hill Close, Feltwell (Site 5188/c1). Photo: British Tourist Authority

Contents

List of Contents   v
List of Plates   vi
List of Figures   vi
List of Tables   viii
Contents of Microfiche   viii
List of Contributors   ix
Acknowledgements   x
Summary   x
Abbreviations   x
References to sites and finds   xi
Chronology   xi
Correction   xi

1. Introduction
I.   The survey area   1
        I.1. Location   1
        I.2. History of local research   1
II.   The present volume   1
III.   Collectors, collections and recording   3
        III.1. Frank Curtis   3
        III.2. Other collectors   4
        III.3. The Norfolk sites and monuments record   4
        III.4. The gazetteer   5
        III.5. The appendices   6
        III.6. Caveat   6

2. Shifting scenery
I.   Geology   7
II.   Flandrian fluctuations   7
        II.1. Breckland   7
        II.2. Fenland   7
III.   Wildlife   9
IV.   Modern topography   10

3. Living sites
I.   Hockwold cum Wilton Old OS fields
        466, 613, 614 and 616   11
        I.1. Site 24866 ('site 8') and its components   11
        I.2. Site 5373 (22)   15
        I.3. Site 5308/c2 (62)   15
        I.4. Site 5308/c1 (63)   16
        I.5. Site 5308/c3 (69)   16
        I.6. Site 5308/c4 (61/68)   16
        I.7. Site 5332 (66)   17
        I.8. Site 5324 (93)   19
        I.9. Site 5333 (95/97)   19
        I.10. Site 5308/c5 (96)   19
        I.11. Test pits 1981   19
II.   The remainder of the survey area   24
        II.1. Site 24837. Hockwold Fen, unlocated   24
        II.2. Hockwold cum Wilton. Site 5423 (9)   24
        II.3. Hockwold cum Wilton. Site 5374 (19)   26
        II.4. Hockwold cum Wilton. Site 5316/c2, c5, c6
              ('site 7188')   26
        II.5. Hockwold cum Wilton. Site 5316/c7, c8
              ('site 7088')   27
        II.6. Hockwold cum Wilton. Site 5394. Sluice Drove   27
        II.7. Hockwold cum Wilton. Site 5317/c3 (23).
              Corner Ground   27

II.8. Hockwold cum Wilton. Site 5317/c2 (25).
      Corner Ground   28
II.9. Feltwell. Site 4921/c1. Glebe Farm   28
III.   Discussion   28

4. Bodies and burials
I.   Early Bronze Age skeletal remains   30
        I.1. Methwold. Site 2586. 'Nancy' or 'the
             Southery Fen female'   30
        I.2. Methwold. Site 2825   30
        I.3. Feltwell. Site 5188/c1. Hill Close   30
        I.4. Methwold. Site 2550. Hemplands Farm   36
        I.5. Methwold. Site 2542. Methwold Severalls   36
II.   Dating, by F. Healy and R.A. Housley   37
III.   Discussion   38
        III.1. Modes of burial   38
        III.2. Other possibly prehistoric human remains
               from the survey area   41
        III.3. Beyond the survey area   41

5. Objects, everyday and exceptional
I.   Metalwork   43
        I.1. Early Bronze Age   43
        I.2. Middle Bronze Age   43
        I.3. Late Bronze Age   43
        I.4. Discussion   47
        I.5. Catalogue of illustrated metalwork   48
II.   Lithics   50
        II.1. Raw materials   50
        II.2. Hockwold cum Wilton. Old OS fields
              466, 613, 614 and 616   53
        II.3. The survey area as a whole   53
        II.4. Discussion   62
        II.5. Terms used in describing lithic material   75
        II.6. Catalogue of illustrated lithic material   79
III.   Pottery and fired clay   95
        III.1. Hockwold cum Wilton old OS fields 466,
               613, 614 and 616   95
        III.2. The survey area as a whole   105
        III.3. Discussion   112
        III.4. Catalogue of illustrated pottery   117
IV.   Worked bone and antler   157
        IV.1. Hockwold cum Wilton old OS fields 466,
              613, 614 and 616   157
        IV.2. The survey area as a whole   157
        IV.3. Discussion   157
        IV.4. Catalogue of illustrated worked bone
              and antler   158
V.   Wood   160
        V.1. The Methwold Bow. Site 4460   161

6. People, animals and vegetation
I.   Human skeletal remains
        by Jacqueline I. McKinley   162
        I.1. Introduction   162
        I.2. Method   162
        I.3. Results   162
        I.4. Discussion   167

II.	Dietary reconstruction by means of stable isotope analysis of bone by Rosemary H. Lennon	169
	II.1. Principles	169
	II.2. Methods	170
	II.3. Discussion	171
	II.4. Conclusions	171
III.	Animal bone	171
	III.1. Hockwold cum Wilton. Site 24866 ('site 8') and other sites investigated in 1959–62 by C. Balyuzi, M. Chapman, W. McIsaac, G. Jones and D. Pert with A.J. Legge	171
	III.2. Sites investigated in 1964–67 by P. Lawrance	172
IV.	Sediments and miscellaneous biological remains from test pits dug in Site 5308/c4 (68) in 1981 by Peter Murphy	174
	IV.1. Introduction	174
	IV.2. The deposits	174
	IV.3. Biological remains	174
	IV.4. Discussion	174
V.	Palynological evidence	175

	V.1. Site 2542. Methwold Severalls by F.A. Hibbert	175
	V.2. The Methwold Bow. Site 4460 by R.E. Sims	175

7. The story so far...

I.	Record and reality	
	I.1. Archaeological visibility	177
	I.2. Settlement history?	177
II.	Settlement character	178
	II.1. Pre-Fen Clay	178
	II.2. Post Fen Clay	178
III.	The contents of stores, drawers, garden sheds and display cases	180
	III.1. Fine flint and stone objects	180
	III.2. Beakers	180
	III.3. Metalwork	181
	III.4. Human remains	181

Bibliography	182
Index, by Peter Gunn	191
Microfiche	

List of Plates

Pl.I	Blackdyke Farm, Hockwold cum Wilton: Air Photograph	11
Pl.II	Blackdyke Farm, Hockwold cum Wilton: Sketch map by Frank Curtis	12
Pl.III	Old OS fields 466, 613–4, 616, Hockwold cum Wilton: Sketch map by Frank Curtis	13
Pl.IV	Old OS fields 466, 613–4, 616, Hockwold cum Wilton: Sketch map by Frank Curtis	16
Pl.V	Hockwold cum Wilton: The excavation of a 'fire pit', 1964	17
Pl.VI	Hockwold cum Wilton: Site 5332 (66), 1965	17

Pl.VII	Hill Close Feltwell: Section by Frank Curtis	32
Pl.VIII	Hemplands Farm, Methwold (Site 2550): skeleton	37
Pl.IX	Feltwell Fen (Site 5296): bone beads found 1876	157
Pl.X	Hill Close, Feltwell (Site 5188/c1), burial 7	164
Pl.XI	Methwold (Site 2585). Frontal vaults of two juveniles	165
Pl.XII	Methwold Severalls (Site 2542), burial 5	166

List of Figures

Fig.0	Location of the survey area, with sites mentioned in text	xii
Fig.1	The survey area today	2
Fig.2	Surface geology	8
Fig.3	Settlement and miscellaneous excavations	14
Fig.4	Hockwold cum Wilton old OS fields 466, 613, 614, and 616	15
Fig.5	Hockwold cum Wilton. Site 5308/c4 (61/68). Plan and section	18
Fig.6	Hockwold cum Wilton. Site 5308/c4 (61/68). Distribution of lithic material	19
Fig.7	Hockwold cum Wilton. Site 5308/c4 (61/68). Distributions of pottery and fired clay and of sherds from dispersed vessels	20

Fig.8	Hockwold cum Wilton. Site 5332 (66). Plan and section	21
Fig.9	Hockwold cum Wilton. Site 5333 (97). Plan and section	21
Fig.10	Hockwold cum Wilton. Site 5333 (97). Distribution of lithic material	22
Fig.11	Hockwold cum Wilton. Site 5333 (97). Distributions of pottery and fired clay and of sherds from dispersed vessels	22
Fig.12	Hockwold cum Wilton. Site 5308/c5 (96). Plan and section	23
Fig.13	Hockwold cum Wilton. Site 5308/c5 (96). Distribution of lithic material	24
Fig.14	Hockwold cum Wilton. Site 5308/c5 (96). Distributions of

	pottery and fired clay and of sherds from dispersed vessels	25
Fig.15	Hockwold cum Wilton. Site 5308/c4 (68). Location of 1981 test pits, and section drawings	26
Fig.16	'Hockwold Fen'. Site 24837. Unlocated find of an oven or hearth and a smaller hearth, 1960	27
Fig.17	Funerary evidence	31
Fig.18	Hill Close, Feltwell (Site 5188/c1). Plan of 1965 excavation	34
Fig.19	Hill Close, Feltwell (Site 5188/c1). Aspects of the excavation and detail of burial 7	35
Fig.20	Hemplands Farm, Methwold (Site 2550). Plan of 1967 excavation, showing disturbed skeleton	36
Fig.21	Methwold Severalls (Site 2542). Plan of 1968 excavation	38
Fig.22	Calibrated age ranges for radiocarbon determinations on human remains	40
Fig.23	Distribution of Early Bronze Age metalwork	44
Fig.24	Distribution of Middle Bronze Age metalwork	45
Fig.25	Distribution of Late Bronze Age metalwork	46
Fig.26	Bronze Age metalwork from various site in the survey area	49
Fig.27	Late Bronze Age sword from Site 24114	50
Fig.28	Dimensions of complete, unretouched flakes from Sites 5308/c4 (61/68), 5333 (95/97) and 5308/c5 (96)	56
Fig.29	Proportions of complete, unretouched flakes from Sites 5308/c4 (61/68), 5333 (95/97) and 5308/c5 (96)	57
Fig.30	Non-metrical characteristics of complete, unretouched flakes from Sites 5308/c4 61/68), 5333 (95/97) and 5308/c5 (96)	57
Fig.31	Dimensions of complete flake scrapers from Sites 24866 ('site 8'), Sites 5308/c4 61/68), 5333 (95/97) and 5308/c5 (96)	58
Fig.32	Proportions of complete flake scrapers from Site 24866 ('site 8'), 5308/c4 (61/68), 5333 (95/97) and 5308/c5 (96)	59
Fig.33	Non-metrical characteristics of complete flake scrapers from Sites 24866 ('site 8'), 5308/c4 (61/68), 5333 (95/97) and 5308/c5 (96)	59
Fig.34	Distribution of Mesolithic material	64
Fig.35	Distribution of leaf arrowheads	65
Fig.36	Distribution of chisel arrowheads	66
Fig.37	Distribution of oblique arrowheads	67
Fig.38	Distribution of barbed and tanged arrowheads	68
Fig.39	Distribution of flint knives	69
Fig.40	Distribution of flint axes	70
Fig.41	Distribution of stone axes	71
Fig.42	Distribution of stone artefacts other than axes and saddle querns	72
Fig.43	Distribution of saddle querns	73
Fig.44	Lithic material from Site 24866 ('site 8')	78
Fig.45	Lithic material from Site 24866 ('site 8')	79
Fig.46	Lithic material recovered from Hockwold cum Wilton in 1959–60	80
Fig.47	Lithic material from Site 5373 (22)	81
Fig.48	Lithic material from Site 5308/c4 (61/68)	82
Fig.49	Lithic material from Site 5308/c4 (61/68)	83
Fig.50	Lithic material from Site 5308/c4 (61/68)	84
Fig.51	Lithic material from Site 5332 (66)	85
Fig.52	Lithic material from Site 5333 (95/97)	86
Fig.53	Lithic material from Site 5308/c5 (96)	87
Fig.54	Lithic material from Glebe Farm, Feltwell, Hill Close, Feltwell and Methwold Severalls	88
Fig.55	Stone artefacts from various findspots in Feltwell	89
Fig.56	Stone artefacts from various findspots in Feltwell	90
Fig.57	Lithic material from various findspots in Feltwell	91
Fig.58	Lithic material from various findspots in Feltwell and Hockwold cum Wilton	92
Fig.59	Stone axes from Hockwold cum Wilton and Methwold	93
Fig.60	Stone implements from Hilgay, Weeting with Broomhill and the survey area at large	94
Fig. 61	Composition of larger pottery collections from Hockwold cum Wilton	98
Fig.62	Rim diameters of pots from Hockwold cum Wilton	99
Fig.63	Major morphological character-istics of the most frequent pottery styles from Hockwold cum Wilton	100
Fig.64	Decorative techniques on identified pots from Hockwold cum Wilton	101
Fig.65	Decorative techniques on unattributed sherds from Hockwold cum Wilton	102
Fig.66	Decorative motifs of comb-impressed and incised Beaker pottery from Hockwold cum Wilton	103
Fig.67	Distribution of Neolithic Bowl pottery	107
Fig.68	Distribution of Later Neolithic pottery	108
Fig.69	Distribution of Beaker pottery	109
Fig.70	Distribution of Food Vessel and Collared Urn	110
Fig.71	Distribution of other Bronze Age pottery	111
Fig.72	Pottery from Site 24866 ('site 8')	119

Fig.73	Pottery from Site 24866 ('site 8')	120
Fig.74	Pottery from Site 24866 ('site 8')	121
Fig.75	Pottery from Hockwold cum Wilton Site 24866 ('site 8')	122
Fig.76	Pottery from various findspots in Hockwold cum Wilton	123
Fig.77	Pottery from Sites 5439 (44) and 5309 (48)	124
Fig.78	Pottery from Sites 5309 (48) and 5310 (49)	125
Fig.79	Pottery from Sites 5311 + 5312 (50 + 51)	127
Fig.80	Pottery from Sites 5311 + 5312 (50 + 51)	128
Fig.81	Pottery from Sites 5311 + 5312 (50 + 51)	129
Fig.82	Pottery from Sites 5311 + 5312 (50 + 51)	130
Fig.83	Pottery from Sites 5311 + 5312 (50 + 51)	131
Fig.84	Pottery from Sites 5311 + 5312 (50 + 51)	132
Fig.85	Pottery from Sites 5311 + 5312 (50 + 51)	133
Fig.86	Pottery from Site 5373 (22)	135
Fig.87	Pottery from Site 5373 (22)	136
Fig.88	Pottery from Site 5373 (22)	137
Fig.89	Pottery from Site 5308/c4 (61/68)	139
Fig.90	Pottery from Site 5308/c4 (61/68)	140
Fig.91	Pottery from Site 5308/c4 (61/68)	141
Fig.92	Pottery from Site 5308/c4 (61/68)	142
Fig.93	Pottery from Site 5308/c4 (61/68)	143
Fig.94	Pottery from Site 5308/c4 (61/68)	144
Fig.95	Pottery from Site 5332 (66)	145
Fig.96	Pottery from Site 5333 (95/97)	147
Fig.97	Pottery from Site 5333 (95/97)	148
Fig.98	Pottery from Site 5333 (95/97)	149
Fig.99	Pottery from Site 5308/c5 (96)	150
Fig.100	Pottery from Site 5308/c5 (96)	151
Fig.101	Pottery from Sites 5308/c5 (96) and 5364 (75)	152
Fig.102	Pottery from Glebe Farm and Hill Close, Feltwell and Hockwold Fen	153
Fig.103	Pottery from various findspots in Hockwold cum Wilton	154
Fig.104	Pottery from various findspots in Hockwold cum Wilton	155
Fig.105	Pottery from various findspots in Methwold	156
Fig.106	Worked bone and antler from Hockwold cum Wilton	158
Fig.107	Worked bone and antler from Hockwold cum Wilton	159
Fig.108	Worked bone and antler from Feltwell and Methwold	160
Fig.109	The Methwold bow (Site 4460)	161
Fig.110	Proportions of main species identified from Site 24866 ('site 8')	172
Fig.111	Sheep/goat survival chart for Site 24866 ('site 8')	173
Fig.112	Cattle bone survival chart for Site 24866 ('site 8')	173
Fig.113	The Methwold bow (Site 4460): 1971 pollen analysis	175

List of Tables

Table 1	Radiocarbon determinations on human skeletal material	39
Table 2	Modes of recovery of Bronze Age metalwork	47
Table 3	Petrological identifications	52
Table 4	Hockwold cum Wilton: Raw material in main collections	54
Table 5	Hockwold cum Wilton: Composition of main collections	54
Table 6	Hockwold cum Wilton: Cores of main collections	54
Table 7	Hockwold cum Wilton: Retouched pieces of main collections	55
Table 8	Arrowheads	61
Table 9	Flint knives	61
Table 10	Axes	62
Table 11	Stone artefacts other than axes and saddle querns	62
Table 12	Hockwold cum Wilton: Pottery and fired clay	96–7
Table 13	Approximate chronology of Neolithic and Bronze Age pottery styles in East Anglia	113–116
Table 14	Summary of age and sex determinations	168
Table 15	Sex, age and isotope ratios	170
Table 16	Proportions of species from Site 24866 ('site 8')	172
Table 17	Unworked animal bone from sites investigated in 1964–67	173

Contents of Microfiche

Introduction		1:A6
Concordance of county numbers, old Ordnance Survey field numbers, and Curtis field numbers		1:A12
Gazetteer		
	Feltwell	1C:6
	Hilgay	2F:9
	Hockwold cum Wilton	2G:3
	Methwold	4B:13

Northwold   4G:9
Southery   5A:3
Weeting with Broomhill   5A:13
Survey area unlocated   5C:3
Appendix 1.   Sites investigated in Hockwold
               cum Wilton OS 466 and 616 in
               1959–60   5C:8
Appendix 2.   Other settlement and
               miscellaneous excavations   5D:6
Appendix 3.   Funerary evidence   5F:7
Appendix 4.   Early Bronze Age metalwork   5G:9
Appendix 5.   Middle Bronze Age metalwork   6A:7
Appendix 6.   Late Bronze Age metalwork   6C:10
Appendix 7.   Indeterminate Bronze Age
               metalwork   6E:3
Appendix 8.   Mesolithic and ?Mesolithic
               material   6E:9
Appendix 9.   Leaf-shaped arrowheads   7A:8
Appendix 10.   Petit tranchet arrowheads   7G:7
Appendix 11.   Chisel arrowheads   7G:10
Appendix 12.   Oblique arrowheads   8C:3
Appendix 13.   Barbed and tanged arrowheads   8F:1
Appendix 14.   Tanged arrowheads   9E:2
Appendix 15.   Triangular arrowheads   9E:10
Appendix 16.   Hollow-based arrowheads   9G:5
Appendix 17.   Plano-convex knives   9G:11
Appendix 18.   Scale-flaked knives   10A:14
Appendix 19.   Discoidal knives   10D:1
Appendix 20.   Flint daggers   10D:8

Appendix 21.   Single-piece flint sickles   10E:3
Appendix 22.   Flint chisels   10E:7
Appendix 23.   Flint axes   10F:2
Appendix 24.   Stone axes   11B:5
Appendix 25.   Stone artefacts other than axes
               and saddle querns   11D:11
Appendix 26.   Saddle querns   11G:11
Appendix 27.   Neolithic Bowl pottery   12A:8
Appendix 28.   Later Neolithic pottery   12B:10
Appendix 29.   Beaker pottery   12B:13
Appendix 30.   Food Vessel, Food Vessel Urn
               and Collared Urn pottery   12F:14
Appendix 31.   Other Bronze Age pottery   12G:13
Appendix 32.   Indeterminate pottery   13B:6
Appendix 33.   Worked bone and antler   13C:4
Appendix 34.   Human skeletal remains:
               identification details by
               Jacqueline McKinley   13E:7
Appendix 35.   Unworked animal bone from
               settlement sites in Hockwold
               cum Wilton.
               A. Sites investigated in 1959–62,
               identifications by Chris Balyuzi,
               Marion Chapman, Wendy
               McIsaac, Graham Jones and
               Diana Pert with A.J. Legge   14B:9
               B. Sites investigated in
               1964–67, identifications by
               Peter Lawrance   14B:12

Contributors

Steven Ashley, F.C.S.D., A.I.F.A.,
Illustrator, Norfolk Archaeological Unit

Chris Balyuzi, Marion Chapman, Graham Jones, Wendy McIsaac and Diana Pert,
Formerly students at the Centre for Extra-Mural Studies, Birkbeck College, University of London

Denise Derbyshire,
Former Illustrator, Norfolk Museums Service

Frances Healy, B.Sc. (Econ.), Ph.D., M.I.F.A., F.S.A.,
Freelance prehistorian

F. Alan Hibbert, B.Sc., M.A., Ph.D., C. Biol., F.I.Biol.,
President, Institute of Biology, Queensberry Place, London

John Hostler,
Former Illustrator, Norfolk Archaeological Unit

Rupert A. Housley, B.Sc., Ph.D., F.S.A.,
Department of Archaeology, University of Glasgow

Peter Lawrance, B.Sc.,
Former Assistant Keeper of Natural History, Norwich Castle Museum

A.J. Legge, M.A.,
Reader in Environmental Archaeology, Centre for Extra-Mural Studies, Birkbeck College, University of London

Rosemary H. Lennon, B. Sc., Ph.D.,
Formerly of the Department of Archaeology, University of Edinburgh

Margaret Mathews, B.A., Dip. Archaeol.,
Technician, Department of Archaeology, University of Reading

Jacqueline I. McKinley, B.Tech., M.I.F.A.,
Osteoarchaeologist, Wessex Archaeology

Peter Murphy, M.Phil.,
Environmental Archaeologist, Centre of East Anglian Studies, University of East Anglia

Richard E. Sims, M.Sc.,
Colfox School, Bridport, Dorset

Hoste Spalding, Dip. Memb. S.I.A.D.,
Former Illustrator, Norfolk Archaeological Unit

Jean Stokes,
Former Illustrator, Norfolk Museums Service

Susan G. White, A.A.I.S., Dip. Memb. S.I.A.D.,
Senior Illustrator, Norfolk Landscape Archaeology

David Wicks,
Photographer, Norfolk Archaeological Unit

Acknowledgements

Funding, for which the writer is most grateful, was provided initially by the Manpower Services Commission, subsequently by English Heritage, Norfolk County Council and the British Academy. Radiocarbon determinations on human skeletal material were funded by an award from the British Academy's Fund for Applied Science in Archaeology.

Thanks are gladly given to Mr E. B. Secker, Mr M.J.Younge, the late Mrs Alice Curtis and the late Mr A.J. Orange, all of Feltwell, as well as to Mr J.D. Wortley of Methwold, who were more than generous with their own time and with access to their collections.

The work would have been impossible without the unfailing co-operation and patience of present and past staff in Norwich Castle Museum, chief among them Barbara Green, Bill Milligan, Peter Lawrance and Dr Tony Stuart. Staff in King's Lynn Museum, Mildenhall Museum, Moyses Hall Museum in Bury St Edmunds, and the Cambridge University Museum of Archaeology and Ethnology have also provided access to collections and records.

Present and past staff of Norfolk Field Archaeology Division have contributed labour, support and advice. Particular thanks are due to Joan Daniells, Denise Derbyshire, the late Tony Gregory, David Gurney, Andrew Lawson, Margaret Mathews, Bob Silvester and John Wymer.

Invaluable discussion, advice, encouragement and comment on the text at various stages of its composition have been provided by Dr Helen Bamford, David Buckley, Dr Ian Longworth, Edward Martin, Dr Stuart Needham, Dr David Tomalin and Dr Martyn Waller.

All the authors of specialist reports have been painstaking, conscientious and generous of their own time.

Permission to publish photographs has kindly been granted by the British Tourist Authority (cover) and the Cambridge University Committee for Aerial Photography (Pl. I).

Jenny Glazebrook and Joan Daniells have been patient, painstaking and forbearing in the process of production.

Summary

This volume attempts to document and synthesise the overwhelming and intractable mass of evidence for pre-Iron Age activity accumulated over the decades preceding the inception of the Fenland Project from the Norfolk fen edge between the rivers Wissey and Little Ouse. This area is the northernmost tip of a more extensive zone of dense Neolithic and Bronze Age settlement on the south-eastern edge of the Fenland Basin.

The picture which emerges conforms to the recent work of the Fenland Project in indicating substantial Early or Middle Neolithic settlement before the Fen Clay transgression and substantial Beaker and Early Bronze Age settlement after it, with relatively little Later Neolithic activity in the period when the transgression was at its maximum and virtually no Middle or Late Bronze Age settlement in the wetter conditions which obtained after c. 1100 cal. BC. Settlement assemblages excavated in the 1960s contrast with more recent collections in the large quantities of Beaker and especially Early Bronze Age pottery which they contain. The artefactual and environmental records together suggest that fen edge settlements were located to maximise the resources of upland and of peat fen.

Four finds of human skeletons from the fen have been radiocarbon-dated to the Early Bronze Age. The long-observed concentration of fine and exotic flint, stone and bronze objects in the area is interpreted partly in terms of wealth and display, partly in terms of deliberate deposition, the latter being especially appropriate to Middle and Late Bronze Age metalwork in the apparent absence of contemporary fen edge settlement.

Abbreviations

These are employed principally in the microfiched Gazetteer and Appendices, but some also occur in the text.

Parishes

FWL	Feltwell
HLG	Hilgay
HCW	Hockwold cum Wilton
MTW	Methwold
NWD	Northwold
SRY	Southery
WWB	Weeting with Broomhill

Site type

CMK	cropmark
EWK	earthwork
SMK	soilmark
SS	surface scatter
CF	chance find
EXC	excavation

Periods

MES	Mesolithic
EMES	Earlier Mesolithic
LMES	Later Mesolithic

NEO	Neolithic		USAF	United States Air Force

NEO	Neolithic
EMNEO	Early/Middle Neolithic
LNEO	Later Neolithic
LNEBA	Later Neolithic/Early Bronze Age
BKR	Beaker
BA	Bronze Age
EBA	Early Bronze Age
MBA	Middle Bronze Age
LBA	Later Bronze Age
IA	Iron Age
R-B	Romano-British
Indet.	Indeterminate

Institutions

BM	British Museum
CUCAP	Cambridge University Collection of Aerial Photography
CUM	Cambridge University Museum of Archaeology and Ethnology ICM Ipswich City Museum
KLM	King's Lynn Museum
MM	Mildenhall Museum
MH	Moyses Hall Museum, Bury St.Edmunds
NCM	Norwich Castle Museum
NMR	National Monuments Record
OS	Ordnance Survey
SMR	Norfolk Sites and Monuments Record

USAF	United States Air Force

Pottery Styles

BA	Indeterminate Bronze Age
BKR	Beaker
CU	Collared Urn
FV	Food Vessel
FVU	Food Vessel Urn
GW	Grooved Ware
IA	Iron Age
Indet.	Indeterminate prehistoric
LBA	Late Bronze Age
LBKR	Late style Beaker
LNEBA	Indeterminate Later Neolithic/ Early Bronze Age
MBA	Middle Bronze Age
MBKR	Middle style Beaker
NB	Early/Middle Neolithic Bowl
PET	Peterborough Ware
RBKR	Rusticated Beaker

Pottery Decoration

BW	'Barbed wire'
FN	Fingernail-impressed
FP	Finger-pinched
FT	Fingertip-impressed

References to Sites and Finds

Norfolk sites and finds are generally referred to by their serial numbers in the county sites and monuments record, e.g. 'Site 4460' or 'Site 5188/c1'. For those within the survey area old Ordnance Survey field numbers are often added to facilitate reference to the gazetteer and appendices. In the case of material from the most prolific part of Hockwold cum Wilton parish (the fields shown in Plate II) county numbers are followed by museum map numbers (Ch. 1.III.3), e.g. 'Site 5308/c1 (63)', since these numbers have already been used by several authors, including Bamford (1982) and Gibson (1982).

The microfiched gazetteer and appendices are ordered by old Ordnance Survey field numbers within parish (Ch. 1.III.4–5). A concordance between SMR numbers, field numbers and some of the other notations which have been applied to the material documented here precedes the gazetteer.

Chronology

Uncalibrated radiocarbon determinations are expressed in years BP. Calibrated radiocarbon determinations are expressed cal. BC at a confidence range of 68% and have been calculated using CALIB version 2.1 (Stuiver and Reimer 1987). Broad chronological ranges are expressed in approximate years cal. BC.

Correction

A grid reference previously published for the 'Sahara' site excavated by Lady Grace Briscoe at Lakenheath, Suffolk (East Anglian Archaeology 16, 138) is erroneous. The Suffolk Sites and Monuments Record gives the correct grid reference as TL 733 831.

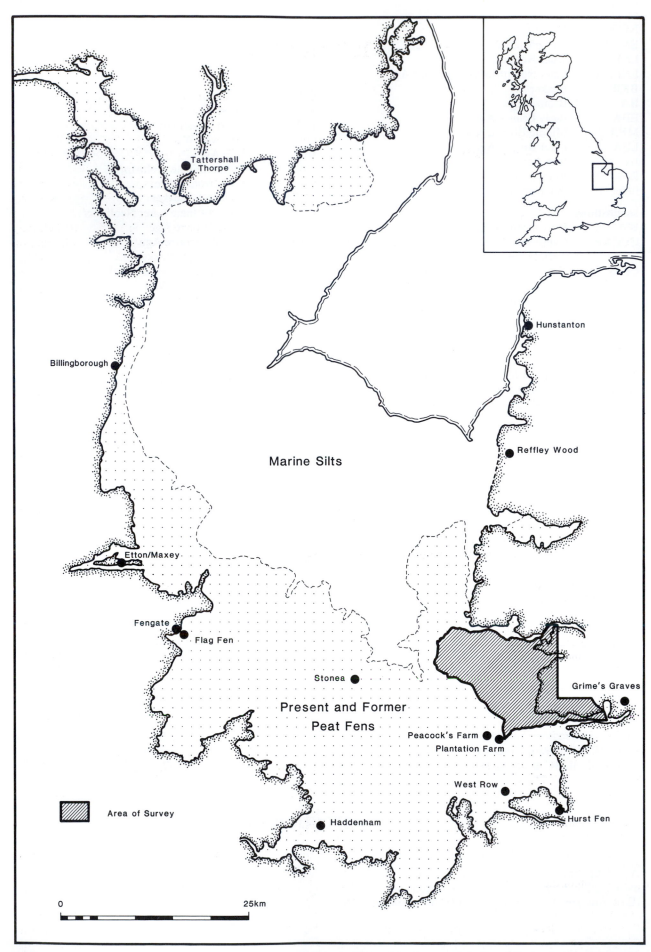

Figure 0 Location of the survey area, showing selected sites mentioned in the text. Landward limit of silts after Darby (1983, fig. 140)

1. Introduction

I. The survey area

I.1. Location

The area described in this volume lies in the south-east of the Fenland basin (Fig. 0), bounded to the north and south by the present courses of the rivers Wissey and Little Ouse, and comprising varying extents of the Norfolk parishes of Hilgay, Southery, Northwold, Methwold, Feltwell, Hockwold cum Wilton, and Weeting with Broomhill (Fig. 1). Its eastern, Breckland, part is formed by chalk upland, cut by the Little Ouse valley, and its western, Fenland, part by present and former peat fen, broken principally by the island of Hilgay and Southery (Fig. 2). Today the division between upland and fen is marked by the cut-off channel (Fig. 1), constructed in the 1960s to intercept some of the flow of rivers entering the fen from the upland and carry it to the Wash. The survey area forms the northernmost part of a zone of fen and fen margin between the rivers Cam and Wissey long known to be particularly rich in Neolithic and Bronze Age artefacts.

I.2. History of local research

Like the rest of the south-eastern fens, the area first came to antiquarian notice in the course of the nineteenth century as an exceptionally rich collecting ground, as artefacts discovered during peat-cutting, drainage and cultivation were acquired by museums and private collectors. Many of the bronzes and stone implements which blacken this corner of modern distribution maps came to light in this period. Fox's seminal *Archaeology of the Cambridge Region*, published in 1923, translated the already vast accumulation of artefacts from the south-eastern fens into human terms and demonstrated the potential of the area for settlement studies. Since he was based in Cambridge and depended on a bicycle for transport, the Norfolk fens were peripheral to his synthesis. This bias was perpetuated in the work of the Fenland Research Committee, founded in 1932 and also Cambridge-based (Godwin 1978, 45–49). The researches of its members were focussed on the Cambridgeshire and Suffolk fens, with only occasional forays into Norfolk to investigate the sites of particular discoveries. So it was that, while the same topography, conditions and archaeology obtained to the north of the Little Ouse as to the south, the classic excavations of Neolithic and Bronze Age sites in the Fenland, such as Plantation Farm and Peacock's Farm, Shippea Hill (Clark 1933; Clark *et al.* 1935), all lay in Cambridgeshire or Suffolk.

After the second world war, many pasture fields in the survey area were brought into cultivation, while the construction of the cut-off channel in the 1960s not only involved large-scale earth-moving but accelerated peat wastage by improving drainage. Archaeological response to these developments was slight, consisting almost entirely of piecemeal excavation of already-known sites on the line of the cut-off channel, among them a ditched enclosure system in Hockwold cum Wilton excavated in 1961–2 (Salway 1967). The haphazard tally of con-temporary discoveries reported to Norwich Castle and King's Lynn Museums by members of the public shows that countless prehistoric sites were being exposed. Museum staff, with almost non-existent resources for fieldwork, struggled to record and salvage as much information as possible.

In this period, Mr W.F. (Frank) Curtis of Feltwell, whose work is described in section III.1 below, almost single-handedly excavated and recorded sites which would have otherwise been destroyed without record, showing that Shippea Hill-like settlements extended into Norfolk. These excavations were concentrated in a block of four fields in Hockwold cum Wilton (Fig. 4: old OS nos 466, 613, 614 and 616), two of the sites in which have already been published by Bamford (1982). He and many others also continued to collect.

Systematic fieldwalking was undertaken towards the end of the 1970s by the late Tony Gregory, then of the Norfolk Archaeological Unit, over an area of fen edge in Hockwold cum Wilton and southern Feltwell extending up the Little Ouse valley into Weeting with Broomhill. With the inception of the Fenland Project in the early 1980s the western, fenward part of this area was incorporated in the wider swathe of Norfolk peat fen subjected to extensive fieldwalking survey by Bob Silvester (Silvester 1991).

II. The present volume

The project was undertaken in 1979 as an adjunct to Tony Gregory's survey. Its initial aims were to publish those of the Beaker and Bronze Age settlement sites excavated by Frank Curtis in Hockwold cum Wilton fields 466, 613, 614, and 616 which had not already been studied by Bamford, and to integrate them with the accumulation of contemporary stray finds from the area in museum and private collections. The latter proved inexhaustible. The material incorporated here is no more than a hint of what remains unrecorded. When more extensive fieldwalking was undertaken in the course of the Fenland Project the area covered by this work was expanded to its present limits so that it would complement Bob Silvester's survey. The gazetteer records finds of Mesolithic to Bronze Age date made in the survey area up to the end of October 1987, excluding Fenland Project data.

Work on the volume has been intermittent, and some aspects of it reflect the age of both project and author. These are more than counterbalanced by the capacity to address questions which were not formulated, or at best half-formulated, when the project was conceived. Bob Silvester's work has provided the opportunity to compare the results of two centuries of accidental discovery and acquisitive collecting with those of a few years of systematic field survey (Healy 1991a, 136–138). In the process it has been possible to consider issues such as the following, which are discussed in Chapter 7:

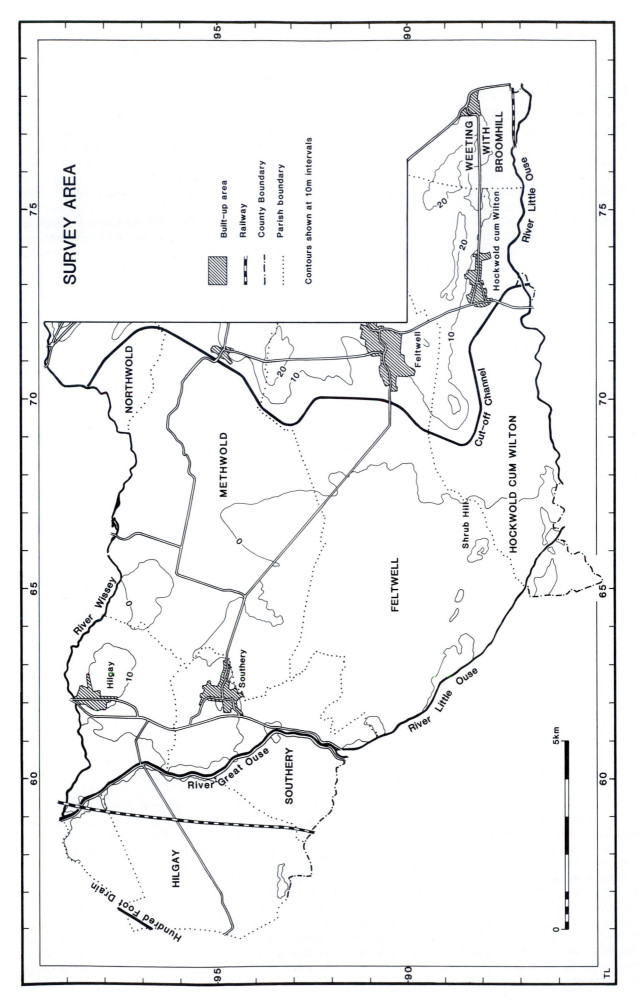

SURVEY AREA

Built-up area

Railway

County Boundary

Parish boundary

Contours shown at 10m intervals

WEETING WITH BROOMHILL

Hockwold cum Wilton

River Little Ouse

NORTHWOLD

METHWOLD

Feltwell

Cut-off Channel

HOCKWOLD CUM WILTON

Shrub Hill

FELTWELL

River Little Ouse

River Wissey

Hilgay

Southery

SOUTHERY

River Great Ouse

HILGAY

Hundred Foot Drain

5km

Figure 1 The survey area today. Scale 1:100,000. Based on 1:50,000 OS maps

2

(a) How far the artefacts recovered from an eroding landscape in a short span of years reflect its full settlement history and how far the erosion has reached.

(b) The nature of local Neolithic and Early Bronze Age settlement and economy.

(c) The relationship between fen edge and upland.

(d) The significance of the numerous bronzes and finely-worked flint and stone implements found in the survey area and along the south-eastern fen edge as a whole.

III. Collectors, collections and recording

The main sources of information drawn on in this volume are the Norfolk Sites and Monuments Record and the manuscript catalogue, drawings, and other papers of Frank Curtis. These are supplemented by information obtained from various Museum records, including a photographic record of part of the Curtis collection made soon after his death, from the literature, and from individuals. Most of the material illustrated and documented in this volume forms part of the collections of Norwich Castle Museum. The rest is in King's Lynn and other museums, in the Curtis collection, and in the private collections described below.

III.1. Frank Curtis
(Cover)
W. F. (Frank) Curtis was a native of Feltwell and lived his life there apart from serving in the army during the first World War. He is remembered as a man endowed with a remarkable and endearing personality and with inexhaustible energy and enthusiasm. He explored the gamut of local natural history and archaeology while employed as a farm worker and carpenter. He was a man who habitually fieldwalked as he ate his lunch, while his workmates sat down, and who began to excavate in the evening, after a day's work on the land. His rare capacity for investigation and recording in addition to collection is seen in the quantity of settlement evidence from the southern part of the area studied in this volume.

The Curtis papers consist mainly of photocopies made soon after his death in 1972 by Norwich Castle Museum staff of material then in the possession of his widow, the late Mrs Alice Curtis, and are clearly incomplete. They take the form of a catalogue, assorted descriptions, including sketches, of particular sites and finds, and sketch maps (e.g. Pls II–IV). The artefact collection was then also in Mrs Curtis' possession, and remained so when examined by the writer in 1981. Unfortunately only that part of the collection kept in Mrs Curtis' house was then available for study, further material stored in a shed being inaccessible. Some of the collection was sold by Mrs Curtis before her death, some remains in the Curtis family. Where objects are recorded as having been seen in the Curtis collection, this records the state of affairs in 1981.

Frank Curtis' catalogue records the collection of surface finds, mainly flint implements, from at least 1948, and the conduct of small-scale excavations from 1959. Most objects are recorded by field, generally denoted by Mr Curtis' own series of field numbers. These covered the fen edge and a part of the upland in Hockwold cum Wilton, Feltwell and the southern part of Methwold. These are recorded on a sketch map by Mr. Curtis held in King's Lynn Museum and on the 1:10,560 record maps in

Norwich Castle Museum. The Curtis field numbers are occasionally supplemented or replaced by Ordnance Survey field numbers and by grid references. The latter are often at variance with the field numbers. It is assumed here that Frank Curtis was more familiar with the fields over which he collected than with the national grid, so that when his field numbers and grid references are at variance the former are more likely to be correct. Discrepancies are noted in the appropriate gazetteer entries.

The catalogue is divided into sections by object type: for example, 'Tanged and barbed arrowheads' or 'Hammerstones', and objects in each section are given a separate sequence of serial numbers, starting from 1. The catalogue also includes a substantial 'Various' section in which, at least as it survives, serial numbers start at 200. Entries are occasionally accompanied by sketches. A typical entry in the 'Axes' section is:

Date	Remarks	Cat. No.	Field No.	
Dec.11 52	Brown semipolished	22	1	5 1/2 x 1 3/4

A typical entry in the 'Various' section is:

Date	Remarks	Cat. No.	Field No.	
June 6 56	Grey	443	82	Knife from axe

Excavations, especially those carried out in 1959–60, tended to be recorded incidentally to objects from them, for example, again from the 'Various' section:

Date	Own Field No.	OS No.	Cat. No.	
Dec. 20 1959	79	616	559	Leaf arrowhead found at Drain Bank Drove site 3 feet deep with animal bones and Beaker and plain pottery

The use of at least seventeen concurrent series of catalogue numbers poses problems in the identification of the recorded objects. These are exacerbated by the absence of some parts of the catalogue and the duplication of others, often with slight discrepancies. Frank Curtis apparently made occasional alterations to his system of field numbers, and at one stage re-wrote the 'various' section, altering the catalogue numbers without always altering the numbers on the corresponding objects.

It is nonetheless often possible to identify and provenance many objects recorded in the catalogue. Hand-written labels still tied to some objects in the Curtis collection in 1981 were generally exact replicas of catalogue entries; while Curtis field and catalogue numbers are marked on other objects from the Curtis collection in King's Lynn Museum and in the collection of the late Mr A. J. Orange.

Three sketch maps by Frank Curtis are reproduced here as Plates II, III and IV. The originals of Plates II and IV are held in Norwich Castle Museum, Plate III is known only from a photocopy. Plate II, which shows the fields around Blackdyke Farm, Hockwold cum Wilton, seems to have been drawn early in 1965, since it shows Site 5332 (66), excavated in January of that year, but does not show the eastern part of Site 5308/c4 (61/68), excavated in

February 1965, Site 5324 (93), excavated in August 1965, or Sites 5308/c5 (96) and 5333 (95/97), both excavated in 1967. Plates III and IV show fields 466, 613, 614 and 616 in Hockwold cum Wilton in greater detail. Neither can have been completed before March 1967, since they include Sites 5308/c5 (96) and 5333 (95/97), which were both excavated then.

The sketch maps are in broad agreement with each other and with the Sites and Monuments Record, but there are discrepancies of detail, especially with regard to sites excavated in 1959–60, which are discussed separately in Chapter 3.I.1. Pottery identifications recorded on the maps are not always to be taken at face value (Ch. 5.III.1). Additions made by the late Mr A.J. Orange to the Sites and Monuments Record in the mid-1960s must have been based on a sketch map very similar to Pl. III, since they are all closely matched by entries on it.

III.2. Other Collectors
Artefacts in the collection of Mr E. B. Secker are recorded by local field names or by six-figure grid references based on 1:25,000 maps. Those in the collection of Mr M.J. Younge are recorded by local field names or by six-figure grid references based on 1:63,360 maps. Those in the collection of the late Mr A.J. Orange, many of them derived from the Curtis collection, are mainly recorded according to the system used by Frank Curtis. Most of those in the collection of Mr J.D. Wortley are either unlocated, except to the general area, or located to fields or blocks of fields.

Many surface finds from the east of the survey area form part of the collection made by Mr R.F. Parrott of Fengate Farm, Weeting, between 1936 and 1954, which is now on loan to Norwich Castle Museum together with its manuscript catalogue. Most objects are numbered in a series of sequences, the first running from 1 to 1000, the second from 1A to 1000A, the third from 1B to 1000B, and so on. The numbers refer to catalogue entries, such as:

No. Description Date   Where Found   By Whom
124B scraper   July 15/42   339 Belvedere   Gandy 2d
                                    Breck, Fengate

Parcels of land are identified by their old OS field numbers and by descriptive names. Several names may be applied to different parts of a large field. Selective collection was encouraged by a system of payments to farmworkers and others in which arrowheads were bought for as much as 2s 6d, while scrapers, such as the one in the entry quoted above, were bought for 1d or 2d.

This illustrates the selectivity of almost all the collectors who have been active in the area. Its very richness has prompted the collection of individual finished implements, preferably fine ones. At least two local collectors have told the writer that they no longer pick up scrapers, partly because they already have more than enough, partly in order to leave something for the next person to come along. Debitage in most collections is thus confined to a few distinctive pieces, such as particularly regular cores, especially discoidal forms and blade cores, and the occasional blade. In these circumstances, any consideration of surface material must focus on the more readily recognisable artefacts. J.S. Warburton, who worked the western fringes of the survey area early in this century, seems, exceptionally, to have achieved something approaching total collection.

Mr Rock Fletcher, a nephew of Frank Curtis and an active collector in the area in the 1960s, stated in 1981 that he had given his collection to Moyses Hall Museum, Bury St Edmunds. This illustrates the mobility of material in many of the collections. Objects have passed informally and often without record from collector to collector. Several entries in the Curtis catalogue are marked with an 'S' for 'sold', while numerous objects recorded in it were subsequently given to other collectors or to King's Lynn Museum or Norwich Castle Museum. Any possibility of the double recording of a single object is noted in the appropriate gazetteer entries. Such occurrences are not, however, always detectable. For this reason it is also recorded whether objects have been seen by the writer, so that those examined at first hand provide a minimum total.

III.3. The Norfolk Sites and Monuments Record
In the Sites and Monuments Record each site or find is given a county number, which is an unique serial number used to mark its position on a 1:10,560 (now transcribed to 1:10,000) or, if greater detail is required, 1:2,500 record map and to identify the relevant records. Separate contexts are sometimes identified within a site or an arbitrary area, as in field 613 in Hockwold cum Wilton, where the whole field is designated Site 5308 and the sites and finds within it 5308/c1, /c2, /c3, etc. (Fig. 4).

This system has, however, obtained only since the mid-1970s, when the Sites and Monuments Record became the joint responsibility of the Norfolk Archaeological Unit and the Norwich Castle Museum. Most of the material published in this volume was recorded before this, much of it during the 1960s, according to the system still in use in Norwich Castle Museum, where the Sites and Monuments Record had been established by Rainbird Clarke in the 1930s. In this system, modelled on that of the Ordnance Survey, there is a separate sequence of serial numbers for each 1:10,560 or 1:10,000 sheet, so that a site or find is designated by both the number of the sheet and its number on that sheet. Site 5308/c1, for example, is TL 68 NE (63). For the areas most intensively investigated by Frank Curtis the Castle Museum records also incorporate his own system of field numbers (Ch. III.1), so that Site 5308/c1 or TL 68 NE (63) may also be referred to as 'site 63, field 80'. This is the form in which most of the material in the Castle Museum is accessed and boxed. In this volume sites and finds are generally referred to by the county number, e.g. Site 4460. In the case of sites recorded on sheet TL 68 NE, county numbers are followed by the bracketed museum map number, e.g. HCW 613 Site 5308/c1 (63), since these last have already been used by several authors, among them Bamford (1982), Gibson (1982), and Tomalin (1983).

Up to the early 1960s, the record was maintained on 1:10,560 sheets acquired in the 1930s, on which the national grid was not marked. Six-figure grid references for sites and finds marked on them were estimated from 1:63,360 maps and incorporated into the appropriate records. These grid references are necessarily approximate, and are sometimes misleading: the 1961 grid reference for Site 5373 (22), for example, is 52/694 875, which places it in the south of field 616, although the contemporary entry on the record map places it in the south-west of field 614, the next field to the west, at approximately TL/6930 8790 (Fig. 4).

Gridded 1:10,560 maps were acquired in the 1960s and the record gradually transferred to them. For the sheets covering Hockwold, Feltwell and part of Methwold, this was done by the late Mr A.J. Orange, probably in 1964, since this is the date of the latest find recorded on the old maps. As well as transcribing the existing record, Mr Orange, who had always taken a strong and active interest in the archaeology and local history of the Feltwell area, incorporated additional information from his own sources, much of it obtained from Frank Curtis. It was at this stage that sites investigated by Frank Curtis in the south of field 616 and perhaps in field 466 in Hockwold cum Wilton in 1959–1960 first entered the Sites and Monuments Record in any detail. The scanty and often contradictory records of these sites pose particular problems which are discussed in Chapter 3. Because no 1:2,500 map was available, the particularly dense concentration of sites and finds in fields 466, 613, 614 and 616 in Hockwold cum Wilton (Fig. 4; Bamford 1982, text fig. 2) was recorded on an unscaled enlargement sketched on the reverse of the 1:10,560 map. Findspots added at this time are thus very approximate, especially as they were almost certainly based on rough sketch maps in the first place (see below).

In the early 1960s, too, Frank Curtis was reporting discoveries and giving material to King's Lynn Museum as well at to Norwich Castle Museum. Sites and finds described by him in letters to Sophia Mottram, the then curator, can sometimes be tied in to the Sites and Monuments Record but all too often remain unlocated (Ch. 3.I.1).

From 1964 recording improved. Sites and finds were reported and complete collections of material brought directly to Norwich Castle Museum. Site locations were recorded on sketch maps showing paced distances from field boundaries, and were transferred from these onto the record maps. Sites were excavated in a series of square or rectangular areas (Figs 5, 9, 12; Bamford 1982, text figs 3, 6); finds from each square or rectangle were kept separate; and plans and sections were drawn. Confusion, however, still sometimes arose. Bamford (1982, 13–17) describes problems encountered in the detailed reconstruction of Sites 5308/c1 (63), 5308/c2 (62) and 5308/c3 (69).

III.4. The Gazetteer

The information brought together here is of uneven precision and reliability. Further problems are posed by diverse recording systems and by the fact that some of the records date from several decades ago, so that allowance has to be made for changes in archaeological thought and vocabulary. The record format is intended to accommodate these disparities, notably in allowing for different levels of precision in location, in making it clear whether or not material has been examined at first hand, and in reproducing vague or uncertainly interpretable information in quotation marks.

A fictitious specimen record is set out below. Few, if any, actual records include every section present in it. The abbreviations used are listed at the front of this volume.

FWL OS 999. Curtis Field no. F207. Centre TL 6995 9200. Brown's Close
Co.no.: 59098/c1
NCM no.: 69SE (125)
NGR: TL 6991 9195
Found: 1981–85
Site type(s): CF
Date(s): ?MES, EMNEO, LNEBA, BKR, EBA
This vol.: Ch. 3, Ch. 6.I and 6.II, Fig. 200: M34, Figs 210–211: L201–L243, Fig. 260: P413–P420, Fig. 270: B40
Source(s): Smith catalogue. Jones 1965, 34–36, fig. 9:4
Collection(s): Smith 12–102
Seen
Cu alloy: Flat axe
Flint: A2 core, 34 flakes, 12 blades, leaf arrowhead, 10 scrapers, scale-flaked knife, backed knife, notch, 3 misc. retouched.
Stone: Axe (ground, frag.)
Ceramics: 9 NB, 4 BKR, 1 LBKR, 2 RBKR, 11 LNEBA
Worked bone/antler: bone point
Other: wooden stake (tip)
Animal bone present
Comment/description: 4 blades heavily corticated. Stone axe petrology no. N306, Group VI. NB flint-tempered, inc. sherd with out-turned rim & hollow neck. BKR comb-impressed. RBKR FN. LBKR incised with motif 33. 1 LNEBA sherd incised with row of chevrons.

Entries are ordered by *parish*, beginning in those parishes which fall wholly or almost wholly within the survey area (Feltwell, Hilgay, Hockwold cum Wilton, Methwold and Southery) with finds which can be provenanced only to the parish or to a vague location within it. Finds from within the survey area but not locatable even to parish are listed at the end of the gazetteer.

Within each parish most entries are ordered by *field*, mainly because so much of the material was collected and recorded by field, partly too so that finds made close to each other are grouped together. *Old Ordnance Survey field numbers* are used because the parcels of land which they designate, mapped early in this century, correspond more closely than do modern field boundaries to the fields by which much of the material was recorded. In the case of the Parrott collection the correspondence is total. They also provide continuity with the map already published by Bamford (1982, text fig. 2). Old OS field numbers are equated, where appropriate, with *Frank Curtis' own field numbers,* which spanned parts of Hockwold cum Wilton, Feltwell, and Methwold in a single sequence. They are distinguished by the prefix 'F'. The use of the less self-explanatory sections of the gazetteer entries is described below.

Co. no. (County number) *NCM no.* (Norwich Castle Museum number) are explained in section 1.III.3 above.

NGR prefixes six- or eight-figure grid references denote the location of a findspot. If none is given, then the find is locatable only to the field, block of fields or general location under which it is listed, a grid reference for the centre of which is given, where possible, in the appropriate heading.

Source(s) exclude the Norfolk Sites and Monuments Record, which would otherwise figure in every entry.

This vol.: contains references to relevant text and illustrations in this volume. Artefact illustrations are identified by their serial numbers within material type, the latter indicated by the letters M (metalwork), L (lithics), P (pottery) and B (worked bone).

Flint and *Stone* are generally described in terms of the categories defined in Chapter 5.II.5. Where terms used in unverified records cannot confidently be translated into these categories they are transcribed in inverted commas.

Ceramics include both pottery and other fired clay. Decorative motifs are denoted by numbers: 1–38 as illustrated by Clarke (1970, 424–42), with the addition of:

39. 'False cord', *i.e.* rows of contiguous, horizontal fingernail-impressions, *e.g.* Fig. 91: P241.
40. 'Crow's foot' rustication, *i.e.* relatively non-plastic paired fingernail impressions, *e.g.* Fig. 101: P349.

The stylistic terms Early, Late and Middle Beaker are used as defined by Case (1977). Note that '4 BKR', for example, means 'four Beaker sherds', not 'four Beakers', while 'BKR' without a preceding number denotes Beaker pottery in unspecified quantities.

III.5. The appendices
Appendices 2–33 (microfiche) list particular categories of site or find. They consist of appropriate records extracted from the gazetteer, and ordered in the same sequence, sometimes edited and with relevant matter highlighted. They have the same layout as the gazetteer entries, but incorporate additional information which is there conveyed in headings. If the fictitious gazetteer entry above formed part of an appendix, it would begin with the following lines:

Parish: FWL Old OS field no.: 999
Curtis field no.: F207
Name: Brown's Close

A grid reference prefixed with 'NGR' records a site or findspot, as in gazetteer entries. Where this cannot be given, one prefixed with 'Centre' records the central point of the field, block of fields or other area to which a find is less specifically located.

In appendices which relate to distribution maps, plotted sites and finds are marked with an asterisk. They are not plotted when findspots are imprecise, when identifications are uncertain, or when there is possible duplication of other records.

III.6. Caveat
There is an element of subjectivity in the interpretation of many of the records relating to the survey area. The results presented here often represent a personal attempt to find a 'best fit' between conflicting or deficient sources. Discrepancies between the contents of this volume and other publications or the Norfolk Sites and Monuments Record should be seen in this light.

2. Shifting Scenery

I. Geology
(Fig. 2)

Long-term tectonic downwarping of an area centred on the southern North Sea basin has tilted the originally superimposed geological deposits of East Anglia into a series of successive north to south bands. Within the survey area these are Jurassic and Cretaceous strata comprising, from west to east, Kimmeridge Clay, Lower Greensand, Gault and Chalk (Hall 1987, fig. 2). Erosion of the soft Kimmeridge Clay and of other Jurassic clays to the west and south, largely by glacial action, has produced a low-lying basin, within which patches of more enduring material remain as elevated 'islands', such as that which forms the present parishes of Hilgay and Southery (Figs 1–2). The upland of the eastern edge of the basin is formed by an escarpment of the more resistant Gault, Greensand and Chalk. The chalk so exposed consists, in its lower, now westernmost, zone of a Chalk Marl composed of alternating beds of soft and hard material (Peake and Hancock 1970, 299; Seale 1975, 16), prone to erode into narrow hillocks and ridges. In the course of the Pleistocene, south-eastward moving ice breached the Gault and Greensand of the escarpment between the present courses of the rivers Wissey and Lark. It is this eastward extension of the basin which forms the Wissey Embayment of the title.

By the end of the Pleistocene, the chalk of the upland within the survey area was diversely covered by glacial sands and gravels, perhaps with some till (Corbett 1973, 7). A widespread deposit of chalk-sand drift seems to have resulted from the cryoturbation of chalk and overlying deposits in periglacial conditions, since its lithology conforms to and varies with the underlying solid (Corbett 1973, 8–15). These deposits were the source of extensive wind-blown sand, sometimes forming dunes (Corbett 1973, 15–16). A sparsely-vegetated Late Glacial land-scape seems a likely genesis for this material, which was certainly present by the Later Neolithic, since it was cut by the flint mine shafts of Grime's Graves (Site 5640; e.g. Clarke 1915, fig. 7). Chalk-sand drift and wind-blown sand togther characterise the Breckland region of north-west Suffolk and south-west Norfolk, of which the eastern part of the survey area forms a part.

Wind-blown sand extended into the low-lying basin to the west, especially its south-easternmost part. By this time too variegated Pleistocene deposits had been laid on the floor of the basin. Within the survey area these consisted primarily of gravels, especially in the south, with some patches of till to the north (Gallois 1988, fig. 25).

II. Flandrian Fluctuations

As temperate conditions were re-established, all of the area became covered by deciduous forest. From the mid-Flandrian onwards, however, the history of its two parts was very different.

II.1. Breckland
In the north-east of the Breckland, analysis of pollen from the sediments of Hockham Mere by Bennett (1983) indicates that once deciduous forest was established, c. 9000 BP, it was broken only by small-scale, short-lived clearances until c. 2000 BP (c. 50 cal. BC), when more extensive clearance and cultivation led to the development of heathland. The same sequence seems to have obtained closer to the survey area. Molluscan evidence form Grime's Graves suggests that woodland regenerated after a Later Neolithic episode of flint mining (Site 5640; Evans 1981, 106–107); while charred plant remains from late Iron Age and Romano-British contexts at Fison Way, Thetford, indicate that by then heathland conditions obtained in the surrounding area (Site 5853; Murphy 1984a, 21). Most of the eastern part of the survey area may thus have remained a patchwork of woodland and clearings throughout the period covered by this volume, with the heaths of historical times developing only from the Iron Age. Bennett suggests (1983, 479) that lime may have been an important component of the tree cover from c. 6600 BP (5500 cal. BC).

Molluscan evidence published as representing a Later Neolithic/Early Bronze Age environment of thin woodland or bush with some open spaces on the chalk edge of the Little Ouse valley in Hockwold cum Wilton (Site 5316/c7 ('site 7088'); Salway 1967, 44, 71) must be regarded as of uncertain or later prehistoric date, since some of the associated pottery seems to be Late Bronze Age or Early Iron Age (Ch. 5.III.2).

II.2. Fenland
The pace and scale of landscape change were many times greater in the fenland basin to the west. The broad outline of events was established by the pioneering work of Godwin in the 1930s, summarised by him in a later synthesis (Godwin 1978). Recent work, much of it relating to the Fenland Project, has greatly refined local depositional and vegetational history (Waller 1994). Only the briefest of outlines is attempted here.

The floor of the basin remained wooded and relatively well-drained through the early post-glacial, pine-dominated forest progressively giving way to mixed deciduous woodland in which lime was an important species, as on the upland (Waller 1988, 341). A combination of eustatic rise in sea level and continued down-warping of eastern England caused the watertable to rise. Peat began to grow, at first confined to river channels and other wet places.

Peat was growing by 8610 ± 160 BP (Q–588) in the channel of the Little Ouse at Peacock's Farm, Shippea Hill, Cambridgeshire (Clark and Godwin 1962, 19); it may have begun to form as early as 9010 ± 90 BP (CAR–1102; Smith et al. 1989, fig. 5). Pollen spectra also indicate early peat growth in the same river channel at Old Decoy nearby (Godwin 1940, fig. 4) and at Wilton Bridge, Hockwold cum Wilton, higher upstream (Godwin 1940, fig. 7). Farther north, localised early peat growth at Queen's

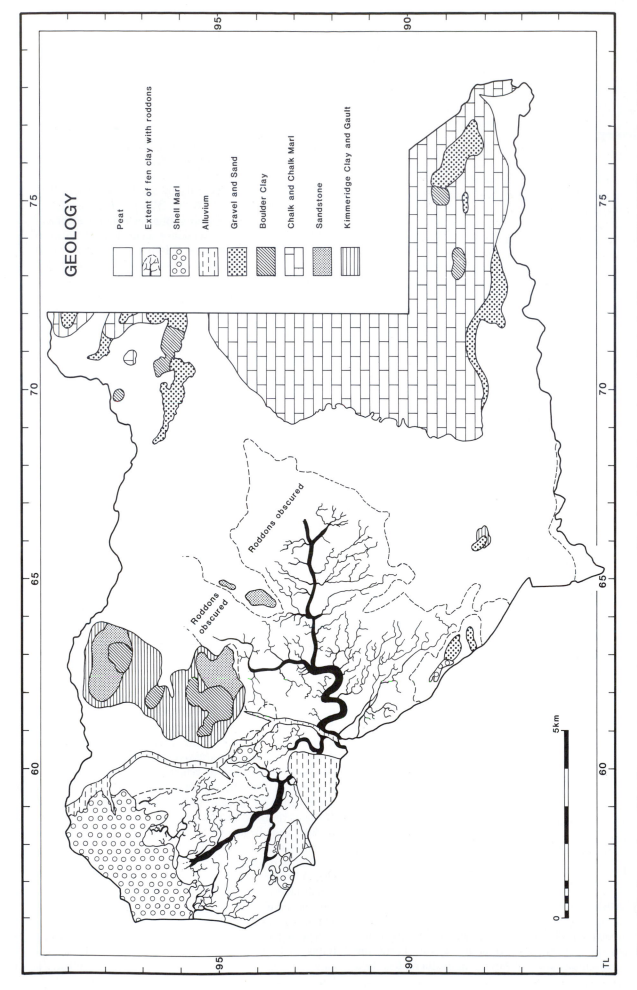

Figure 2 Surface geology with relict water courses and approximate extent of fen clay, based in the north on the Geological Survey's 1886 1:63,360 map and on fieldwork by Bob Silvester, in the south on the Geological Survey's 1980 1:50,000 map of the Ely district, and on Seale (1975). Scale 1:100,000

GEOLOGY

- Peat
- Extent of fen clay with roddons
- Shell Marl
- Alluvium
- Gravel and Sand
- Boulder Clay
- Chalk and Chalk Marl
- Sandstone
- Kimmeridge Clay and Gault

Roddons obscured

Roddons obscured

5 km

0

Ground, Methwold, was attributed to the presence of nearby springs (Godwin 1940, 264).

Peat does not seem to have extended beyond such restricted locations in the south of the basin until the third millennium cal. BC. At Feltwell Common (TL 668 917) within the survey area, peat was forming and forest, dominated first by lime then by oak, was giving way to alder carr by 4490 ± 75 BP (Q–2550; 3400–3040 cal. BC). Alder carr was in turn giving way to reed swamp in increasingly brackish conditions by 4225 ± 75 BP (Q–2549; 2920–2700 cal. BC) (Waller 1988, 339–342). This and other sequences show a progressive landward expansion of marine and fen environments. Overlying deposits, however, make it difficult to judge the rate at which this took place or the extent of peat growth within the basin. It may have been patchy and discontinuous.

Over the basin floor as a whole, a widespread index of increasing wetness is provided by bog 'oaks', the collapsed trunks of tall, high-canopied forest trees preserved at the bottom of deposits which grew over them after they had collapsed. Radiocarbon determinations have been made on a number. Published examples, including those listed by Godwin (1978, 60) fall in the early to mid third millennium cal. BC, corresponding to the chronology of peat growth at sites such as Feltwell Common.

In the course of the third millennium cal. BC progressively wetter and more brackish conditions culminated in a marine incursion. This laid down a deposit of clay, known as fen clay or buttery clay, the extent of which within the survey area is shown in Figure 2. The contact between the lower peat and the fen clay at Feltwell Common is dated to 4135 ± 70 BP (Q–2548; 2880–2600 cal. BC; Waller 1988, 337). Transgression was far from synchronous across the basin, a reflection of contemporary topography among other factors. Other determinations for the contact of lower peat and fen clay towards the landward limits of the transgression in the south-eastern fens range from 4350 ± 60 BP (Q–2537; 3040–2910 cal. BC) away from the incised channel of the Little Ouse at Peacock's Farm, Shippea Hill, Cambridgeshire, and 4310 ± 60 BP (Q–2596; 3020–2900 cal. BC) at Redmere, Suffolk to 3955 ± 70 BP (Q–2528; 2580–2400 cal. BC) at Pymore, Cambridgeshire (Waller 1988, 337–338; Waller 1994, 118–155).

The sedimentary characteristics of the fen clay are those of material deposited in still salt marsh conditions. Contemporary drainage is represented by roddons (Fig. 2), bands of silty alluvium marking the former courses of the sinuous creeks and larger streams which flowed through the salt marsh (Silvester 1991, fig. 48).

After perhaps two or three hundred years the watertable began to fall, freshwater conditions were re-established and peat growth recommenced. The contact of the upper peat with the fen clay at Feltwell Common is dated to 3815 ± 70 BP (Q–2551; 2450–2140 cal. BC). Closely similar determinations have been obtained from three other sequences: 3840 ± 55 BP (Q–2526; 2460–2200 cal. BC) at Redmere, Suffolk, 3800 ± 65 BP (Q–2580; 2450–2140 cal. BC) at Wood Fen, Cambridgeshire, and 3810 ± 50 BP (Q–2821; 2350–2150 cal. BC) at Welney Washes, also in Cambridgeshire (Waller 1994, 152–5).

The upper peat of this period was extensive and continuous, although much of it is now humified if not completely wasted. It is possible to envisage fen wood fringing the upland and islands, with carr, sedge fen and reedswamp conditions successively prevailing farther out in to the basin (Silvester 1991, fig. 48). The post-fen clay occupation of Plantation Farm, Shippea Hill, Cambridgeshire, some 8km out from the upland beside the then course of the Little Ouse, took place on a sandhill apparently surrounded by shallow, peat-forming swamp (Godwin and Godwin 1933, 286). That of Peacock's Farm nearby was sited in an immediate environment of willow carr (Godwin, Godwin and Clifford 1935, 314–316). Close to the upland, the rather later occupation of a hillock in Mildenhall Fen, Suffolk, seems to have taken place in fen wood (Godwin, Godwin and Clifford 1936, 34–35; Godwin 1978, 74).

After nearly a thousand years this drier Early Bronze Age episode was followed by increased waterlogging, seen in the re-establishment of reed swamp or sedge fen and locally culminating in the formation of freshwater meres. The transition from fen carr to sedge fen occurred before 3075 ± 50 BP (Q–2820; 1420–1300 cal. BC) at Welney Washes and before 3030 ± 50 BP (Q–2594; 1400–1230 cal. BC) at Redmere (Waller 1994, 154). This broadly corresponds to the progressive abandonment of the system of ditched enclosures at Fengate, Cambridgeshire, on the western edge of the basin, which were, in their lower-lying areas, overlain by a freshwater flood deposit in the later Bronze Age (Pryor 1980b, 177–178, 187, 247–249; Pryor 1984, 208; French 1992).

III. Wildlife

Skeletons of the animals and birds which inhabited the basin in the earlier Flandrian have been preserved in the peats. They include aurochs, one of them excavated from a post-fen clay deposit near Littleport (Shawcross and Higgs 1961). This is one of three aurochs from the Cambridgeshire fens which have been radiocarbon dated to the later Neolithic or Early Bronze Age (Burleigh, Matthews and Ambers 1982, 236–237). A 'long-horned ox' found in Feltwell Fen in 1950 may have been another of the same species (Site 5254/c2). Red deer are represented in almost all the excavated collections, and roe deer in some (Ch. 6.III.1 and 2; Jackson 1933; Jackson 1935; Jackson 1936; Bamford 1982, 29–30). A note of a barbed and tanged arrowhead found in a beaver skull in Poppylot, Methwold in 1883 but lost by 1922 provides a glimpse of one element of the post-fen clay fauna and its fate (Site 5234). Beaver is also reported from Plantation Farm, Shippea Hill, Cambridgeshire (Jackson 1933), and is represented in a collection associated with pre-dominantly Biconical Urn pottery from Hockwold cum Wilton (Ch. 6.III.1). Otter was represented at a Bronze Age living site in Mildenhall Fen (Jackson 1936) and at a Late Beaker one in the survey area (Site 5341(93); Bamford 1982, 29).

Mesolithic to Bronze Age deposits of the Cambridgeshire fenland have yielded not only species of water bird familiar in the area today, but, among others, pelican, bittern, crane and white-tailed eagle (Northcote 1980). The last of these is represented in the survey area by a perforated claw found with predominantly Bronze Age material (Fig. 106: B1).

IV. Modern Topography

To the east, much of the historical heath of the Breckland has been replaced within this century by conifer plantations. To the west, progressive drainage, accelerated by the construction of the cut-off channel in the 1960s, has resulted in rapid peat wastage. In the landscape of Plate I, an expanding skirtland zone, in which thin peaty topsoil directly overlies the mineral deposits of basin floor, extends outwards from the upland into wasting peat fen. The underlying microtopography produces a terrain of slight hummocks and hillocks, often several to a field, formed by relict Late Glacial sand dunes in the south of the survey area and by peaks and ridges of harder chalk isolated by the erosion of softer material in the north. It is these higher points which were occupied, often repeatedly, in prehistory and which have been progressively exposed by wasting peat (Silvester 1991, figs 14–16).

Most of the present skirtland soils in the survey area are humic gley soils of the Wilbraham-Reach complex, giving way farther into the fen to organic soils of the Adventurers series, formed on humified peat. The upland soils are mainly rendzinas of the Icknield series and intermingled rendzinas and brown calcareous soils of the Swaffham Prior-Newmarket series. The clays of Hilgay and Southery support mainly gleyed soils of the Ashley, Highlodge, Peacock-Bracks and Aldreth series (Seale 1975).

3. Living Sites

(Appendices 1–2 (microfiche))

I. Hockwold cum Wilton. Old OS Fields 466, 613, 614 and 616
(Pls I–IV, Fig. 4)

These fields lie close to the edge of the upland, on the northern side of the mouth of the Little Ouse valley at 1–2m OD, the present cut-off channel being only 250m to the north of them (Pl. I; Bamford 1982, text fig. 2). Today, their surface is formed by a relatively thin layer of humified peat, through which underlying sandhills have emerged in fields 466, 614 and 616. These three fields, which together formed Frank Curtis' field 79, also known as Green's, were permanent pasture until about thirty years ago, when they were brought into arable cultivation. Most of their area has now reverted to pasture (Pl. I). Field 613, Frank Curtis' field 80, also known as the Oaks or the Poor Ground and formerly a turbary, remained under the cover

of scrubby woodland which it retains today. Sites in these fields are described in the order in which they were investigated. Stray finds from them are plotted in Figure 4, documented in the gazetteer, and selectively described and illustrated in Chapter 5.

I.1. Site 24866 ('site 8') and its Components
(Fig. 4)

The ploughing of fields 466, 614 and 616 in 1959 is recorded in Frank Curtis' papers:

> Greens ploughed up. Old pottery. Beaker, Rusticated. bones bone needles, awls, stone amulets scrapers. knives. axe. adze. bracer. one nearly complete pot unidentified. Site has been identified as late Neolithic Early Bronze age occupational site.

His catalogue entries for the period record that he was collecting and excavating, the latter probably for the first

Plate I Vertical air photograph showing wasting peat fen (right and centre) separated from chalk upland (left) by the cut-off channel, at Blackdyke Farm, Hockwold cum Wilton, 1982. Area of Figure 4 outlined in white.
Cambridge University Committee for Aerial Photography: copyright reserved (RC8-EA 283)

11

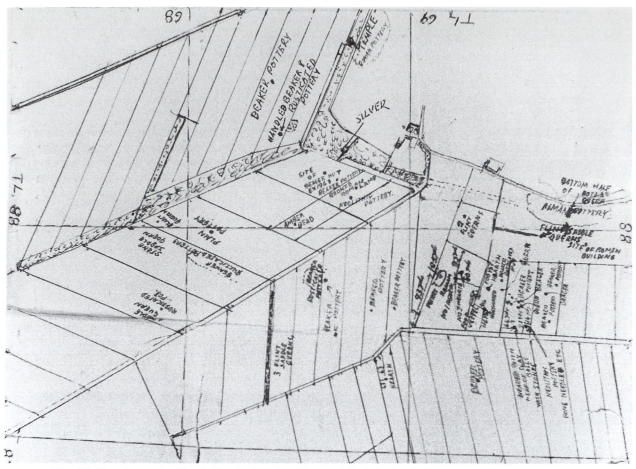

Plate II Sketch map by Frank Curtis showing sites and finds in the fields around Blackdyke Farm, Hockwold cum Wilton. Photo: David Wicks

time, at a number of separate locations within the fields, identified as sites 1 to 5 plus Drain Bank site or Drain Bank Drove site. Problems have subsequently arisen because these discrete concentrations of artefacts were not initially distinguished in the Sites and Monuments Record or in the collections of Norwich Castle and King's Lynn Museums. A large collection of material given to Norwich Castle Museum by Mr Curtis in 1960 is accessed as from 'site 8', an ovoid area covering most of fields 466 and 616 (Fig. 4), subsequently dubbed Site 24866. The corresponding record card reads 'Concentrations of Beaker and Rusticated ware from sandy peat topsoil of field, animal bones and potboilers also found'. The size of the collection, which includes nearly 10kg of pottery (Table 12), makes it unlikely to have come from a single sandhill. A smaller collection, given to King's Lynn Museum at about the same time, is simply accessed as from field 79 (*i.e.* from fields 466+614+616) and figures in the Sites and Monuments Record as Site 14662. Sherds of one pot, P14 (Fig. 73), occur in both collections.

The quantity and preservation of the material shows how little disturbance had taken place prior to ploughing. The pottery abounds in large, fresh sherds of Bronze Age vessels, some with organic residue clearly visible on their interior surfaces.

The animal bone collected at the same time poses a problem. It consists of two substantial collections. The first has the same accession number, 121.960, as the rest of the 'site 8' material, and the larger bones among it are marked 'site 8'. Most of the larger bones of the second collection are also marked 'site 8', although two are marked 'site 5' and one 'site 9'. This collection, however, has the accession number 95.960. This should apply to

material from Site 5423 (9), 1.4km to the north-west (Fig. 3). There are several indications that most of the 95.960 animal bone came from 'site 8':

1. The larger bones in it are marked 'site 8'.
2. Labels with the bone and apparently contemporary with its accession read 'Beaker Site 8. 52/695876. 95.960'; this is the same six-figure grid reference as that originally recorded for the 'site 8' material with the accession number 121.960.
3. The 95.960 animal bone includes a beaver mandible which almost certainly corresponds to the 'beaver teeth' marked on a site in the south of field 616 in Plate III.
4. The size of the 95.960 bone collection is far greater than might be expected from the excavation of an area 3.65 m square, as Site 5243 (9) was (Ch. 3. II.2). Neither does it tally with Frank Curtis' description of the quantity and preservation of the bones from that site, 'the bones were very fragile and as they lay among the debris of a fireplace, I put the lot in a box I had with me.' The 121.960 and 95.960 bone collections are described together in Ch. 6.III.1, except for the bones marked as coming from 'site 5' and 'site 9'.

The sites investigated in fields 466 and 616 in 1959–60 entered the Sites and Monuments Record individually only in about 1964 (Ch. 3.III). They were not at the time equated with Mr Curtis' site numbers, but simply given serial numbers in the sequence for the map on which they were marked. Finds from them were given by Mr Curtis to Norwich Castle Museum at about the same time, material from Sites 5439 (44), 5309 (48) and 5310 (49) in 1964, followed by a mixed collection from Sites 5311 (50) and 5312 (51) in 1965.

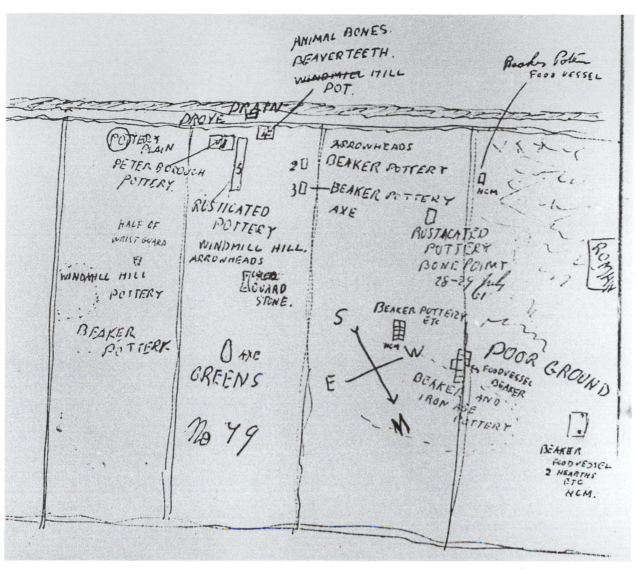

Plate III Sketch map by Frank Curtis showing sites and finds in HCW OS 466, 613, 614 and 616.
Photo: David Wicks

Attempts were made by Museum staff, in consultation with Mr Curtis, to equate the sites recorded in the Sites and Monuments Record with his sites 1–5. Successive equations were sometimes contradictory.

Descriptions of the pottery recovered are of little help in identifying the sites. Misidentifications were frequent (Ch. 5.III.1) and correct identifications often showed a bias in favour of fine and rusticated Beaker, readily recognisable even in small fragments, and against the much plainer Bronze Age wares, which form a large proportion of the pottery surviving from these fields (Table 12). The collections in Norwich Castle Museum from Sites 5439 (44), 5309 (48), 5310 (49) and 5311+5312 (50+51) are clearly incomplete, since they consist almost exclusively of pottery.

The first three comprise selected pieces, the bulk of the material found with them having been retained in the Curtis collection. They are dominated by large, relatively well-preserved sherds of fine and rusticated Beaker, with many fresh breaks for which no joins can be found. They furthermore include a high proportion of partly reconstructable pots, like those illustrated in Figure 77. Such vessels may have been singled out at the expense of less attractive and distinctive wares.

Appendix 1 (microfiche) summarises what is known about each of the sites investigated in 1959–60 within or close to the area of 'site 8', excluding both stray finds and Site 5324 (93), which was not discovered until 1965. It suggests correlations with the Sites and Monuments Record and incorporates suggestions kindly made by the late Mr A.J. Orange.

The task is particularly difficult in field 616. Whether or not the correlations suggested are correct, it is clear that five or six separate sites were identified in the south of the field in 1959–60, and that some excavation took place on Frank Curtis' sites 1 (? = 5310 (49)), 3 (? = 5439 (44)), and 4 (? = 5309 (48)), all of which are noted as 'Ex.' in the Catalogue. Excavation also seems likely on Drain Bank Drove or Drain Bank Site, which extended onto the drove to the south of the field (Pls III–IV), since objects from it are catalogued as 'found at Drain Bank Site 3' deep', although it is possible that material may simply have been exposed in the side of the Sluice Drain on the south side of the drove (Pl. III).

Some of the material recovered at this time is missing, inaccessible, or unidentified. In addition to the incompleteness of the surviving collections, there is no material assigned to Sites 5441 (52) or 5442 (53). The

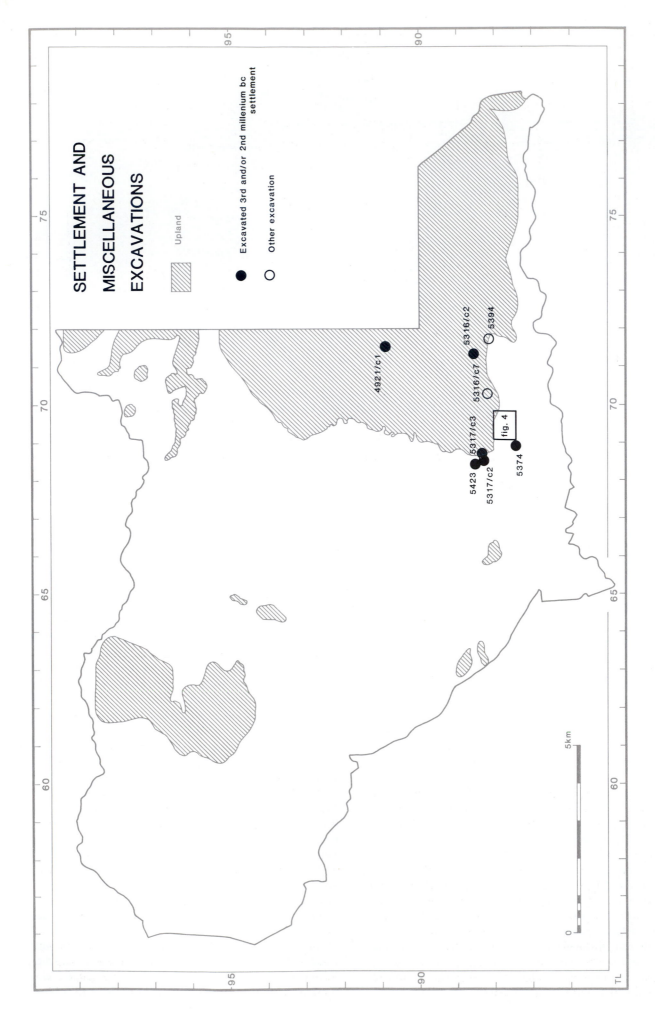

SETTLEMENT AND
MISCELLANEOUS
EXCAVATIONS

Upland

● Excavated 3rd and/or 2nd millenium bc settlement

○ Other excavation

4921/c1

5316/c2

5316/c7

5394

fig. 4

5317/c3

5423

5317/c2

5374

5km

Figure 3 Settlement and miscellaneous excavations listed in Appendix 2 (microfiche). Scale 1:100,000

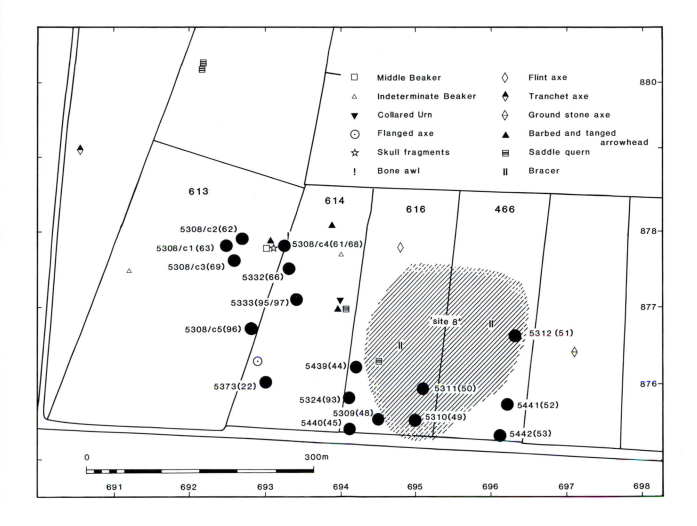

Figure 4 Hockwold cum Wilton OS fields 466, 613, 614 and 616 (Curtis fields 79 and 80).
Scale 1:5,000

untraced material may be accounted for in several ways. Some may have been noted but not collected: animal bone was certainly sometimes left in the field because of the difficulties of transporting it (Bamford 1982, 30). Some may have remained in the inaccessible part of the Curtis collection. Some may have passed into other collections. Much undoubtedly forms part of the Site 24866 ('site 8') collection in Norwich Castle Museum and the Site 14662 (Field 79) collection in King's Lynn Museum.

Illustrated artefacts
Flint and stone Figs 44–46: L1–L27
Pottery Figs 72–85: P1–P148
Worked bone and antler Fig. 106: B1–B7

I.2. Site 5373 (22)
Found 1961–2. TL 6930 8760. Old OS field 614
There is no record of excavation here, although a subrectangular outline shown in the south-west of the field in Plate III and labelled 'Rusticated pottery bone point 28–29 July 61' suggests that one took place. SMR and accession register agree that two batches of material were received from the site, the first, consisting predominantly of Bronze Age pottery, including P149–171 (Figs 86–87), in 1961, the second, consisting predominantly of fine and rusticated Beaker, including P172–193 (Figs 87–88), with some struck flint and animal bone, in 1962. It is not clear

whether these were indeed collected in successive years or simply given to the museum in two instalments, the more interesting decorated pieces (mainly fine and rusticated Beaker) having initially been retained. The latter would be consistent with notes on Plate III and on the 1961 record card to the effect that Frank Curtis then retained some of the material.

Illustrated artefacts
Flint and stone Fig. 47: L28–L32
Pottery Figs 86–88: P149–P193
Worked bone Fig. 106: B8–B9

I.3. Site 5308/c2 (62)
Excavated 1964. TL 6927 8779. Old OS field 613 (? Pl V; Bamford 1982, 12)
This was a hearth cut into the underlying chalk, from which one Late style Beaker and two Bronze Age sherds were recovered. It was one of a group of closely-spaced 'sites' in the north-east of the field (Fig. 4) which might best be seen as a unit, their separate excavation resulting from the exigencies of digging in clearings in woodland. The others were Sites 5308/c1 (63), 5308/c3 (69) and 5308/c4 (61/68). Their close relationship is illustrated by the conjoins between sherds from two or more of the 'sites' (Bamford 1982, 12, 14, 17).

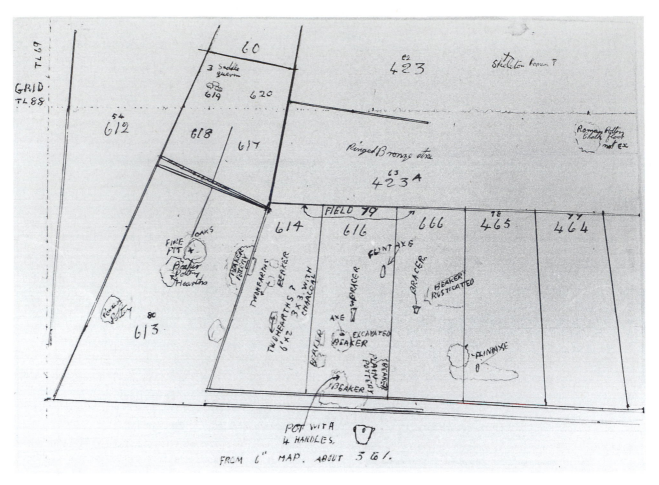

Plate IV Sketch map by Frank Curtis showing sites and finds in HCW OS 466, 613, 614 and 616.
Photo: David Wicks

I.4. Site 5308/c1 (63)

Excavated 1964. TL 6925 8778. Old OS field 613 (?Pl. V; Bamford 1982, 12–13)

Here, another hearth was excavated, this time with some of its surrounding area. The hearth contained ash, charcoal, burnt flint, burnt quartzite, lumps of haematite and sherds of Late style Beaker pottery. It is probably this hearth which is shown in Plate V and described in a letter of 27 July 1964 to Barbara Green, Keeper of Archaeology in Norwich Castle Museum:

> My Bronze Age hearth is slightly different to all the other I have dug, this one has been dug into the chalk below the peat and the bottom 3" consists of gritty ash and small burnt flints such as we find in large heaps in the fen. (pot boilers).

The accompanying sketch shows a bowl-shaped depression cut into the chalk with a heap of pottery, flint flakes and bones described as 'thrown from fire pit'.

There were several stake-holes in the surrounding area, but they did not form a coherent plan. The surrounding area contained struck flint and sherds, predominantly of Late style Beaker but including Neolithic Bowl, Food Vessel Urn, and plain Bronze Age Wares.

I.5. Site 5308/c3 (69)

Excavated 1965. TL 6926 8776. Old OS field 613 (Bamford 1982, 13–17)

In 1965 Frank Curtis began to draw measured plans and sections (Bamford 1982, text figs 6–7) and to excavate in arbitrary rectilinear areas, in this case 6 ft (1.83m) squares,

keeping the finds from each separate. The excavated area was contiguous to the hearth of Site 5308/c1 (63) and included a large oval pit which measured approximately 4.5m x 2m and was approximately 1m deep. The section records an undifferentiated 'occupation layer' of dark, humic sand 15–30cm deep, between peaty topsoil and undisturbed natural sand. This contained struck flint, animal bone, fired clay and pottery. While dominated by Late style Beaker, the pottery included Middle style Beaker, Neolithic Bowl, Food Vessel Urn and plain Bronze Age Wares.

I.6. Site 5308/c4 (61/68). Dykeside

Excavated 1964, 1965 and 1967. TL 6932 8778. Old OS fields 613+614 (Figs 5–7; Bamford 1982, 17)

This area was cut by the drainage ditch between fields 613 and 614 (Fig. 4). Initial excavations in field 613 in 1964 (site 61) were virtually unrecorded. In one of the plans on which Figure 5 is based, which must date from 1967 at the earliest, the southernmost of the three rectangular areas on the west side of the ditch in field 613 is marked '1964'. This may not, however, indicate the whole of the area then excavated. The statement 'afterwards the whole of this area was dug and scattered pottery found over all' is written on blank paper to the west of it, and a smaller sketch plan gives dimensions of 20 x 10yd (18 x 9m) for the excavation here. It also notes that Food Vessel was found in the north of this area and rusticated Beaker in the south. The quantity of finds from the 1964 excavation, which include 5.60kg of pottery and eighty-five pieces of

Plate V The excavation of a 'fire pit', probably Site 5308/c2 (62) or Site 5308/c1 (63), in HCW OS 613 in 1964

Plate VI Site 5332 (66) in HCW OS 614, 1965

worked flint and stone, suggests that an area of roughly this size was opened up.

In 1965, rectangular areas *1* to *8* were excavated on the east side of the ditch in field 614 (site 68). Two further rectangular areas were excavated on the west side of the ditch in 1967 (1967 *1* and *2*). The broken circle shown in Figure 5 is annotated 'Area of hut 17' [5.2m] circular? The ditch cutting through and rabbit burrows made it impossible to measure exactly'. It is not clear what this represents. One section is annotated 'no stakeholes', and artefact densities were not noticeably greater within the circle than outside it (Figs 6–7). The sections show the same stratigraphy as at Site 5308/c3 (69; Bamford 1982, text fig. 7) with the addition of chalk upcast from the bottom of the drainage ditch.

There are three stone axes from the site, L66–68 (Fig. 50). Cores and 'pot-boilers' were concentrated in 1967 area *1*, scrapers in areas *5, 6* and *8*, animal bone in areas *7* and *8*. Pottery includes Neolithic Bowl, Middle and Late style Beaker, Food Vessel Urn, and other Bronze Age wares. There is also worked bone and antler, including B10–B14 (Fig. 107).

There are discrepancies between the positions of three finds as planned (Fig. 5) and their areas by which they are boxed. 'Antler axe', plotted in area *2* in Figure 5, can only be B12 or B14, yet these are respectively marked and boxed with material from areas *6* and *8*. The 'Antler spatula bored' also plotted in area *2* must be B11, yet this is boxed and marked with material from area *1*. 'Broken axe approx.', plotted in area *7*, is likely to equate with L66 or L67, but both were found in 1964, when excavation was on the other side of the ditch. L66 is perhaps the more likely candidate, since it is recorded as having been a surface find, and may therefore have been collected from the east side of the ditch during excavations on the west side.

Illustrated artefacts
Flint and stone Figs 48–50: L33–L68
Pottery Figs 89–94: P194–P265
Worked bone and antler Fig. 107: B10–B14

I.7. Site 5332 (66)

Excavated 1965. TL 6933 8775. Old OS field 614 (Pl. VI, Fig. 8)

Frank Curtis wrote two brief accounts of the discovery and excavation of this site:

> 29 Jan 1965. the plough had just cut the top of hearths and had broken up some pottery and a bone awl but not a bone spearhead.
> Pottery was mostly plain, coarse, ware, some 8 or 9 pieces of rims of different pots were found, and 4 or 5 pots with a shoulder and markings, broken bones and teeth and flint scrapers were found, practically any piece of flint had been worked. No arrowheads or flint weapons were found.
> Cultivating stopped work.

And:

> EBA FLOOR AREA 10' x 10' [3 x 3m] cleared. Two hearths? of chalk, one 3' x 2' [0.90m x 0.60m] and one 7' x 3'7" [2.13m x 1.10m], at a depth of 1'3" [0.38m]. Plain pottery mostly, a few pieces usual Beaker decoration, a bone spear head and a broken bone awl. no arrowheads or axes, but scrapers, broken bones and teeth found.

The section differs from other recorded in the immediate area in showing a layer of 'peaty dark sand' between the hearths and the 'occupational layer' around them and the underlying natural sand. This must represent the surface on which they were built. The SMR card adds that the smaller hearth was made of chalk and large pebbles and the larger of chalk alone, and that sherds were scattered between them. The pottery is almost all of Biconical Urn affinities. It is not clear that these features were hearths. There is no mention of any charcoal, of discoloration of the chalk or of burnt objects. Plate VI, taken at the end of the excavation, confirms this impression and shows the two patches of chalk isolated on pedestals of darker sand above clean natural sand.

Illustrated artefacts
Flint Fig. 51: L69–L79
Pottery Fig. 95: P266–P282
Worked bone Fig. 107: B15–B17

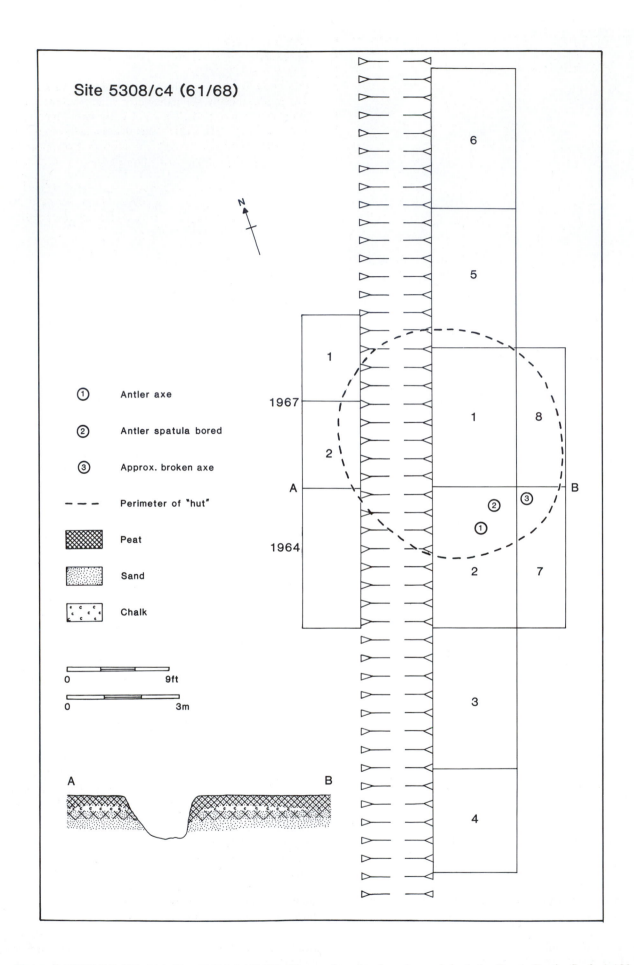

Figure 5 HCW OS 613–614, Site 5308/c4 (61/68). Plan and section based on originals by Frank Curtis. Scale 1:100

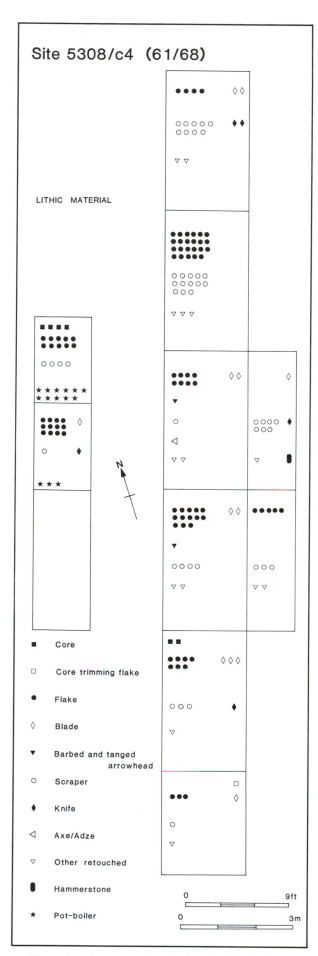

Site 5308/c4 (61/68)

LITHIC MATERIAL

■ Core

□ Core trimming flake

● Flake

◇ Blade

▼ Barbed and tanged
    arrowhead

○ Scraper

◆ Knife

◁ Axe/Adze

▽ Other retouched

▮ Hammerstone

★ Pot-boiler

Figure 6 HCW OS 613–614, Site 5308/c4 (61/68).
Distribution of lithic material. Scale 1:100

I.8. Site 5324 (93)

Excavated 1965. TL 6941 8758. Old OS field 616
(Bamford 1982, 9–12)

This consisted of a roughly circular area of dark humic
sand approximately 6m in diameter, which included three
hearths, and was underlain by a gully and edged by a
setting of birch stakes which were densest in the north side
and seemed to have formed a windbreak. Artefacts and
animal bone were almost entirely confined to the 'floor'
area. A copper alloy fragment, M1 (Fig. 26), has subsequently been found among the pottery, which itself
forms an homogeneous, apparently single-period Late
style Beaker assemblage, attributable to Clarke's (1970)
Late and Final Southern groups.

Illustrated artefact
Copper alloy fragment Fig. 26: M1

I.9. Site 5333 (95/97)

Excavated 1967. TL 6934 8771. Old OS field 614 (Figs 9–11)
Following the recovery of finds from the ploughsoil (site
95), Frank Curtis excavated a rectangular area of 16ft
(4.88m) x 8ft (2.44m) in 4ft (1.22m) squares (site 97). No
features were recorded, and the section records the
familiar sequence of ploughsoil, 'occupation layer' and
natural sand. Finds, however, were dense, with lithics
concentrated in square 7 (Fig. 10), pottery in squares 3, 6
and 7 (Fig. 11), and animal bone in square 8. As with Site
5324 (93), the pottery seems to form a single-period Late
style Beaker assemblage, in this case perhaps attributable
to Clarke's (1970) Developed Southern group.

Illustrated artefacts
Flint Fig. 52: L80–L92
Pottery Figs 96–98: P283–P323 Worked bone Fig. 107: B18–B19

I.10. Site 5308/c5 (96). South Site

Excavated 1967. TL 6920 8767. Old OS field 613 (Figs 12–14)
This lay some 100m south of the complex of sites
excavated in 1964–7 (Fig. 4). An L-shaped area of
approximately 432sq ft (40sq m), was divided into the
arbitrary rectangles shown in Figures 12–13. The only
definite feature was a roughly circular pit in area 7,
approximately 3ft (90cm) in diameter and 1ft 6in (45cm)
deep, which contained animal bone. The nature of the area
marked 'floor' in area 4 is unclear. It is shown on only one
of the three surviving plans. Another is annotated
'scattered sherds no real evidence of floor'. The section
(Fig. 12) shows the same stratigraphy as on Sites 5308/c4
(61/68), 5308/c3 (69), 5324 (93) and 5333 (95/97). Lithics
were concentrated in areas 2 and 7 (Fig. 13), pottery in
areas 2 and 3 (Fig. 14), fired clay in area 1 (Fig. 14), and
animal bone in area 7. The pottery includes Middle and
Late style Beaker and Bronze Age wares.

Illustrated Artefacts
Flint Fig. 53: L93–L103
Pottery Figs 99–101: P324–P357)

I.11. Site 5308/c4 (68). Dykeside. Test Pits

Excavated 1981. TL 6931 8778. Old OS field 614 (Fig. 15)
When it was first proposed to publish the excavations
described above, their records prompted several
questions:
1. How much undisturbed deposit remained? Sections
such as those reproduced in Figures 5, 8, 9 and 12 showed

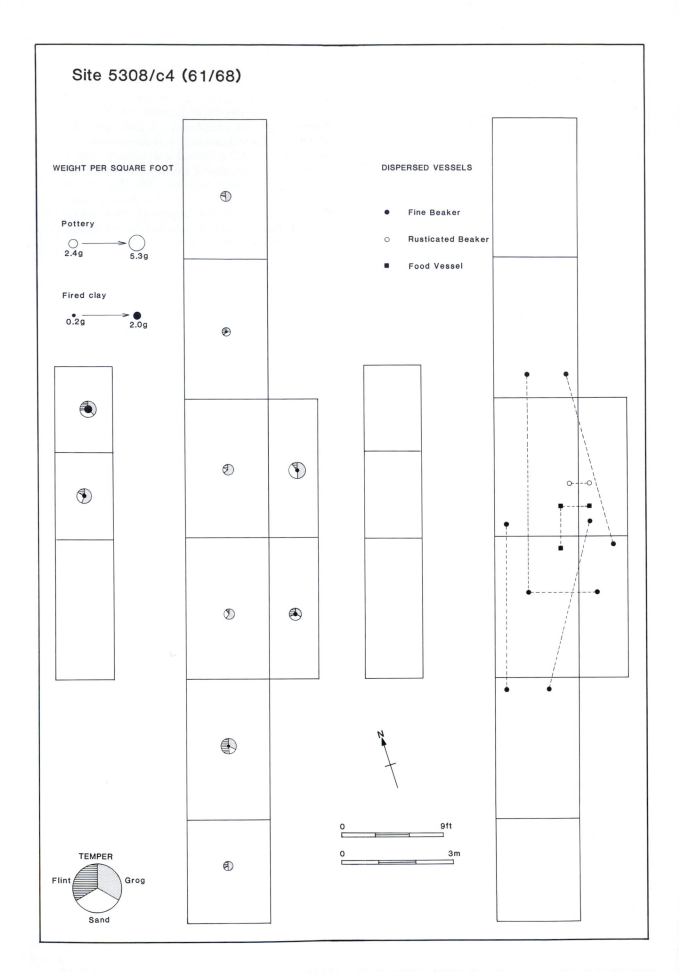

Figure 7 HCW OS 613–614, Site 5308/c4 (61/68). Distributions of pottery and fired clay and of sherds from dispersed vessels. Scale 1:100

20

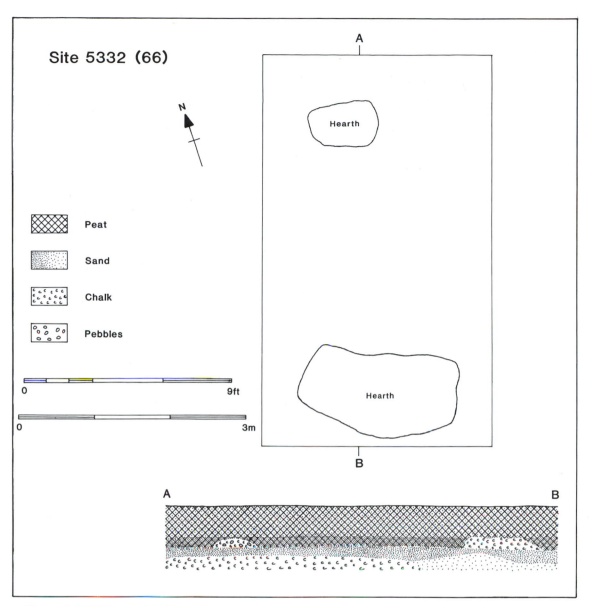

Figure 8 HCW 614, Site 5332 (66). Plan and section based on originals by Frank Curtis. Scale 1:50

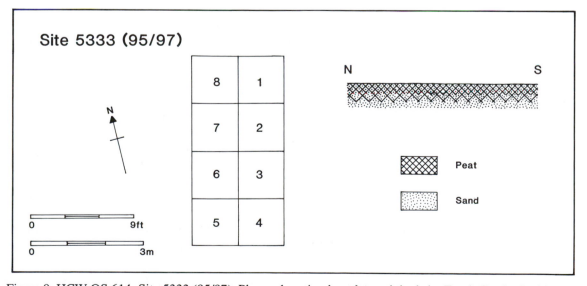

Figure 9 HCW OS 614, Site 5333 (95/97). Plan and section based on originals by Frank Curtis. Scale 1:100

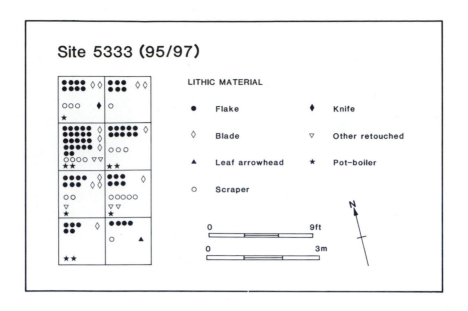

Figure 10 HCW OS 614, Site 5333 (95/97). Distribution of lithic material. Scale 1:100

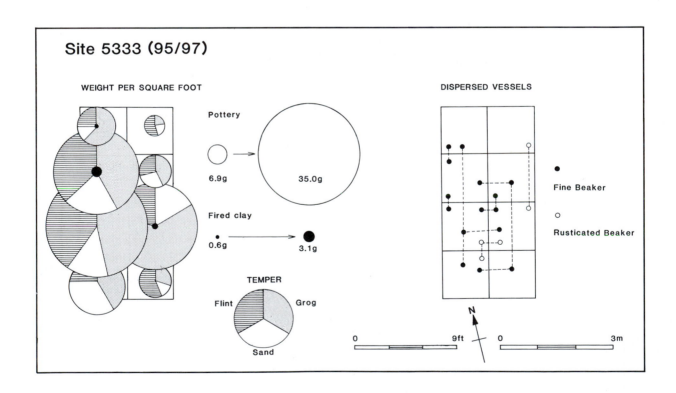

Figure 11 HCW OS 614, Site 5333 (95/97). Distributions of pottery and fired clay and of sherds from dispersed vessels. Scale 1:100

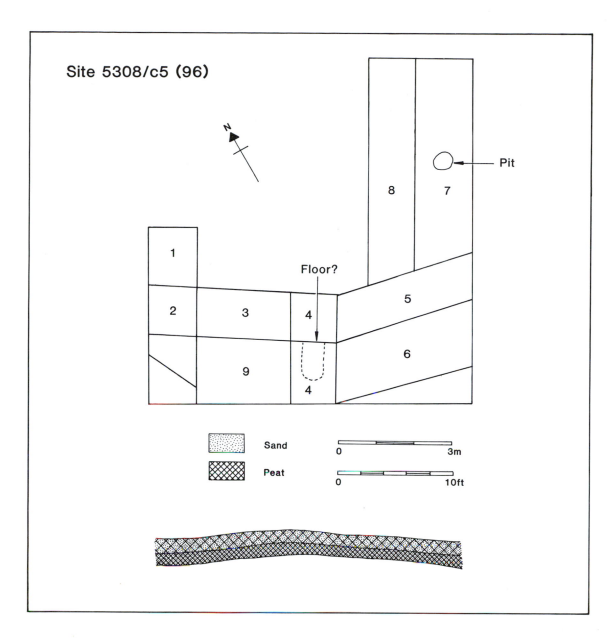

Figure 12 HCW OS 613. Site 5308/c5 (96). Plan and section based on originals by Frank Curtis. Scale 1:100

the 'occupation layer' continuing undiminished in thickness to the edges of the excavated areas; artefact densities too often showed little or no diminution towards the edges of the cuttings (Figs 6, 10, 11, 13, 14). Both observations suggested that even deposits on hillocks where excavation had taken place had not been exhausted.
2. Of what did the 'occupation layer' consist, and was it indeed as homogeneous as it appeared in the sections, even where pottery indicated intermittent occupation over hundreds of years?
3. Did it contain plant macrofossils and other biological evidence which had not been recovered by the methods employed in excavation, and what was the present level of preservation of organic and biological remains?

An attempt was made to answer some of these questions by Peter Murphy, David Wicks and writer. Site 5308/c4 was selected for further investigation because its position on the boundary of two fields, cut by a drainage ditch, made it the easiest to relocate, and because the pottery from it ranged from Neolithic Bowl to Bronze Age, so that, if there were any stratigraphic division between

earlier and later occupations, it would be likely to show there.

Field 614 had reverted to pasture and the site was visible as a slight rise. Four pits were dug through the overlying deposits into natural sand and chalk marl (Fig. 15). Their stratigraphy is described in detail by Peter Murphy in Chapter 6.IV. The 'occupation layer', in the form of a grey, humose sand containing small quantities of struck flint, 'pot-boilers' and animal bone and one sherd of Beaker pottery, was located in all of them, and appeared to be homogeneous (Fig. 16: section C-D, layer 2; section E-F, layer 3).

The section in pit *1*, to the south of the previously-excavated area, was identical to those recorded by Frank Curtis (Fig. 16: section C-D). In pits *2*, *3*, and *4*, to the north, which were slightly lower-lying, some desiccated, sandy peat (Fig. 16: section E-F, layer 2) survived between the ploughsoil and the underlying 'occupation layer'. Organic preservation was poor, although one charred grain of emmer-type wheat was recovered (Ch. 6.IV).

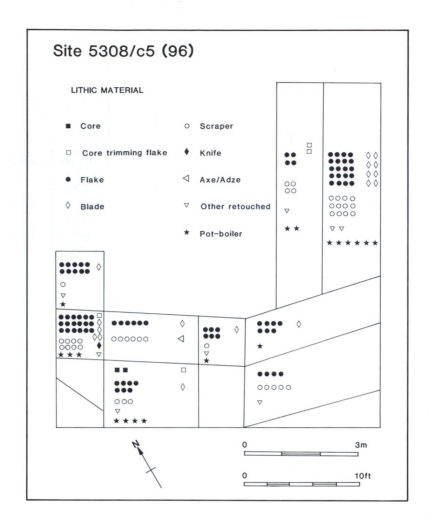

Figure 13 HCW OS 613. Site 5308/c5 (96). Distribution of lithic material. Scale 1:100

II. The Remainder of the Survey Area
(Fig. 3)

II.1. Site 24837. Hockwold Fen, unlocated
Excavated 1960 (Fig. 16)

This excavation is known only from two letters to Sophia Mottram, one dated 13 January 1960, the other 16 February 1960, both incorporating sketches with measurements on which Figure 16 is based. The first reads:

> I had a couple of days digging but got only the old kind of pottery two arrowheads and an axe...

> I suppose you couldnt tell me if any of the people (Windmill Hill, Beaker, Peterborough) used anything like an oven as I came across a patch of dark earth about 18" [46cm] to 2' [60cm] down. I had already found one like this before, so I carefully uncovered it and dug round, as before it was a heap of charcoal ashes etc. with a couple of burnt sherds, under it was, as expected, a bed of chalky marl 6" [15cm] to 8" [20cm] thick and about 2ft [60cm] across, *now under this* was another heap of charcoal and ashes. About level with the top of the chalk and about a foot [30cm] away was a small pit about a foot across and a few inches deep was another heap of charcoal etc. ...

The accompanying sketch is annotated 'usual few bones around'. The second letter adds:

> About the 'oven'?, I couldnt see any layers of sand or earth in the deposit underneath the chalky cover, there should have been if it had been used at intervals also why the chalk. (I should say that this had been soaked in water and pulverised and then spread on the sand and when dry the underneath had been scraped out. dont forget there had been fires on top of the chalk...

In the accompanying sketch, headed 'Fire Place. Neolithic. Hockwold Fen', the fill below the chalk is annotated 'charcoal, ashes', the fill above the chalk 'ash charcoal bone fragments pottery'. A further note adds 'bones were unburnt pottery blackened by fire'.

This may equate with one of the sites excavated in 1959–60 in fields 466, 614 and 616 (Ch. 3.I.1), but it is impossible to be sure.

II.2. Hockwold cum Wilton. Site 5423 (9)
Excavated 1960. TL 6841 8844. Old OS field 48

The excavation is described in a note which reads:

> Spinney. Small surface finds. Area 12 x 12 [3.65m x 3.65m] to depth of 3' [0.90m] a fair amount of pottery of Beaker type. Decoration carried under the base [Fig. 103: P365]...Rims of sixteen different pots found now in Norwich Castle Museum. scrapers bones no arrowheads.

and at greater length in a letter to Sophia Mottram:

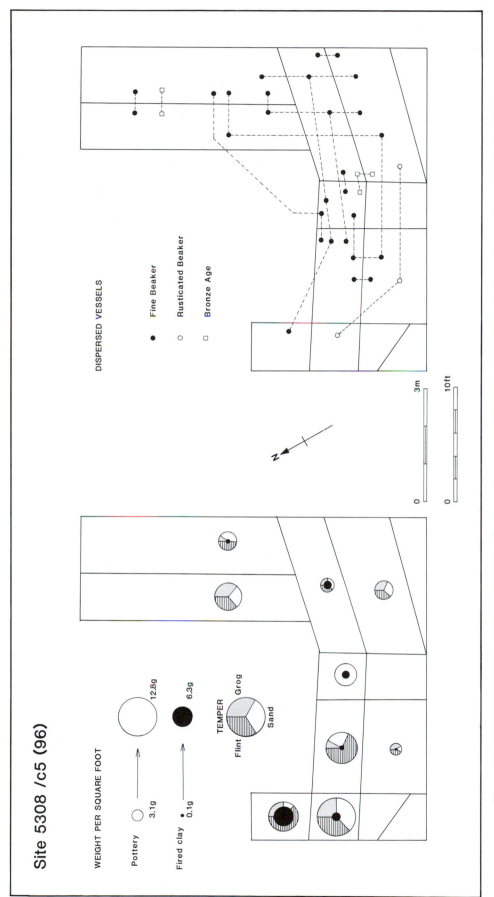

Figure 14 HCW OS 613. Site 5308/c5 (96). Distributions of pottery and fired clay and of sherds from dispersed vessels. Scale 1:100

25

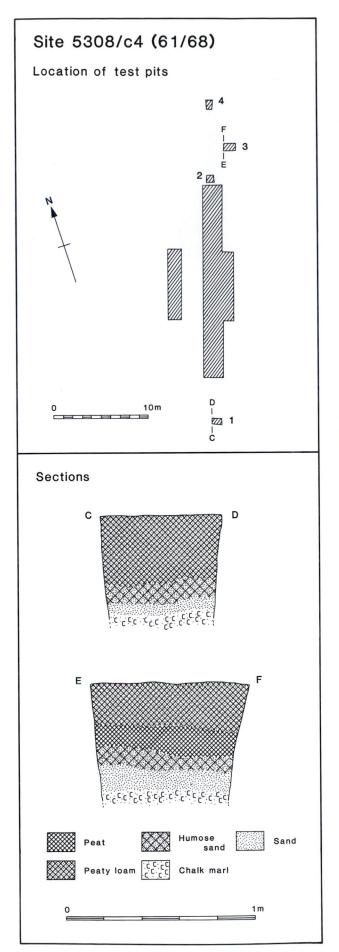

Site 5308/c4 (61/68)

Location of test pits

0   10m

Sections

C   D

E   F

Peat   Humose sand   Sand

Peaty loam   Chalk marl

0   1m

Figure 15 Site 5308/c4 (61/68). Location of 1981 test pits and sections of west faces of nos *1* and *3*.
Scales 1:400, 1:20

On the Monday after your visit I had a look round at dinner time and found a piece of rusticated pottery in another field about 3/4 miles [1.20km] away so I tried at night to find more. I soon came on some more pieces of pottery and the usual bones the bones were very fragile and a part of a jawbone with a few teeth, I couldnt make out, and as they lay among the debris of a fireplace, I put the lot in a box I had with me, and sent it straight to Norwich, asking for it to be given to Miss Green.

In reply Mr Clark said the pottery was of Necked Beaker... the bones were so fragmentary the only ones they could identify were ox and pig, while the charcoal was of alder, hornbeam or hazel, this is interesting, as I know of no hornbeam round these parts, but neither is there any yew trees nearer than the church, whereas the fen is so full of them they are as common as bog oaks. He also asked if they could keep the pottery from the site. Meantime, I kept digging and after I had dug about 12 feet [3.65m] square I started to find the bits together and was surprised to find the rims (pieces) of 14 different pots (evidently two portions of the base of a pot had the decoration continued underneath).

The NCM collection is almost certainly incomplete, consisting only of one scraper, twelve sherds of fine and rusticated Beaker and a small quantity of animal bone (Appendix 35a (microfiche). Possible confusion between the animal bone from this site and that from 'site 8' in fields 466–616 is discussed above. Handled vessels were also present according to Plate II, where the site is marked 'handled Beaker and rusticated pottery'.

Illustrated artefact
Beaker sherd Fig. 103: P365

II. 3. Hockwold cum Wilton. Site 5374 (19)
Excavated 1961. TL 6890 8740. Old OS field 596
It is simply recorded that a hearth was excavated here. The eight sherds preserved from it in NCM are from plain Bronze Age vessels.

II.4. Hockwold cum Wilton. Site 5316/c2, c5, c6 ('site 7188')
Excavated 1961–2. TL 7130 8850 (centre). Old OS field 430 (Salway 1967, 48–56)
These and the following excavations were conducted in advance of the construction of the cut-off channel. They sampled an extensive crop-mark complex of ditched enclosures and tracks on the chalk skirtland.

Salway's first excavation revealed a small pit containing a Late style Beaker (Salway 1967, fig. 12: F1; Clarke 1970, corpus no. 559, fig. 752). The pit was sealed by a layer of clean sand containing a further Beaker sherd (Salway 1967, fig. 12: F2) and a few pieces of struck flint. The sand layer locally capped the chalk and was cut by the ditches of the enclosure system, which was of more than one phase. Excavation farther to the east the following year revealed traces of Iron Age occupation and confirmed that the ditches of the enclosure system were multi-phase and contained Romano-British pottery.

The total collection of pre-Iron Age material from 'site 7188' comprises forty-seven pieces of struck flint, including possibly Mesolithic material, the complete

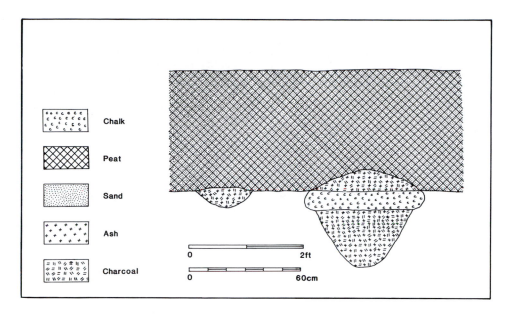

Chalk	
Peat	
Sand	
Ash	
Charcoal	

0   2ft

0   60cm

Figure 16 'Hockwold Fen'. Site 24837. Section through unlocated find of an oven or hearth and a smaller hearth, 1960, based on originals by Frank Curtis. Scale 1:20

Beaker and Beaker sherd mentioned above, and a further Beaker sherd.

II.5. Hockwold cum Wilton. Site 5316/c7, c8 ('site 7088')

Excavated 1962. TL 7025 8815 (centre). Old OS field 428 (Salway 1967, 44–48)

Multi-phase Romano-British ditches were again excavated. Two trenches cut into a natural hollow in the northern part of the site, area 1 (Site 5316/c7), revealed features of irregular plan, described as pits and post-holes, in the chalk at its base, one of them with numerous fragmentary wooden stakes (Salway 1967, figs 4–5). They contained and were surrounded by an extensive spread of 'Secondary Neolithic/Beaker occupation debris' on the chalk surface, which was itself sealed by a medium grey clay, flecked with chalk. This was succeeded by further clayey layers, one of them containing Iron Age pottery.

Re-examination of the pottery published as 'Secondary Neolithic' shows it to be of Late Bronze/Early Iron Age date, although earlier material is also present (Ch. 5.III.2).

The total collection of pre-Iron Age material from 'site 7088' comprises 458 pieces of struck flint, predominantly Later Neolithic or Early Bronze Age in character, but including some Mesolithic material, one sherd possibly of Neolithic Bowl and two of Beaker.

II.6. Hockwold cum Wilton. Site 5394. Sluice Drove

Excavated 1962. TL 7185 8810 (centre). Old OS field 441 (Salway 1967, 56)

At the same time, Colonel T.C. Kelly, U.S.A.F., excavated in another part of the complex in a field to the south-east. No records or finds are available. Apart from the briefest of mentions by Salway, who states that 'There was no evidence for habitation and only a few fragments of Iron Age or Roman pottery were recovered', the only information about the excavation is a typescript by Colonel Kelly which forms part of the SMR:

Just 75 yards [69m] southeast of the Southeast corner of Sluice Drove bridge [*i.e.* at approx. TL 7175 8895],

a small chalk house floor was excavated but yielded only a few pre-Roman potsherds and flint scrapers. To make sure no other habitation was encountered in this series of ditches and also to satisfy the requirements laid on by the land owner, the field was finally levelled with a bulldozer and only another early camp site containing pottery and a single bone needle was identified. None of the ditches contained any pottery and my conclusions are that they were part of a farm drainage project and probably pre-roman based on the potsherds found. No metal of any kind was found, even with a mine detector.

The clarity of this introduction, which seems to state unequivocally that only *two* 'sites' were discovered in the field, is fogged by the *three* separate lists of finds which follow, one from 'Sluice Drove' 62 — Original House Floor', which should relate to the 'small chalk house floor', one from 'Sluice Drove South' which, since it includes a 'bone needle or punch', should relate to 'another early camp site', and a third from 'Sluice Drove North Site'. All record struck flint, with some blades and blade cores described as comparable with Mesolithic material from Kelling Heath (Site 6246). Pottery is mainly listed as Iron Age or Romano-British, but includes 'one sherd Bronze Age beaker' and 'Group of secondary Neolithic or Early Beaker material, 23 sherds', both from 'North site', and 'One Early Beaker rim sherd', from 'South Site'. The only pottery listed from 'Original House Floor' is 'fifteen potsherds, native norfolk, well made pottery, comb decorated'.

While it is impossible to evaluate these identifications, they at least indicate that pre-Iron Age as well as Iron Age material was present.

II.7. Hockwold cum Wilton. Site 5317/c3 (23). Corner Ground

Excavated 1962. TL 6865 8823. Old OS field 644

December — 62. Handled Beaker Hut Site...Animal teeth, Roe Deer Antler fragments, Bone fragments and flints. Two hearths. Arrowheads No. 93 and 94 and

Axe No. 74 were excavated from an area roughly 9 x 9' circular.

The SMR card adds that there were many sherds of handled Beakers.

Green records three oblique and two barbed and tanged arrowheads (1980, 380, catalogue no. 363)

II.8. Hockwold cum Wilton. Site 5317/c2 (25). Corner Ground

Excavated 1962. TL 6850 8830. Old OS field 644
'Beaker hut site' excavated by Frank Curtis. Even less is known of this excavation than of the last. Surviving finds include struck flint and Late and Rusticated Beaker sherds.

II.9. Feltwell. Site 4921/c1. Glebe Farm

Excavated 1965. TL 7148 9090. Old OS field 264 (Cleal 1984, 148)
While excavating a Romano-British bath house on the chalk upland on the northern fringe of Feltwell village, Frank Curtis found a pit containing most of a Grooved Ware dish, a small quantity of struck flint, a bone point, and animal bone consisting primarily of cattle and pig (Table 17).

Illustrated artefacts
Flint Fig. 54: L104
Pottery Fig. 102: P359
Worked bone Fig. 108: B20

III. Discussion

The distribution of excavated settlements, confined to Hockwold cum Wilton (Fig. 3), reflects the area in which Frank Curtis was most active and the location of rescue excavations on the line of the cut-off channel in 1961–2. Settlements comparable with those excavated by Frank Curtis line the south-eastern fen edge. Within the survey area, obvious unexcavated examples include a sandy hillock in Feltwell (Site 17569, OS 282) where Mr Eric Secker turned up patches of red ashes during ploughing and from which he collected a stone axe (Fig. 55: L114), struck flint, and a Beaker sherd; a chalky hillock farther north in the same parish (Site 5159/c2, OS 321+498) on which there is a 'pot-boiler' concentration and from which both Mr Secker and Mr M. J. Younge have collected Beaker pottery, and Mr Younge struck flint; and a field in Methwold (Site 2531/c1, OS 242), from the chalk hillocks of which Mr J. D. Wortley has amassed a collection of struck flint and of pottery including Neolithic Bowl, Peterborough Ware (Fig. 105: P386), Grooved Ware, Beaker, and Early Bronze Age material, some of it illustrated by Gibson (1982, figs MET 1–3). South of the survey area, classic excavated examples include Plantation and Peacock's Farms, Shippea Hill, Cambridgeshire (Clark 1933; Clark *et al.* 1935), as well as Fifty Farm and Hayland House, Mildenhall, Suffolk (Leaf 1934).

On the Hockwold sites structural remains were confined to the stakes around Site 5324 (93) (Bamford 1982, text fig. 3), stake-holes observed on Site 5308/c1 (63) (Bamford 1982, 13), the puddled chalk 'hearths' of Site 5332 (66) (Fig. 8), a 'hearth with heap of clay balls with stones' marked in the south of field 616 (Pl. II), and an unlocated 'oven' (Fig. 16). Hearths without recorded structure were the most common features. There were only

two pits, on Site 5308/c3 (69) (Bamford 1982, text figs 6–7) and Site 5308/c5 (96) (Fig. 12). It is not clear whether a gully beneath Site 5324 (93) was of natural or artificial origin (Bamford 1982, 12).

Occupation was primarily represented by concentrations of artefacts and animal bone, which preserved some spatial patterning. Artefact density varied considerably, ranging from approximately 30 objects per m^3 on Site 5308/c4 (61/68; Figs 6–7) to 220 on Site 5333 (97; Figs 10–11).

The artefact-rich horizon preserved no visible stratigraphy, even where the pottery within it spanned hundreds of years or where protection from the plough was provided by a remnant of desiccated peat below the ploughsoil (*e.g.* Fig. 15: section E-F, layer 2). It is easy to visualise circumstances in which this might have come about: movement of people and animals on a thin, sandy soil could quickly mix the debris of current and past occupations, and there is the further possibility of deflation prior to peat growth. It invites comparison with the 'culture layer' of Mildenhall Fen, Suffolk (Clark 1936, fig. 2) or Hurst Fen, in the same parish (Clark 1960, 203, figs 2 and 6).

This reflects the fact that excavations were sited on the *tops* of hillocks, where material was exposed by the plough. Any vertical separation between successive episodes would have survived on the *flanks* of hillocks, where the debris of earlier occupations might have become covered by peat growth before being mixed with the debris of later ones, as at Peacock's Farm, Shippea Hill, Cambridgeshire (Clark *et al.* 1935, pls XLII and XLIV, fig. 5).

Collectively, however, the sites in fields 466, 614 and 616 show another form of vertical separation. In general, and allowing for the vagaries of topography and agriculture, those investigated in 1959–62, when the fields were first ploughed up or soon afterwards (Sites 24866 ('site 8'), 5311+5312 (50+ 51) and 5373 (22)), produced predominantly Bronze Age pottery, with small quantities of earlier styles, while those excavated in 1965–67 (Sites 5324 (93) and 5333 (95/97)) produced only or almost only Beaker (Table 12, Fig. 61). The exception is Site 5332 (66), excavated in 1965, which produced an almost pure Bronze Age assemblage. It seems that the highest hillocks, exposed when the fields were first ploughed, had remained in intermittent occupation well into the second millennium cal. BC, while lower ones, which had become peat-covered and ceased to be occupied centuries earlier, progressively became exposed as peat wastage was accelerated by cultivation.

The same did not occur in field 613, which remained wooded. Here every site, including 5308/c5 (96), excavated in 1967, produced at least some Bronze Age pottery. This and other surviving patches of woodland in the area may yet preserve deposits the equivalents of which have been destroyed in surrounding fields.

It has been pointed out (Pryor and French 1985, 304) that the system of ditched enclosures and tracks, some of it plotted by Salway (1967, fig. 2), which occupies part of the skirtland in Hockwold cum Wilton bears at least a superficial resemblance to the Later Neolithic to Middle Bronze Age system at Fengate, Cambridgeshire, on the western edge of the fens. The Hockwold system has scarcely been investigated. The ditches excavated by Salway in 1961–62 on Site 5316 were Romano-British in date: they not only contained Romano-British material but also, at least in one area, cut through a sand layer which sealed a pit containing a Beaker. Prehistoric material, from Mesolithic to Iron Age, was, however, recovered during the excavations. As far as can be judged from a summary report unsubstantiated by finds or records, prehistoric material seems to have been even more prevalent at Site 5394 to the south-east, excavated by Colonel Kelly in 1962. The area of the system was densely occupied in prehistory, although the evidence of this occupation has suffered more from the continued use of the zone in later periods and from natural erosion than has contemporary material from slightly farther out in the fen. Any relationship between this occupation and the system itself remains to be demonstrated.

4. Bodies and Burials

(Appendix 3 (microfiche))

Barrows and ring-ditches within the survey area so far seem confined to upland and skirtland. None has been investigated. Human remains of certain or possible prehistoric date have, however, been found at several other locations, most of them in peat fen (Fig. 17).

I. Early Bronze Age skeletal remains

I.1. Methwold. Site 2586. 'Nancy' or 'the Southery Fen female'
Found 1931. TL 6300 9425. Old OS field 1231
A skeleton was found by workmen widening and deepening the Ten Foot Drain, a drainage ditch near the boundary between Southery and Methwold. The body was described as lying face down, one arm across the face and the other extended with a bracelet of eight barrel-shaped jet beads (Lethbridge, Fowler and Sayce 1931, pl. XXXIIIa) around the wrist.

T.C. Lethbridge visited the site and recorded that the skeleton had lain under 1ft 9in (55cm) of peat, on a layer of compressed sedges 2–3in (5–8cm) thick which rested directly on undisturbed clay. He also recovered a two-pointed, quadrangular-sectioned copper alloy awl (Lethbridge, Fowler and Sayce 1931, pl. XXXIIIb). A peat-filled former water course, cutting into the clay, ran 28yd (25m) from the site. The skull was identified as that of a young adult female. There was no evidence of deliberate burial, and it was surmised that the find represented a drowning, the body having been carried along by the river in flood, dropped among the sedges bordering it when the flood subsided, and subsequently covered by peat (Lethbridge, Fowler and Sayce 1931, 362).

Sir Harry Godwin established that the skeleton had lain near the base of the Upper Peat just above the Fen Clay. He collected pollen samples from within 3ft (92cm) of where its feet had lain and from undisturbed peat and identified a pollen spectrum comparable with that of the base of the Upper Peat at Shippea Hill (Godwin 1940, 273; 1978, 65).

I.2. Methwold. Site 2585
Found 1958. TL 631 941. Old OS field 1231
Twenty-seven years later, ploughing in the field immediately to east of the 'Nancy' site revealed further human remains. The find was investigated by Sophia Mottram, then Curator of King's Lynn Museum, who described it in a letter to Rainbird Clarke dated 25 January 1958:

> P.S. Had a call from Mr Hudson...who said he'd ploughed up some bones. Unfortunately the village PC got there first and showed us a fragmentary human skeleton — but we had a poke round in the hole and I have sent the proceeds to Doc. [Calvin] Wells. The land there is a thin layer of rich black mud on top of nearly 3 feet [90 cm] of clean black peat on top of light brown clay. It is shrinking fast, great cracks appear in a dry summer... The skeleton appears to have been

near the bottom of the peat with his head, which caught the plough, higher than his feet (according to the ploughman but doubt if there's much in this as I found a loose toe some yards away dragged by the plough) *ie* at a depth of about 2ft [60cm]...

> There was a quite useless flint flake in the disturbed soil, and at the bottom of the peat, in a crack in the clay, a flint pebble (¾" [2cm] more or less cubic) with a hole through it. At that point we had to come back but are going out to have another look.

The Norwich Castle Museum record card adds 'Extended skeleton of adult & 2 children... Bone awl?'. Jacqueline McKinley identifies the individuals as one adult, possibly female, and two juveniles, one possibly male, aged approximately eight to ten, the other possibly female, aged approximately nine to eleven (Ch. 6.I.3).

Radiocarbon determinations
Skeleton *1* 3760 ± 80 BP OxA–2860
Skeleton *2* 3540 ± 80 BP OxA–2861

Illustrated artefact
Worked bone Fig. 108: B21

I.3. Feltwell. Site 5188/c1. Hill Close
Found 1961, excavated 1965. TL 6966 9080. Old OS field 283 (Pl. VII, Figs 18–19)
Unlike the other finds, this was located not in peat fen but on skirtland. The field name reflects its relative elevation, the Lower Chalk bedrock here projecting into the fen as a slight spur. The sections recorded in Pl. VII show solid chalk capped by 'fresh water clay, chalky, with snail shells' under a thin, peaty topsoil. The 'clay' may have been the weathered, frost-altered top of the chalk or the remnant of a soft bed within the Lower Chalk itself (Seale 1975, 15–16).

The field in which the burial lay was permanent pasture until 1961 when it was rotivated and ploughed. This led to the discovery of a copper alloy cauldron and fleshhook ascribed to the Penard phase (Site 5191; Gerloff 1986, 88–92, fig. 6ii) and of an Early Iron Age settlement (Site 5188/c2,c3; Shand 1985). Also ploughed up were a human skull and fragments of other bones which came from a slight hillock.

The circumstances in which Frank Curtis came to excavate the hillock four years later are described by him in a letter to Barbara Green (Keeper of Archaeology, Norwich Castle Museum) dated 24 October 1965:

> On Friday Rock Fletcher came over (he is on night shift) and wanted to do something, so thinking we couldn't do any harm, I got the tools out and we went to have a look at that hill where the burial was, near the Iron Age site. (Cauldron field).

> We dug a shallow trench from east to west and about the centre we found a fragment or two of bone. We extended to the south and came across a skull at 10" [25cm] Deep the plough had just missed it but the

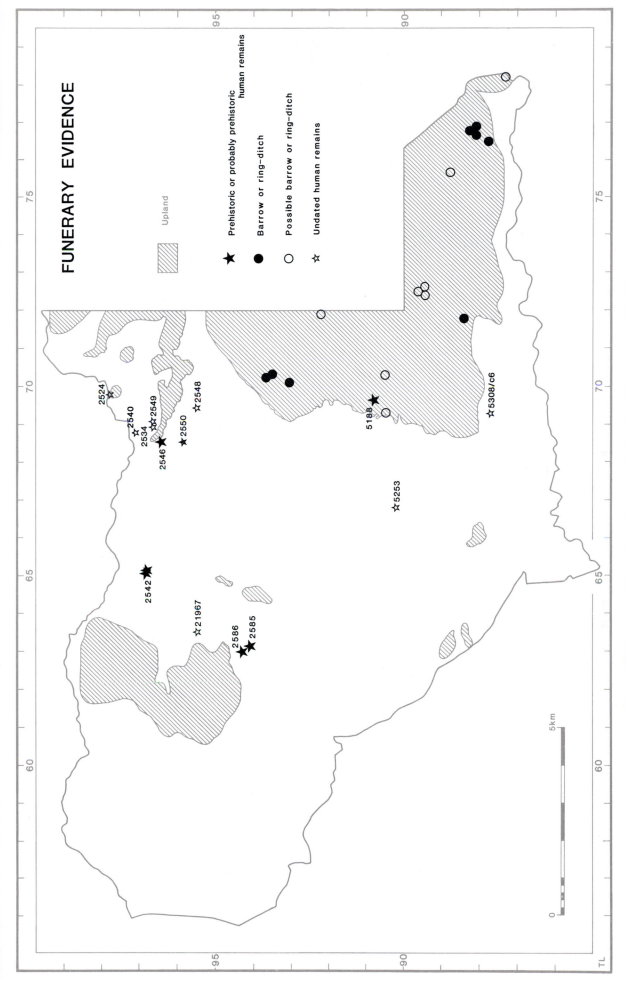

Figure 17 Funerary evidence, listed in Appendix 3 (microfiche). Scale 1:100,00

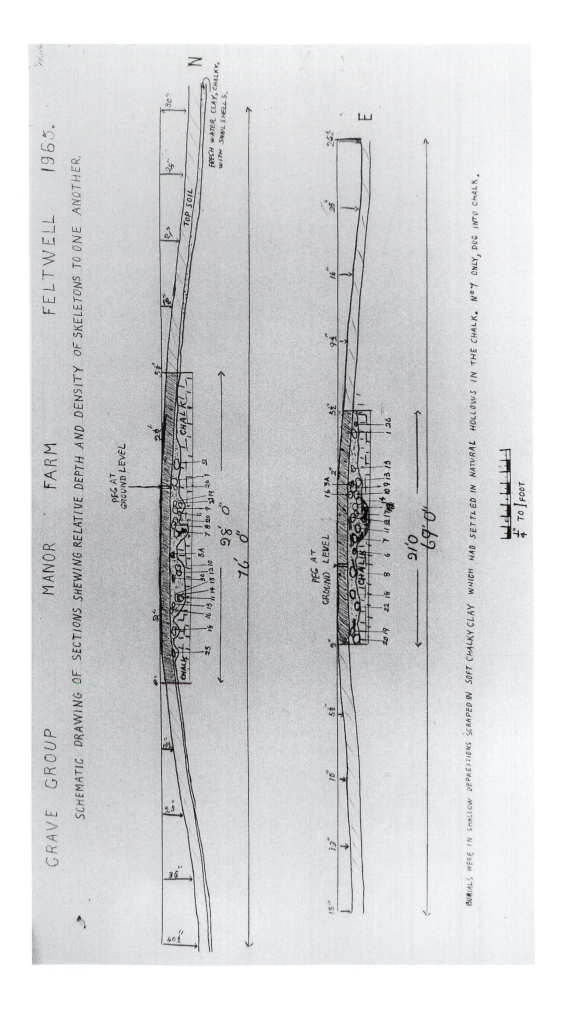

Plate VII Schematic section by Frank Curtis through a hillock used for burials in Hill Close, Feltwell (FWL OS 283, Site 5188/c1).
Photo: David Wicks

tractor wheels running in the furrow had broken it of course. We cleared well round and had to go down 6" [15cm] before we found any bones, even so they were in very bad condition and although the ribs were plain to see for a few inches they faded into a brown stain.

Since the field was about to be deep-ploughed, he continued to excavate intermittently for a further five weeks, occasionally helped by friends and relatives. Handicaps included rain, frost, snow and the media:

Last night Lynn Advertizer sent their people to take photos and get a statement. I wonder how they knew. Today ITV came down and I had to uncover everything for them this took all the morning, and when I got home for dinner I found the Eastern Daily Express waiting with the BBC, and Dr Calvin Wells, so we all went back and I had to uncover everything once more, and then cover up again this finished the day and no work done.

The account which follows is based on Frank Curtis' notes, drafts and sketches. The plan (Fig. 18) is compiled from two versions, one in King's Lynn Museum the other (seen in the background of the cover photograph) now in Norwich Castle Museum.

The excavated area was progressively extended as more burials were discovered, reaching eventual dimensions of 28ft [8.5m] from north to south and 21ft [6.4 m] from west to east, with a slight westward extension to take in burial 20 (Fig. 18). The profile of the hillock and the depths of burials and finds were recorded from the level of a peg driven into the highest point (Pl. VII, Fig. 19).

Burials and some other finds were numbered consecutively. 'Group 3' was used to denote a 'jumble of bones everywhere mixed with pieces of skull', which was subsequently resolved into burials 10 to 17 (Fig. 18). The number 33 has been given retrospectively to a previously unnumbered collection of bones in the north-east corner of the excavated area (Fig. 18).

The apparently natural origin of the hillock was confirmed. There was no evidence for an artificial mound, and a trench dug for 21ft (6.4m) outwards from the north-east corner of the excavated area found no trace of a ditch.

Three areas of burning were recorded. 24, an 'area of dark soil, charcoal, ash, burnt bones', underlay and was cut by burial 8. It contained the cremated remains of an unsexed adult and uncremated bone from other individuals. No cremated bone survives from the other two burnt areas, 25 and 32, although they were recorded in similar terms to 24. Small quantities of cremated human bone have, however, been identified among the inhumed remains of nos. 2, 17 and 25? (Ch. 6.I.3).

Most of the burials were inhumed. The impression of poor preservation and recent damage conveyed in the initial letter is confirmed in accounts of subsequently excavated burials. A description of 2 reads 'Skull crushed flattened by weight of tractor while ploughing', while some bones were 'of the texture of wet brown sawdust'. The inhumations were 'in shallow depressions scraped in soft chalky clay' (Pl. VII). Where their original attitude can be determined, they were generally flexed or contracted, the exceptions being 7 and 8. Some were thought to be incomplete or disarticulated. 'The fact that some skulls had no signs of any other bones with them (No 18 – No 6

– No 26) while No 23 – No 9 had a few bones of upper body only, makes it appear that in fact this was all that was buried'. 8 is described as 'probably a dismembered burial', although it appears articulated in the plan (Fig. 18). There are indications that some burials were successive rather than contemporary: the grave of 8 'had been dug through the cremation area [24]'; the legs of 19 were 'lying on the skull of No 22 which was some 5" lower in the ground', while 22 was described as 'probably disturbed by burial No 19'.

7 was among the better-preserved (Fig. 19):

As we worked, I came on a patch of chalk and as it was about six inches across and circular it seemed odd, and on tapping it with the handle it sounded hollow so it was carefully scraped away until a skull began to appear... The grave had been dug through the chalky clay subsoil, and cut at least six inches into the solid chalk. The pit itself was only three feet nine inches [1.15m] long, by one foot six [45cm] wide, and the body crowded in. The body lay on its back, the right knee had been twisted and pushed down so that the leg stuck up nearly straight and leaning back towards the head. The other femur lay straight out, with tibia and bent across the other ones. The skeleton lay west to east, but the skull itself was upright, facing west. Unfortunately, the condition of the neck bones was such that we were unable to be certain that it was disconnected from the body. A flint leaf arrowhead was found amongst the brown residue, in the lower part of the body.

The skeleton was that of a woman with severe dental caries (Ch. 6.I.3).

Jacqueline McKinley has identified the remains of a total of thirty inhumed individuals, with a preponderance of females, juveniles and infants. Small quantities of animal bone were found with 1, 2, 4 and 7, burnt with 1, unburnt with the remainder. The species represented are cattle and horse (Ch. 6.I.3).

The arrowhead found in the grave of 7 (Fig. 19) was one of the few artefacts associated with the burials. A second leaf arrowhead (Fig. 54: L105) was found in uncertain relation to 1, 'very close to the back but not sticking in a bone unfortunately'. A Late style Beaker sherd (Fig. 102: P362) was found with 19. Cremation 24 included four small, featureless body sherds in predominantly grogged fabrics compatible with those of Early Bronze Age wares. One of them was refired, perhaps when the cremation took place. A further grogged sherd was found among the bones of 2. The 'small piece of flaking pottery' marked close to one of the burials in the south-east of the excavated area does not survive. Other finds, all of Early Bronze Age date, were not associated with particular burials. They comprise an inverted Food Vessel, (Fig. 102: P360; 3A in Fig. 18), a fragmentary flat-based, lugged pot (Fig. 102: P361; 5 in Fig. 18), and a scale-flaked knife (Fig. 54: L107; shown in the south-west of Fig. 18). Burials may have extended beyond the excavated area, since excavation ceased only because deep-ploughing started, not because the site was thought to be exhausted. One account ends 'It is hoped to continue next autumn when the crop is off as it is possible more burials may be found', another reads 'I have looked over the place since ploughing, and some broken bones are shewing, but we may have removed the best part'.

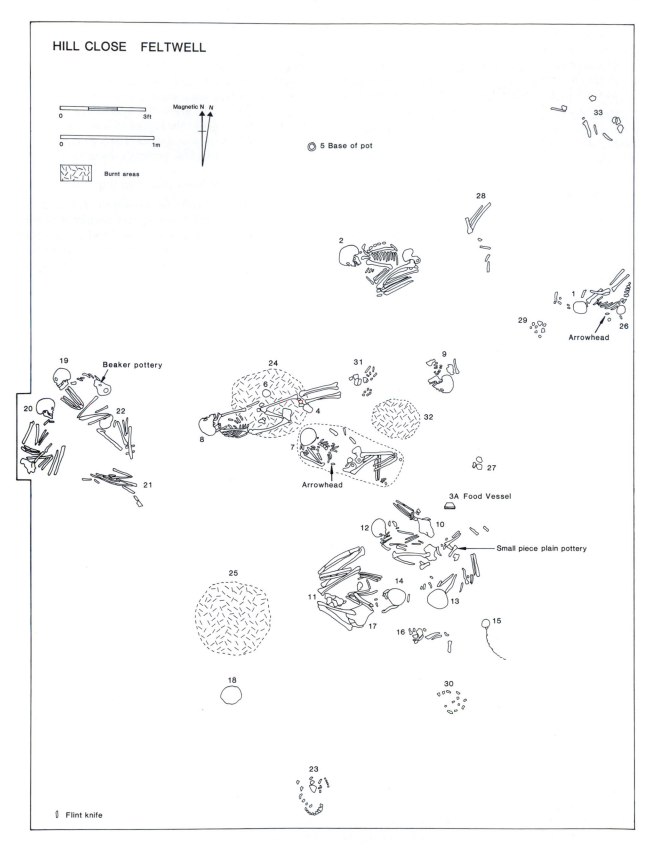

HILL CLOSE FELTWELL

Magnetic N N

Burnt areas

◎ 5 Base of pot

Beaker pottery

Arrowhead

Arrowhead

3A Food Vessel

Small piece plain pottery

◊ Flint knife

Figure 18 Hill Close, Feltwell (FWL OS 283, Site 5188/c1). Plan of 1965 excavation based on originals by
Frank Curtis. Scale 1:40

Radiocarbon determinations
Skeleton *1* 3100 ± 70 BP (OxA–3069)
Skeleton *7* insufficient collagen
Skeleton *19* 3380 ± 70 BP (OxA–2885)

Illustrated artefacts
Flint Fig. 54: L105–107
Pottery Fig. 102: P360–362

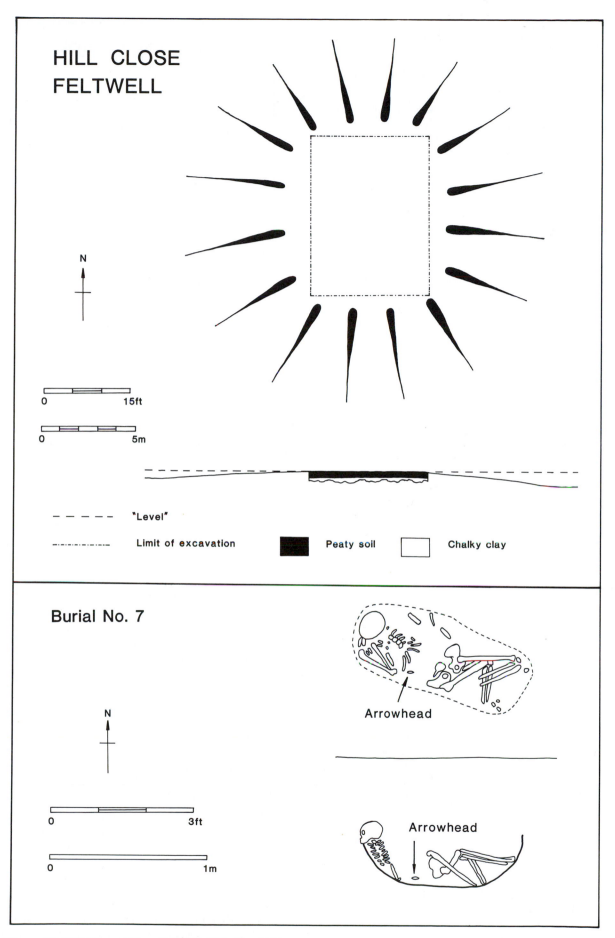

HILL CLOSE
FELTWELL

N

0   15ft

0   5m

– – – – –   "Level"

–·–·–·–·–   Limit of excavation   ▮ Peaty soil   ☐ Chalky clay

Burial No. 7

N

Arrowhead

0   3ft

0   1m

Arrowhead

Figure 19 Hill Close, Feltwell (FWL 283, Site 5188/c1). Above: location of excavated area on hillock, profile of hillock and 'level' from which depths were measured. Scale 1:200.
Below: detail of burial 7. Scale 1:24. From originals by Frank Curtis

I.4. Methwold. Site 2550. Hemplands Farm

Found and excavated 1967. TL 6856 9591. Old OS field 949 (Pl. VIII, Fig. 20)

The manuscript account, dated 3 April 1967, reads as follows:

> During the week previous to Sunday 2–4–67 a man walking by the side of a newly-cut dyke (ditch) in Methwold, saw something glinting in the opposite bank. looking closer, it was found to be a lower human jaw...

> The owner was informed (the land owner) and he took it out carefully and grubbed round a little for the skull, but it was not there. On the opposite side of the ditch they could see some more small bones and just enough were taken to make sure they were also human and then left alone...

> I went down on Monday and took the top soil, over an area 5' x 5 [1.5m x 1.5m] to a depth of 2' [60cm], the last 6" [15cm] trowelled carefully but nothing for the trouble, however eventually a rib and then another and away we went. It was soon found the burial had been disturbed, some ribs were some distance from the others and were the wrong way around a vertebra or two were found but not in a regular pattern, and a femur, caused a lot of work searching for the leg bones that were not there. Then when the pelvis came to light it could be seen the femur was the wrong way round the ball end was farthest from the socket of the pelvis. One of the collarbones was lying across the pelvis, which was itself crushed and out of shape while it was practically impossible to separate pieces of wood from it without parts sticking to it. No bones below the knee, and no arm bones at all were found, they may of course, be broken and scattered by the digger, and then when the spoil from the ditch was buldozed away and cultivated, all trace was lost...

> One thing I must mention, the skeleton lay on sticks placed side by side, regularly and level and were about an inch thick they were of course rotten and exposing them to the air caused them to disintegrate... The bones were also covered with wood but this had been put on less regular and it is possible it may have floated there. I wondered if this could have been part of a brushwood causeway or something like that, and the burial being there was incidental and had really nothing to do with the sticks...

The accompanying sketch, reproduced in Figure 20, shows a disturbed but articulated skeleton lying on a regular setting of parallel pieces of wood, both cut by the ditch. Plate VIII confirms the regularity and artificiality of the setting. Jacqueline McKinley identifies the remains as those of an adult woman (Ch. 6.I.3).

Radiocarbon determination
3840 ± 80 BP (OxA–2868)

I.5. Methwold. Site 2542. Methwold Severalls

(i) Site 2542/c1
Found 1967, excavated 1968. TL 6505 9685. Old OS field 1012 (Fig. 21)

A typescript report by Frank Curtis reads as follows:

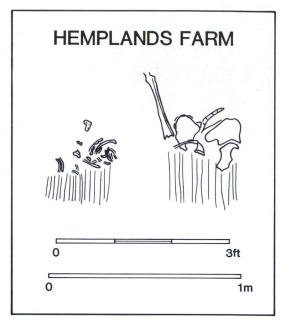

Figure 20 Hemplands Farm, Methwold Hythe (MTW 949, Site 2550). Plan of 1967 excavation, showing disturbed skeleton on regularly-laid pieces of wood, both cut by drainage ditch Orientation uncertain. Scale 1:20

During 1967, I had occasion to investigate a skeleton, found after a ditch had been freshly cut at Hemplands Farm, Methwold Fen [Site 2550, described above]. A week or two after finishing this, a human femur was ploughed out on a field recently reclaimed for cultivation. The owner of the land, Mr Jerry Waterfall, had got interested by now, and as the field was now under crops, we left it until it was clear, in the hope that something might turn up, to give an indication as to the whereabouts of this burial.

This year, in May 1968, Mr Waterfall, looking about for evidence, found what he thought was a piece of skull, and a piece of scapula. He came over and brought these pieces, and as I agreed they were human, he said he would come the next day and take me to the site, and leave me for two or three hours before taking me home again...

Walking...to the place where another piece had been found, (a portion of skull with three teeth in upper jaw) I found a fairly large piece of skull, but this rather complicated matters as it was about 40 yards [35m] from where the other pieces of skull had been found. However, we got to the place and Jerry showed me where he had scratched about with a piece of stick to try and find more...

I opened a 6' x 4' [1.80m x 1.2m] area and moved the top soil down to the undisturbed peat, and found nothing. I then went down two more feet, and again nothing. As some bones had been ploughed out, there seemed no point in going deeper at this time. A further 6' x 4' was staked, and this time, while removing the top soil, an arm, humerus, radius and ulnar [*sic*] were found, but they had been moved, unfortunately. However, on cleaning the top soil off the underlying peat, the indentations where these bones had come from could be plainly seen, being filled with black loose soil, in brown solid peat, as good as one could

Plate VIII Hemplands Farm, Methwold Hythe (MTW OS 949, Site 2550): skeleton on regularly-laid pieces of wood, cut by drainage ditch.
Photo: Frank Curtis

wish. I eventually plotted these, as it was evident they (the bones) had just been rolled out of place by the ground plate of the plough. Again, nothing was found underneath, and another 6' x 4' made, but this time pieces of bone began to appear in the top soil, and so I extended the site to 20' x 10' [6m x 3m] which I hoped would uncover the burial. At this time I had no idea there would be more than one body. As the top soil was removed, the large number of pieces of bone that turned up made it certain that more than one skeleton was here, and as the undisturbed peat showed up portions of bones could be seen. The top loose black soil was easily removed as the underlying peat was cut cleanly by the plough, and it was very difficult to clear from the bones embedded in it... The bones such as ribs and smaller bones, and the thin parts of others, were soft and broke up when lifted, not being as tough as the peat, which was very wet...

The skulls, in all cases, had either been sliced off by the plough, or crushed in by the weight of tractors... The skeletons had been disturbed shortly after burial, some limbs were still in articulation, although away from the rest... As the peat had never been disturbed, the bodies must have been moved by dogs or other animals, or even by water... The bones that were in the undisturbed peat were all in a layer of about 6 inches [15cm] and nothing was found below after lifting. A small bronze pin was the only find... The depth varied considerably. In one place there was no layer of sand above peat and peat was 4 feet 6 inches [1.4m] deep below base of topsoil, but could not be kept clear of water.

Shortly after the excavation, Dr F. A. Hibbert, then of the Cambridge Botany School, visited the site with Frank Curtis and collected samples from close to where the burials had been found. His preliminary palynological report (Ch. 6.V.1) indicates that the skeletons lay in peat formed after fen woodland had given way to wetter

conditions, and that there was a marked increase in the pollen of plants associated with cultivation in the deposits immediately below the level in which the bones were found. A post-Neolithic date was inferred.

The remains of six individuals were recovered. Jacqueline McKinley identifies them as two adult women, an adult man, a juvenile aged approximately seven to eight, another aged approximately eleven, and an infant (Ch. 6.I.3).

A two-pointed, quadrangular-sectioned copper alloy awl, (Fig. 26: M3), was found approximately 50cm from the nearest burial (Fig. 21). During the preparation of the palaeopathological report a small roll of sheet lead marked with the same accession number as the bones, was found with the mature female. It resembled a Roman *defixio*, but when unrolled carried no inscription. It may have been accidentally introduced into the collection after excavation, especially as by 1967 Frank Curtis had excavated on several Romano-British sites, including two temples. Alternatively, although perhaps less probably, it may have been contemporary with the burials, given the presence of small rolls of sheet lead among the artefacts deposited in and around the Fengate Power Station timber alignment in Cambridgeshire from the Middle Bronze Age onwards (Coombs 1992, fig. 8: 12) and of lead beads in a probably Early Bronze burial at West Water Reservoir, Peebleshire (Sheridan 1992).

Radiocarbon determinations
Skeleton *1* 3580 ± 80 BP (OxA–2862)
Skeleton *2 or 3* 3670 ± 80 BP (OxA–2863)
Skeleton *5* 3650 ± 80 BP (OxA–2864)

Illustrated artefact
Copper alloy awl (Fig. 26: M3)

(ii) Site 2542/c2
Found 1971. Approx. TL 6510 9684. Old OS field 1012. Further skeletons were found in 1971, at a spot recorded as ten yards (9m) south and fifty yards (45m) east of the first find. The only record is a note on the SMR card which carries a sketch showing the location of the second findspot and reads '3 burials + 2 white scrapers [Fig. 54: L108–L109] just under bones undisturbed. Fd. in peat *c.* 2ft [60cm] deep. All disturbed by ploughing.'

Jacqueline McKinley identifies the skeletons as those of an adult man and two juveniles, aged approximately six to seven and five to six (Ch.6.I.3).

Radiocarbon determinations
Skeleton *7* 3760 ± 80 BP (OxA–2865)
Skeleton *8* 3600 ± 80 BP (OxA–2866)
Skeleton *9* 3620 ± 80 BP (OxA–2867)

Illustrated artefacts
Flint Fig. 54: L108–L109

II. Dating
by Frances Healy and Rupert A.Housley

The date of most of the burials described here was uncertain. In the case of Hill Close, Feltwell (Site 5188/c1), while rite and artefacts indicated an Early Bronze Age date for some of the burials, there was a suggestion of Early or Middle Neolithic practice in the leaf

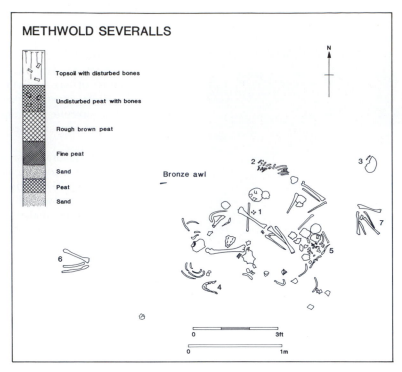

Figure 21 Methwold Severalls (MTW OS 1012, Site 2542). Plan of 1968 excavation based on original by Frank Curtis. Scale 1:40

arrowheads found with two burials and in the possible disarticulation of others (Healy 1984, 87, 116). In the case of the Fenland sites, while a prehistoric date seemed probable and an Early Bronze Age date possible, there was no conclusive evidence of either. The dating of skeletal remains in peat fen on stratigraphic grounds alone is problematic, since it is generally impossible to determine from what level they sank or were buried.

Thanks to an award from the British Academy's Fund for Applied Science in Archaeology it was possible to submit twelve samples, all femurs, to the Oxford University Radiocarbon Accelerator Unit. These were pretreated and dated by Dr Rupert Housley, using the methods outlined by Hedges *et al.* (1989). The results are listed in Table 1 and depicted graphically in Figure 22. Those for the fenland sites are published and discussed by Healy and Housley (1992).

Hill Close, Feltwell (Site 5188/c1)
Samples were submitted from skeletons *1* and *7*, both found with leaf arrowheads, and skeleton *19*, found with a sherd of Late style Beaker pottery. That from *7* was too low in collagen to provide a reliable determination; that from *19* falls towards the end of the early Bronze Age; that from *1* within the Middle Bronze Age (Table 1). The difference between the two, which do not quite overlap at two standard deviations, would be compatible with the intermittent insertion of burials into the hillock, and with continued activity in this relatively elevated area through the second millennium.

Both weigh against the Neolithic use of the hillock and tend to support Green's use of the site to argue for the continued currency of leaf arrowheads into the Early Bronze Age (1980, table IV.31). The arrowheads may alternatively have been accidentally redeposited, although their positions in the two burials make this unlikely. Leaf arrowheads abound in the area (Fig. 35), at least four

further examples having been found in the same field (Appendix 9 (microfiche)).

Whatever the age of skeleton *7*, the other burials are probably of Bronze Age date. A predominance of unaccompanied burials is not unusual for the period. At Bowthorpe, Norwich, for example, only four out of eleven fully-excavated Early Bronze Age graves contained grave-goods of any kind (Site 11431; Lawson 1986, 23–30). The contemporary insertion of burials into natural mounds is seen at Waterhall Farm, Chippenham, Cambridgeshire (Martin 1976a), and perhaps at Mepal in the same county (Fox 1923, 37)

Fenland sites
All four finds from which samples were submitted have produced determinations within the Early Bronze Age, predating those for Hill Close. Measurements for groups of skeletons from Sites 2585, 2542/c1 and 2542/c2 cluster sufficiently closely to suggest that each group may represent a single event (Fig. 22).

III. Discussion

III.1. Modes of Burial

Hill Close, Feltwell (Site 5188/c1)
Frank Curtis clearly thought that some of the skeletons were disarticulated at the time of burial. The evidence is, however, ambiguous. The apparent rotation through 180° of the skull of burial *7* (Fig. 19) may have resulted from burial face-downwards. The rest of skeleton was in normal juxtaposition, if not in articulation, as were most of the others. The incompleteness of many may be due partly to damage by cultivation and by the passage of tractors and other heavy equipment over a thin, peaty soil, partly to poor preservation, and partly to the disturbance of earlier burials by later ones. Comparison of Figure 18 and Plate VII shows that those burials which were closest to the

Site	Skeleton	Lab. No.	BP	cal. BC 1 δ	cal. BC 2 δ
Hill Close, Feltwell					
Site 5188	1	OxA–3069	3100 ± 70	1446 (0.92) 1298 1284 (0.08) 1267	1522 (0.98) 1204 1188 (0.02) 1162
	7	Insufficient collagen			
	19	OxA–2885	3380 ± 70	1862 (0.05) 1850 1759 (0.87) 1607 1556 (0.08) 1536	1878 (0.09) 1834 1824 (0.91) 1522
Fenland sites					
Methwold OS 1231					
Site 2585	1	OxA–2860	3760 ± 80	2330 (0.85) 2122 2082 (0.15) 2040	2458 (0.97) 2020 2004 (0.03) 1976
	2	OxA–2861	3540 ± 80	2021 (0.07) 2003 1977 (0.55) 1864 1848 (0.38) 1765	2131 (0.06) 2073 2044 (0.94) 1687
Hemplands Farm, Methwold					
Site 2550		OxA–2868	3840 ± 80	2457 (0.19) 2414 2407 (0.61) 2270 2253 (0.21) 2203	2563 (0.02) 2541 2500 (0.95) 2128 2078 (0.03) 2042
Methwold Severalls					
Site 2542/c1	1	OxA–2862	3580 ± 80	2112 (0.08) 2087 2038 (0.80) 1877 1838 (0.07) 1820 1798 (0.05) 1783	2187 (0.01) 2165 2141 (0.99) 1740
	2/3	OxA–2863	3670 ± 80	2192 (0.11) 2162 2143 (0.89) 1947	2321 (0.99) 1878 1836 (0.01) 1822 1796 (0.01) 1785
	5	OxA–2864	3650 ± 80	2176 (0.01) 2174 2139 (0.99) 1923	2287 (0.97) 1873 1841 (0.02) 1815 1804 (0.02) 1778
Site 2542/c2	7	OxA–2865	3760 ± 80	2330 (0.85) 2122 2082 (0.15) 2040	2458 (0.97) 2020 2004 (0.03) 1976
	8	OxA–2866	3600 ± 80	2129 (0.20) 2076 2042 (0.80) 1881	2194 (0.03) 2160 2144 (0.97) 1747
	9	OxA–2867	3620 ± 80	2131 (0.26) 2073 2044 (0.74) 1891	2268 (0.01) 2258 2202 (0.99) 1755

All made on femurs. Calibrated age ranges and probabilities calculated using OxCal v2. The probability for each range is expressed in brackets between its two extremes.

Table 1 Radiocarbon determinations on human skeletal material

surface were among the most fragmented (*e.g. 16, 18, 23*, and *30*). All may have been complete when interred.

7 stood out from the other burials in being the only one whose grave had been cut down into the solid chalk and in being compressed into a small space, while the others, where intact, seemed to have been more carefully disposed (Figs 18–19). It was also the only one to show severe dental caries (Ch. 6.I.3). The possibility remains that it may have been of a different date from the rest.

Fenland sites
In the case of skeletons recovered from peat fen, the likelihood of disturbance by ancient water movement, peat shrinkage and recent cultivation is difficult to evaluate. It is equally difficult to judge whether these and similar finds represent deliberate burial, disposal of bodies by throwing them into bogs, or drownings. At Hemplands Farm (Site 2550), the regular setting of wood beneath the skeleton must indicate deliberate deposition.

The survival of the wood shows too that the burial was waterlogged from deposition to recent drainage. At Methwold Severalls the larger group of skeletons, excavated in 1968 (Site 2542/c1), came from a peat deposit with abundant reed and sedge, formed in wet conditions (Ch. 6.V.1). The record of 'Nancy' (Site 2586), found on a bed of compressed sedges, suggests similar circumstances. The proximity of Site 2585 to the Nancy site and of the second group from Methwold Severalls (Site 2542/c2) to the first makes it probable that they too were deposited in wet conditions.

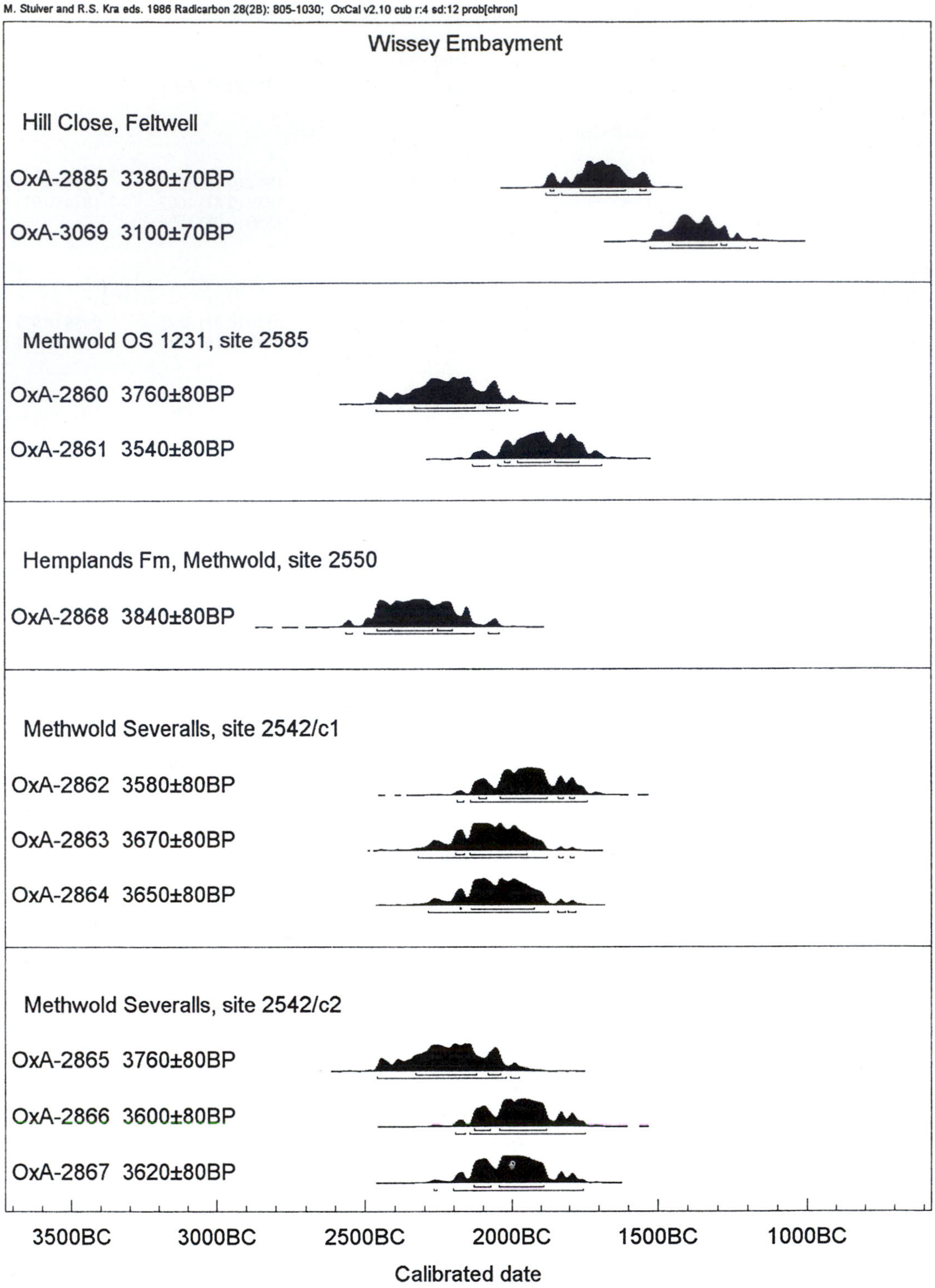

M. Stuiver and R.S. Kra eds. 1986 Radiocarbon 28(2B): 805-1030; OxCal v2.10 cub r:4 sd:12 prob[chron]

Wissey Embayment

Hill Close, Feltwell

OxA-2885 3380±70BP

OxA-3069 3100±70BP

Methwold OS 1231, site 2585

OxA-2860 3760±80BP

OxA-2861 3540±80BP

Hemplands Fm, Methwold, site 2550

OxA-2868 3840±80BP

Methwold Severalls, site 2542/c1

OxA-2862 3580±80BP

OxA-2863 3670±80BP

OxA-2864 3650±80BP

Methwold Severalls, site 2542/c2

OxA-2865 3760±80BP

OxA-2866 3600±80BP

OxA-2867 3620±80BP

3500BC   3000BC   2500BC   2000BC   1500BC   1000BC

Calibrated date

Figure 22 Calibrated age ranges for radiocarbon determinations on human remains

The possibility of deliberate burial is enhanced by independent evidence that not all interments of the period were made in barrows or natural mounds. Bodies were placed in field ditches at Fengate, Cambridgeshire (Pryor 1980, 174–175). What may have been two flat graves were found at Exning, Suffolk, one containing the skeleton of a woman with a possibly Bronze Age sherd, the other the skeletons of a man and six children without surviving grave goods. The male skeleton was dated to 3520 ± 80 BP (HAR–4399; 1960–1750 cal. BC; Martin and Denston 1986). A feature exposed in a quarry face at Barnack, Cambridgeshire, contained three successive inhumations, all probably male, accompanied only by a single pig bone. One provided a radiocarbon determination of 3560 ± 70 BP (Beta–53122; 2030–1780 cal. BC; Reynolds 1992).

The sex and age composition of the groups from Sites 2585, 2542/c1 and 2542/c2 are compatible with their having been family groups. In the case of Site 2585, this possibility may be reinforced by the presence of metopic sutures in both juveniles (Ch. 6.I.3; Appendix 34 (microfiche)).

III.2. Other prehistoric and possibly prehistoric human remains from the survey area

An unambiguously deliberate burial was discovered in 1992 in the course of an excavation conducted as part of the Fenland Management Project, when a crouched inhumation was found in a grave beneath a 'pot-boiler' site in Feltwell, which also sealed a surface on which were sherds of Beaker pottery (Site 23650; Hall and Coles 1994, 88). With 'Nancy', dated by her associated artefacts, and the finds described above, this makes a total of six separate contemporary finds of human remains from the peat fen in Methwold and Feltwell (Healy and Housley 1992). They raise the possibility of a comparable age for some of the others, all unaccompanied and some fragmentary, listed in Appendix 3. Most were discovered during cleaning or cutting of drainage ditches, or during other operations which involved digging well below the ploughsoil into undisturbed peat.

A few may be singled out. Part of a male skeleton was found with animal bone during trenching 4ft (1.20m) deep in peat in 1955 in Catsholm, Methwold (Site 2534, OS 974), in a field where a human mandible was found some five years later, 'nearby' an unfinished Middle Bronze Age rapier (Site 2540, OS 974). The Site 2534 skeleton is among the three undated individuals examined by Jacqueline McKinley (Ch. 6.I.3; Appendix 34 (microfiche)). Human bones were found in dredgings from the river Wissey on the Northwold-Stoke Ferry border, close to Herringay Hill in 1928–9, as was Beaker pottery (Site 2524). A human mandible found in Feltwell Fen in 1901 'laid on clay head beneath the turf' (Site 5302) may have come from just above the Fen Clay. A human skeleton was found beneath, rather than in, peat by Gordon Fowler in Methwold in 1932 (Site 2546, OS 290). An unconfirmable record of a palstave found near a skeleton during the ploughing of a field near Southery in 1889 (Site 2567) does not make it clear whether the skeleton was human or animal.

Prehistoric and undated human remains from the survey area are concentrated in Methwold, many of them away from the settled zone of the fen edge (Fig. 17). The concentration is likely to be genuine, since Frank Curtis, who found many of them, worked most intensively in

Hockwold and Feltwell, and would have been more likely to find others there, had they been present. It recalls the concentration of round barrows in particular parts of the Cambridgeshire fens, sometimes removed from areas with numerous flint scatters (Hall 1988, 312).

A surface find of eight human skull fragments, animal bone, a barbed and tanged arrowhead, a 'barbed wire' Beaker sherd and a grogged sherd (Fig. 17: Site 5308/c6) was made in 1964 in Hockwold cum Wilton close to a group of excavated settlements (Sites 5308/c1–/c4; Ch. 3.I.2–6). This may reflect the same kind of activity as human remains found in apparent settlement contexts at Fifty Farm (Leaf 1934, 118–119) and West Row Fen (Martin and Murphy 1988, 356), both in Mildenhall, Suffolk.

Some artefact finds may have accompanied unrecovered bodies. Chief amongst them are three bone spacer beads, of similar form and pointillé decoration to jet examples from Early Bronze Age burials, found in Feltwell Fen in 1876, 'in clay soil, about five feet below the surface, and just above a bed of sand' (Site 5296; Pl. IX; Manning 1879). A complete Late style Beaker 'found in June 1857 in Hilgay Fen near Wood Hall at a depth of 10ft by clay diggers' may have been deposited with a burial (Site 4450; Lethbridge and O'Reilly 1937, 75, pl. IIa; Clarke 1970, corpus no. 50, fig. 980). The same may be true of a complete rusticated Beaker found on the borders of Feltwell and Methwold before 1885 (Site 4856; Abercromby 1912, pl. IX, fig. 80; Fox 1923, 322; Clarke 1970, corpus no. 569, fig. 439). It must be remembered, however, that complete Beakers occur in other contexts than funerary ones. During the excavation of part of a ditched enclosure system on chalk skirtland in Hockwold cum Wilton, where bone was well-preserved, a complete Late style Beaker was found in a small pit without any accompanying burial (Site 5316; Salway 1967, 52, fig.12: F1; Clarke 1970, corpus no, 559, fig. 752).

III.3. Beyond the survey area

There are numerous records of finds of prehistoric or probably prehistoric human remains in the fens. Among the best-known, and now the best-dated, is 'Shippea Hill Man', found in 1911 'hunched up and crowded into a small space, less than two feet square' by men digging drains on a farm north-east of Ely, Cambridgeshire. McKenny Hughes, who investigated the find, found some bones remaining *in situ* about 4in (10cm) from the base of 4½ft (1.4m) of peat which rested on fen clay (Clark 1933, 278–279). Radiocarbon determinations of 3500 ± 100 BP (OxA–4290) and 3540 ± 85 BP (OxA–4291), giving an average span of 1950–1760 cal. BC, have been made on the femurs of the skeleton. Three other finds of human remains from the Cambridgeshire Fens have proved to range in date from the Late Bronze Age to the Middle Saxon periods (Hedges *et al.* 1994, 358).

Fox (1923, 55) refers to a skeleton found in Soham Fen, Cambridgeshire, associated with the unlikely combination of jet beads and spacer plates and a 'socketed chisel-like axe of late type'. He also mentions the discovery of a further jet necklace in Burwell Fen in the same county. A skeleton was found with a bone needle in Stoke Ferry Fen in 1910 (Site 2526; *Proc. Cambridge Antiq. Soc.* 16 (1912), 11). In 1941, a complete Food Vessel was found during the digging of a drainage shaft on Shippea Hill Farm near Littleport, Cambridgeshire, at a depth of about 9ft (2.75m). Bones of unrecorded species found near it were replaced when the shaft was closed (Fell and Briscoe 1951). The Suffolk Sites and Monuments Record includes three unaccompanied finds of human skeletons and one of a skull from Lakenheath Fen (refs LKH 067, 090, 094, 107; Edward Martin pers. comm.).

Whatever their date, these finds can represent only a minute fraction of the human remains preserved in the fens. Their reporting and investigation remain haphazard. The odd human skull, mandible or femur, peat-stained and unprovenanced, is not unusual in fenland private collections. A few of these finds may have come from peat-covered barrows. Most are unlikely to have done so. It is clear that many bodies were deposited, deliberately or accidentally, in peat fen, some of them in prehistory.

5. Objects, Everyday and Exceptional

The artefacts plotted on distribution maps in this chapter are recorded in Appendices 4–33 (microfiche).

I. Metalwork

> When those Dutchmen drained the fens they dug hundreds of miles of deep dykes. During the digging they found a lot of things made of bronze which they sent down the river by lighters to Denver sluice, where they had established a blacksmith's shop. There old swords were...forged into bolts, nuts and hoops, then sent back into the fens to be used in the construction of bridges and sluices.

Whatever the truth of the tradition quoted by Barrett (1961), it reinforces the impression that vast quantities of Bronze Age metalwork have been recovered from the south-eastern fens and that relatively little of it is now known, whether because it has been melted down and reused or because it has gone unrecognised: a rapier found in Hockwold Fen in 1945 was initially used for topping turnips (Site 5381).

The wealth of metalwork from the area has led to the attribution to Fenland provenances of objects found elsewhere. A notable case is that of the Clouston collection acquired, mainly by purchase, early in this century and bought by Ipswich Museum in 1934. Many bronzes in the collection, some of them provenanced to the south-eastern fens, were subsequently found to have been stolen from Devizes Museum, Wiltshire (Lawson 1979a, 79). More recently, a smaller group of objects from the collection, some of them provenanced to 'near Catsholm House', Methwold, and interpreted as showing contact with north Germany during Montelius II (Lawson 1979a, 79–83), have been shown to be nineteenth-century imports. Here, objects from the Clouston collection are listed in the appropriate appendices, but are not plotted in Figures 23–25 or included in any of the totals quoted. They serve as a warning that the Fenland provenances of other bronzes from older collections acquired largely or wholly by purchase may also be dubious.

The Bronze Age metalwork from the south-eastern fens calls for a full study. Such a work, however, is beyond the scope of this volume and the competence of its author. The main aim of this section is to list and plot the known material, a minimum of 185 objects, including indeterminate pieces (mainly fragments or uncertain identifications) listed in Appendix 7 (microfiche), and to place it in the context of contemporary local occupation.

I.1. Early Bronze Age
(Fig. 23, Appendix 4 (microfiche))
Minimum: fourteen flat and flanged axes, two awls, two daggers, one fragment. *Total:* nineteen.

The few funerary and domestic associations of copper alloy objects in the survey area date from this period. The best-known is a two-pointed, quadrangular-sectioned awl with 'Nancy', a female skeleton found near the Southery-Methwold boundary (Site 2586; Lethbridge, Fowler and Sayce 1931, pl. XXXIIIb). A similar awl (Fig. 26: M3) was found near a group of skeletons in Methwold Severalls (Site 2542/c1; Ch. 4.I.5). An unattributable fragment (Fig. 26: M1) was found amongst a large collection of Late style Beaker sherds from an occupation site (Site 5324 (93); Bamford 1982, 9–12).

I.2. Middle Bronze Age
(Fig. 24, Appendix 5 (microfiche))
Minimum: thirty-six palstaves, one knife, fifteen dirks and rapiers, seven spearheads, one razor, 1 torc, one flesh-hook, one cauldron. *Total:* sixty-three.

The most remarkable find of Middle Bronze Age metalwork was a riveted sheet bronze cauldron containing a flesh-hook, ploughed up in Feltwell in 1961 (Site 5191, OS). The cauldron stands 440mm high and has a capacity of 70 litres. Both it and the flesh-hook are assigned to the Penard phase on metallurgical, technological and typological grounds (Gerloff 1986, 88–92, fig. 6ii). A 10ft x 10ft (3m x 3m) excavation following its discovery revealed the impression of the cauldron base 1ft (0.30m) deep in humified peat resting on what appeared to be boulder clay. Reed preserved in the peat suggested that conditions had been wet when the cauldron was deposited.

I.3. Late Bronze Age
(Fig. 25, Appendix 6 (microfiche))
Minimum: nineteen socketed axes, six swords, seven spearheads, one spear ferrule, 2 socketed gouges, one chisel, two finds of crumpled, riveted sheet bronze, four hoards. *Total* (including hoards): ninety.

Two of the four hoards are recent finds. The first is of two Ewart Park phase socketed axes found in 1965 during the re-cutting of a drainage ditch in Hilgay (Site 13891, OS 267; Lawson and Ashley 1980, fig. 1:A, B). The second is a larger, dispersed hoard, consisting mainly of fragmentary socketed axes, found with a metal detector in or around 1977 in Hockwold cum Wilton (Site 5316/c4, OS 425).

The two remaining hoards have an antiquarian history which makes it difficult to judge whether the objects comprising them were originally associated with each other. The Stoke Ferry hoard (Site 4725; Hawkes 1954) was found on the bank of the river Wissey near the village of Stoke Ferry (*i.e.* on the border with Northwold or, less probably, Methwold) in or before 1873. It may have been dredged from the river. The presence of a halberd in what is otherwise a Late Bronze Age collection suggested to Hawkes that the halberd was already old when deposited (1954, card 2). Alternatively, it may not have formed part of the same deposit as the other pieces. Nothing is known of the discovery of the Feltwell Fen hoard (Site 5295; Smith 1957), which was acquired by Canon Greenwell between 1881 and 1909. It includes the only recorded item of Bronze Age goldwork from the survey area, in the form of a fragmentary foil ornament (Smith 1957, no. 15).

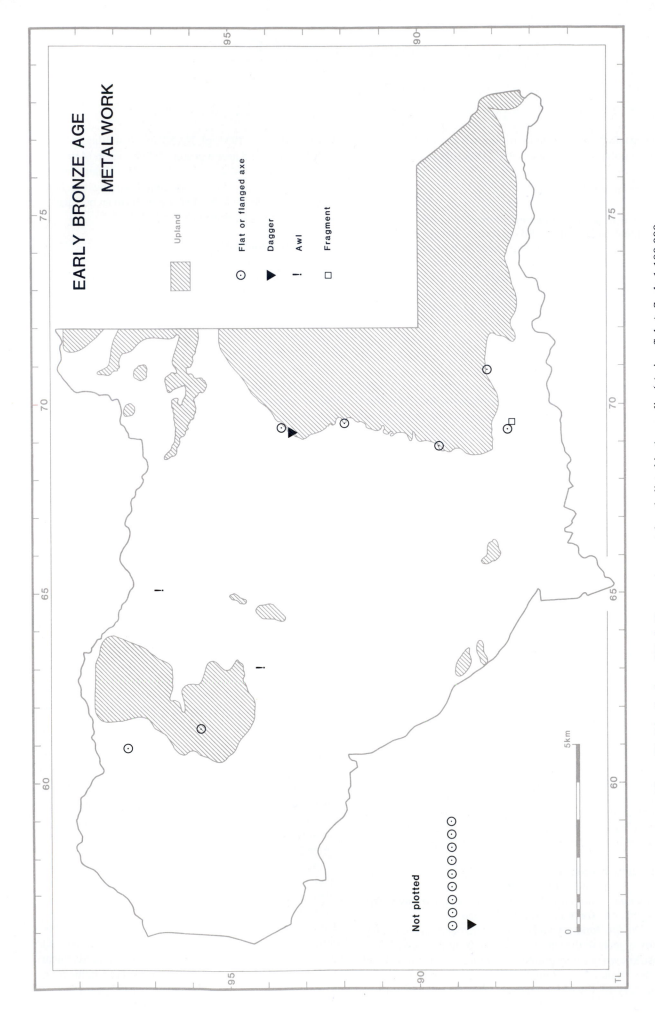

Figure 23 Distribution of Early Bronze Age metalwork, listed in Appendix 4 (microfiche). Scale 1:100,000

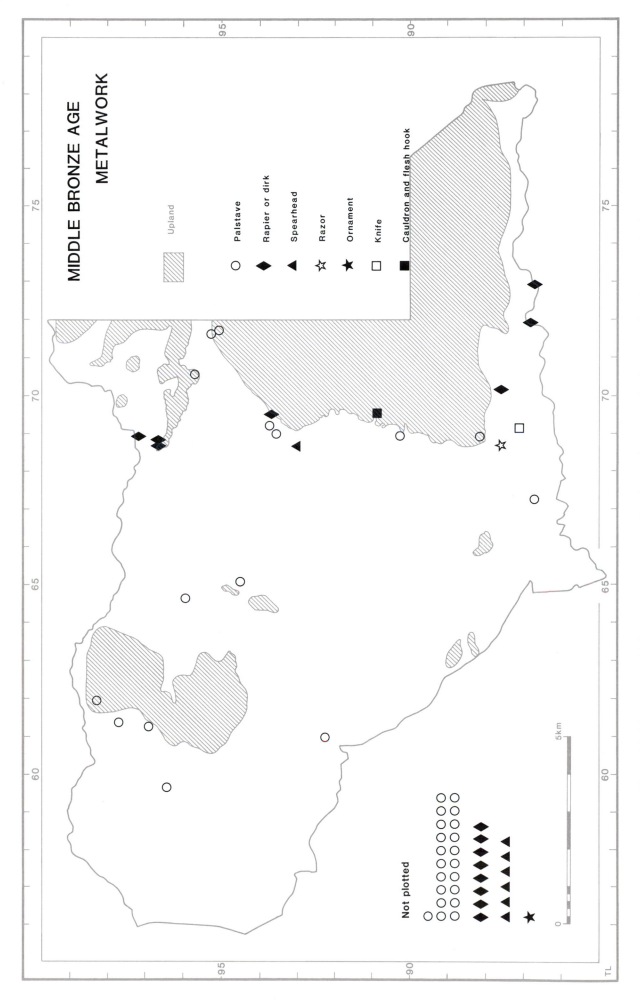

Figure 24 Distribution of Middle Bronze Age metalwork, listed in Appendix 5 (microfiche). Scale 1:100,000

MIDDLE BRONZE AGE
METALWORK

Upland

Palstave
Rapier or dirk
Spearhead
Razor
Ornament
Knife
Cauldron and flesh hook

Not plotted

5km

45

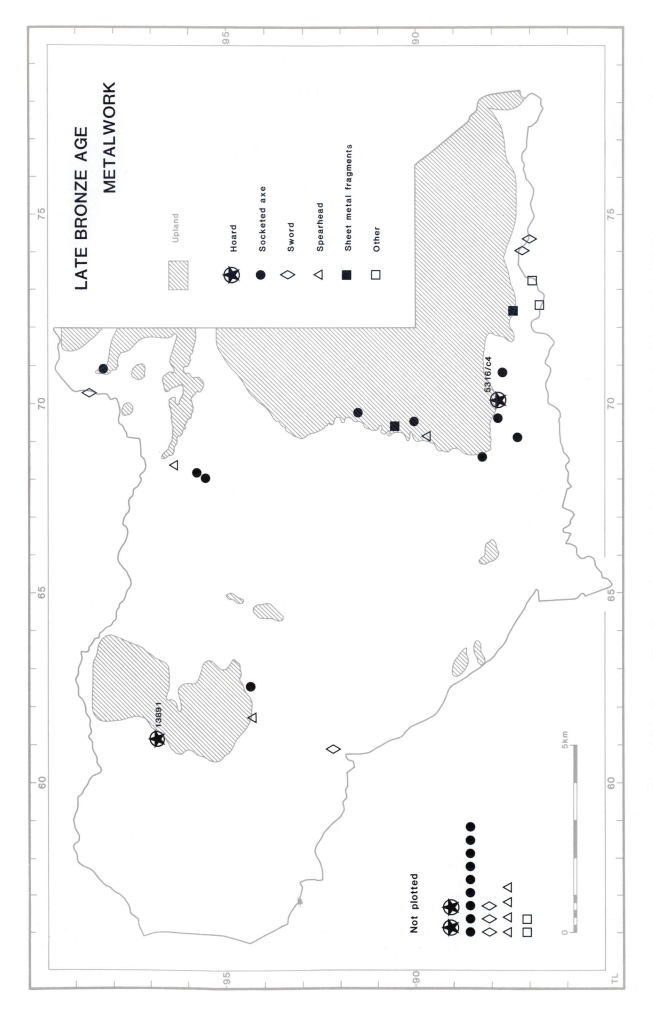

LATE BRONZE AGE
METALWORK

Upland

Hoard
Socketed axe
Sword
Spearhead
Sheet metal fragments
Other

5316/c4

13891

Not plotted

5km

0

Figure 25 Distribution of Late Bronze Age metalwork, listed in Appendix 6 (microfiche). Scale 1:100,000

46

	1 Excav. from burial	2 Excav. from settlement	3 Found near contemp. settlement	4 Found during agricultural operations (excl. 3)	5 Found during peat- or ditch-cutting	6 Found in rivers, dredgings, on riverside	7 Other/ unknown
EBA							
flat & flanged axes			6	1	1		6
awls	2						
daggers			1				1
fragment		1					
MBA							
palstaves				11	1	4	20
dirks & rapiers				2		4	9
spearheads					1		6
cauldron				1			
other				1			2
LBA							
socketed axes				9			10
swords					1	5	
spearheads				1	2		4
sheet metal				2			
hoards					1 (2 pieces)	1 (8 pieces)	2 (42 pieces)
other				1		1	3

Notes:

'Found near contemp. settlement' denotes objects found either near contemporary occupation sites or, more often, within scatters of contemporary surface finds of apparently domestic character.

'Found during agricultural operations' denotes not only finds made during cultivation and harvesting but also those made on weathered, cultivated surfaces.

Table 2 Modes of discovery of Bronze Age metalwork

I.4. Discussion

Metalworking

In the 1970s Rowlands saw the south-eastern fen edge as a major metalworking centre, established in the Early Bronze Age. In the Middle Bronze Age it produced mainly tools and weapons with few ornaments, a specialist centre for the production of large spearheads and weapons developing in the Cambridge region towards the end of that period. He notes a dearth of evidence for contemporary workshop areas, moulds or waste. (1976, 118–119).

The evidence from the survey area is consistent with this picture. An unfinished rapier, without rivet holes and with unsharpened edges from Catsholm, Methwold (Site 2540, OS 974; Burgess and Gerloff 1981, cat. no. 176), may reflect the local manufacture of weapons in the Middle Bronze Age. The contemporary excess of tools over weapons and the rarity of ornaments, confined to a single torc also from Catsholm (Site 2537; Lawson 1979a, fig. 2.3:d), conforms to the balance of categories in Rowlands' East Anglian region as a whole (Rowlands 1976, fig. 21). The totals quoted above show that much the same balance obtained in the survey area throughout the Bronze Age.

There is more tangible evidence for Late Bronze Age metalworking, notably in the composition of the hoard from Site 5316/c4 (OS 425), which includes a casting jet and three cake fragments. The prevalence in it of broken artefacts is also characteristic of what are traditionally interpreted as founders' hoards. Some aspects of the Feltwell Fen hoard would place it in the same category, namely the presence of a cake fragment, a fairly high frequency of broken objects, and the insertion of two fragmentary implements into the socket of another (Smith 1957, no. 10). The same characteristics are exemplified more fully in the massive Wilburton phase hoard from Isleham Fen, Cambridgeshire (Colquhoun and Burgess 1988, 42).

Deposition

The number of Middle Bronze Age dirks and rapiers found in the south-eastern fens is exceeded in England only by that from the lower reaches of the river Thames (Burgess and Gerloff 1981, pl. 116). The same two areas have major concentrations of Late Bronze Age metalwork (Megaw and Simpson 1979, fig. 6.26; Colquhoun and Burgess 1988, pls 116–7). This has long been interpreted as the result of the deliberate deposition of metalwork, especially weaponry, in wet places.

Problems attend any attempt to assess the likelihood of deliberate deposition within the survey area. Many of the metalwork finds are only vaguely located. Because of the hummocky topography, wet and dry conditions would have alternated over very short distances: it is normal for a single field to contain several hillocks and ridges, all formerly separated by peat (Pl. I). The fen was drier in some periods than in others, and river courses have altered. Table 2 summarises the available information. The larger number of objects represented in it than are plotted in

Figures 23–25 reflects the fact that circumstances of discovery were sometimes noted even when precise findspots were not, especially in the case of objects recovered from dredgings or during peat-cutting. Imperfect as the data are, they show certain broad trends.

One of the twelve pieces of Early Bronze Age metalwork from classifiable findspots came from a Late style Beaker occupation site and seven from fields in which Beaker and/or Early Bronze Age pottery and contemporary lithics have been found.

After that, the frequency of metalwork finds from rivers and peat increases, accounting for ten out of the twenty-six pieces of Middle Bronze Age metalwork and for nineteen (including two hoards) out of the thirty-three pieces of Late Bronze Age metalwork from classifiable findspots. These proportions must be understatements. Many objects ploughed up from peat may originally, like the Feltwell cauldron, have lain in wet locations. There are further probable river finds: the unfinished rapier from Catsholm, Methwold was found some 150m from the present bank of the river Wissey, and may have come from its channel. The same may be true of two fragmentary rapiers located only to the area of Catsholm House (Site 2530; Burgess and Gerloff 1981, cat. nos. 148, 456). A sword (Fig. 27: M8) found immediately to the north of the survey area on a potato harvester working in a field bordering the Wissey, may also have come from the river channel (Site 24114; Mathews 1988).

There is some suggestion of prior damage: one of the swords in the Stoke Ferry hoard is broken by bending and apparently deliberately battered (Site 4725; Hawkes 1954; Colquhoun and Burgess 1988, 79), a sword found on the bank of the Little Ouse on the Brandon-Hockwold border appears to have been bent and broken in antiquity (Site 16018; Martin 1980), and another from the same river is bent (Site 22921).

River and peat findspots are, furthermore, more frequent for dirks and rapiers (at least four out of eleven) than for palstaves (five out of thirty-six). The contrast between swords (eight out of eight, including two in the Stoke Ferry hoard) and socketed axes (two out of thirty-one) is even stronger. These distinctions are consistent with the preferential deposition of weapons in wet places. The significance of dirks, rapiers and swords may have been linked to the far higher levels of skill, labour and other resources involved in their production (Northover 1988, 131–133), as well as to their practical and social functions.

This disparity between the findspots of different implement types emerges even more clearly in the North Level of the north-west Cambridgeshire fens, where tools predominate among metalwork from dry land, and weapons predominate among metalwork from wet areas (Downes 1993, figs 5–6). The whole echoes the contrast in the Early Bronze Age between the predominant deposition of small tools, daggers and ornaments in graves and of halberds, spearheads and axes in hoards (Needham 1988), with river and fen contexts for rapiers and swords taking the place of grave contexts for daggers. Bradley (1990, 97–154) sees bog and river finds of metalwork as part of a long European tradition of deposition of fine and exotic objects, sometimes accompanied by human remains, in wet places from which they could be retrieved only with difficulty, if at all.

In England such practices are most clearly represented on the western edge of the Fenland basin, where a wealth of weapons and ornaments mainly of the Late Bronze Age, some of them damaged or broken, were consigned to the fen on a spectacular scale along a timber alignment linking the elaborate structures of Flag Fen with the dry land of Fengate (Pryor 1991, 107–121; Pryor 1992a; Coombs 1992).

No such focus has yet been found in the south-eastern fens, but the diffuse mass of metalwork finds is more consistent with deliberate deposition than with other interpretations. This impression is reinforced by individual finds such as that of an exceptionally large and fine 'ceremonial' dirk without rivet holes still vertical in the peat of Oxborough Fen, just north of the survey area (Site 29157; Needham 1990).

It is particularly difficult to see the Middle and Late Bronze Age metalwork from the area as resulting from erosion of riverside settlements or from accidental loss, because there is scant evidence for settlement beyond the end of the Early Bronze Age. The dense fen edge occupation represented by sites like those described in Chapter 3 almost certainly ended with the onset of wetter conditions c. 1300 cal. BC. Known living sites of the next few hundred years lay to the east in the Breckland (Ch. 7.I.2). Evidence for the manufacture of large, 'ceremonial' Middle Bronze Age spearheads, like some of those from the fens, at Grime's Graves (Needham 1991) may suggest that Rowlands' skirt fen centre of Middle Bronze Age metalworking lay not on the fen edge but scattered through the settlements of the adjoining upland. A similar situation in the Late Bronze Age may be represented by an apparent sword-making site on the gravel upland of Chippenham, Cambridgeshire (Prigg 1888).

I.5. Catalogue of Illustrated Metalwork
(Figs 26–27)

Hockwold cum Wilton. Site 5324 (93)
TL 6941 8758. Old OS field 616. NCM accession no. 571.965

M1 **Fragment**. Air bubble visible in uppermost break. Found among Late style Beaker sherds excavated 1965 from area 9 of 'floor' (Bamford 1982, text fig. 3)

Hockwold cum Wilton. Site 17541
TL 6929 8763. Old OS field 614. Younge coll.

M2 **Flanged axe**. Found 1977 in south-west corner of field (Fig. 5), near Site 5373 (22) which produced Beaker and Bronze Age pottery, including P149–P193 (Figs 86–88). From a drawing by Dr Stuart Needham.

Methwold. Site 2542. Methwold Severalls
TL 6505 9685. Old OS field 1012. NCM accession no. 93.969

M3 **Awl**. Found 1968 close to a group of six skeletons excavated from peat (Ch. 4.I.5; Fig. 21; Norfolk Museums Service 1977, fig. 107)

Feltwell. Site 17193/c2
TL 6947 9192. Old OS field 322. Younge coll.

M4 **Flat axe**, cutting edge blunt, surface pitted, both probably the result of corrosion. Found 1978 with metal detector on one of a block of fields (old OS fields 321, 322, 498) which have produced Beaker and indeterminate Later Neolithic/Early Bronze Age sherds and large quantities of contemporary lithics.

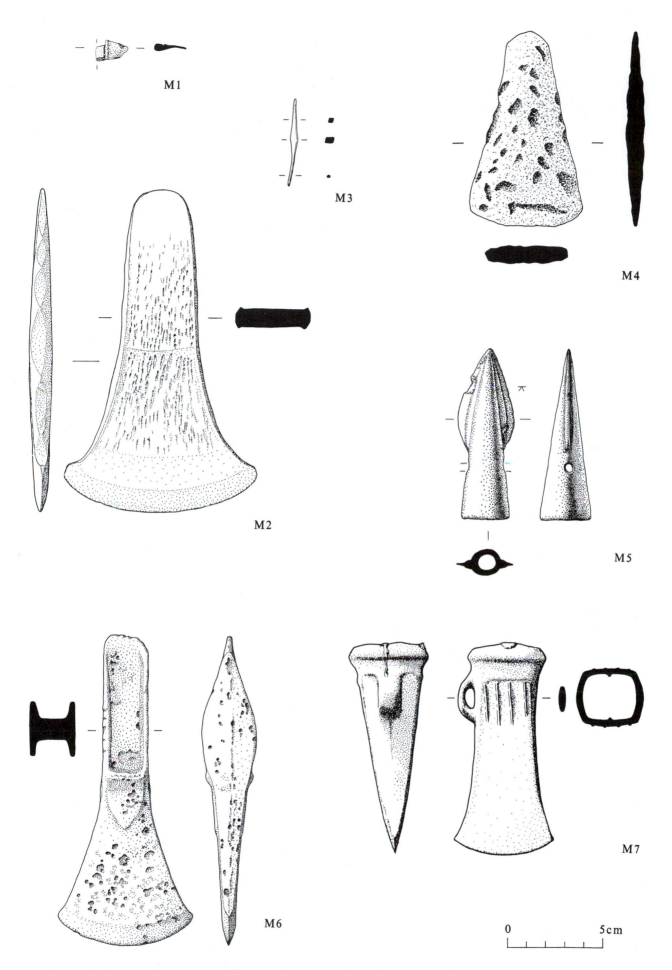

M1

M3

M4

M2

M5

M6

M7

0   5 cm

Figure 26 Bronze Age metalwork from various sites in the survey area. Particulars in catalogue. Scale 1:2

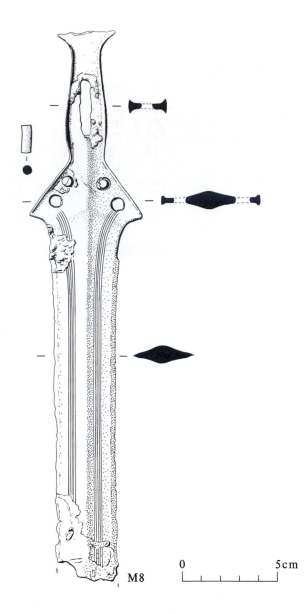

Figure 27 Late Bronze Age sword found in a field bordering the river Wissey on the northern edge of the survey area (Site 24114). Scale 1:2

Feltwell. Site 17483
TL 6913 8977. Old OS field 763. Secker coll.

M5 **Socketed Spearhead**, Ewart Park phase. Found 1981 with metal-detector after subsoiling.

Hockwold cum Wilton. Site 16590
TL 672 867. Old OS field 570. KLM accession nos 35.968, A682

M6 **Palstave**. Dug up *c.* 1940–44 in Hockwold Fen by dragline engaged in drainage work.

Methwold. Site 4874
Unlocated. NCM accession no. 206.951 (3), ex Bradfer-Lawrance coll.

M7 **Socketed axe**.

Fordham. Site 24114
TL 623 950. Whicker coll.

M8 **Sword.** Wilburton phase. Found 1987 on potato-harvesting machine working in field bordering river Wissey, on northern edge of survey area (Mathews 1988).

II. Lithics

Terms used in describing lithic material are defined in Section II.5.

II.1. Raw materials

Flint

The Breckland
Although most of the upland within the survey area consists of chalk (Fig. 2), it has little *in situ* chalk flint. The Lower Chalk, exposed at the western edge of the upland, is virtually flintless; it is only in the *Terebratulina lata* zone of the Middle Chalk in the east of the area, that flint begins to occur consistently and in quantity, the relatively small nodules of its western part, some 3km from the fen edge, increasing in size and frequency towards the east (Peake and Hancock 1970, fig. 3, pl. 1). The flint mines of Grime's Graves, Weeting with Broomhill (Site 5640) lie here, some 4km from the eastern edge of the survey area and some 12km from the fen edge (Fig. 0). These exploited a relatively localised deposit of flint of exceptional quality between *c.* 2500 and 2000 cal. BC (Burleigh *et al.* 1979, 46). Analysis of Later Neolithic knapping floors on the site has shown that floorstone, the semi-tabular seam to which pits and shafts were sunk, was selected in preference to the flint from various overlying deposits (Saville 1981a, 1–2). Floorstone consists of generally black and clear flint with some fossil and chalky inclusions, normally with a thick, fresh, creamy cortex which is its most distinctive feature. It is this cortex which, where it survives, permits tentative macroscopic identification of floorstone away from its source.

Similar cortex occasionally occurs on the surface flint of the Breckland, which constitutes the most abundant and accessible local flint supply. The topsoil of the area abounds in flint derived from the underlying deposits by frost action and occurring characteristically as weathered nodules and fragments with frequent thermal fractures and corticated or even sand-polished surfaces. It includes material derived from gravel and till deposits as well as directly from the chalk. It is from this superficial material that the bulk of contemporary industries within the Breckland seem to have been made (Healy 1991b). Westward towards the fen edge surface flint become progressively smaller, sparser, more degraded, and more heterogeneous.

The fens and fen edge
There is little accessible flint in the south-west of the survey area today, and not all of it is knappable. Test pits dug at Site 5308/c4 in Hockwold cum Wilton (Ch. 3.I.11) cut into chalk marl and recovered from it a few small, rolled and cracked pebbles and fragments of flint, similar to a handful of unworked fragments occurring in excavated assemblages from the immediate area. There is no evidence that this material was ever worked. Farther out into the fen, in the south-west of the parish, small, rolled flint pebbles naturally present in the Decoy Farm Sandhill, a ridge (levee?) bordering the old course of the Little Ouse, do not seem to have provided any of the raw material for the substantial accumulation of struck flint present there (Site 20054; Healy and Silvester 1991). Other sand and gravel ridges in the south-west of the

survey area, the larger of them mapped in Figure 2, tend to contain relatively little flint, although it may occur in local concentrations.

When peat cover was less extensive, some flint would have been accessible on the floor of the Fenland basin, in the form of discontinuous gravel deposits close to the upland and discontinuous till deposits farther west (Gallois 1988, fig. 25). Flint is one of the main erratics of this till, along with chalk and Jurassic cementstones. The terrace gravels of the Little Ouse consist largely of flint. An old exposure at Shrubhill, Feltwell, is described as consisting of a coarse subangular flinty gravel in a sandy matrix (Seale 1975, 19). Some flint also occurs in the gravely sands which form the base of the Flandrian sequence in the basin (Gallois 1988, 74).

The macroscopic identification of flint can only be tentative, and may be attempted only when enough cortex survives or where the flint is itself of a distinctive colour. In Methwold and most of Feltwell it is made even more difficult by the fact that much of the flint has come from chalky hillocks and ridges and is therefore, like the artefacts from Glebe Farm and Hill Close in Feltwell (Fig. 54: L104–L109), often so heavily corticated as to preclude even approximate characterisation. Within these limitations, it is possible to see that flint used in the survey area came from a variety of sources. Four broad flint types can be distinguished:

Chalk flint. Generally dark in colour with light cortex, sometimes fresh, sometimes weathered and battered with areas of corticated thermal fracture, in either case retaining the surface irregularities of nodular flint. Very few artefacts from the area have the exceptionally thick, creamy cortex which might suggest manufacture from Grime's Graves floorstone. A scraper from Site 5308/c5 (96) (Fig. 53: L101) is a rare example. Most are made on smaller, more heavily weathered raw material, retaining the relatively thin cortex and the curvature of the parent nodule.

Gravel flint. Rare artefacts are made from smooth, rounded pebbles with thin, abraded cortex.

Orange flint. Of a distinctly orange colour throughout, favoured for arrowhead manufacture at Hurst Fen (Clark and Higgs 1960, fig. 9). Where cortex survives it is generally no more weathered or abraded than that of most of the chalk flint from the area. It is sometimes mottled with light, opaque inclusions. This material must at least occasionally take the form of very large nodules, since one scraper (Fig. 51: L73) seems to have been made on a flake struck from the side of an orange flint saddle quern. Flint of this colour does not occur in the local chalk, but is found among the surface flint of the Breckland. A till source seems most likely.

Re-worked artefacts. On fen edge hillocks and ridges, previously discarded artefacts would often have been the nearest flint source. These were sometimes re-worked, often when already corticated. Particularly clear examples include a 'fabricator' from Site 24866 ('site 8'; Fig. 45: L18) and a scale-flaked knife from Site 5333 (95/97; Fig. 52: L88).

Other distinctive flints, among them the mottled, pale grey material of a ground axe fragment from Site 5308/c5 (96; Fig. 53: L103), are present in smaller quantities. The majority of the struck flint remains unclassifiable. Most of it is probably from the chalk on the evidence of its dark

grey to black colour, but where insufficient cortex survives it is impossible to tell whether it was collected from an *in situ* or a secondary source.

Other Rocks
Local sources of non-flint rock are limited. There are patchy outcrops of sandstone, in the form of the Lower Cretaceous Sandringham Sands, on and around Southery and Hilgay (Fig. 2), divided by the Wissey valley from the continuous outcrop which runs northwards from the river (Larwood 1970, fig. 2). Other rocks are all in derived deposits. The high-level (probably glacial outwash) gravels of the Breckland consist primarily of flint and quartzites, with smaller quantities of carstone, Bunter quartzites, hard chalk and relatively rare erratics possibly from Coal Measures or Millstone Grit (Corbett, 1973, 14–15). Quartzite pebbles are easily found in the topsoil.

Beyond the survey area, there are two relatively local sources of igneous and metamorphic erratics. The North Sea Drift of the Anglian glaciation, now exposed in the cliffs of east Norfolk and north-east Suffolk (Sparks and West 1972, 146–7; Wymer 1985, 339, fig. 109), includes igneous rocks of Scottish and Scandinavian origin (Sparks and West 1972, 146), among them dolerites, basalts, granites and gneisses (Harmer 1928). The Hunstanton Till of the Devensian glaciation reached only the extreme north-west of Norfolk (Wymer 1985, fig. 116). Its predominantly Cheviot erratics include basalts, granites, gneisses, and schists (Whitaker and Jukes-Browne 1899, 86–92; Straw 1960, 380–381).

Many of the stone implements are made of non-local rock. The available petrological identifications, listed in Table 3, give an impression of the range of materials present and the variety of their sources.

One grouped rock may possibly have been obtained within the region. Group XVIII, quartz dolerite from the Whin Sill, which occurs as an erratic in the tills of East Yorkshire, and was probably collected and worked there (Phillips, Cummins and Keen 1988, 53) may also have been collected and worked from the North Sea Drift of East Anglia (Chappell 1987, 36). The possibility is reinforced by its diffuse regional distribution, which contrasts with the compact concentrations formed by other grouped rocks and compares with that of ungrouped rocks, some of them of local origin (Clough and Green 1972, figs 5, 8). At least some may have been obtained and distributed together with the ungrouped material.

Among the ungrouped rocks, dolerites and, especially, quartzites and sandstones are most likely to have been obtained within the region. Many others must have come from non-local sources. A jadeite axe, (Fig. 55: L111) is almost certainly of continental origin (Woolley *et al.* 1979, 95). A number of the greenstones and epidiorites are likely to have originated in the south-west of England, among them one of the axes from Site 24866 ('site 8'; Fig. 45: 122; Clough and Green 1972, 125, 154), while the two wristguards sketched in Plates III and IV are of material similar to hornstone from the Beacon Hill area of Charnwood Forest in Leicestershire (Clough and Green 1972, 138, fig. 14).

Jet and amber, which provided the raw material for buttons, beads and other ornaments, such as L26 (Fig. 46) and L115 (Fig. 56), may have been collected from North Sea beaches, but may equally have been obtained from more distant sources.

Identifications	axes/adzes	mace heads	battle-axes	axe-hammers	pebble-hammers	cupped hammers	other	totals
A. Grouped Rocks								
I or near I Uralitized gabbro, epidiorite or greenstone. ?Cornwall	4							4
VI Epidotized intermediate tuff. Lake District	10						1	11
VII Augite granophyre. Caernarvonshire	1							1
VIII Silicified tuff. SW Wales	1							1
XIV Camptonite. Warwickshire				1				1
XV Micaceous sub-greywacke. Lake District				1				1
XVIII Quartz dolerite. Whin Sill	1			1				2
?XIX Greywacke. Cornwall	1							1
XX Epidotized ashy grit. Leicestershire	2	1						3
Totals	20	1		3			1	25
B. Ungrouped Rocks								
Jadeites	1							1
Dolerites		1		1				2
Greenstones/Epidiorites	7							7
Greywackes/Sub-greywackes			1	1				2
Rhyolites	1							1
Quartzites	1				2	5	4	12
Sandstones	1						1	2
Tuffs and ashes	2							2
Slates	1							1
Other	3						2	5
Totals	17	1	1	2	2	5	7	35

Table 3 Petrological Identifications

II.2. Hockwold cum Wilton. Old OS Fields 466, 613, 614 and 616

The few lithic finds which can confidently be attributed to Frank Curtis' excavations of 1959–60 are recorded in Appendix 1 (microfiche). They include stone and jet buttons (Fig. 46: L25–6) from his site 3 (? = Site 5439 (44)) and a fragmentary stone macehead (Fig. 46: L27) from 'Drain site' (? = Site 5309 (48)), both in the south of field 616. Other stray or imprecisely-located finds from the fields are recorded in the gazetteer, among them a fragmentary axe-hammer (Fig. 46: L23) and a grooved sandstone block (Fig. 46: L24), both also found in 1959–60. The text concentrates on the main collections from the fields, excluding those listed by Bamford (1982, 26–28). Despite the large amount of pottery from Sites 5311+5312 (50+51) and 5373 (22) recorded in Table 12, surviving lithic material consists of only one scraper from 5311+5312 (50+51) and nine scrapers, a 'fabricator' and a possibly flaked quartzite pebble (Fig. 47) from 5373 (22).

Raw materials
(Table 4)
The balance between the distinguishable kinds of flint is fairly constant. Orange flint, because it is recognisable without cortex, is inevitably over-represented. The bulk of the indeterminate flint is almost certainly from the chalk. Re-worked artefacts include not only already-corticated pieces but also at least two flakes from flint saddle querns, which served as blanks for scrapers. One, unillustrated, is from Site 24866 ('site 8'), the other, (Fig. 51: L73), from Site 5332 (66).

Composition
(Table 5)
Declining percentages of retouched pieces from the top to the bottom of Table 5 suggest that retrieval improved from 1959–60 to 1967. This is also the most likely explanation for the increased frequency over the same period of un-retouched flakes less than 30mm long or 20mm broad (Fig. 28). It is unlikely, however, that recovery ever became total. Even in the two most recent collections, the ratios of lithics to sherds, 1:4 for Site 5333 (95/97) and 1:3 for Site 5308/c5 (96), seem disproportionately low while the percentages of retouched pieces remain exceptionally high.

The earlier stages of the reduction sequence are far more fully represented in the many collections of similar date made from the surrounding area in the course of the Fenland Project, which have far lower proportions of retouched pieces than those recorded in Table 5. Predominantly Beaker and Bronze Age collections from the Project include between them only fourteen percent of retouched forms (Healy 1991a, fig. 65), less than half even the lowest frequencies in the collections published here.

Debitage
Cores (Table 6) are few, small and predominantly multi-platform and keeled. The occasional flake such as the blank of a scraper from Site 5308/c5 (96) (Fig. 53: L100) reflects Levallois-like technique.

Flakes (Figs 28–30). The unretouched flakes from Site 5308/c4 (61/68) are distinguished from the other two groups by a higher frequency of proportionately narrow, blade-like forms (Fig. 29), often with little dorsal cortex and punctiform butts (Fig. 30). Those from Site 5308/c5 (96) stand out by their thinness (Fig. 28).

Retouched forms
(Table 7)
The Site 24866 ('site 8') scrapers are substantially larger than those of the other collections (Fig. 31). Their modified edges are sometimes formed by the removal of quite large flakes (*e.g.* Fig. 44: L4, L6) and are often stepped in profile (*e.g.* Fig. 44: L5, L7, L11). The smaller groups of scrapers from Sites 5373 (22) and 5332 (66), both associated with predominantly Bronze Age pottery, are similar (Figs 47 and 51). The scrapers of the other collections are generally smaller (Fig. 31), more neatly-worked, and more often scale-flaked (*e.g.* Fig. 49: L48–51, Fig. 52: L82–86). They are generally thicker, although not larger, than the unretouched flakes of the collections in which they occur, and show a higher frequency of primary flakes (Figs 28, 31).

II.3. The Survey Area as a Whole

Lower Palaeolithic
In addition to stray finds, which are listed by Wymer (1985, 44, 81, 103), the survey area includes two Lower Palaeolithic sites. Gravel-quarrying on Shrubhill, an island in the west of Feltwell Fen (Site 5292, TL 660 880), in the last century produced hundreds of hand-axes, some of them illustrated by Evans (1897, 569–572). Wymer suggests (1985, 79–81) that the hand-axes, although derived, may belong to a single industrial tradition with a preference for pointed forms. Hand-axes have also been recovered from gravels of Hockwold Heath, to the north-east of Hockwold cum Wilton village, mainly from a gravel pit formerly worked on Wilton Hill (Site 5303, TL 750 885). These are in less rolled condition and include a high proportion of cordate and ovate forms (Wymer 1985, 81).

Long Blade Industries

Hockwold cum Wilton. Site 5307
Excavated 1964. TL 7118 8757. Old OS field 472 (Wymer 1977, 207)
Frank Curtis records that, in 1964, 'A few long flint flakes found in February led to small dig after corn harvest. A fair amount of long flints, cores and smaller flakes were found'. The SMR card adds 'found at junction of sand and peat'. The industry is in fresh condition, and made on good quality grey to black flint. A total of over 600 pieces is dominated by blade cores, often bipolar, and blades, the latter sometimes over 150mm long, while truncated blades are the most frequent retouched form. A small quantity of later material may be present in the collection, but most of it seems likely to be of Late Glacial date.

Methwold. Site 4738
Discovered 1959. TL 7046 9528. Boundary of old OS fields 302 and 301 (Wymer 1977, 210)
During the cleaning of a drainage ditch in 1959 Mr J. D. Wortley extracted struck flint from beneath peat at a depth of about six to eight feet (1.80–2.40m). Bob Silvester has subsequently recorded a ridge exposed in the side of the drainage ditch at this point (Silvester 1991, 62). The artefacts are heavily corticated. A total of forty-three pieces includes a blade core and thirty blades, some of them in the same size-range as the larger examples from Site 5307. A similar date seems probable.

Site	Chalk flint	Gravel flint	Orange flint	Re-worked artefacts	Indeterminate flint	Stone	Totals
Site 24866 ('site 8')	28 31.5%	3 3.4%	3 3.4%	5 5.6%	48 53.9%	2 2.2%	89
Site 5308/c4 (61/68)	62 23.9%	14 5.4%	63 24.4%	7 2.7%	110 42.4%	3 1.2%	259
Site 5332 (66)	15 26.3%		13 22.8%	1 1.8%	28 49.1%		57
Site 5333 (95/97)	30 24.4%	6 4.9%	18 14.6%	4 3.3%	65 52.8%		123
Site 5308/c5 (96)	38 24.5%	10 6.5%	36 23.2%		71 45.8%		155
Totals	173 25.3%	33 4.8%	144 21.1%	14 2.1%	313 46.0%	5 0.7%	682

Table 4 Hockwold cum Wilton fields 466, 613, 614 and 616. Raw material in main collections

Site	Cores	Irreg. waste	Core rejuvenation flakes	Flakes	Blades	Retouched	Totals
Site 24866 ('site 8')	1 1.1%			13 14.6%	1 1.1%	74 83.1%	89
Site 5308/c4 (61/68)	9 3.3%		1 0.4%	108 42.6%	14 5.3%	126 48.4%	258
Site 5332 (66)	6 10.5%			30 52.6%		21 36.8%	57
Site 5333 (95/97)				72 58.5%	13 10.6%	38 30.9%	123
Site 5308/c5 (96)	2 1.3%		4 2.6%	82 52.9%	17 11.0%	50 32.3%	155
Totals	18 2.6%		5 0.7%	305 44.8%	45 6.6%	309 45.3%	682

Table 5 Hockwold cum Wilton fields 466, 613, 614 and 616. Composition of main collections

Site	Single platform (A2)	Multi-platform (B-C)	Keeled (D-E)	Uncl./ Fragmentary	Totals	Mean Core Weight (g)	Drawings
Site 24866 ('site 8')			1		1	28	L1
Site 5308/c4 (61/68)	2	2	3	2	9	29	L34–L37
Site 5332 (66)	1	2	1	2	6	43	L69, L70
Site 5308/5 (96)				2	2		
Totals	3	4	5	6	18	35	

Table 6 Hockwold cum Wilton fields 466, 613, 614 and 616. Cores of main collections

Site	1	2	3	4	5	6	7	8	9	10	11	12	13	14	15	Totals	Drawings
Site 24866 ('site 8')	0 0.0%	2 2.7%	0 0.0%	1 1.4%	55 74.3%	1 1.4%	1 1.4%	0 0.0%	0 0.0%	0 0.0%	4 5.4%	8 10.8%	2 2.7%	0 0.0%	0 0.0%	74	L2–L22
Site 5308/c4 (61/68)	0 0.0%	2 1.6%	1 0.8%	4 3.2%	87 69.0%	3 2.4%	3 2.4%	6 4.8%	1 0.8%	1 0.8%	6 4.8%	7 5.6%	3 2.4%	1 0.8%	1 0.8%	126	L33, L38–L68
Site 5332 (66)	0 0.0%	0 0.0%	0 0.0%	0 0.0%	18 85.7%	2 9.5%	0 0.0%	0 0.0%	0 0.0%	1 4.8%	0 0.0%	0 0.0%	0 0.0%	0 0.0%	0 0.0%	21	L73–L79
Site 5333 (95/97)	1 2.6%	0 0.0%	0 0.0%	0 0.0%	30 78.9%	1 2.6%	0 0.0%	1 2.6%	0 0.0%	1 2.6%	4 10.5%	0 0.0%	0 0.0%	0 0.0%	0 0.0%	38	L80–L92
Site 5308/c5 (96)	0 0.0%	0 0.0%	0 0.0%	0 0.0%	40 80.0%	0 0.0%	0 0.0%	1 2.0%	0 0.0%	0 0.0%	8 16.0%	0 0.0%	1 2.0%	0 0.0%	0 0.0%	50	L94–L103
Totals	1 0.3%	4 1.3%	1 0.3%	5 1.6%	230 74.5%	7 2.3%	4 1.3%	8 2.6%	1 0.3%	3 1.0%	22 7.1%	15 4.8%	6 2.0%	1 0.3%	1 0.3%	309	

1 = Leaf Arrowhead, 2 = Barbed & Tanged Arrowheads, 3 = Triangular Arrowheads, 4 = ?Unfinished Arrowheads or Arrowhead Blanks 5 = Scrapers, 6 = Borers, 7 = Plano-Convex Knives, 8 = Scale-Flaked Knives, 9 = Denticulate, 10 = Serrated Pieces, 11 = Misc. Retouched, 12 = 'Fabricators' or Rods, 13 = Axes, 14 = Waisted Tool, 15 = Hammerstone

Table 7 Hockwold cum Wilton fields 466, 613, 614 and 616. Retouched pieces of main collections

Flake Dimensions

Primary ☐   Secondary ▨   Tertiary ▨

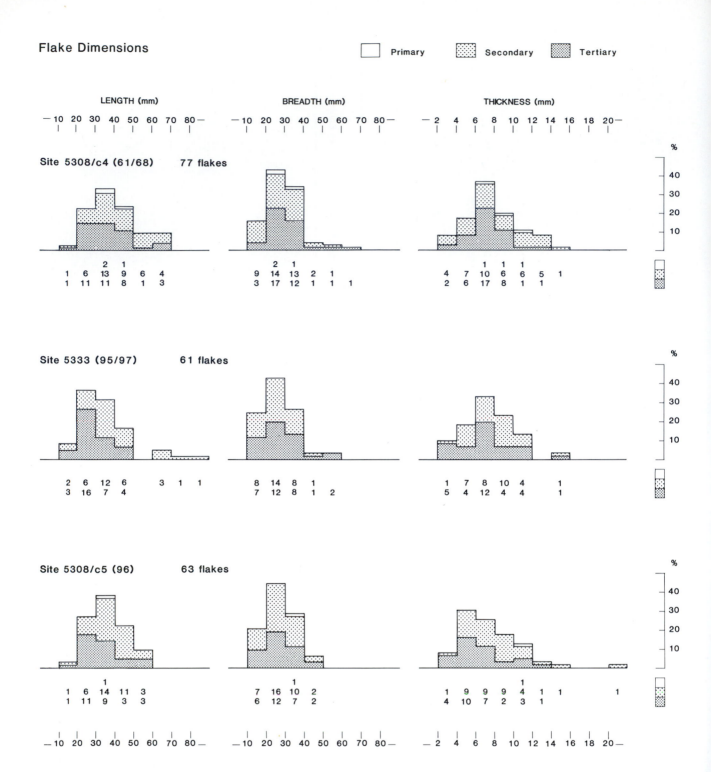

Figure 28 Dimensions of complete, unretouched flakes from Sites 5308/c4 (61/68), 5333 (95/97) and 5308/c5 (96)

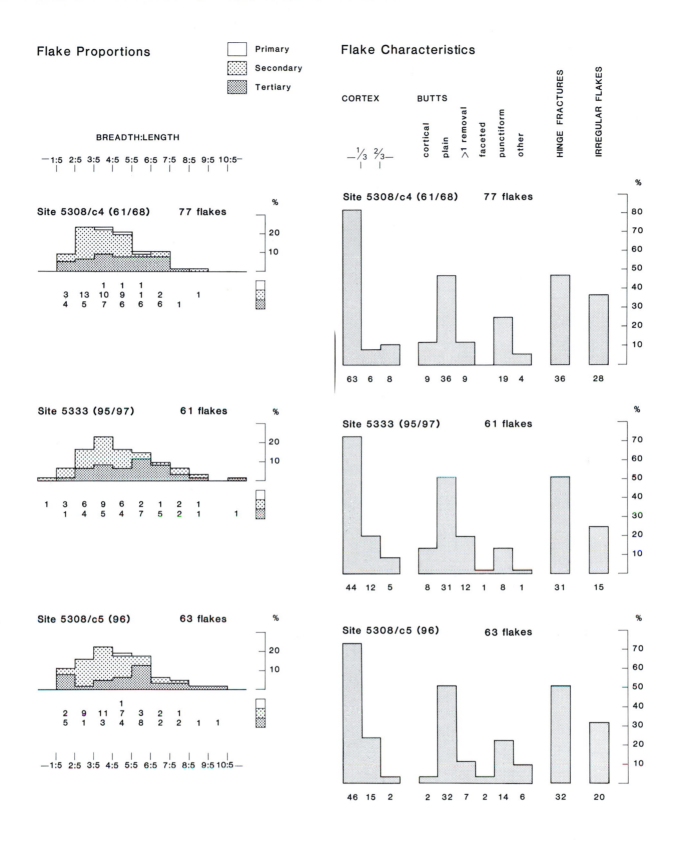

Figure 29 Proportions of complete, unretouched flakes from Sites 5308/c4 (61/68), 5333 (95/97) and 5308/c5 (96)

Figure 30 Non-metrical characteristics of complete, unretouched flakes from Sites 5308/c4 (61/68), 5333 (95/97) and 5308/c5 (96)

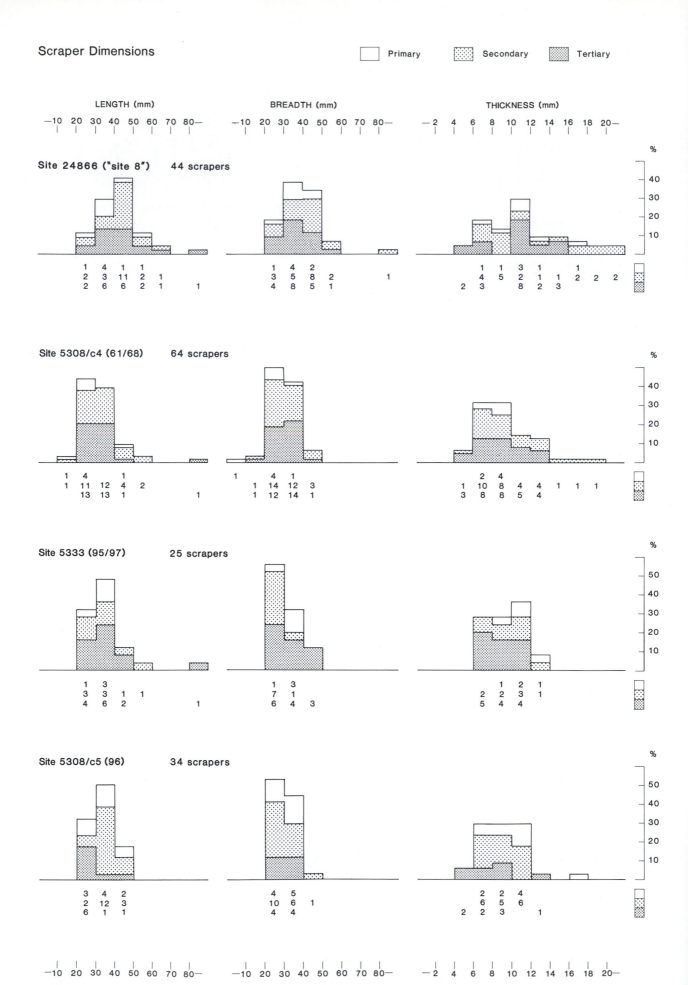

Figure 31 Dimensions of complete flake scrapers from Sites 24866 ('site 8'), 5308/c4 (61/68), 5333 (95/97) and 5308/c5 (96)

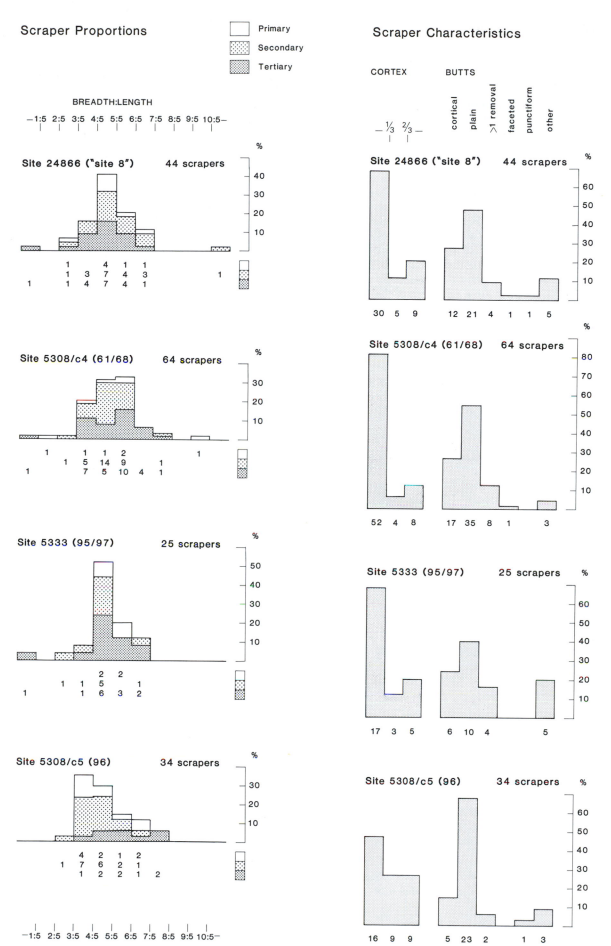

Figure 32 Proportions of complete flake scrapers from Sites 24866 ('site 8'), 5308/c4 (61/68), 5333 (95/97) and 5308/c5 (96)

Figure 33 Non-metrical characteristics of complete flake scrapers from Sites 24866 ('site 8'), 5308/c4 (61/68), 5333 (95/97) and 5308/c5 (96)

Scattered Mesolithic Material
(Fig. 34, Appendix 8 (microfiche))
This consists of isolated finds and of artefacts in surface collections dominated by later material. Appendix 8 (microfiche) records a minimum of six *tranchet* axes, twenty-six microliths, and three truncated pieces. Most of the microliths are simple obliquely-blunted points, with few geometric forms.

It must be remembered that *tranchet* axes may have continued to be made into the Neolithic (Gardiner 1987, 59). Other artefact types traditionally seen as Mesolithic are even less certainly so. Pebble-hammers, such as L138 (Fig. 60), are not plotted in Figure 34, although listed in Appendix 8 (microfiche), because some are likely to be of Later Neolithic or Early Bronze Age date (Roe 1979, 36). The distribution of the few plottable examples (Fig. 42) bears no relation to that of diagnostic Mesolithic artefacts (Fig. 34). Probably Mesolithic debitage, in the form of small, regularly-worked blades and blade cores, often distinguished by heavy white cortication, occurs as a minority component in many collections. Such material is recorded in Appendix 8 (microfiche) but not plotted.

Figure 34 shows three concentrations of diagnostic Mesolithic material, all in predominantly Neolithic and Bronze Age collections, two on what later became the fen edge in Feltwell, centred at TL 694 921 (Sites 5159, 17537, 17193: OS 321, 322, 498) and TL 692 900 (Sites 14624, 14625, 22311, 30029; OS 722, 722A, 723, 728-30, 762A, 763), and a third up the Little Ouse valley in Weeting with Broomhill, centred at TL 771 875 (Site 14943; OS 279). The first two each span several fields and coincide with slight concentrations of probably Mesolithic debitage. The third consists of eight microliths from a single 14ha field. While this suggests that a more substantial industry was present, the methods by which the Parrott collection, of which the material forms a part, was acquired (Ch. 1.III.2) would have made the recovery of debitage unlikely.

Neolithic and Bronze Age

Excavated Material
The small quantity of stratified lithic material of these periods recovered from outside fields 466, 613, 614 and 616 in Hockwold cum Wilton is listed in Appendices 2 and 3 (microfiche). The following are most noteworthy:

Feltwell. Site 4921/c1. Glebe Farm (Ch. 3.II.9). Two keeled cores, eight flakes, two scrapers and a serrated blade (Fig. 54: L104) were found in a pit with a Grooved Ware dish (Fig.102: P359), a bone point (Fig. 108: B20) and animal bone.

Feltwell. Site 5188/c1. Hill Close (Ch. 4.I.3). Two leaf arrowheads (Fig. 54: L105, L106) and a scale-flaked knife (Fig 54: L107) were found in a multiple burial, the arrowheads both with individual skeletons.

Methwold. Site 2542/c2. Methwold Severalls (Ch. 4.I.5). Two scrapers (Fig. 54: L108, L109) were found 'just under' a group of three skeletons excavated from peat.

Collected material
The Neolithic and Bronze Age are otherwise represented by the accumulated tonnage of surface collections. The Breckland has a near-continuous cover of predominantly Later Neolithic and Early Bronze Age material, comparable with extensive spreads in from other parts of

England (Bradley 1987, 182–183). Here and on the upland of the west and north of the survey area, extensive contemporary scatters were noted and collected from by Warburton in the first quarter of this century. They included an area of approximately 1.2ha at Methwold Hythe (Site 4844; Warburton 1913, 425–426), one on Herringay Hill in Northwold covering more than 1ha (Site 13458/c1; Warburton 1913, 425), another of 1.5ha in the same parish (Site 4747), and another in Weeting with Broomhill covering approximately 3ha (Site 5596). The collection from Site 4844 comprises 304 pieces, dominated by scrapers and by multi-platform and keeled flake cores on small, weathered pebbles, and including finished implements such as 'thumbnail' scrapers, borers, a denticulate, a flaked axe fragment and a waisted tool.

To the west, the dissected topography of the skirtland and fen edge (Pl. I) precludes extensive scatters, creating instead a series of ridge- or hillock-sized 'sites', each of which is likely to combine the debris of successive episodes of occupation. Here collecting methods and preferences have tended to the singling-out of finished implements, so that the extent and overall composition of individual concentrations are often unknown. Analysis is necessarily focused on the more distinctive artefact types.

Arrowheads (Table 8, Figs 35–38, Appendices 9–16 (microfiche)). The low frequency of chisel and oblique forms among unseen arrowheads (Table 8B) reflects their low recognisability and the inconsistent nomenclature applied to them. An unknown, probably large, proportion of the 'transverse arrowheads', 'harpoon barbs', 'triangular arrowheads' and 'hollow-based arrowheads' recorded in Appendices 11–12 and 15–16 (microfiche), is likely to consist of chisel and oblique arrowheads, although reliable identification is impossible from such records.

Leaf, chisel and oblique arrowheads all have their maximum concentrations on the fen edge in the north of Feltwell and the south of Methwold, leaf and chisel arrowheads between northings 9200 and 9300, oblique arrowheads between northings 9100 and 9399 (Figs 35–37). Barbed and tanged arrowheads, on the other hand, are evenly distributed down the fen edge to the Little Ouse valley (Fig. 38).

To the nineteen Ballyclare barbed and tanged arrowheads, among them L125 (Fig. 57), recorded in Table 8A may be added one Green Low and one Conygar Hill form in the same large size-range. Occasional enlarged forms also occur among the leaf-shaped, chisel and oblique arrowheads.

Bifaces such as L15 (Fig. 45) or L60 (Fig. 49), which may have been blanks for leaf-shaped or barbed and tanged arrowheads, occur throughout the survey area, both on the fen edge and up the Little Ouse valley in the Breckland.

Knives (Table 9, Fig. 39, Appendices 17–20 (microfiche)). Edge-ground discoidal knives are concentrated on the fen margin in Feltwell, between northings 9000 and 9300. Flint daggers, plano-convex knives, and the far more numerous scale-flaked knives, on the other hand, have been found in equal density to the south in Hockwold cum Wilton (Fig. 39), where the two last regularly occurred in excavated occupation deposits of predominantly Beaker and Early Bronze Age date (*e.g.* Fig. 48: L45 and Fig. 52: L88).

Class	Sub-divisions					Totals			
A. Seen									
Leaf						203		33%	
Petit tranchet						4		1%	
Chisel	B: 5	C: 34	D: 17		Other: 7	63}		10%}	
Oblique	E: 2	F: 1	G: 7	H: 22	Other: 22	54}	120	9%}	20%
Chisel or Oblique						3}		1%}	
Barbed & Tanged	Green Low: 14	Conygar: 22	Ballyclare: 19		Other: 193	248}	258	39%}	41%
Tanged						10}		2%}	
Triangular						27		4%	
Hollow-based						5		1%	
Total						617			
B. Known only from records									
Leaf						134		55%	
Chisel						1}		1%}	
Oblique						2}	10	1%}	5%
Chisel or Oblique						7}		3%}	
Barbed & Tanged	Green Low: 2	Conygar: 2	Ballyclare: 3		Other: 59	66}	70	27%}	29%
Tanged						4}		2%}	
Triangular						25		10%	
Hollow-based						3		1%	
Total						240			

Table 8 Arrowheads

Class	Sub-divisions		Totals	
A. Seen				
Discoidal	Edge-ground: 7	Flaked: 7	14	7%
Scale-flaked			143	72%
Plano-convex			33	17%
Flint dagger	Tanged: 4		11	4%
Total			201	
B. Known only from records				
Plano-convex			8	
Flint dagger			2	
Total			10	

Table 9 Knives

Flint and Stone Axes (Table 10, Figs 40–41, Appendices 23–24 (microfiche)). Most axes have been found along the densely-occupied fen margin, some of them actually coming from occupation sites (*e.g.* Fig. 45: L21–22, Fig. 50: L66–68, Fig. 53: L103, Fig. 55: L114). To the west of this zone, axes from the fen or from islands are more often of stone than of flint (Fig. 41). To the east, flint axes from the upland tend to be flaked rather than ground (Fig. 40).

Axes were made in a variety of flints which, while not attributable to particular sources, often seem distinct from the bulk of the flint in the collections of which they form a part (*e.g.* Fig. 53: L103). Where petrological identifications are available, Group VI (Great Langdale tuff) is the most frequent rock among stone axes (Table 3), and is almost certainly the raw material of a further four unsectioned examples, including one from Shrubhill, Feltwell, which is almost entirely unground (Site 5292; Evans 1897, 96), and another (Fig. 57: L122), which is of exceptionally large size. Similarly massive dimensions are attained by a ground flint axe from Hilgay Fen which measures 219 x 81 x 79mm (Site 4448; Evans 1897, 100).

Axes of both Group VI and flint were often flaked-down, sometimes into miniature forms (*e.g.* Fig. 58: L127), sometimes less specifically, resulting in cores (*e.g.* Fig. 56: L117) and in flakes and flake tools (*e.g.* Fig. 62: L62). Re-working had proceeded so far in the case of a flake of Group VI rock found together with struck flint in a 'pot-boiler' concentration in Feltwell that its dorsal face retains no trace of grinding, being covered with the scars of previous removals (Site 5183, OS 336; Clough and Green 1972, 150, 154).

Class	Subdivisions		Totals		
A. Seen					
Flint, flaked	Miniature: 3		26	26.3%}	
Flint, wholly or partly ground		Blunted: 2	31	31.3%}	57.6%
Stone	Miniature: 3	Blunted: 2	42	42.4%	
Totals	6	4	99		
B. Known Only from Records					
Flint, flaked	Miniature: 1		8	13.1%}	
Flint, wholly or partly ground			22	36.1%}	70.5%
Flint, indeterminate	Miniature: 2		13	21.3%}	
Stone			18	29.5%	
Totals	3		61		

Table 10 Flint and stone axes

Class	Subdivisions		Totals
A. Seen			
Beads	Jet: 12	Amber: 1	13
Buttons	Jet: 1	Stone: 1	2
Wristguards			3
Battle-axe			1
Axe-hammers			6
Maceheads			2
Pebble hammers			4
Cupped pebbles			2
Grooved sandstone blocks			3
'Sponge fingers'			2
Rubbers/pounders			6
Other			12
B. Known only from records			
Beads		Amber: 3	3
Buttons	Jet: 1		1
Battle-axe			1
Axe-hammers			3
Maceheads			2
Maceheads or pebble hammers			4
Pebble hammers			6
Cupped pebbles			5
Rubbers/pounders			6
Other			8

Table 11 Other stone artefacts (excluding saddle querns)

Other Stone Artefacts (Table 11, Fig. 42, Appendix 25 (microfiche)). As well as tools and weapons, these include personal accoutrements, in the form of beads, buttons and wristguards. A bracelet of eight barrel-shaped jet beads of Early Bronze Age form was found with 'Nancy', a female skeleton discovered near the Southery-Methwold border (Site 2586; Lethbridge, Fowler and Sayce 1931, pl. XXXIIIa), and a simple amber bead forms part of the Late Bronze Age Feltwell Fen hoard (Site 5295; Smith 1957, no. 16). The remainder, however, seem to have come either from occupation sites (*e.g.* Fig. 46: L25, L26), or at least from areas of dense occupation, as in the case of the two wristguards sketched on Plates III and IV.

Most shaft-hole implements have also been found in occupied areas (*e.g.* Fig. 46: L23, L27). As with stone axes, some are from islands or the fen (Fig. 42). Three may have been recovered from deep peat: one axe-hammer had apparently been dug up from a drainage ditch between two fields in Feltwell (Site 24735, OS 762); another was dug up close to Sam's Cut Drain in the relatively low-lying land between Hilgay and Southery (Site 4451, OS 468); while a battle-axe, too imprecisely located to plot, is recorded as having been found about 4ft (1.2m) deep in a drainage ditch in Methwold (Site 5233).

Saddle Querns (Fig. 43, Appendix 26 (microfiche)). The minimum of eleven stone and sixteen flint saddle querns are all stray finds. Stone examples are generally of sandstone or quartzite, flint ones, where their material can be determined, of tabular flint.

II.4. Discussion

Hockwold cum Wilton Fields 466, 613, 614 and 616
Small and almost certainly incomplete as the collections from the excavated sites in these fields are, aspects of their composition and technology conform to and elucidate wider trends.

Debitage
Despite the under-representation of debitage, there is evidence for on-site flint working in the presence of a hammerstone, (Fig. 43: L33), cores, rare core rejuvenation flakes (*e.g.* Fig. 53: L93), and flakes representing every stage of the reduction sequence (Figs 28–29).

Flake proportions (Fig. 29) show the prevalence of broad, squat forms usual in Later Neolithic and Bronze Age industries (Pitts 1978) and seen on the western edge of the fens in the industries of the Storey's Bar Road and Newark Road subsites at Fengate, Cambridgeshire (Pryor 1980, figs 73, 74). Higher frequencies of blade-like flakes (Fig. 29) and of punctiform butts (Fig. 30) in the Site 5308/c4 (61/68) collection almost certainly stem from the presence of Early or Middle Neolithic material, seen more clearly in a small quantity of Neolithic Bowl pottery (including Fig. 89: P194, P195). The incidence of hinge fractures and irregular flakes in all three collections (Fig. 30) is close to that among flakes from pits containing Late style Beaker at Beeston with Bittering (Site 15995; Wymer with Healy forthcoming), higher than among flakes from pits containing Grooved Ware on Redgate Hill, Hunstanton (Site 1396; Healy, Cleal and Kinnes 1993, fig. 33) and yet higher than among flakes from pits containing Neolithic Bowl pottery on Spong Hill, North Elmham (Site 1012; Healy 1988, fig. 36). This local sequence corresponds to a more general transformation of flint-knapping style (Ford *et al.* 1984, 162–163; Herne 1991, 66–74).

Retouched forms
Arrowheads. Among barbed and tanged arrowheads there is a suggestion that the funerary association of Conygar Hill forms with Food Vessel and other Early Bronze Age urn styles and of Green Low forms with Beaker (Green 1980, 244–250) may have extended to settlement material. There is a Conygar Hill form (Fig. 44: L3), in the Site 24866 ('site 8') collection, the pottery of which is predominantly Bronze Age, and a Green Low form (Fig. 48: L38), in the Site 5308/4 (61/68) collection, the pottery of which includes a far higher proportion of Beaker. The presence of relatively thin, often broken, bifaces in both collections (*e.g.* Fig. 45: L15, Fig. 49: L59, L60) strongly suggests that arrowheads were being made on the sites, as at Plantation Farm, Shippea Hill, Cambridgeshire (Clark 1933, 271–272).

Scrapers. The size difference between the scrapers of the Site 24866 ('site 8') collection, associated with predominantly Bronze Age pottery, and those of the other three collections, associated largely or solely with Beaker (Fig. 31), is a common one. The prevalence of 'thumbnail' scrapers in Beaker-associated industries, first demonstrated metrically by Clark and Higgs (1960, fig. 12), and since confirmed in the study of many other assemblages (Healy 1986, 88), seems to reflect stylistic and/or functional preference. It is not imposed by available raw material size, because the scrapers of nearby industries associated with different ceramics are almost invariably larger, as here in the case of the Site 24866 ('site 8') scrapers; and because scraper blanks in Beaker-associated industries do not seem to have been selected from among the larger flakes, as they do in industries associated with other pottery styles (Healy 1985, 190–191).

Scraper blanks in the predominantly Beaker-associated collections do, however, seem to have been selected for *thickness,* seen not only in their measurements but in the higher frequency of primary (= cortical) flakes among scrapers than among unretouched flakes (Figs 28, 31). This seems likely to reflect a need for a reasonable depth of working edge and for an implement robust enough to withstand pressure without breaking in use.

The Bronze Age affinities of thick, steep, scrapers such as L6, L7, L8 and L11 (Fig. 44), with their working edges formed by the removal of large flakes, were first recognised by Stone in his discussion of the Deverel-Rimbury-associated industries of Boscombe Down and Thorny Down, Wiltshire (1936, 482; 1937, 656) and restated by Fasham and Ross in their account of the industries from R4, Hampshire (1978, 59–61). Here too they occur in collections associated with predominantly Bronze Age pottery.

The Survey Area as a Whole

Palaeolithic and Mesolithic
The recovery of two long blade industries from beneath peat suggests that other contemporary and earlier sites may still be preserved under surviving Fenland deposits.

It is difficult to tell how far the scattered Mesolithic artefacts represent 'sites' obscured by the under- or non-collection of debitage and by the vast quantities of later material which dominate the surface collections.

In view of the doubt surrounding the date of British *petit tranchet* arrowheads (Green 1980, 111), it is noteworthy that three of the four examples from the survey area occur in collections which include Mesolithic material, the remaining one in a collection which includes possibly Mesolithic material (Appendix 10 (microfiche)).

Neolithic and Bronze Age: individual artefact classes
Arrowheads. The survey area forms the north-western part of one of the largest concentrations of flint arrowheads in England and Wales, in the Breckland and the south-eastern fen edge (Green 1980, fig. 52). The frequency of the main forms among those arrowheads actually seen (Table 8A) is very close to those recorded by Green both for East Anglia and for England and Wales as a whole (1980, tables VII.7, VII.8).

Among barbed and tanged arrowheads, large, Ballyclare, forms are exceptionally common, forming 7% of all barbed and tanged arrowheads seen (8% if enlarged Green Low and Conygar Hill forms are taken into account) in contrast to 1.7% for East Anglia as a whole (Green 1980, table VI.2). Green Low forms are more frequent than usual in relation to Conygar Hill ones, occurring in the ratio 1:1.5 in contrast to 1:3.7 for East Anglia as a whole (Green 1980, table VI.1). This probably reflects the substantial Beaker presence in the area.

Knives. Discoidal knives were made at Grime's Graves by users of Grooved Ware in the late third millennium cal. BC (Saville 1981a, 56), and a Later Neolithic context is supported by finds of edge-ground forms with Grooved Ware and Beaker at Carnaby Top site 12, Yorkshire (Manby 1974, 27–29, fig. 10:12), and with Grooved Ware at Lawford, Essex, and Creeting St Mary, Suffolk (Healy 1985, fig. 15). The other forms have different associations and rather later, if overlapping, currencies. The almost exclusively Beaker associations of flint daggers were demonstrated by Grimes (1931, 342), and shown by Clarke to lie mainly with Late style Beakers of his Southern tradition (1970, 448). The predominantly Early Bronze Age associations of plano-convex knives, first demonstrated by Clark (1932a), are re-emphasised by Saville (1985, 129–130); while less extensively retouched scale-flaked knives occur in both Beaker and Early Bronze Age contexts (Healy 1986, 167).

Flint and stone axes. It is difficult to tell from which phase or phases of activity these derive, because some stone sources were exploited for very long periods, c. 3700–2100 cal. BC in the case of Group VI (Smith 1979, 14), and because the currency of flint axes seems to have been equally long. Even where axes have been recovered from predominantly Beaker and Early Bronze Age occupation deposits it is impossible to tell if they were contemporary with or residual in them, especially where small quantities of Earlier Neolithic material are present.

63

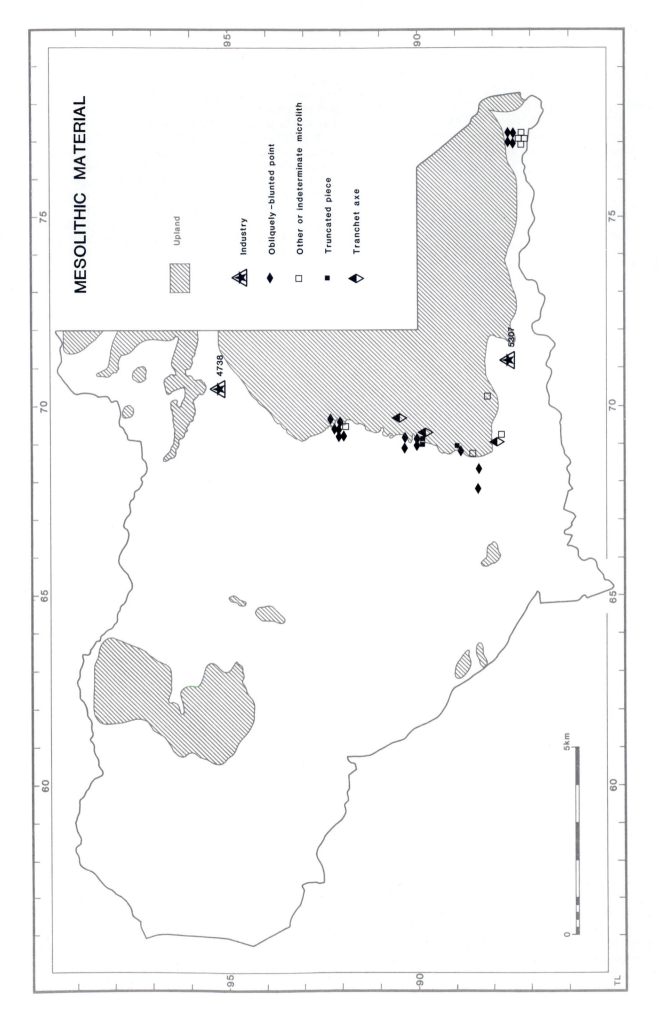

Figure 34 Distribution of Mesolithic material, listed in Appendix 8 (microfiche). Scale 1:100,000

64

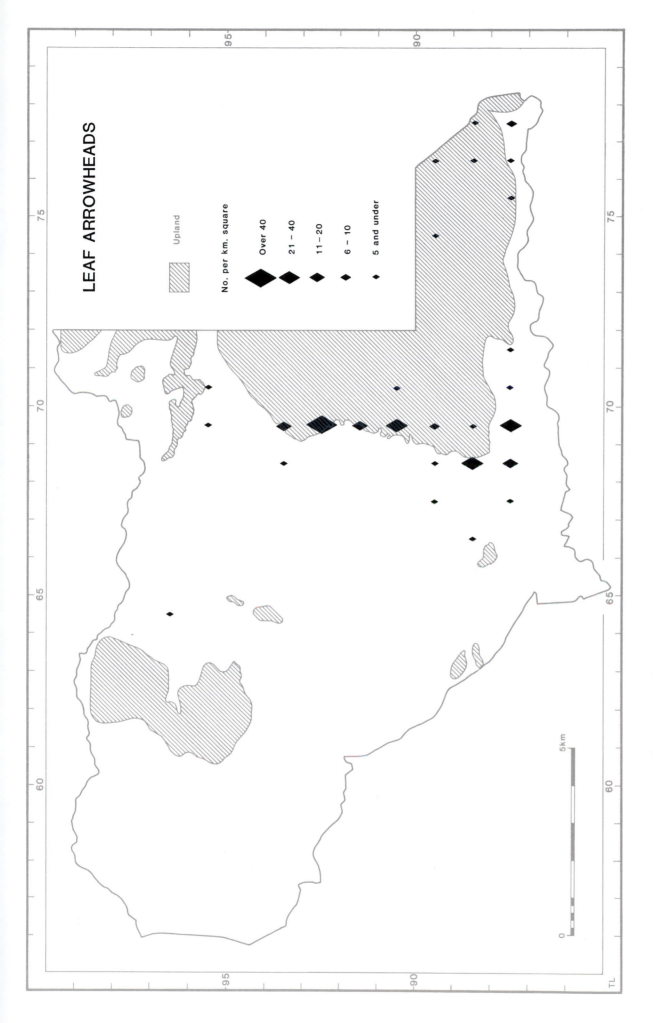

Figure 35 Distribution of leaf arrowheads, listed in Appendix 9 (microfiche). Scale 1:100,000

LEAF ARROWHEADS

Upland

No. per km. square

Over 40

21 – 40

11 – 20

6 – 10

5 and under

5km

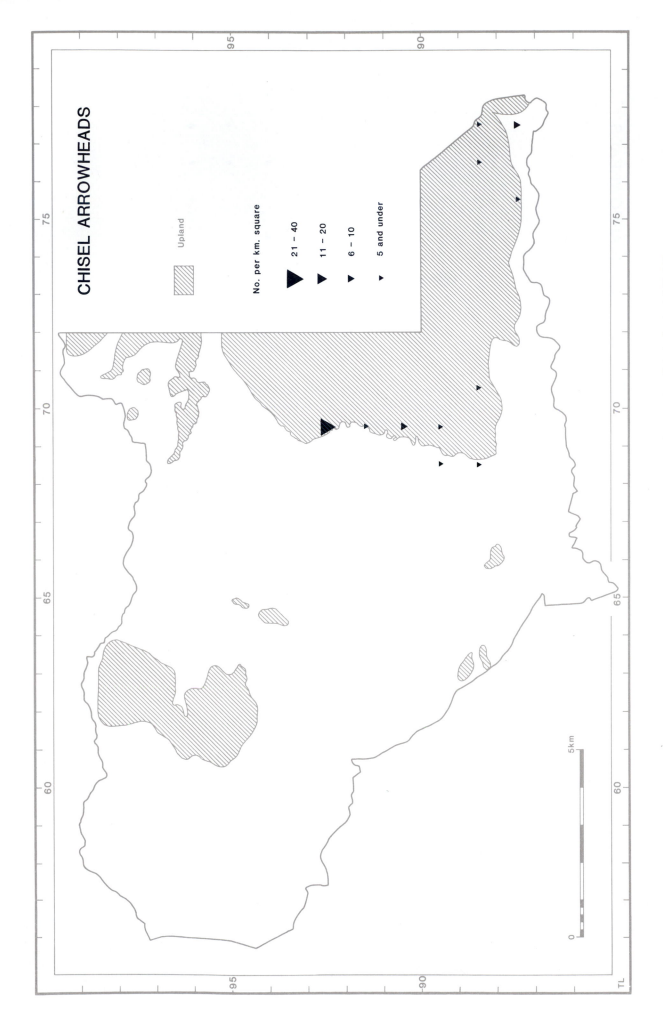

Figure 36 Distribution of chisel arrowheads, listed in Appendix 11 (microfiche). Scale 1:100,000

66

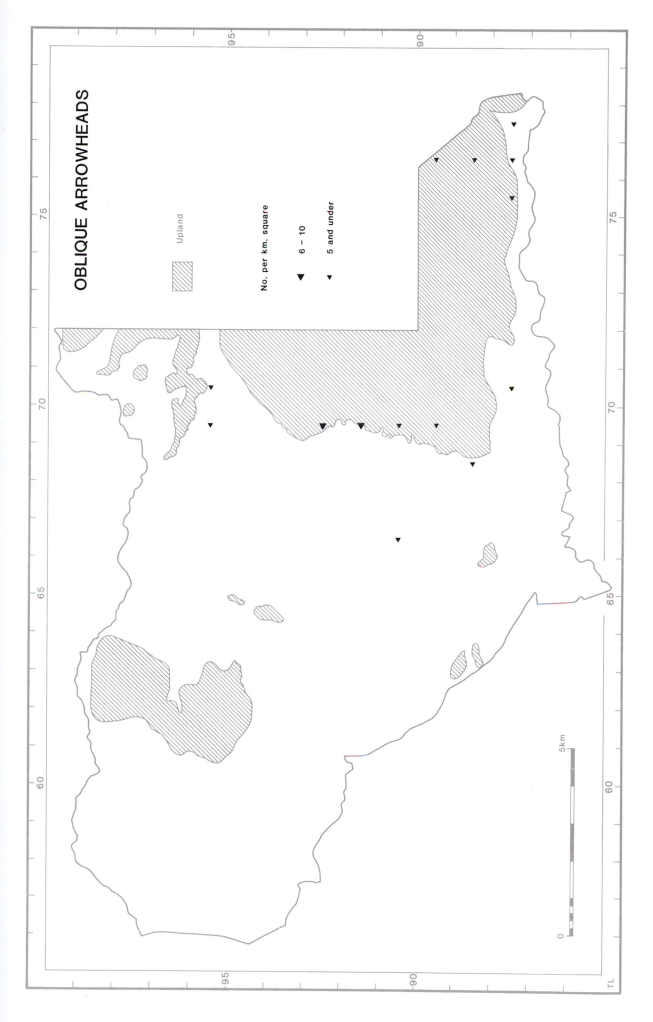

Figure 37 Distribution of oblique arrowheads, listed in Appendix 12 (microfiche). Scale 1:100,000

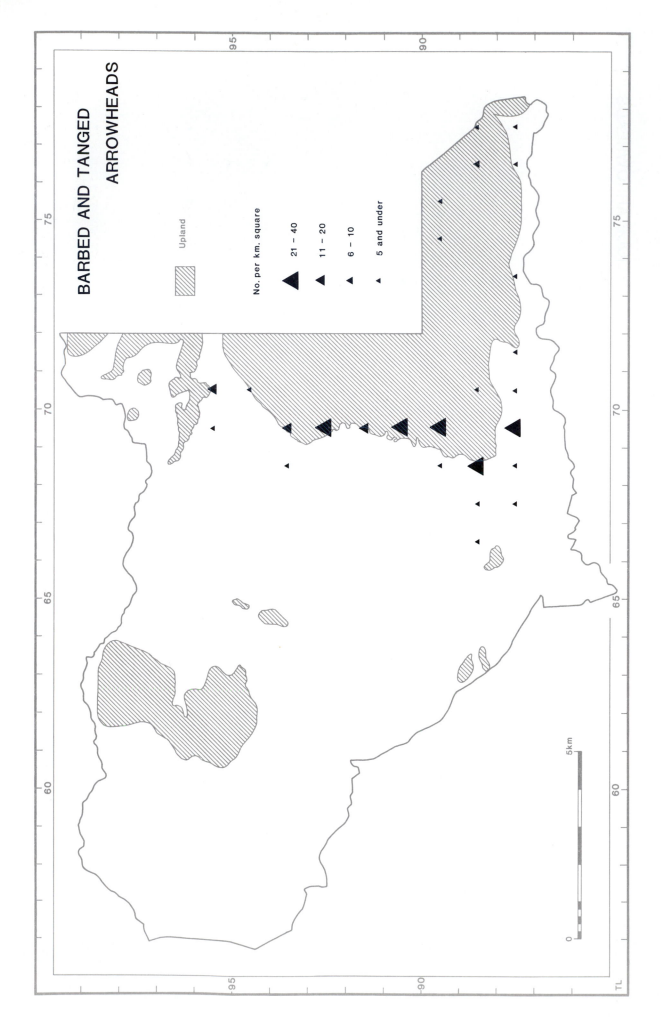

Figure 38 Distribution of barbed and tanged arrowheads, listed in Appendix 13 (microfiche). Scale 1:100,000

68

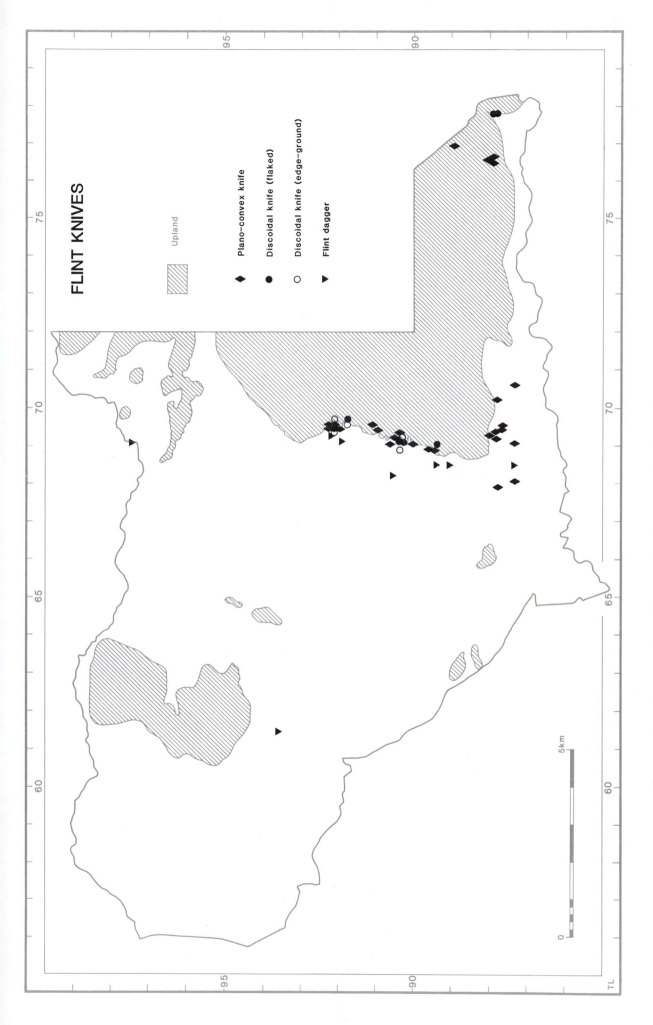

FLINT KNIVES

Upland

◆ Plano–convex knife

● Discoidal knife (flaked)

○ Discoidal knife (edge–ground)

▶ Flint dagger

Figure 39 Distribution of flint knives, listed in Appendices 17, 19 and 20 (microfiche). Scale 1:100,000

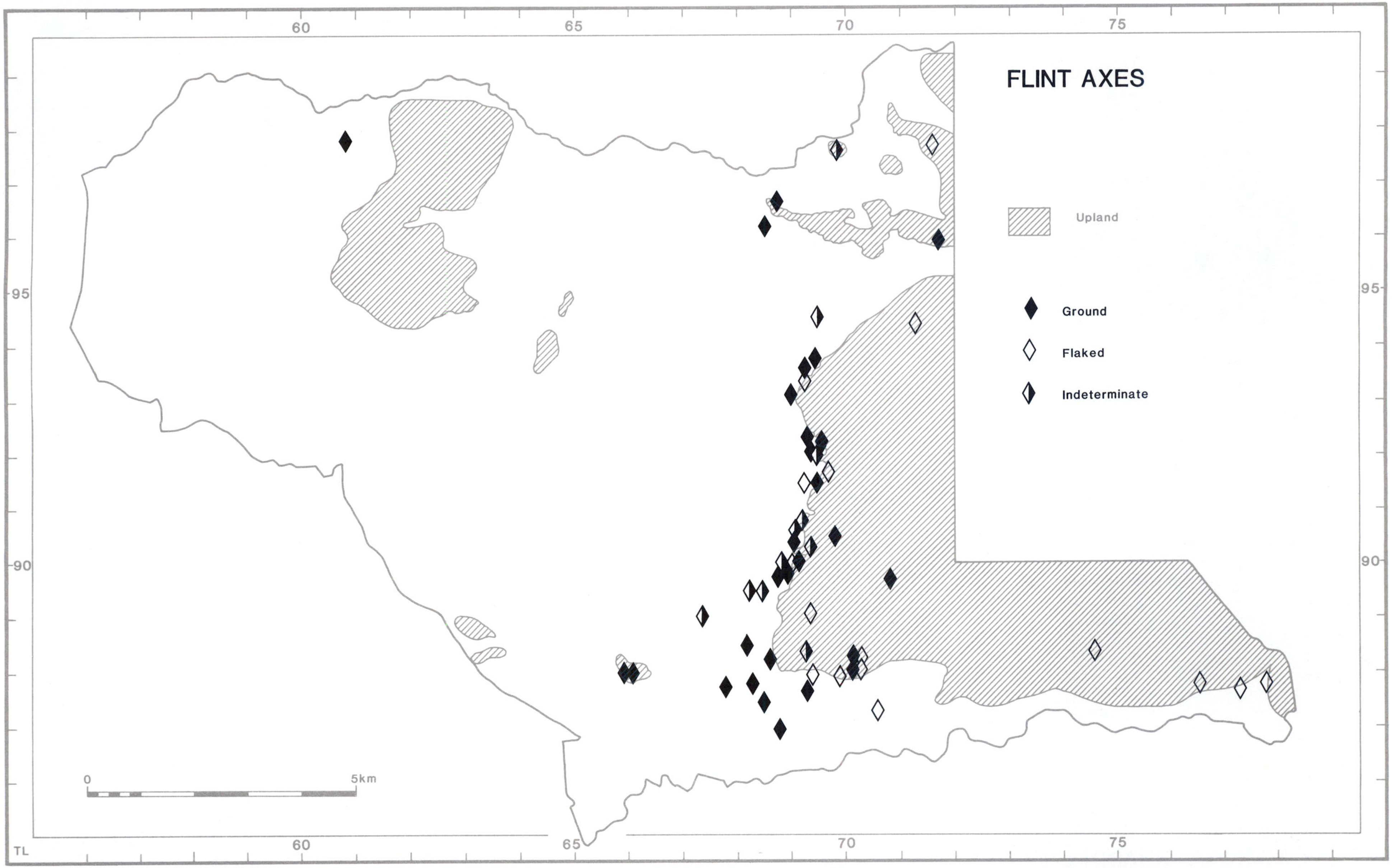
FLINT AXES
Upland
Ground
Flaked
Indeterminate
0
5km
60
65
70
75
95
90
TL

Figure 40 Distribution of flint axes, listed in Appendix 23 (microfiche). Scale 1:100,000

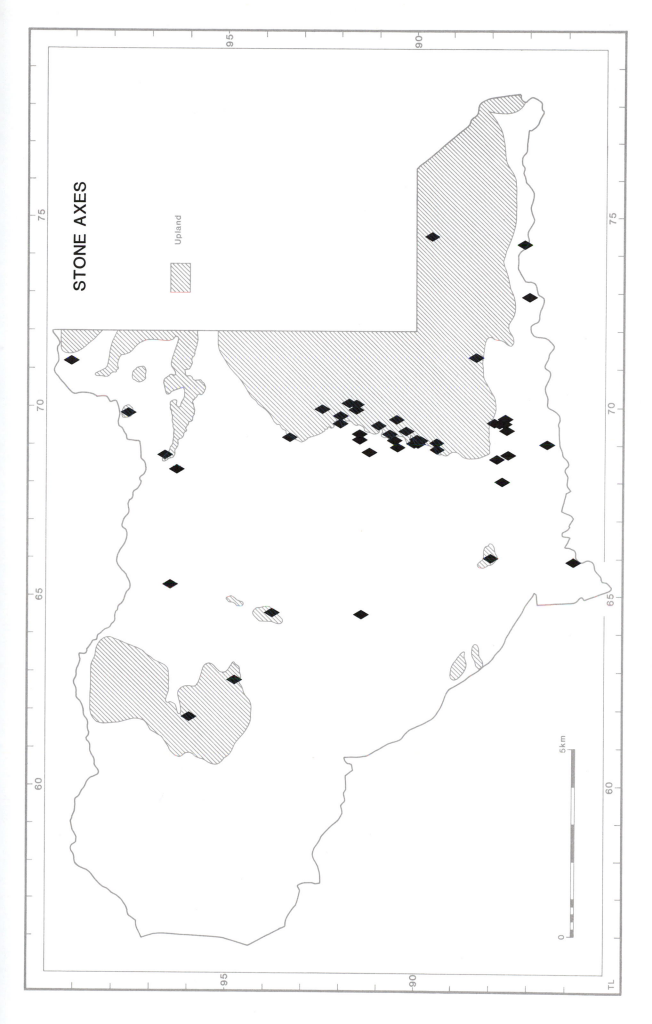

Figure 41 Distribution of stone axes, listed in Appendix 24 (microfiche). Scale 1:100,000

STONE AXES

Upland

5km

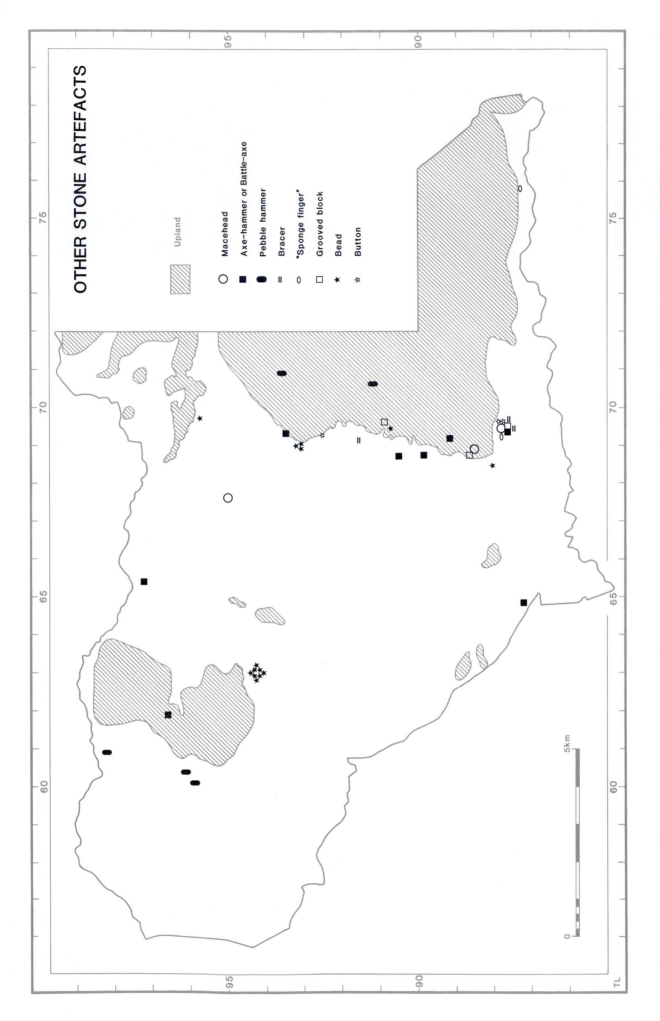

Figure 42 Distribution of stone artefacts other than axes and saddle querns, listed in Appendix 25 (microfiche). Scale 1:100,000

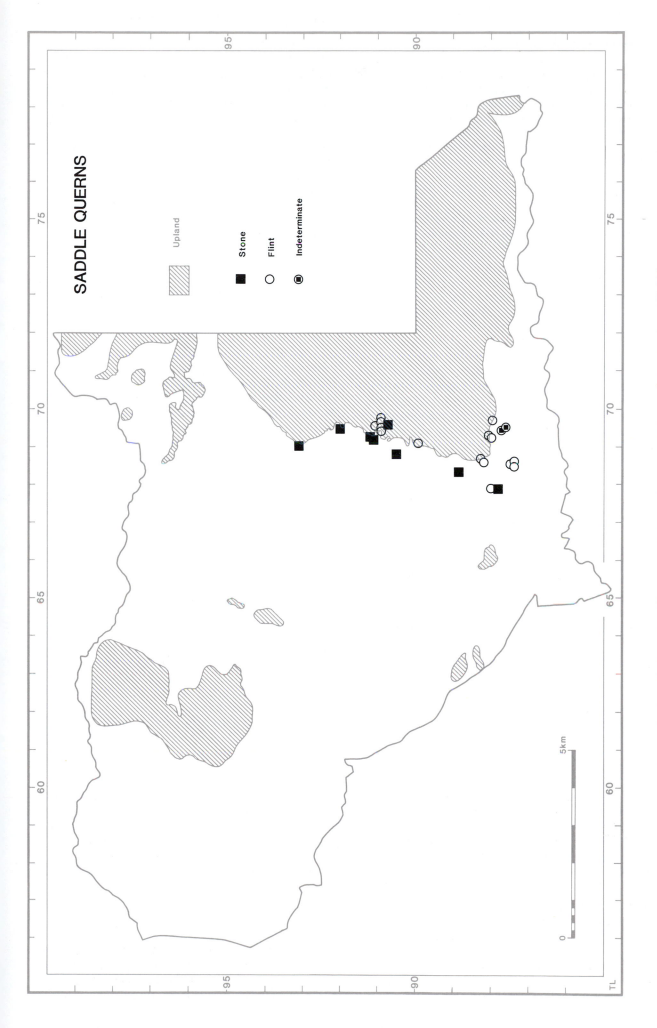

SADDLE QUERNS

Upland

Stone
Flint
Indeterminate

Figure 43 Distribution of saddle querns, listed in Appendix 26 (microfiche). Scale 1:100,000

5km

The survey area forms the northernmost part of a major concentration of stone axes from all parts of Britain which extends along the south-eastern fen edge from the Wissey to the Cam (Cummins 1979, fig. 1; Green 1988, 37–38). Although flint axes are also abundant (Figs 40, 41), stone ones are exceptionally frequent by regional standards: they make up thirty-seven percent of the axes from the survey area, but only eight percent of the axes from Norfolk as a whole, excluding those from known mine and quarry sites which would, if included, increase the frequency of flint axes yet further (Healy 1984, 123, fig. 5.12).

There is a strong impression of constraint on the availability of axes of rare materials from distant sources as distinct from axes of locally near-ubiquitous flint.

Other stone artefacts. Many, such as buttons, wristguards, battle-axes, axe-hammers and 'sponge-fingers', are demonstrably of Beaker and/or Early Bronze Age affinities, as are some simple jet and amber beads (Clarke 1970, 448; Smith and Simpson 1966, 149–151; Smith 1979; Longworth 1984, 65–75; Leahy 1986). Maceheads became current in the Later Neolithic (Smith 1979, 15). While some pebble hammers have been found in Mesolithic contexts, others may date from as late as the Early Bronze Age (Roe 1979, 36). Simple, functional stone implements, such as rubbers or pounders, are inherently undatable, and are included in Appendix 25 (microfiche) because they have been found in areas of Neolithic and Bronze Age occupation.

Saddle querns, like other simple stone implements, had a long currency. Examples from the relatively elevated location of Hill Close, Feltwell (Sites 5195, 24840), where there is Early Iron Age and Romano-British settlement, may be of post-Bronze Age date. Most, however, are from lower-lying parts of the fen edge (Fig. 43), which do not seem to have been occupied beyond the end of the Early Bronze Age. Numerous as the recorded saddle querns from the survey area are, they are probably under-represented, since their weight and bulk must often predispose finders to move them to the nearest field edge, out of the way of cultivation, rather than transport them farther, let alone collect them.

Neolithic and Bronze Age: General Considerations
Variation along the fen edge. While all artefacts types are concentrated in a narrow north-south zone along the fen edge, distributions within the zone suggest that the focus of activity expanded southward over time. Insofar as Earlier Neolithic activity is represented by leaf-shaped arrowheads, and Later Neolithic activity by chisel and oblique arrowheads and discoidal knives, both seem to have been most intense in the central part of the zone (Figs 35–37, 39), while Beaker and Early Bronze Age activity, insofar as they are represented by barbed and tanged arrowheads, plano-convex knives, flint daggers and shaft-hole implements, was more evenly dispersed over the central and southern parts of the zone (Figs 38, 39, 42).

Relationship between upland and fen edge. Especially after the fen clay transgression, a large part of the flint used on the fen edge must have been brought from the adjoining upland, even if over only short distances. The most striking difference between Breckland and fen edge collections is one of size, illustrated by a ninefold drop in mean core weight over a distance of 8km, from 322g at

Fengate Farm, Weeting with Broomhill, a Breckland site in the extreme east of the survey area (Site 5636/c2; Healy forthcoming) to 35g in the main collections from fields 466, 613, 614 and 616 in Hockwold cum Wilton (Table 6). This indicates that these fen edge industries were largely made on the relatively small, low quality flint of the immediate upland. Tabular flint saddle querns, on the other hand, must have come from the Breckland, and may be the most readily recognised aspect of a more substantial importation of flint.

Breckland collections are ill-represented in the narrow strip of the region which forms part of the survey area. Viewed over a wider area, they tend to include small numbers of heavy implements, such as picks, *tranchet* tools, waisted tools and irregular heavy bifaces which regularly occur on mine and quarry sites (Care 1982, 279–281; Gardiner 1991, 62). It is significant that Warburton (1913) considered the extensive upland scatters from which he collected in Methwold and Northwold to include 'Cissbury type' implements. Such forms are very rare in fen edge collections and of exceptionally small size, like a waisted tool from Site 5308/c4 (61/68; Fig. 50: L65).

Even the thin sliver of Breckland which falls within the survey area is distinguished from the fen edge by the prevalence in it of flaked rather than ground flint axes (Fig. 40), suggesting that axes made in the Breckland may have been finished on the fen edge. Variety of flints among the fen edge axes indicates a range of sources. Flake axes of plano-convex section and triangular outline, such as were made at Grime's Graves (Site 5640; Saville 1981a, figs 43–45) are very rare. There are only two definite examples from the survey area, one of which is not a Grime's Graves product, since it is made of mottled, inclusion-filled orange flint (Healy forthcoming).

The probably vast output of Grime's Graves remains elusive. Trace element analysis of ground flint axes has revealed very few possible products (Craddock *et al.* 1983). The characteristic cortex of floorstone is, furthermore, rare in contemporary local industries, suggesting that most of the flint taken from the site was already in a non-cortical state (Healy 1991b). If this consideration is combined with Saville's conclusion that the mining period industry was a multi-product one, in which axes were relatively unimportant (1981a, 67–72), then possible products include implements which were non-cortical in the finished or partly finished state; which required large, sound flake blanks such as those provided by mined flint; and which were of sufficient contemporary worth to justify manufacture from material extracted at considerable cost in time and labour. The known products of the site, flake axes and discoidal knives (Saville 1981a, 51–56), meet these specifications, as do chisel and oblique arrowheads, which have also been found there. Other possibilities include plano-convex knives, flint daggers, single-piece sickles and the more elaborate barbed and tanged arrowheads. Green has suggested the production and long-distance transport of triangular blanks for barbed and tanged arrowheads (1980, 118).

Elaborate flint implements such as these, some of them made of floorstone-like flint, abound on the south-eastern fen edge, where they seem concentrated in the same manner as arrowheads and stone implements. More than fifty years ago, pioneering studies by Clark (1928; 1932b) and Grimes (1931) showed that nationally high densities of discoidal knives, flint daggers and single-piece sickles coincided on the fen edge between the Little Ouse and the Cam. Relatively few findspots were then recorded north of the Little Ouse. Now all three concentrations extend to the Wissey (Fig. 39). There is an even greater concentration of plano-convex and scale-flaked knives, which far outnumber discoidal forms (Table 9).

This apparent concentration of fine objects may be illusory, representing no more than the distinctive, collectable fraction of a vast concentration of worked flint, among which highly-finished artefacts are no more frequent than among contemporary material in other regions. The exceptionally high frequency of exotic stone, as opposed to local flint, axes argues against this, however, as does comparison with another area of contemporary occupation.

The Loam Region of north-east Norfolk is one of light, fertile, ultimately loess-based soils which has seen dense, but so far under-investigated, Neolithic and Bronze Age occupation. Long-term collection and investigation has been undertaken on two adjoining farms, by Mr J.E. Owles at Park Farm, Witton (Lawson 1983) and by the late Mr J.E. Turner at Bacton Wood Mill Farm, Edingthorpe, Bacton (Bamford 1982, 36–37; Healy 1980, appendix I). Both have produced extensive evidence for Neolithic and, especially, Beaker and Bronze Age activity. The combined collection of lithic material is, however, very different from the fen edge material. The axes are all of flint, corresponding to a general rarity of stone axes in north-east Norfolk (Healy 1984, fig. 5.12), with stone confined to two fragmentary shaft-hole implements. Arrowheads and knives are few and generally unelaborate; and items such as beads, buttons and wristguards are completely absent. The artefacts illustrated by Lawson (1983, figs 3, 4, 13) convey the overall character of the material.

The grave goods of the Later Neolithic and Early Bronze Age have emerged regularly from the ploughsoil of the fen edge but rarely from that of the Loam Region.

II.5. Terms used in describing lithic material

Debitage

Cores
Classified according to Clark and Higgs (1960, 216) with the addition of Levallois:

Single-platform
A1. Flakes removed all around
A2. Flakes removed part of way around (*e.g.* Fig. 51: L69)

Multi-platform
B1. Two parallel platforms
B2. Two platforms, one at an oblique angle
B3. Two platforms at right-angles
C. Three or more platforms

Keeled
D. Flakes struck from either side of a ridge (*e.g.* Fig. 44: L1, Fig. 48: L36)
E. As D, but with one additional platform or more (*e.g.* Fig. 51: L70)
Levallois. Discoidal keeled core prepared for the detachment of flakes of predetermined shape (Tixier, Inizan and Roche, 1980, 44–46)

Unclassifiable or fragmentary

Irregular waste
Fragment produced during the breaking-up of a nodule or pebble.

Core rejuvenation flake
Removal made to prepare a core platform for further flaking (*e.g.* Fig. 53: L93)

Flake
Generally used to denote any removal from a core. Sometimes subdivided visually, as in Table 5, into:

Blade (*e.g.* the blanks of Fig. 52: L88 and Fig. 54: L104). A proportionately narrow, parallel-sided flake, often with parallel arrises on the dorsal face.

Flake. Any other removal.
In Figures 28–29 and 31–32 flakes are divided into:
    Primary (*e.g.* the blank of Fig. 53: L95). Dorsal face completely cortical
    Secondary (*e.g.* the blank of Fig. 53: L101). Dorsal face partly cortical
    Tertiary (*e.g.* the blank of Fig. 51: L72). Dorsal face non-cortical

Flake dimensions, represented in the same diagrams, have been measured according to Saville (1981b, 146–147):
    Length. Maximum dimension along bulbar axis at right-angles to striking platform
    Breadth. Maximum distance between any two points on opposite lateral edges, taken at right-angles to length measurement
    Thickness. Maximum dimension between dorsal and ventral faces, measured at right-angles to ventral face

Flake butts (or striking platforms) are divided in Figures 30 and 33 into:
    Cortical. Completely cortex-covered
    Plain. Formed by a single removal
    With more than one removal. Having more than one truncated flake scar on the striking platform
    Faceted. With a series of negative bulbs along the dorsal edge, forming part of the flake scars truncated at the ventral edge by the detachment of the flake (Saville 1981a, 6)
    Punctiform. Slender and of restricted area, likely to have been by a soft hammer or punch-struck blow

Hinge fracture. Flake or blade in which the fracture plane turns abruptly up at the distal end, leaving a smoothly rounded tip.

Irregular flake (*e.g.* the blank of Fig. 48: L43). A flake of markedly asymmetrical outline.

Retouched forms

Leaf arrowhead
A bifacially-flaked point ranging in outline from pointed oval to piriform, and including kite-shaped and ogival forms, as defined by Green (1980, 22). Retouch may completely cover both faces (*e.g.* Bamford 1982, fig. 33: h), be confined to tips and edges (*e.g.* Fig. 52: L80), or occupy any intermediate extent (*e.g.* Fig. 54: L105, L106), the bulb almost always being reduced. Complete examples are allotted, where possible, to the metric classes defined by Green (1980, 21–29, table II.18).

Petit tranchet arrowhead (*e.g.* Green 1980, fig. 37: a-c)
Transverse arrowhead of trapezoid outline, made, generally on a blade segment, by bilateral abrupt retouch. Equivalent to form A of Clark's (1934) *petit tranchet* derivative arrowhead classification.

Chisel arrowhead (*e.g.* Green 1980, fig. 37: d-f; Healy 1991a, fig. 63: L10)
Roughly symmetrical arrowhead of trapezoid or triangular outline, generally formed by bifacial retouch and retaining one unworked primary flake edge. Equivalent to forms B-D of Clark's (1934) *petit tranchet* derivative arrowhead classification (adapted from Green 1980, 30).

Oblique arrowhead (*e.g.* Green 1980, fig. 38; Healy 1991a, fig. 63: L11)
Asymmetrical arrowhead of subtriangular outline, formed by bifacial retouch along one long edge and often around an asymmetrically hollowed base, with the remaining primary flake edge generally unworked, but sometimes also retouched, especially towards the tip. Equivalent to forms E-I of Clark's (1934) *petit tranchet* derivative arrowhead classification (adapted from Green 1980, 30).

Barbed and tanged arrowhead
Bifacially flaked point of triangular or sub-triangular outline with two basal notches forming a central tang and lateral barbs. Subdivided into:

Green Low (*e.g.* Fig. 48: L38). Barbs oblique-ended, with obtuse angle next to tang and acute angle at lowest point of barb. Tang squared, subsquare, rounded, or, if longer than barbs, pointed or triangular (Green 1980, 51).

Conygar Hill (*e.g.* Fig.44: L3). Barbs and tang both squared (Green 1980, 51).

Ballyclare (*e.g.* Fig. 57: L125). Length (mm) x breadth (mm) = 1400 (Green 1980, 50).

Other (*e.g.* Bamford 1982, fig. 33, l, m; Healy 1991a, fig. 64: L15).

Tanged arrowhead (*e.g.* Green 1980, fig. 45: a-f)
With tang but no barbs, equivalent to Green's (1980, 51) Sutton a form of barbed and tanged arrowhead.

Triangular arrowhead (*e.g.* Fig. 48: L39)
Bifacially-flaked point of triangular or subtriangular outline.

Hollow-based arrowhead (*e.g.* Evans 1897, figs 328–330)
Bifacially flaked point of triangular outline with a marked basal concavity producing two barbs of equal length. Distinguished from oblique arrowhead by symmetrical outline, lenticular transverse section and more extensive retouch.

Laurel leaf (*e.g.* Clark and Higgs 1960, fig. 14: F39–F42)
Bifacially-flaked point with similar range of outlines to leaf arrowheads but markedly larger, reaching up to 9 or 10cm in length. Grades into:

?Unfinished arrowhead (*e.g.* Fig. 45: L15, Fig. 49: L60)
Large, relatively thin and flat biface more likely to have been an arrowhead blank than a finished implement.

Scraper
Implement part of the edge of which is bevelled by unifacial blunting retouch, forming an angle of approximately 20–90 degrees with the flat underside of the blank, the modified edge being usually convex (Saville 1981a, 8–9). Subdivided into:

End scraper (*e.g.* Fig. 44: L4, Fig. 53: L95). Worked at the distal or, rarely, the bulbar end of a flake.

Side-end scraper (*e.g.* Fig. 44: L5, Fig. 51: L74). Worked at the distal or bulbar end of a flake and along more than half of one lateral edge.

Horseshoe scraper (*e.g.* Fig. 44: L10, Fig. 49: L49). Worked at the distal or bulbar end of a flake and along both lateral edges or, rarely, at both distal and bulbar ends and along one lateral edge.

Disc scraper Worked around the entire circumference of a flake.

Side scraper (*e.g.* Fig. 49: L50, Fig. 51: L77). Worked along one lateral edge or both lateral edges of a flake.

Fragmentary flake scraper (*e.g.* Fig. 51: L76).

Scraper on non-flake blank (*e.g.* Fig. 47: L30, Fig. 53: L102).

Small, sometimes scale-flaked scrapers (*e.g.* Fig. 44: L10, Fig. 48: L41, Fig. 49: L48) are traditionally referred to as 'thumbnail' forms, regardless of extent or location of retouch.

Borer
Implement with a narrow retouched projection, apparently used for perforation. Subdivided into:

Awl (*e.g.* Fig. 44: L14, Fig. 49: L52, Fig. 52: L87). Borer with point formed by retouch from more than one direction (Clark and Higgs 1960, 223).

Piercer (*e.g.* Fig. 53: L99). Borer with point formed by retouch from only one direction (Clark and Higgs 1960, 223).

Spurred piece (*e.g.* Fig. 49: L53). Borer with point formed on scraper-like edge or by the working of two closely-spaced notches (Smith 1965, 105).

Plano-convex knife (*e.g.* Fig. 44: L12, Fig. 48: L45)
Sharp-edged implement of thin, plano-convex section with sharp edges and generally of ovoid outline, scale-flaked over all, or almost all, of its dorsal face (Clark 1932a).

Scale-flaked knife (*e.g.* Fig. 49: L56, Fig. 52: L88, Fig. 54: L107)
A generally parallel-sided blank, with regular, scale-flaked retouch along one or two lateral edges.

Discoidal knife (*e.g.* Fig. 57: L123)
Sharp-edged implement, generally of subcircular outline, formed by bifacial retouch extending around its entire periphery and sometimes over both faces. Often finished by edge-grinding. Triangular, quadrangular and lozenge-shaped forms occur, especially ground variants (Clark 1928).

Edge-ground knife (*e.g.* Clark and Higgs 1960, fig. 15: F49)
A flake with at least part of its periphery ground to a cutting edge, but lacking the regularity and extensive retouch of discoidal forms.

Single-piece sickle (*e.g.* Fig. 58: L130)
Of biconvex transverse section, with pointed tip and rounded butt, bifacially flaked and generally of crescentic outline, sometimes with silica gloss on the cutting edge (Clark 1932b).

Flint dagger (*e.g.* Green, Houlder and Keeley 1982, fig. 1; Healy 1991a, fig. 64: L18)
Bifacially flaked replica of a copper alloy dagger, of foliate outline, sometimes two-pointed, sometimes with a blunt, elongated tang, sometimes with lateral notches to facilitate hafting (Grimes 1931).

Backed knife (*e.g.* Clark and Higgs 1960, fig. 15: F51)
A generally parallel-sided blank, one lateral edge of which is blunted by abrupt retouch, the opposite edge being either unretouched, although often worn, or modified by uni- or bilateral retouch.

Notch
Piece in the edge of which one or more indentations have been worked by abrupt or semi-abrupt retouch.

Denticulate (*e.g.* Fig. 49: L57, Fig. 51: L79)
Piece in the edge of which coarse teeth have been formed, sometimes by the working of contiguous notches, sometimes by the detachment of single flakes. Includes the more restricted classes of '(keeled) denticulated flakes' (Wainwright and Longworth 1971, 176) and 'denticulate scrapers' (Saville 1981a, 9).

Saw
Coarsely-serrated piece, its teeth often formed by the removal of two or more small flakes on either side.

Serrated piece (*e.g.* Fig. 49: L58, Fig. 54: L104)
Straight-sided blank, generally a blade, with one or occasionally both lateral edges finely serrated by the removal of a single chip on either side of each tooth (Smith 1965, 108). This effect may be obtained by striking downwards onto the edge of the flake to be serrated with the edge of another flake held at right-angles to it.

Burin (*e.g.* Wymer 1977, fig. 2: 4–5; Healy 1991a, fig. 63: L2)
Implement with a chisel-like edge formed by the intersecting angle between the bulbar end of a negative flake scar (or scars) and its platform (Saville 1981a, 8).

Microlith (*e.g.* Wymer 1977, fig. 2: 9–13; Healy 1991a, fig. 63: L3–4)
Small blade or flake fragment, its bulb normally removed, modified to a regular form by abrupt retouch. Examples other than obliquely-blunted points are, where possible, classified according to Jacobi (1978, fig. 6).

Microburin (*e.g.* Wymer 1977, fig. 2: 7–8)
By-product of microlith manufacture, formed by working a notch in the edge of a blade over the edge of an anvil across which the proximal or distal end eventually breaks off, becoming a microburin. Characterised by truncated dorsal notch forming an acute angle with a ventral fracture facet (Tixier *et al.* 1980, 62–64).

Truncated piece (*e.g.* Bamford 1982, fig. 31: b)
Flake or blade the distal end of which is truncated, generally obliquely, by abrupt retouch.

Miscellaneous retouched piece (*e.g.* Fig. 52: L91)

'Fabricator' or rod (*e.g.* Fig. 45: L18, L19)
Uni- or bifacially-flaked, blunted-ended, parallel-sided implement, of thick plano-convex or biconvex section, sometimes relatively thin and

edge-retouched only (*e.g.* Fig. 50: L64), sometimes heavily-worn. Includes all but the unilaterally-retouched forms among 'rods', as defined by Saville (1981a, 10).

Tranchet axe (*e.g.* Wymer 1977, fig. 2: 1)
Relatively heavy cutting tool of ovoid outline, flaked over both faces with cutting edge formed by removal of one transverse flake.

Axe or adze (*e.g.* Fig. 59: L132–L137)
Relatively heavy cutting tool with transverse cutting edge, sometimes wholly or partly ground.

Flake from ground implement

Tribrach or Y-shaped tool (*e.g.* Piggott 1954, fig. 44: 7; Gardiner 1987, fig. 5.1: 2)
Bifacially-flaked implement with two approximately equal arms and one longer one.

Waisted tool (*e.g.* Fig. 50: L65)
Implement bifacially-flaked into a waisted shape by the formation of two opposed lateral notches, either central to the long axis or displaced to one end. Ends blunt or sharp.

Tranchet tool (*e.g.* Gardiner 1987, fig. 5.1: 1; Saville 1981a, fig. 40: F104)
Cleaver-like implement of triangular or trapezoid outline with an unretouched *tranchet* cutting edge.

Chisel (*e.g.* Manby 1974, fig. 3: 17, fig. 31: 1)
Parallel-sided bar of flint of biconvex section, with a double-bevelled cutting edge which is often ground (Manby 1974, 90).

Pick (*e.g.* Saville 1981a, fig. 32: F77, F78).
Heavy implement with one pointed working end, often bifacially-flaked and of elongated form (Saville 1981a, 8).

Battle-axe (*e.g.* Roe 1979, figs 1–2)
Ground shaft-hole implement with rounded or squared butt, straight- or concave-sided profile, and cutting edge, often expanded, parallel to the shaft-hole (Roe 1979, 23).

Axe-hammer (*e.g.* Fig. 46: L23, L112; Roe 1979, figs 7–8)
Heavy, roughly-finished shaft-hole implement with rounded or squared butt, straight- or occasionally slightly concave-sided profile and unexpanded cutting edge parallel to the shaft-hole (Roe 1979, 29–30).

Macehead (*e.g.* Fig. 46: L27; Roe 1979, figs 9–10)
Ground shaft-hole implement without cutting edge, of ovoid to quadrangular outline, shaft-hole generally located towards narrower end (Roe 1979, 30).

Pebble hammer (*e.g.* Fig. 60: L138)
Otherwise unmodified pebble with central shaft-hole, extremities often battered (Roe 1979, 36).

Cupped pebble
As pebble hammer, but with two opposed depressions which do not meet to form a perforation.

Hammerstone (*e.g.* Fig. 48: L33)
Flint or stone, whether or not otherwise modified, battered from use as hammer, generally in flint-working.

Grooved Sandstone (*e.g.* Fig. 46: L24, Fig. 56: L116)
Otherwise unmodified sandstone block with one or more V-sectioned grooves.

'Sponge finger' (*e.g.* Fig. 60: L140; Bamford 1982, fig. 34: g)
Blunt-ended, spatulate implement, generally of plano-convex section (Smith and Simpson 1966, 139–141).

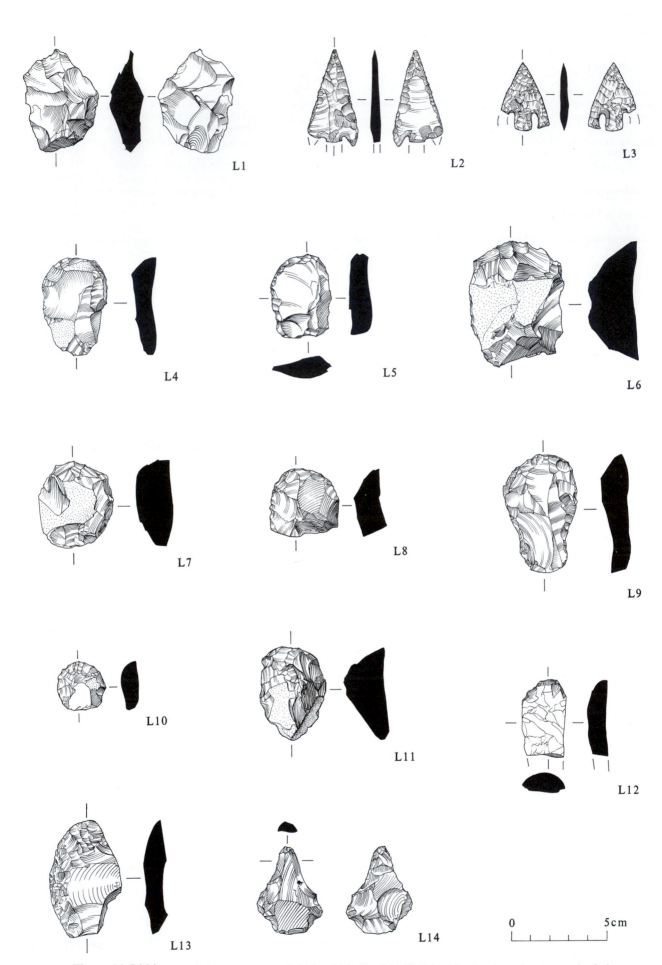

Figure 44 Lithic material from HCW OS 466 + 616, Site 24866 ('site 8'). Corticated areas unshaded.
Particulars in catalogue. Scale 1:2

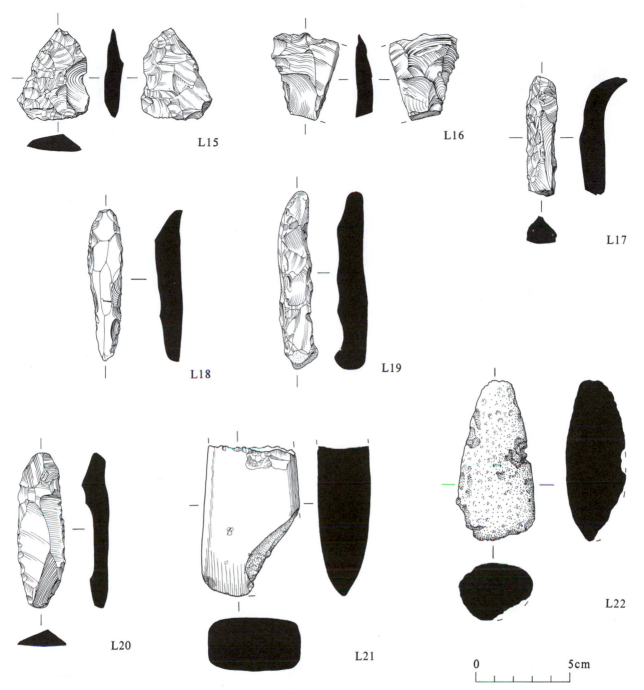

Figure 45 Lithic material from HCW OS 466 + 616, Site 24866 ('site 8'). Corticated areas unshaded.
Particulars in catalogue. Scale 1:2

II.6. Catalogue of illustrated lithic material

Catalogue entries are ordered in the following sequence: Category, petrology number, raw material, descriptive or other comment, context, bibliographical reference(s).

Hockwold cum Wilton. Site 24866 ('site 8')
Centre TL 6954 8765. Old OS fields 466 and 616. NCM accession no. 121.960 (Ch. 3.I.1. Figs 44–45)

L1   **Keeled (D) core.** Indeterminate flint.
L2   **Barbed and tanged arrowhead.** Orange flint.
L3   **Barbed and tanged arrowhead** (Conygar Hill). Orange flint.
L4   **End scraper.** Indeterminate flint.
L5   **Side-end scraper.** Mottled grey flint. Ventral face damaged.
L6   **Side-end scraper.** Chalk flint. Natural polish (?from wind-blown sand) on part of unmodified surface.
L7   **Side-end scraper.** Chalk flint.
L8   **Horseshoe scraper.** Chalk flint.
L9   **Horseshoe scraper.** Indeterminate flint

L10   **Horseshoe scraper.** Indeterminate flint.
L11   **Horseshoe scraper.** Indeterminate flint.
L12   **Plano-convex knife.** Mottled orange-grey flint with lighter inclusions. Corticated, (?plough) damage to surviving end and ventral face.
L13   **Scale-flaked knife.** Mottled grey flint.
L14   **Awl**. ?Chalk flint.
L15   **?Unfinished arrowhead.** Indeterminate flint. Probably broken during manufacture.
L16   **Misc. retouched.** Indeterminate flint.
L17   **'Fabricator'**. ?Chalk flint.
L18   **'Fabricator'.** Made on already-corticated blank of ?chalk flint.
L19   **'Fabricator'.** Mottled grey flint. Distal end worn smooth.
L20   **'Fabricator'.** Mottled grey flint. Proximal end worn smooth.
L21   **Axe.** N57. Group VI. Clough and Green 1972, 137–138, 148, 154.
L22   **Axe.** N58. Epidiorite, possibly from SW England. Clough and Green 1972, 137–138, 148, 154.

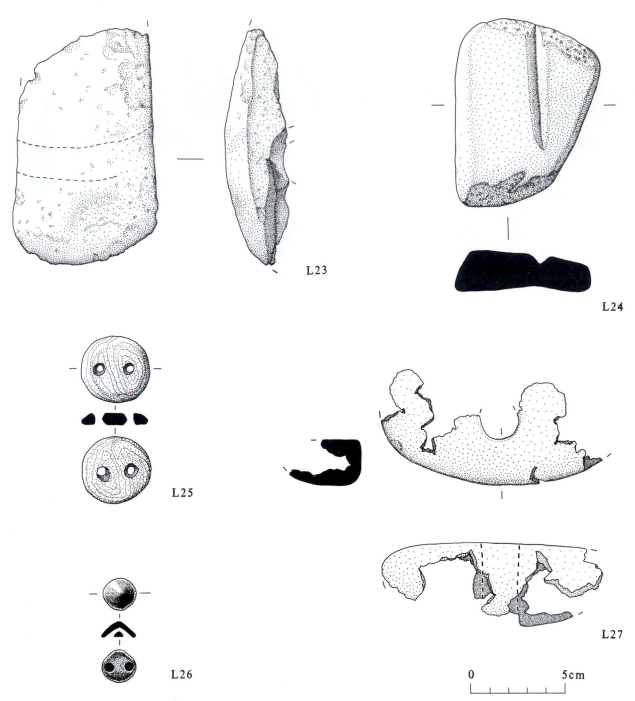

Figure 46 Lithic material from HCW OS 466 + 614 + 616, 1959–60: L23 and L24 from the fields at large, L25 and L26 from Frank Curtis' 'site 3' (? = Site 5439 (44)), L27 from 'Drain site, Greens' (? = Site 5309 (48). Particulars in catalogue. Scale 1:2

Hockwold cum Wilton. Site 14662. 'Field 79'
Centre TL 6945 8765. Old OS fields 466 + 614 + 616. KLM accession no. 4.959 (Ch. 3.I.1. Fig. 46)

L23　**Axe-hammer.** N252. Greywacke.
L24　**Grooved sandstone.**

Hockwold cum Wilton. 'site 3', ? = Site 5439 (44)
Curtis collection. Old OS field 616 (Ch. 3.I.1. Fig. 46)

L25　**Button.** Probably slate. Fine-grained, laminated, blue-grey.
L26　**Button.** Jet.

Hockwold cum Wilton. 'Drain site Greens', ? = Site 5309 (48)
Old OS field 616. NCM accession no. 489.981 (Ch. 3.I.1. Fig. 46)

L27　**Macehead.** Coarse, green igneous rock. In extremely friable condition, much of body of implement seems to have eroded, leaving outer skin.

Hockwold cum Wilton. Site 5373 (22)
TL 6930 8760. Old OS field 614. NCM accession no. 673.962 (Ch. 3.I.2. Fig. 47)

L28　**End scraper.** Chalk flint.
L29　**Side-end scraper.** Indeterminate flint.
L30　**Scraper on thermally-fractured flake.** Indeterminate flint.
L31　**'Fabricator'.** Made on already-corticated blank of orange-grey flint.
L32　**Pebble, ?flaked.** Quartzite.

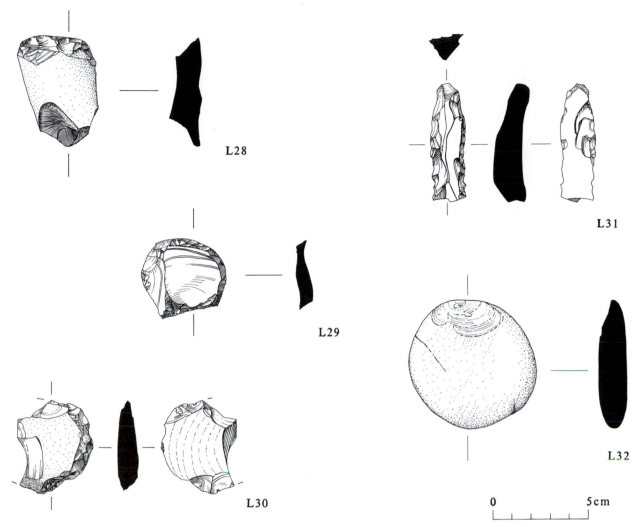

Figure 47 Lithic material from HCW OS 614, Site 5373 (22). Corticated areas unshaded. Particulars in catalogue.
Scale 1:2

Hockwold cum Wilton. Site 5308/c4 (61/68). Dykeside
TL 6932 8778. On boundary of old OS fields 613 and 614.
NCM accession nos 511.964, 205.965 (Ch. 3.I.6. Figs
48–50)

Notes: Where no context is given, objects are from site 61,
an ungridded area in Hockwold cum Wilton 613 excavated
in 1964.

Two finely-worked scale-flaked knives of similar
triangular outline to L56, illustrated by Bamford (1982,
fig. 33: r, s) are also from this site).

L33 **Hammerstone.** Chalk flint. Battered over almost all of surface.
Area *8*.
L34 **Single platform (A2) core.** ?Gravel flint.
L35 **Keeled (E) core.** Mottled grey flint retaining small areas of worn
cortex and of weathered thermally fractured surface. Area *3*.
L36 **Keeled (D) core.** Chalk flint. Area *1*, 1967.
L37 **Keeled (D) core.** Chalk flint. Battered as if subsequently used as
hammerstone.
L38 **Barbed and tanged arrowhead** (Green Low). Orange flint.
Area *1*.
L39 **Triangular arrowhead.** Orange flint. Area *8*.
L40 **End scraper.** Chalk flint.
L41 **End scraper.** Indeterminate flint.
L42 **Horseshoe scraper.** Indeterminate flint.
L43 **End scraper**. Orange flint. Area *5*.
L44 **Side-end scraper.** Chalk flint.
L45 **Scraper.** ?Chalk flint. Made on distal fragment of plano-convex
knife, refitted to proximal fragment. Areas *3, 8*.

L46 **Side-end scraper.** Chalk flint.
L47 **Scraper**. Mottled grey flint. Area *5*.
L48 **Horseshoe scraper.** Indeterminate flint. Area *8*.
L49 **Horseshoe scraper.** Indeterminate flint.
L50 **Side scraper.** ?Chalk flint. Ending in hinge fracture. Area *6*.
L51 **Horseshoe scraper.** Orange flint. Burnt.
L52 **Awl.** Orange flint. Area *5*.
L53 **Spurred piece.** Chalk flint. Area *1*.
L54 **Scale-flaked knife**. Orange flint. Area *6*.
L55 **Scale-flaked knife**. Orange flint. Area *6*.
L56 **Scale-flaked knife.** Made on already-corticated flake of
orange-grey flint.
L57 **Denticulate.** Chalk flint.
L58 **Serrated blade.** Chalk flint. Area *1*.
L59 **Rough biface.** Chalk flint. Beginning of arrowhead
manufacture? — dorsal retouch seems intended to thin.
L60 **?Unfinished arrowhead.** Orange flint. Area *4*.
L61 **'Fabricator'.** ?Gravel flint.
L62 **'Fabricator'.** Made on flake from slightly squared side of
ground axe of mottled light grey flint. Area *5*.
L63 **'Fabricator'.** Orange flint. Heavily worn along left edge.
L64 **'Fabricator'.** Made on already-corticated flake of chalk flint.
Two small patches of cortication remain on dorsal face, ventral
face completely corticated.
L65 **Waisted tool.** Chalk flint. Area *6*.
L66 **Axe.** N72. Group VI. Flaked after breakage. Surface find. Clough
and Green 1972, 138–140, 148, 154.
L67 **Axe.** N79. Group VI. Clough and Green 1972, 138–140, 148,
154. Bamford 1982, fig. 34: h.
L68 **Axe.** N248. Quartzite. Area *1*.

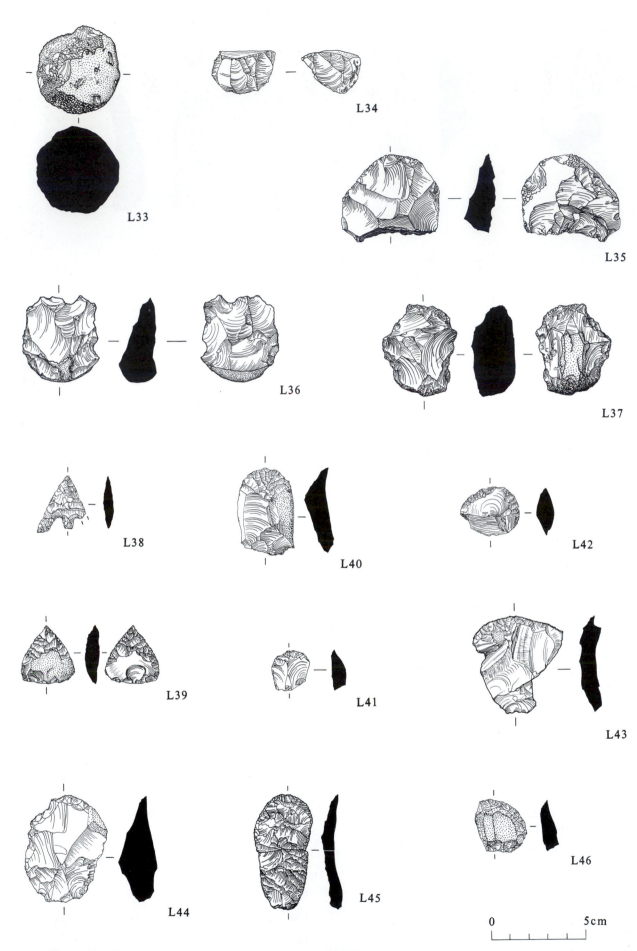

L34

L33

L35

L36

L37

L38

L40

L42

L39

L41

L43

L44

L45

L46

0   5 cm

Figure 48 Lithic material from HCW OS 613 + 614, Site 5308/c4 (61/68). Corticated areas unshaded.
Particulars in catalogue. Scale 1:2

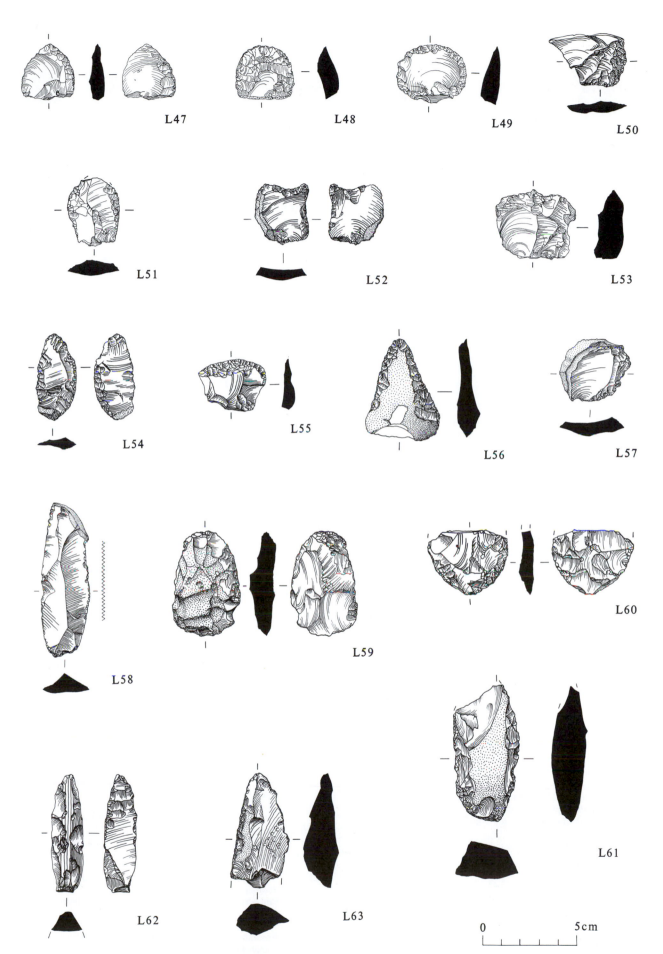

Figure 49 Lithic material from HCW OS 613 + 614, Site 5308/c4 (61/68). Corticated areas unshaded.
Particulars in catalogue. Scale 1:2

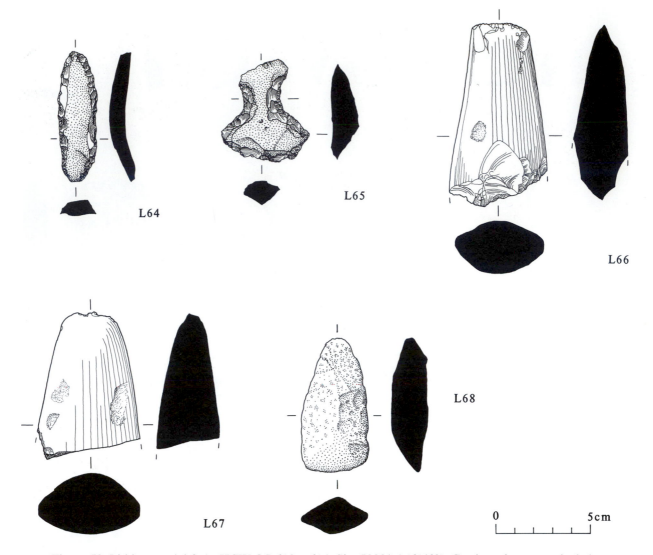

Figure 50 Lithic material from HCW OS 613 + 614, Site 5308/c4 (61/68). Corticated areas unshaded.
Particulars in catalogue. Scale 1:2

Hockwold cum Wilton. Site 5332 (66)
TL 6933 8775. Old OS field 614. NCM accession no.
116.965 (Ch. 3.I.7. Fig. 51)

L69   **Single-platform (A2) core.** Chalk flint.
L70   **Keeled (E) core.** Chalk flint.
L71   **End scraper.** Chalk flint.
L72   **End scraper.** Chalk flint.
L73   **Side-end scraper.** Orange flint. Cortex weathered, right distal area of battering very flat, as if flake struck from edge of quern rather than from hammerstone.
L74   **Side-end scraper.** Chalk flint. Ventral (?plough-) damage.
L75   **Horseshoe scraper.** Orange flint.
L76   **Scraper fragment.** Orange flint. Cortex weathered.
L77   **Double side scraper.** Orange flint.
L78   **Spurred piece.** ?Chalk flint.
L79   **Denticulate.** Orange flint. Smooth, unweathered cortex.

Hockwold cum Wilton. Site 5333 (95/97)
TL 6934 8771. Old OS field 614. NCM accession no.
334.967 (Ch. 3.I.9. Fig. 52)
Note: Where no context is given, objects are from site 95, an initial discovery in the ploughsoil which led to the subsequent excavation of site 97, an area divided into 4ft squares (Ch. 3.I.9).

L80   **Leaf arrowhead.** Indeterminate flint. Corticated. Square *4*.
L81   **End scraper.** Orange flint. Cortex unweathered.
L82   **End scraper.** Indeterminate flint. Square 8.

L83   **End scraper.** Made on already-corticated flake of orange-grey flint. Square *7*.
L84   **Scraper.** Indeterminate flint. Ventral (?plough-) damage.
L85   **Side-end scraper.** Indeterminate flint. Square *9*.
L86   **Horseshoe scraper.** Orange flint. Probably from gravel pebble. Square *7*.
L87   **Awl.** Made on already-corticated blade of indeterminate flint. Square *7*.
L88   **Scale-flaked knife.** Made on already-corticated blade of indeterminate flint. Unretouched edge ?once-serrated. Square 8.
L89   **Denticulate.** Chalk flint.
L90   **Serrated flake.** Indeterminate flint. Square *6*.
L91   **Misc. retouched.** Indeterminate flint. Square *3*.
L92   **Misc. retouched.** Orange flint. ?Atypical chisel arrowhead. Square *3*.

Hockwold cum Wilton. Site 5308/c5 (96)
TL 6928 8767. Old OS field 613. NCM accession no.
209.967 (Ch. 3.I.10. Fig. 53)

L93   **Core rejuvenation flake.** Orange flint. Area *33*.
L94   **Scraper fragment.** Orange flint. Area *1*.
L95   **End scraper.** Indeterminate flint. Cortex weathered and pitted. Area *2*.
L96   **Side-end scraper.** ?Gravel flint. Area *2*.
L97   **Horseshoe scraper.** Chalk flint. Weathered, corticated thermal fractures on dorsal face. Area *2*.
L98   **Scraper frag.** Indeterminate flint. Square *2*.
L99   **Piercer.** Chalk flint. Weathered, corticated thermal fractures on dorsal face. Area *2*.

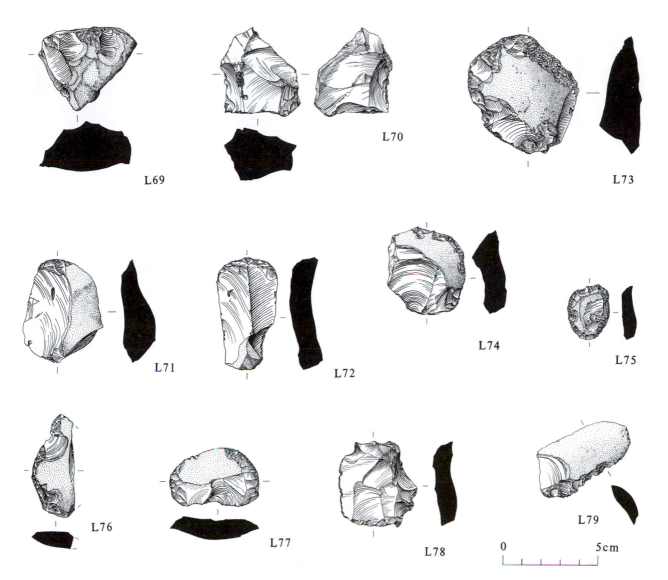

Figure 51 Lithic material from HCW OS 614, Site 5332 (66). Particulars in catalogue. Scale 1:2

L100 **Side-end scraper.** ?Chalk flint. On Levallois-like flake with cortical butt. Area 7.

L101 **Side-end scraper.** Chalk flint. Thick, floorstone-like cortex. Area 7.

L102 **Scraper on core fragment.** Mottled light grey flint. Area 9.

L103 **Axe.** Mottled light grey flint. Ground to high polish, slightly squared sides. Area 3.

Feltwell. Site 4921/c1. Glebe Farm
TL 7148 9090. Old OS field 264. NCM accession no. 275.965 (Ch. 3.II.9. Fig. 54)

L104 **Serrated blade.** Indeterminate flint. Heavily corticated. From pit containing Grooved Ware dish P359 (Fig. 54).

Feltwell. Site 5188/c1. Hill Close
TL 6966 9080. Old OS field 283. NCM accession no. 487.967 (Ch. 4.I.3. Fig. 54)

L105 **Leaf arrowhead.** Indeterminate flint. Heavily corticated, tip missing. Close to spine of burial *1* (Fig. 18). Green 1980, 380.

L106 **Leaf arrowhead.** Indeterminate flint. Heavily corticated. Lower body area of burial *7* (Fig. 19). Green 1980, 380.

L107 **Scale-flaked knife.** Indeterminate flint. Heavily corticated. SE corner of excavated area (Fig. 18).

Methwold. Site 2542/c2. Methwold Severalls
Approx. TL 6510 9684. Old OS field 1012. NCM accession no. 93.969 (Ch. 4.I.5. Fig. 54)

L108 **Side-end scraper.** Indeterminate flint. Heavily corticated. Under three skeletons found 1971.

L109 **Horseshoe scraper.** Indeterminate flint. Heavily corticated. Under three skeletons found 1971.

Feltwell. Site 4907
Unlocated. NCM accession no. 346.958(5) (Fig. 55)

L110 **Axe.** N29. Ophitic diabase (greenstone), matched near Milton Abbot, Devon. Clough and Green 1972, 147, 153.

Feltwell. Site 4904
Unlocated. NCM accession no. 535.971(5) (Fig. 55)

L111 **Axe.** N150. Garnetiferous pyroxene rock (jadeite). Black to very dark green in colour. Jones, Bishop and Woolley 1977, cat. no. 102; Woolley *et al.* 1979, 93

Feltwell. Site 5294. Near Whitedyke
Whitedyke Farm centred TL 6920 8920. NCM accession no. 315.892 (Fig. 55)

L112 **Axe-hammer.** N53. Group XV.

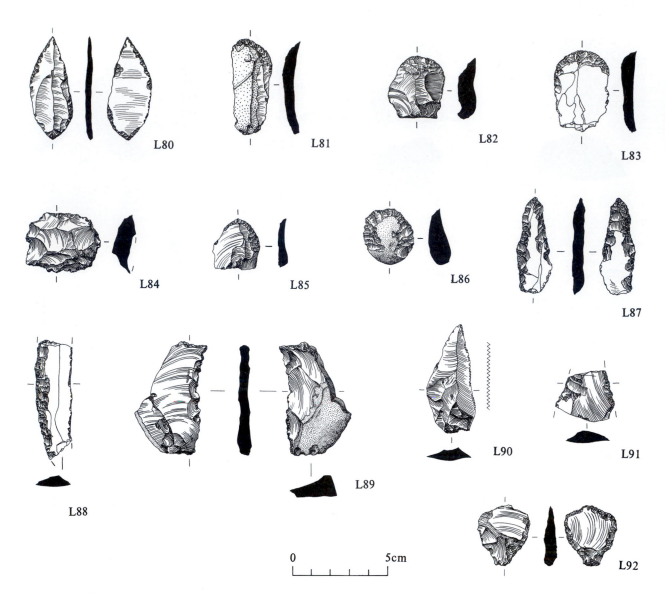

Figure 52 Lithic material from HCW OS 614, Site 5333 (95/97). Corticated areas unshaded.
Particulars in catalogue. Scale 1:2

Feltwell. Site 5179/c2
TL 6970 9052. Old OS field 196. Curtis coll. (Fig. 55)

L113 **Axe.** N161. Tuff. Re-used, perhaps as hone.

Feltwell. Site 17569. Lower Hill Close
TL 6930 9071. Old OS field 282. Secker coll. (Fig. 55)

L114 **Axe.** Greenstone with iridescent particles in granular dark green matrix. Butt end perhaps originally longer. Found with Beaker pottery and struck flint on slightly raised sandy area surrounded by peaty soil where ploughing had turned up patches of 'red ashes'.

Feltwell. Site 24839. Lower Hill Close
TL 6944 9073 approx. Old OS field 282. Secker coll. (Fig. 56)

L115 **Bead.** Jet.

Feltwell. Site 24840. Lower Hill Close
Field centre TL 6955 9090. Old OS field 283. Secker coll. (Fig. 56)

L116 **Grooved sandstone.** ?Quartzite. Upper and lower faces (naturally?) smooth, edges rougher, groove worn smooth.

Feltwell. Site 5184
TL 7995 9160. Old OS field 294. NCM accession no. 19.961 (Fig. 56)

L117 **Axe.** N82. Group VI. Flaked after breakage. Surface find. Clough and Green 1972, 148.

Feltwell. Site 5162
TL 6912 9053. Old OS field 335. Curtis coll. (Fig. 56)

L118 **Axe.** N162. Group XVIII.

Feltwell. Site 20981
TL 6916 9149 approx. Old OS field 411. Younge coll. (Fig. 56)

L119 **Axe.** Coarse-grained rock with green, black and white crystals, ?diorite. Found with L120.
L120 **Discoid.** Apparently Group VI. Light, concentric lines of marbling in rock; ground to sharp edge around entire edge; battered at narrower end. Found with L119.

Feltwell. Site 20981/c3
TL 6913 9153. Old OS field 411. Younge coll. (Fig. 56)

L121 **Bracer.** Grey-green slate. Incomplete perforation between two complete ones, ?attempt to render object usable after breakage.

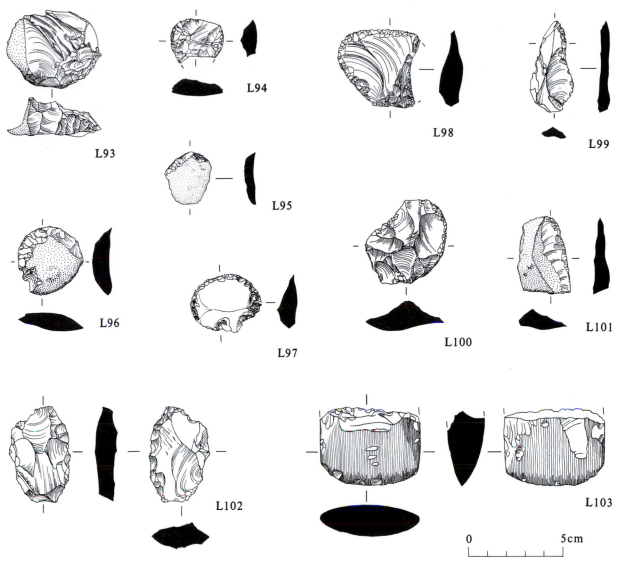

Figure 53 Lithic material from HCW OS 613, Site 5308/c5 (96). Corticated areas unshaded.
Particulars in catalogue. Scale 1:2

0   5cm

Feltwell. Site 5185/c5
TL 6882 9025 approx. Old OS field 720. Younge coll. (Fig. 57)

L122   Axe. Apparently Group VI. Fine-grained green matrix with some white marbling, both linear and speckled. Unworn.

Feltwell. Site 5185/c6
TL 6891 9033. Old OS field 721. Secker coll. (Fig. 57)

L123   Discoidal knife. Flint.

Feltwell. Site 5178
TL 6937 9025. Old OS field 727. Curtis coll. (Fig. 57)

L124   Axe. N164. Group VI.

Feltwell. Site 24838
TL 693 901. Old OS fields 727–8. Secker coll. (Fig. 57)

L125   Barbed & tanged arrowhead (Ballyclare). Indeterminate flint. Heavily-corticated.

Feltwell. Site 22311/c3
TL 6905 8998. Old OS field 730. Curtis coll. (Fig. 58)

L126   Axe. N160. Group XX.

Feltwell. Site 22311/c6
TL 6912 8990. Old OS field 730. Curtis coll. (Fig. 58)

L127   Axe. N165. Group VI. Larger axe flaked down into miniature form.

Feltwell. Site 5177
TL 6995 9248. Old OS field 924. Curtis coll. (Fig. 58)

L128   Axe. N163. Epidiorite, probably Cornish.

Hockwold cum Wilton. Site 5343. Blackdyke
Blackdyke Farm centred TL 6900 8840. Parrott coll. NCM accession no. L 142.961 (Fig. 58)

L129   Axe. N123. Group VI.

Hockwold cum Wilton. Site 17542. Hockwold Heath.
TL 744 891. Old OS field 80. Secker coll. (Fig. 58)

L130   Single-piece sickle. Dark grey chalk flint with floorstone-like cortex, retaining one corticated, thermally-fractured area. No gloss, but many small chips detached from concave edge, probably in use. Surface find.

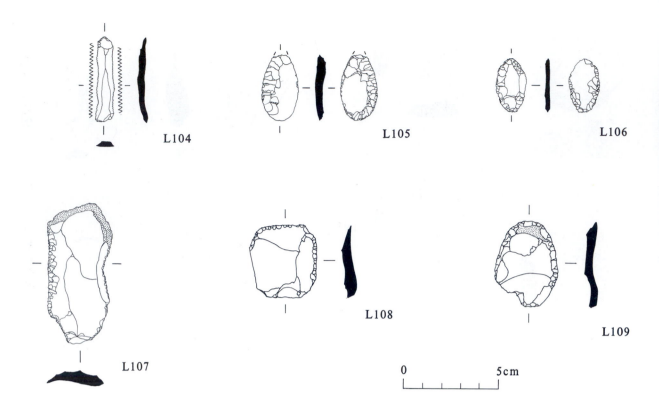

Figure 54 L104 from Glebe Farm, Feltwell (Site 4921/c1), L105–107 from Hill Close, Feltwell (Site 5188/c1), L108–109 from Methwold Severalls (Site 2542/c2). All heavily corticated. Particulars in catalogue. Scale 1:2

Hockwold cum Wilton. Site 5344
TL 729 870. Old OS field 197. NCM accession no. L 142.961 (Fig. 58)

L131 **Axe.** N124. Acidic or intermediate ash or tuff.

Hockwold cum Wilton. Site 5314
TL 6960 8790. Old OS field 423A. Curtis coll. (Fig. 59)

L132 **Axe.** N168. Near Group I. Much weathered.

Hockwold cum Wilton. Site 5316/c1
TL 7132 8840. Old OS field 430. Curtis coll. (Fig. 59)

L133 **Axe.** N166. Greywacke, ?Group XIX.

Hockwold cum Wilton. Site 5316
TL 6971 8764. Old OS field 465. Curtis coll. (Fig. 59)

L134 **Axe.** N167. Group VI.

Hockwold cum Wilton. Site 5313
TL 6895 8783. Old OS field 608. NCM accession no. 203.972 (Fig. 59)

L135 **Axe.** N169. Epidiorite, probably Cornish. Heavily weathered.

Hockwold cum Wilton. Site 5339
TL 6874 8753. Old OS field 609. NCM accession no. 204.972 (Fig. 59)

L136 **Axe.** N170. Schistose grit with albite porphyroblasts, probably a Scottish-derived glacial erratic. Heavily weathered.

Methwold. Site 5245/c7
TL 6921 9336. Old OS field 629. Curtis coll. (Fig. 59)

L137 **Axe.** N159. Silica-cemented sandstone, ?sarsen.

Southery. Site 13454
TL 604 961. Old OS field 3. Starling coll. (Fig. 60)

L138 **Pebble hammer.** Quartzite. Found on ploughed surface.

Weeting with Broomhill. Site 5599. Fengate
Fengate hamlet centred TL 7745 8795. Parrott coll. NCM accession no. L 142.961 (Fig. 60)

L139 **Axe.** N121. Group VII. Clough and Green 1972, 149.

Weeting with Broomhill. Site 5587. West Fen
Field centre TL 7580 8730. Old OS field 349. Parrott coll. NCM accession no. L 142.961 (Fig. 60)

L140 **'Sponge finger'.** N232. Sandstone.

Survey area unlocated. Site 24841
Parrott coll. NCM accession no. L 142.961 (Fig. 60)

L141 **Axe.** N122. Greenstone. Clough and Green 1972, 149, 154.

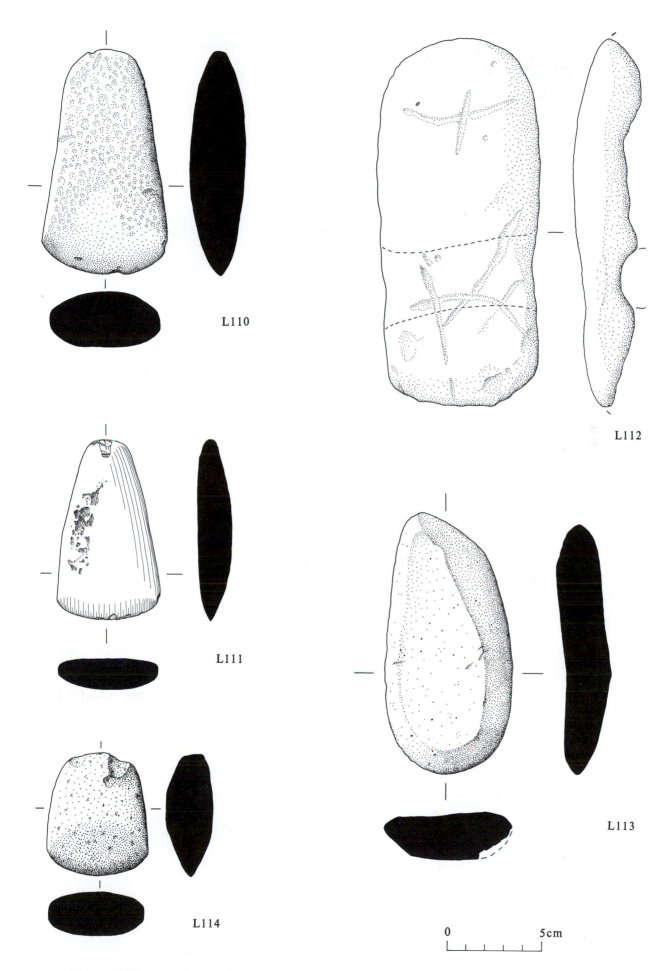

L110

L112

L111

L113

L114

0   5cm

Figure 55 Stone implements from various findspots in Feltwell. Particulars in catalogue. Scale 1:2

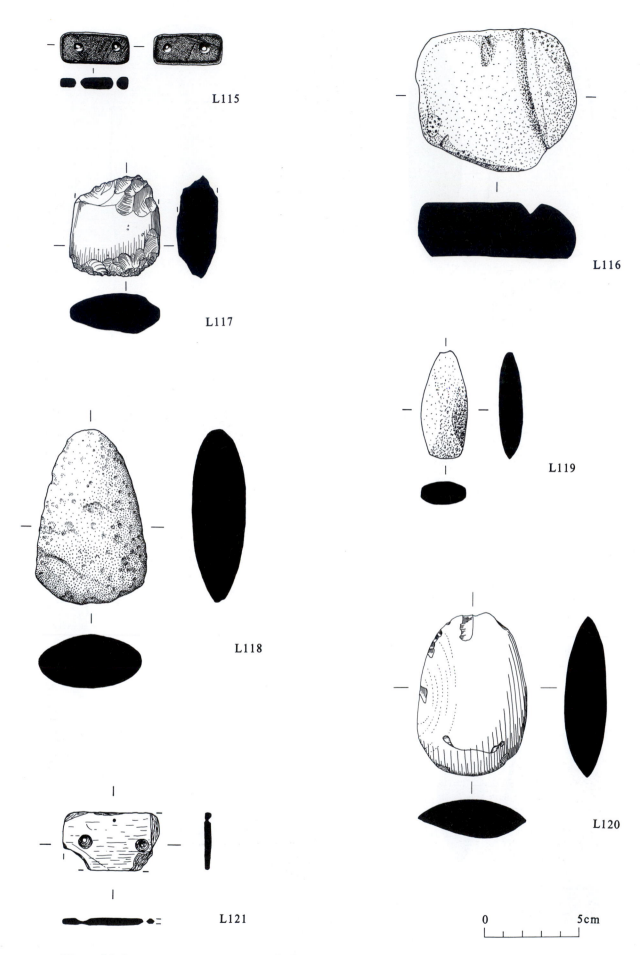

L115

L116

L117

L118

L119

L120

L121

0   5cm

Figure 56 Stone artefacts from various findspots in Feltwell. Particulars in catalogue. Scale 1:2

90

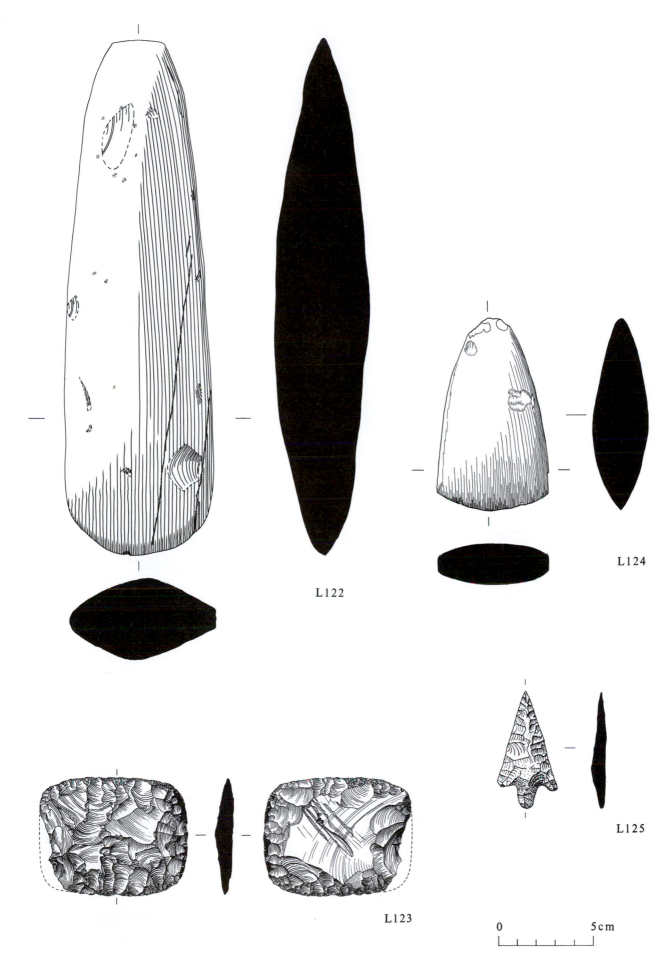

L122

L124

L123

L125

0   5 cm

Figure 57 Lithic material from various findspots in Feltwell. Particulars in catalogue. Scale 1:2

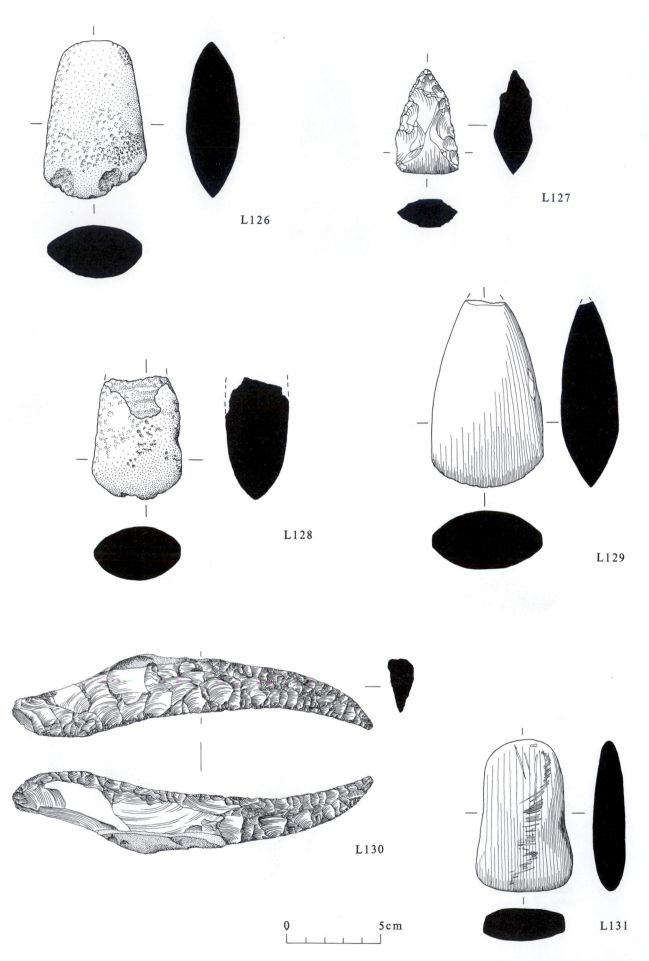

Figure 58 Lithic material from various findspots in Feltwell and Hockwold cum Wilton. Corticated areas unshaded. Particulars in catalogue. Scale 1:2

L126

L127

L128

L129

L130

L131

0   5cm

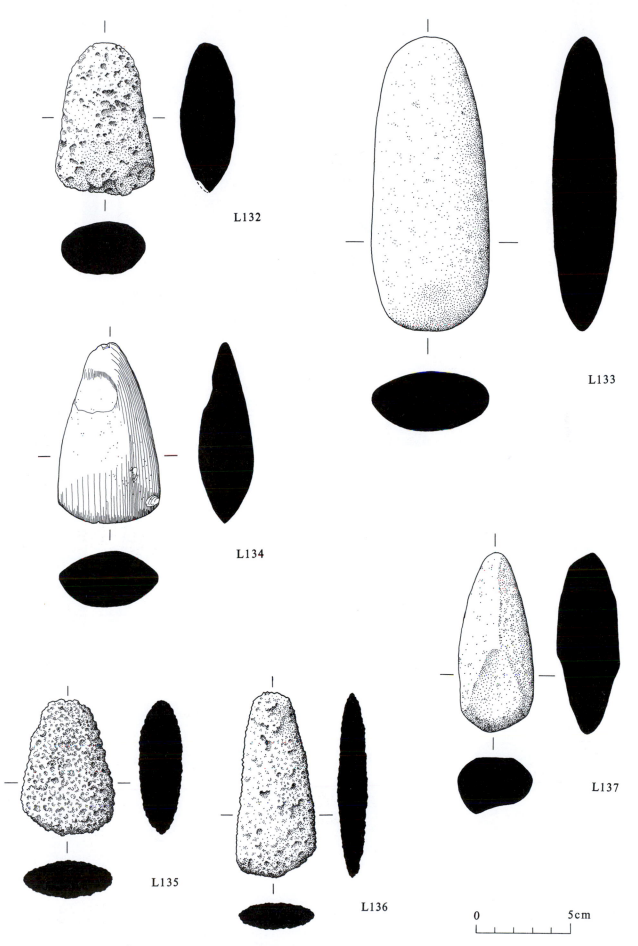

L132

L133

L134

L135

L136

L137

0   5cm

Figure 59 Stone axes from various findspots in Hockwold cum Wilton and Methwold.
Particulars in catalogue. Scale 1:2

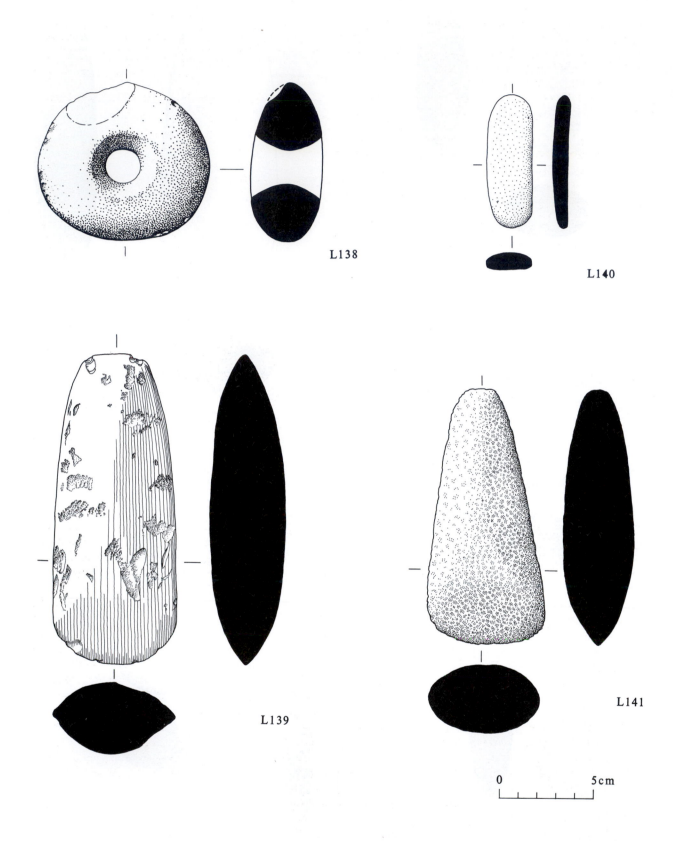

L138

L140

L139

L141

0　　　　　5cm

Figure 60 Stone implements from various findspots in Hilgay, Weeting with Broomhill and the survey area at large.
Particulars in catalogue. Scale 1:2

III. Pottery and Fired Clay

III.1. Hockwold cum Wilton Old OS Fields 466, 613, 614 and 616

The intensity with which Frank Curtis investigated these fields is reflected in the quantity of pottery from them: the collections described here plus those published by Bamford (1982, 21–26) amount to 9711 sherds or 74.463 kg of Neolithic, Beaker and Bronze Age ceramics from an area of 21.71ha. The overall density of 447 sherds per ha is a minimum, since more pottery than this was recovered (Ch. 3.I.1), and excavations were small-scale, leaving an unknown extent of archaeological deposit intact (Ch. 3.I.11).

The pottery identifications noted on Plates II-IV cannot always be taken at face value. A partly crossed-out record of 'Windmill Hill pot' in Plate III, for example, reflects the original attribution to that tradition of P52 (Fig. 76), a Bronze Age vessel shown in a comparable position in Plate IV. A sketch of the same pot in a letter to Sophia Mottram (then Curator of King's Lynn Museum) is accompanied by the words 'According to the books (see Later Prehistoric Antiquities) it belongs to the Windmill Hill culture (Plate 1, fig. 2)'. Similarly, the 'Iron Age pottery' noted on the boundary of two fields in the lower right of Plate III almost almost certainly refers to the relatively hard and dark sherds of Neolithic Bowl, such as P194–5 (Fig. 89), present among the predominantly second millennium BC pottery from the Site 5308/c4 (61/68).

Method

The system by which the pottery was recorded and analysed was devised to provide an overview of the material and to permit comparison between the larger collections. The unit of analysis was the site collection, or, where excavated deposits had been divided into arbitrary areas (*e.g.* Figs 5, 9, 12) the area collection. Within each unit, the following procedures were followed:

1. Sherds were sorted, counted and weighed by temper.
2. Joins were sought among sherds with the same temper or combination of tempers; form sherds were extracted; style, fabrics, form, diameters, decorative techniques and decorative motifs of the pots so identified were recorded.
3. The remaining unattributed sherds were recorded by style, temper, decorative technique and decorative motif.
4. Material was selected for illustration, initially from among the identified pots, with the intention of showing the range of style, form and decoration present in each group. If some decorative techniques or motifs remained unillustrated at this stage, unattributed sherds were chosen to show them.

The illustrated pottery thus shows the range rather than the frequency of the various elements. The frequency of selected features in the more numerous styles is summarised diagramatically in Figures 61–66.

Morphological characteristics represented in Figure 63 are:
1. Simple rim (rounded, pointed or squared (*e.g.* Fig. 72: P1, Fig. 73: P12, Fig. 79: P68)
2. Internally bevelled rim (*e.g.* Fig. 73: P15, P18, Fig. 90: P207, Fig. 96: P290)
3. Out-turned rim (*e.g.* Fig. 99: P332, Fig. 100: P335)
4. Expanded or thickened rim (*e.g.* Fig. 80: P87, Fig. 93: P251, Fig. 97: P301)
5. In-turned rim (*e.g.* Fig. 74: P26, Fig. 80: P88, Fig. 89: P205)

6. Internally concave rim (*e.g.* Fig. 81: P96, Fig. 83: P177, Fig. 90: P216)
7. Collared rim (*e.g.* Fig. 80: P82, Fig. 99: P330)
8. Cordoned rim (*e.g.* Fig. 74: P33, Fig. 78: P63, Fig. 82: P107)
9. Rounded shoulder (*e.g.* Fig. 75: P41, Fig. 77: P54, Fig. 95: P266)
10. Angular shoulder (*e.g.* Fig. 74: P37, Fig. 81: P99, Fig. 92: P248)
11. Simple base angle (*e.g.* Fig. 75: P43, Fig. 79: P74, Fig. 97: P296)
12. Concave base angle (*e.g.* Fig. 80: P90, Fig. 84: P137, Fig. 94: P261)
13. Protruding base angle (*e.g.* Fig. 75: P47, Fig. 85: P145, Fig. 99: P330)
14. Handle (*e.g.* Fig. 76: P52, Fig. 91: P225)
15. Lug (*e.g.* Fig. 72: P11, Fig. 84: P126)
16. Lid (*e.g.* Fig. 75: P48-9, Fig. 85: P146–7)

Decorative techniques represented in Figures 64–5 are:
1. Comb-impression (*e.g.* Fig. 76: P51, Fig. 89: P199, Fig. 90: P209)
2. Twisted cord impression (*e.g.* Fig. 90: P211, Fig. 91: P244, Fig. 93: P251)
3. Whipped cord impression (*e.g.* Fig. 72: P6, Fig. 90: P207)
4. 'Barbed wire' impression (*e.g.* Fig. 91: P236)
5. Miscellaneous non-linear impressions (*e.g.* Fig. 79: P79, Fig. 90: P216, Fig.96: P285)
6. Incision (*e.g.* Fig. 72: P1, Fig. 73: P14, Fig. 97: P296)
7. Grooving (*e.g.* Fig. 97: P299)
8. Appliqué (*e.g.* Fig. 74: P32, Fig. 83: P111, Fig. 84: P134)
9. Fingernail impression (*e.g.* Fig. 78: P62, Fig. 84: P127, Fig. 96: P286, Fig. 100: P336)
10. Finger-pinching (*e.g.* Fig. 80: P87-8, Fig. 83: P121, Fig. 96: P283)
11. Finger-tipping (*e.g.* Fig. 74: P37, Fig. 80: P86, Fig. 87: P163)

Shortcomings in the method became clear as work progressed. A principal one was that the early extraction of identified pots, each of which might consist of several sherds, at stage 2, when all sherds had been recorded by temper but not by style, made it impossible to arrive at a count or weight for sherds of each style.

Composition

The composition of the collections from the fields, excluding those already published by Bamford (1982, 21–26), is set out in Table 12. Collections large enough to be reduced to percentages are summarised in Figure 61. A notable feature, in an area known for its 'Beaker' occupation sites, is the dominance of Bronze Age over Beaker pottery. Even when the predominantly and purely Beaker collections published by Bamford (1982, 21–26) are taken into consideration, Food Vessel, Collared Urn and other Bronze Age (mainly Biconical Urn) pots outnumber fine and rusticated Beakers by more than two to one. Beakers must, furthermore, be over-represented in the count, because their characteristic decoration and form make them more readily recognisable than predominantly plain and often amorphous Bronze Age vessels.

Some groups, such as the Late style Beaker assemblages from Site 5333 (95/97) or Site 5324 (93; Bamford 1982, 21–22), or the small Biconical Urn assemblage from Site 5332 (66) are stylistically homogeneous, or almost so. Others, such as those from Site 5308/c4 (61/68) or the adjoining Sites 5308/c1 and c3 (63 and 69; Bamford 1982, 22–23) include pottery of several styles. Examination of the pottery from the last two sites in the light of the large Bronze Age collections shows that the small quantity of undecorated sherds and vessels mentioned by Bamford (1982, 22) consists of fragmentary Bronze Age wares like those which form a larger part of the collection from Site 5308/c4 (*e.g.* Fig. 90: P212–215).

Site Collection	Neolithic Bowl Pots	Neolithic Bowl US	Beaker Pots	Beaker US	Rusticated Beaker Pots	Rusticated Beaker US	Food Vessel Pots	Food Vessel US	Collared Urn Pots	Collared Urn US	Other BA Wares Pots	Other BA Wares US	Indeterminate Pots	Indeterminate US	Totals Sherds	Totals Wt. (kg)	Mean Sherd Wt. (g)	Fired Clay Frags.	Fired Clay Wt. (kg)
Site 24866 'site 8'			4 (R3)	4	1 (R1)	6	13 (R12)	2	2 (R2)		213 (R102)	663			952	9.931	10	6	0.085
Site 14662 ('Field 79')	3 (R3)		9 (R7)	17	4 (R3)	5					42 (R16)	187	2	172	468	5.940	13	1	0.050
'site 4' (?=Site 5309 (48))											1 (R1)			1+					

(This is a complete vessel, Fig. 76:P52)

Site Collection	Neolithic Bowl Pots	Neolithic Bowl US	Beaker Pots	Beaker US	Rusticated Beaker Pots	Rusticated Beaker US	Food Vessel Pots	Food Vessel US	Collared Urn Pots	Collared Urn US	Other BA Wares Pots	Other BA Wares US	Indeterminate Pots	Indeterminate US	Totals Sherds	Totals Wt. (kg)	Mean Sherd Wt. (g)	Fired Clay Frags.	Fired Clay Wt. (kg)
Site 5439 (44)			1												14	0.225	16		
Site 5309 (48)			5 (R2)	17	1 (R1)	5								2	62	0.575	9		
Site 5310 (49)				9	5 (R5)	25							2 (R1)	3	50	0.400	8		
Sites 5311 + 5312 (50 + 51)	1 (R1)		20 (R10)	76	24 (R17)	193	20 (R8)	16	2 (R2)		332 (R124)	697	11 (R2)	12	1753	20.595	12	19	0.160
Site 5373 (22) A. 477.961											98 (R47)	345			452	5.225	12	6	0.450
B. 673.964			4 (R4)	27	4 (R3)	43					4 (R2)	32	7 (R1)	7	128	1.050	8	1	0.010
Site 5308/c6 (59)				1										1	2	0.020	20		
Site 5308/c4 (61/68)	11 (R9)	17	53 (R22)	152	6 (R5)	106	24 (R23)	23			33 (R18)	354	19 (R6)	99	950	7.995	8	71	755

Site Collection	Neolithic Bowl		Beaker		Rusticated Beaker		Food Vessel		Collared Urn		Other BA Wares		Indeterminate		Totals		Mean Sherd	Fired Clay	
	Pots	US	Pots	US	Pots	US	Pots	US	Pots	US	Pots	US	Pots	US	Sherds	Wt. (kg)	Wt. (g)	Frags.	Wt. (kg)
Site 5332 (66)				2							23 (R12)	67	1 (R1)		95	1.225			
Site 5364 (75)									1						1	0.020	20		
Site 5333 (95/97)			25 (R14)	107	14 (R11)	214	1 (R1)						5	41	444	3.005	7	8	90
Site 5308/c5 (96)		1	24 (R20)	94	8 (R3)	92					6 (R6)	23	2 (R1)	65	394	2.945	7	35	450
Totals	15 (R13)	18	145 (R82)	506	67 (R49)	689	58 (R44)	41	5 (R4)		752 (R328)	2368	49 (R12)	402	5766	59.132	10	147	1.645

US = Unattributed Sherds, *i.e.* sherds not attributed to identified pots
R prefixes the number of rims included in each total of identified pots

Table 12 Hockwold cum Wilton fields 466, 613, 614 and 616. Pottery and Fired Clay

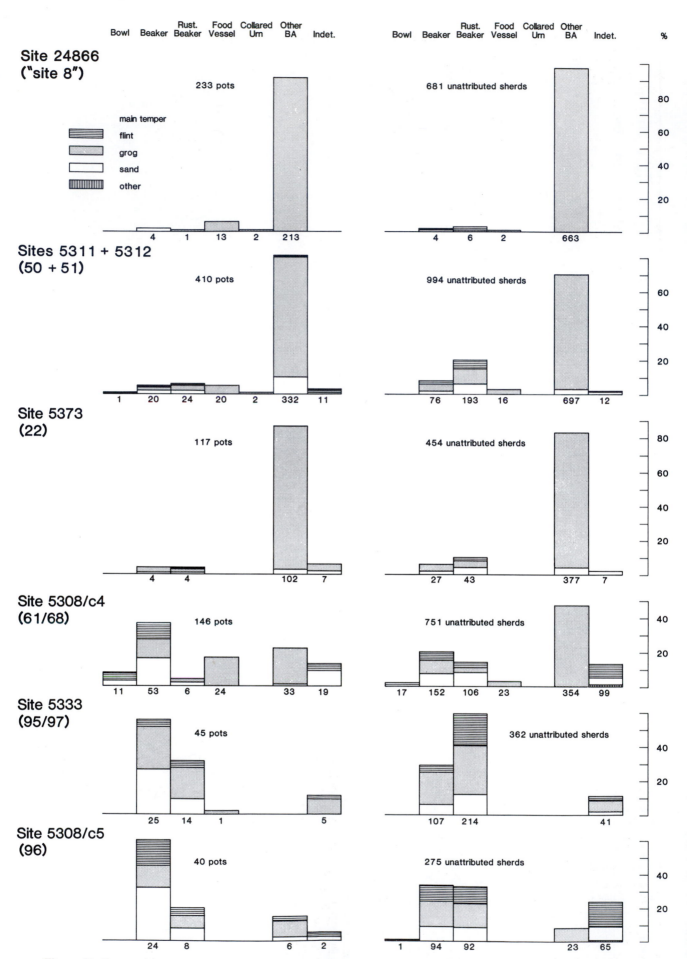

Figure 61 Composition of larger pottery collections from HCW OS 466, 613, 614, 616, broken down by style and main temper

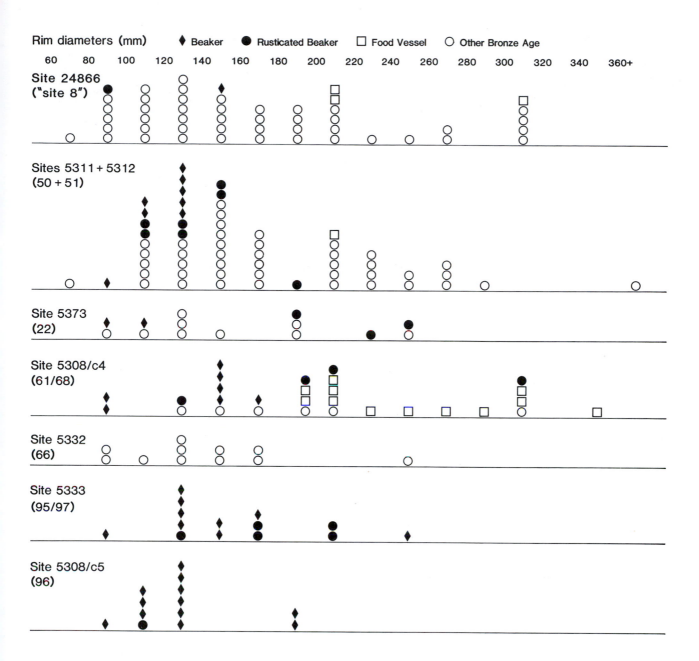

Figure 62 Rim diameters of pots of the most frequent pottery styles in the larger collections from HCW OS 466, 613, 614 and 616

Fabrics

Figure 61 shows a crude correlation between main temper and style. Neolithic Bowl is flint- or sand-tempered; Beaker variably tempered; Bronze Age styles predominantly grogged. Examined in more detail the fabrics show considerable diversity. Fine and Rusticated Beaker fabrics, in particular, display countless temper combinations and variations of texture and hardness, as the individual fabric descriptions in Chapter 5.III.4 show. Small quantities of what appears to be haematite in some Beakers (*e.g.* Fig. 78: P64, Fig. 81: P92, Fig. 91: P234, P236), may relate to the presence of haematite lumps on Site 5308/c1 (63; Bamford 1982, 12–13).

Tomalin's (1983) analysis of the temper density and particle size of Early Bronze Age fabrics, including the Hockwold ones, indicates the use of specific grog recipes both between and within styles. The Hockwold Food Vessels are almost invariably tempered with grog, rarely

accompanied by quartz sand, with a preferred frequency of *c.* 10% and a preferred particle size of *c.* 2mm; the textural characteristics of three local Collared Urn sherds are indistinguishable from these (1983, 21–22). Seven fabric types can be distinguished among the Hockwold Biconical Urns, some of them related to morphological characteristics (1983, 369–372).

Individual Styles

Neolithic Bowl

The small amount of Bowl present (*e.g.* Fig. 79: P66, Fig. 89: P194–5) conforms to the Mildenhall style as defined by Smith (1954, 224) and Longworth (1960, 228). A larger quantity of Mildenhall Ware was recovered from Sites 5308/c1 and c3 (63 and 69; Bamford 1982, fig. 27).

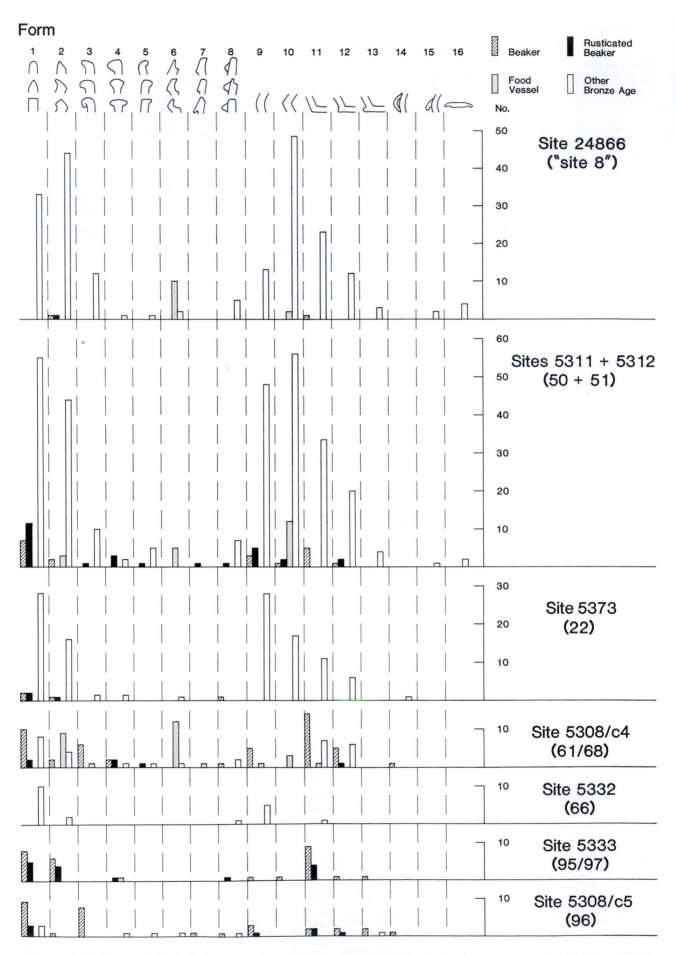

Figure 63 Major morphological characteristics of the most frequent pottery styles in the larger collections from HCW OS 466, 613, 614 and 616. Key in Chapter 5.III.1

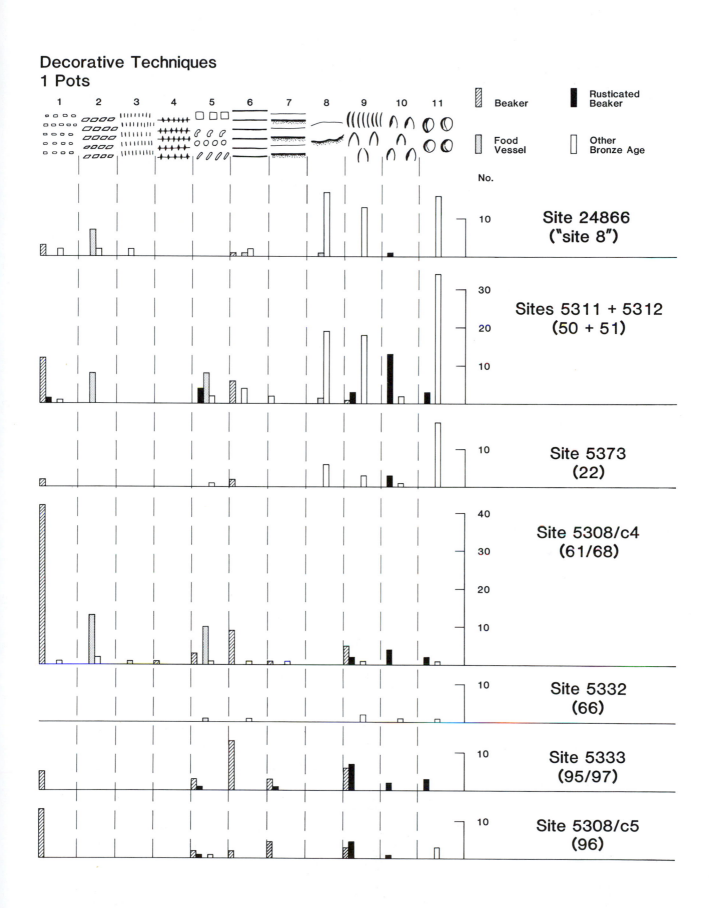

Decorative Techniques
1 Pots

Figure 64 Decorative techniques employed on identified pots of the most frequent pottery styles in the larger collections from HCW OS 466, 613, 614 and 616. Key in Chapter 5.III.1

Decorative Techniques
2 Unattributed Sherds

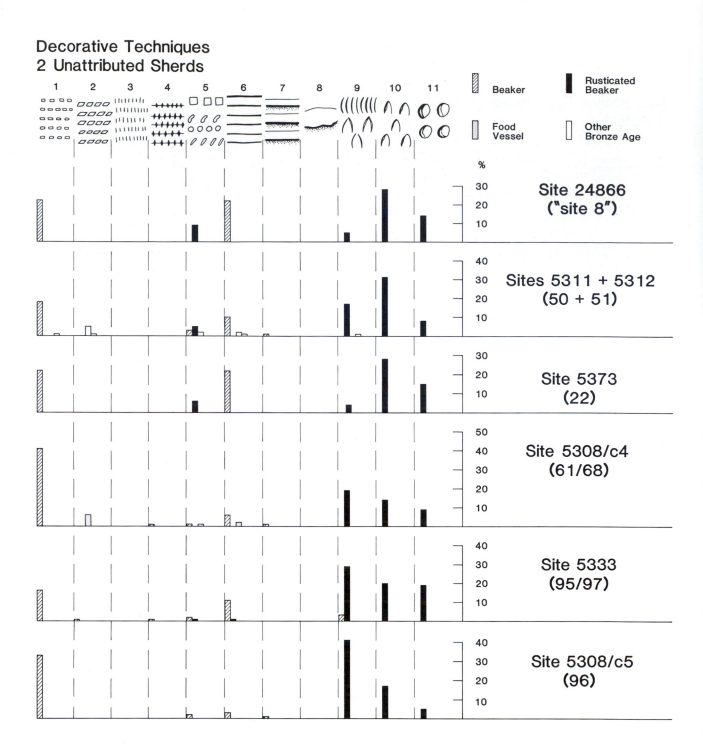

Figure 65 Decorative techniques employed on unattributed sherds of the most frequent pottery styles in the larger collections from HCW OS 466, 613, 614 and 616. Key in Chapter 5.III.1

Beaker

Fabric and size overlap between rusticated and other Beakers. The occasional rusticated vessel (*e.g.* Fig. 78: P62), is of fine, hard, sand-tempered fabric. The occasional comb-impressed or incised vessel (*e.g.* Fig. 97: P297), is of coarse, soft, grogged fabric. Many medium-textured vessels (*e.g.* Fig. 99: P332, Fig. 100: P336), show little correlation between fabric and decorative technique, and sometimes combine rustication with comb-impression or incision (*e.g.* Fig. 77: P53, Fig. 79: P81). Rim diameters similarly overlap (Fig. 62). The finest, hardest and smallest pots, however, tend to be comb-impressed or incised; the coarsest, thickest and largest rusticated. Pot-beakers were present, although their

actual dimensions are difficult to estimate. The curvature of P181 (Fig. 88), for example, indicates a body diameter of at least 220mm, while a thick, coarse, rusticated vessel from Site 5308/c4 (61/68) illustrated by Bamford (1982, fig. 24: A) seems to have had a rim diameter of 300mm.

Form is rarely completely reconstructable. Sinuous profiles (*e.g.* such as Fig. 76: P51, Fig. 77: P54, Fig. 78: P62, Fig. 79: P72, P79, Fig. 98: P310, Fig. 99: P332, Fig. 99, Fig. 100: P336), and straight or convex necks (*e.g.* Fig. 76: P51, Fig. 77: P55, Fig. 78: P62, Fig. 89: P198, Fig. 96: P291, Fig. 97: P302), seem most frequent. The flaring neck of P199 (Fig. 89) is exceptional. While most Beaker rims and base angles are simple, out-turned rims and

Beaker motifs expressed as % of 130 pots (upper rows) and 460 unattributed sherds (lower rows) from the sites represented. ▨ = 1%

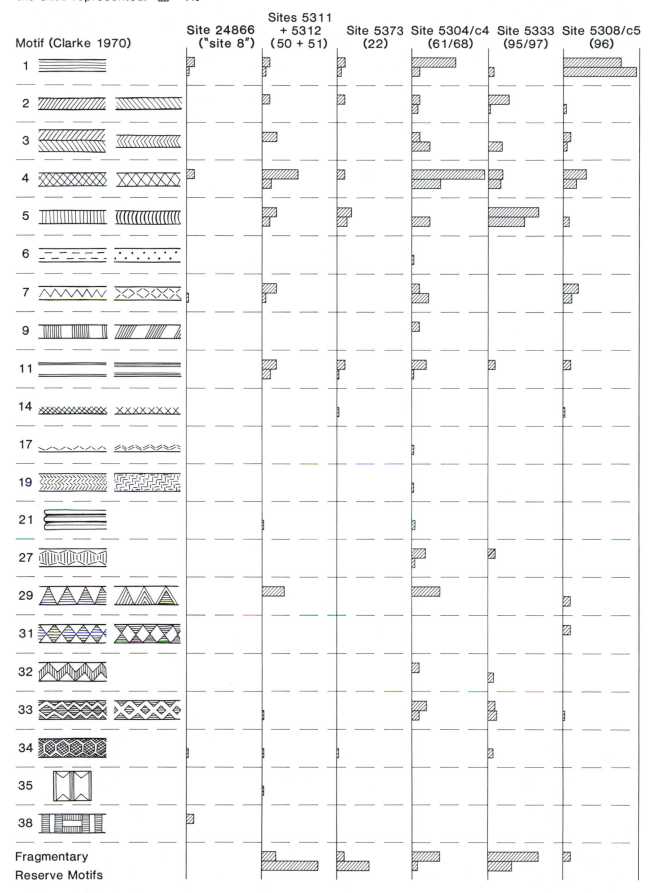

Figure 66 Decorative motifs of comb-impressed and incised Beaker pottery in the larger collections from HCW OS 466, 613, 614 and 616. Motifs as defined by Clarke (1970, 424–428)

concave base angles are most frequent among the comb-impressed and incised Beaker of Site 5308/c4 (61/68), and internally bevelled rims most frequent among the rusticated and other Beaker of Site 5333 (95/97; Fig. 63). Two handles are present (Fig. 91: P225, Fig. 100: P334).

Some rusticated vessels (*e.g.* Fig. 78: P62, P63, Fig. 80: P82, Fig. 100: P336) and many of those illustrated by Bamford (1982, figs 6–11, 22–26), are of Beaker-like forms; others may not have been. P56 (Fig. 78) and P85 (Fig. 80) have been drawn, tentatively, as bowls. The profiles of many rim fragments would be compatible with straight-walled or flowerpot-like shapes (*e.g.* Fig. 80: P86, Fig. 89: P206, Fig. 96: P295, Fig. 97: P301). These are also suggested by a dearth of shoulder fragments among rusticated sherds in all the collections except that from Sites 5311+5312 (50+51; Fig. 63). A near-complete pot found some 1.5 km to the west (Fig. 104: P385), may represent the form of many of the fragmentary rusticated vessels. Simple forms, large size, or both are suggested by the greater frequency of rusticated Beaker among unattributed sherds than among identified pots (Fig. 61).

Decorative techniques. The relative incidence of comb-impression and incision on identified pots varies between collections, but shows little obvious pattern (Fig. 64). On unattributed sherds, however, incision declines from the collections made in 1959–62 to those made in the mid-1960s (Fig. 65). Cord-impression is confined to a single small sherd (Fig. 97: P309) from Site 5333 (95/97). 'barbed wire' impression, best seen on P236 (Fig. 91), is almost equally rare. P233 (Fig. 91) seems to have been impressed with the edge of a shell.

Techniques of rustication, among both identified pots and unattributed sherds, consist predominantly of plastic finger-pinching and finger-tipping in collections made in 1959–62 (*e.g.* Fig. 80: P84, P86, P88), with non-plastic fingernail-impression becoming more frequent in collections made in the mid-1960s (*e.g.* Fig. 91: P240, Fig. 98: P323, Fig. 100: P336; Figs 64–5).

Decorative motifs. The frequency of individual motifs within Clarke's (1970, 424–8) basic European motif group I varies between the main collections. Otherwise the commonest motifs are those of his Southern British motif group 4 (Fig. 66). The fragmentary reserve motifs represented at the bottom of the diagram are all almost certainly of this group or of motif group 5 (panels and metopes). The collection from Site 5333 (95/97) includes two groups of Beakers, P286 + P287 + P290 and P293 + P294 (Fig. 96) each apparently decorated to a single pattern.

Stylistic affinities. Case's (1977, 72) Middle style, corresponding to steps 2–4 of the scheme of Lanting and Van der Waals (1972), is represented by occasional globular forms of Clarke's East Anglian group or Case's own (1993, 263–4) more recently-defined Group E (*e.g.* Fig. 78: P63, Fig. 99: P326, P333). It is more commonly, however, represented by sinuous-profiled vessels with zoned or all-over-impressed rows of decoration, closer to Case's (1993, 260–3) Group D (*e.g.* Fig. 79: P79, Fig. 99: P332, Fig. 100: P336). One vessel (Fig. 89: P199) might, exceptionally, be described as a European Bell Beaker. Middle style Beaker is perhaps most conspicuous in the Site 5308/c5 (96) collection (Figs 99–101). Nowhere does it occur without vessels of Case's 1977, 72) Late style,

corresponding to steps 5–7 in the scheme of Lanting and van der Waals.

Most Late style Beaker is of Clarke's Southern tradition or Case's (1993, 257–9) southern Group B (*e.g.* Fig. 76: P51, Fig. 77: P53–5, Fig. 79: P72, P80, Fig. 97: P302, Fig. 98: P310, Fig. 101: P348), although the fragmentary state of the material often makes finer attribution difficult. The collection from Site 5333 (95/97) might be seen as an homogeneous one, conforming to Clarke's Primary to Developed Southern groups, as the Site 5324 (93) pottery conforms to his Late to Final Southern groups (Bamford 1982, 24).

Food Vessel

Fabric and size. Food Vessels are distinguished by some of the coarsest and most friable fabrics in the collection and by exceptionally large size (Fig. 62). Wherever rim diameters can be estimated, they fall in the range of Food Vessel Urns rather than of Food Vessels (Cowie 1978, text fig. 2). Other pots of rather less coarse fabric but of uncertain diameter may represent a smaller, finer element (*e.g.* Fig. 90: P222, Fig. 93: P252, P256).

Form, as far as it can be reconstructed, seems uniform throughout the collections, with rim bevels more often concave than flat and shoulders more often angular than rounded (Fig. 63).

Decoration is most frequently by twisted cord impression (Figs 64–5).

Stylistic affinities seem to lie with Tomalin's form 2A and 2B Food Urns (1988, fig. 6).

Collared Urn

Recognisable Collared Urn is confined to two fragments from Site 24866 ('site 8'; Fig. 72: P9, P10), two more from Sites 5311+5312 (50+ 51; Fig. 81: P99–100), and a stray find (Fig. 101: P358).

Other Bronze Age Wares

This category is named with deliberate caution, since fragmentation, simple forms and lack of decoration make much of the material covered by it classifiable only in the broadest sense. This is true not only of the featureless, grogged body fragments which make up the bulk of the 2368 unattributed Bronze Age sherds (Table 12), but also of several vessels (*e.g.* Fig. 86: P152, Fig. 90: P212, Fig. 91: P231, Fig. 93: P258, Fig. 100: P338). A few other vessels (*e.g.* Fig. 100: P335), have distinctive but idiosyncratic characteristics. Much of the mass of indeterminate Bronze Age pottery is highly likely to be of Biconical Urn, the style of most of the classifiable rim and shoulder fragments. It is, however, impossible to be sure of this in any individual case without an extension of Tomalin's fabric analysis to morphologically undiagnostic material. It must be born in mind that the two largest collections are in one case, Site 24866 ('site 8'), derived from a substantial area containing discrete concentrations of material, and in the other, Sites 5311+5312 (50+51), derived from at least two such concentrations (Ch. 3.I.1). The remaining, smaller collections are from single locations.

Fabric and size. Rim diameters extend beyond the upper and lower limits of the range for rusticated and other Beaker, but show the same major peak at 120–160mm (Fig. 62). The largest vessels are undoubtedly under-represented in the diagram because the fragmentary state of the material makes the diameters of rim sherds showing little curvature impossible to estimate. Fabrics are generally harder, sounder and sandier than those of Food Vessel, even in the larger, coarser pots. Small pots (*e.g.* Fig. 82: P108–9) tend to be harder and finer and to have a higher proportion of sand temper than larger ones. The fabrics of the Site 5332 (66) collection seem generally harder and sandier than the rest, regardless of size or form.

Form. Closed forms are far commoner than straight-sided, bucket-shaped ones. Convergent necks (*e.g.* Fig. 82: P102) or convex necks (*e.g.* Fig. 73: P15) outnumber near-vertical necks (*e.g.* Fig. 81: P101) by three to one at Site 24866 ('site 8'), by sixteen to one at Sites 5311+5312 (50+ 51), and by five to one at Site 5373 (22). The ratio approaches one to one only in the small assemblage from Site 5332 (66). Bucket-shaped vessels may also be represented by a few straight-sided wall sherds with horizontal cordons (*e.g.* Fig. 74: P35–36, Fig. 84: P129).

Figure 63 shows further morphological differences between the collections. Bevelled rims outnumber simple ones in the Site 24866 ('site 8') collection, but in none of the others. Angular shoulders far outnumber rounded ones in the same collection, the gap narrows among the Sites 5311+5312 (50+51) material, the balance is reversed in the Site 5373 (22) collection, and all the Site 5332 (66) shoulders are rounded.

There are seven lids, four (including Fig. 75: P48–9), from Site 24866, two (Fig. 85: P146–7) from Sites 5311+5312 (50+51) and one in the Site 14662 ('Field 79') collection. Their diameters range from 600 to 1200mm, commensurate, as Tomalin points out (1983, 365) with the smaller pots. There are two handled vessels, one from Frank Curtis's 'site 4' (Fig. 76: P52), sketched in the south of field 616 in Plate IV, and one (Fig. 86: P155) from Site 5373 (22). Lugs (*e.g.* Fig. 72: P11, Fig. 84: P126) are most frequent among the Site 24866 ('site 8') material.

Decoration occurs on eighteen per cent of the identified pots from Site 24866 ('site 8'), nineteen percent from Sites 5311+ 5312 (50+51), twenty-five percent from Site 5373 (22) and seventeen percent from Site 5332 (66). The main techniques are appliqué, fingernail-impression and finger-tipping, the last two varying in frequency between collections (Fig. 64). There are rare instances of comb-impression (*e.g.* Fig. 73: P16, P17, Fig. 90: P209), cord-impression (*e.g.* Fig. 75: P42, Fig. 85: P148), incision (*e.g.* Fig. 73: P14, Fig. 95: P271), and finger-pinching (*e.g.* Fig. 83: P121). Plaited cord was employed on one pot (Fig. 85: P148). Applied decoration most frequently takes the form of cordons (*e.g.* Fig. 74: P33, Fig. 82: P107, Fig. 84: P131); but also includes arc (or 'horseshoe') lugs, most of them fragmentary (*e.g.* Fig. 74: P28, P32, Fig. 83: P111, Fig. 86: P158), and bosses (*e.g.* Fig. 84: P128).

Stylistic affinities. The classifiable fraction of the collections is dominated by Biconical Urn, locally exemplified by the assemblage from Mildenhall Fen, Suffolk (Clark 1936, 36–43). A few apparently straight-sided vessels (*e.g.* Fig. 81: P101, Fig. 82: P103, Fig. 84: P129) might, if found in isolation, be considered Deverel-Rimbury forms. Some of the material is also comparable with the small quantity of plain wares so far published from the later Bronze Age site of Flag Fen, Peterborough, Cambridgeshire (Barrett 1986, fig. 9), which include a handled pot not unlike P52 (Fig. 76).

Fired Clay
Many of the fired clay lumps recorded in Table 12 contain some sand, while others are vacuous or without visible temper. Where surfaces survive some are rounded, others flat, sometimes with two flat surfaces which may meet at an angle. A few have twig impressions. They are comparable with the fired clay lumps described from Site 5308/c 3 (69) by Bamford (1982, 28–29) and with a larger quantity found with sherds of Middle style Beaker beneath a barrow at Weasenham All Saints and interpreted as hand-made bricks which had formed kilns or ovens (Site 3660; Petersen and Healy 1986, 97–99). Such material is surely represented by the note 'hearth with heap of clay balls with stones' appended to a site in the south of OS 616 in Plate II. A concentration of fired clay in area *1* of Site 5308/c5 (96; Fig. 14) echoes that in the south of Site 5308/c3 (69; Bamford 1982, text fig. 6).

III.2. The Survey Area as a Whole

Excavated Material
The relatively small quantity of excavated pre-Iron Age pottery recovered from outside HCW OS 466, 613 and 616 is listed in Appendices 2 and 3 (microfiche). The following are most noteworthy:

'Site 7088'. HCW 428. Site 5316/c7, c8
TL 7025 8815 (centre) (Ch. 3.II.5)
Some of the pottery published as 'Neolithic and Bronze Age' (Salway 1967, 58–59), seems, on re-examination, to be Late Bronze Age or Early Iron Age in date, including numbers A1 and A7 among the illustrated sherds (Salway 1967, fig. 12). Small quantities of Neolithic Bowl (*e.g.* fig. 12: A4) and Beaker (*e.g.* fig. 12: A2) and other Later Neolithic or Early Bronze Age pottery (*e.g.* fig. 12: A3) are also present.

'Sluice Drove'. HCW 441. Site 5394
TL 7185 8810 (Ch. 3.II.6)
It is impossible to evaluate the 'Secondary Neolithic or Early Beaker material' reported from this site by Colonel Kelly.

Corner Ground. HCW 644. Site 5317/c3 (23)
TL 6965 8823 (Ch. 3.II.7)
If the 'many sherds of handled Beakers' noted from this site survive, they may remain in the Curtis collection.

Glebe Farm. FWL 264. Site 4921/c1
TL 7148 9090 (Ch. 3.II.9)
Most of a shell-tempered Grooved Ware dish in the Woodlands substyle (Fig. 102: P359) was found in a pit with two small, weathered body sherds in different fabrics, struck flint (including Fig. 54: L104), a bone point (Fig. 108: B20) and animal bone.

Hill Close, FWL 283. Site 5188/c1
TL 6966 9080 (Ch. 4.I.3, Figs 18–19)
A sherd of Late style Beaker (Fig. 102: P362) was found with burial *19*, a Food Vessel (Fig. 102: P360) close to a group of burials, an indeterminate Bronze Age pot (Fig. 102: P361) in isolation, and indeterminate, grogged sherds with burials *2* and *24*.

Collected Material

The relatively small amount of pre-Iron Age pottery collected from the rest of the survey area both confirms and expands the picture built up from the Hockwold fields. The same broad correlations between fabric and style obtain throughout.

Substantial collections

One of the larger pottery collections has been made over many years from a field in Methwold Hythe (Site 2531/c1, OS 242) by Mr J.D. Wortley. Some of the material remains in his possession; some has been given by him to King's Lynn Museum and is illustrated and briefly described by Gibson (1982, 201–202, figs MET. 1–3). On the northern margin of the survey area, another collection was dredged from the river Wissey on the border between Methwold and Northwold to the south and Stoke Ferry to the north in the late 1920s (Gibson 1982, 247, figs S.F. 1–4). Both, like the material from HCW OS 466, 613, 614 and 616, are dominated by Beaker and Bronze Age pottery, with small quantities of earlier styles.

Individual Styles

Neolithic Bowl (Fig. 67, Appendix 27 (microfiche)). Mildenhall Ware, (*e.g.* Fig. 104: P379, Fig. 105: P387) and indeterminate plain Bowl (*e.g.* Fig. 103: P376–8, Fig. 104: P383–4) have been found in small quantities throughout the survey area. Bowl sherds outnumber the Beaker or Early Bronze Age pottery with which they were found in the collections from two findspots in Hockwold cum Wilton, Site 5317 (OS 644) and Site 5230/c16 (OS 649). A bowl from the former site (Fig. 104: P379) is one of relatively few Mildenhall style vessels with bounded, horizontally zoned decoration (Healy 1988, 71–72).

Grimston Ware, as defined by Manby (1970, 16–17) and Smith (1974a, note 24; 1974b, 31–33), is known only from Whiteplot, Methwold (Site 5235, OS 568–70 and 625–6), where four sherds (including Fig. 105: P388–9) have been found.

Later Neolithic Pottery (Fig. 68, Appendix 28 (microfiche)). Leaving aside the Grooved Ware dish from Glebe Farm, Feltwell, which is on the chalk upland, the only finds of Later Neolithic pottery from the fen edge are from Site 2531/c1 (OS 242) in Methwold, where they are far outnumbered by Beaker and Early Bronze Age styles. There are two sherds of Peterborough Ware, one illustrated by Gibson (1982, fig. MET. 1:16), the other illustrated here (Fig. 105: P386). Gibson also illustrates two of the five Grooved Ware sherds (figs MET.1:29, MET.2:21). A rim fragment which remains in the collection of Mr J.D. Wortley is attributed to the Durrington Walls substyle by spiral or concentric circle decoration.

Beaker (Fig. 69, Appendix 29 (microfiche)) is by far the most abundant style. It is difficult to tell how far this reflects its original frequency, how far its recognisability. All-over-cord decoration remains extremely rare, represented only by a single body sherd from Methwold Hythe (Gibson 1982, fig. MET. 2:33), scarcely larger than the one cord-impressed sherd from the Hockwold fields (Fig. 97: P309). Among Middle style Beaker, Clarke's East Anglian and Barbed Wire groups continue rare. One sherd from Site 5235/c13–14 in Methwold (OS 568) is classed by him as European Bell Beaker (1970, corpus no. 567). Late style Beaker of his Southern tradition remains the most frequent, including complete pots from Hilgay (Site 4450, ? OS 392; Clarke 1970, corpus no. 50, fig. 980) and Hockwold (Site 5316, OS 430; Clarke 1970, corpus no. 559, fig. 752).

Food Vessel and Collared Urn (Fig. 70, Appendix 30 (microfiche)). This distribution, more than any of the previous ones, reflects the concentration of Frank Curtis' activities in Hockwold cum Wilton OS 466, 613, 614 and 616 and the fields to the west of them. The reason for this probably lies in the material itself. The coarse, friable, grogged fabrics of these styles are likely to have a shorter life in the ploughsoil than the more robust flint- and sand-tempered fabrics of Neolithic Bowl and of some Beaker. They are thus less likely to be noticed and collected casually, and more likely to be recovered by excavation or, when freshly ploughed up, by an assiduous and observant fieldwalker.

Food Vessel remains far more frequent than Collared Urn, the only definite additional find of which (Longworth 1984, corpus no. 977) is from the river Wissey at Stoke Ferry (Site 2523). Fragmentary Early Bronze Age pottery from Site 2531/c1 in Methwold (OS 242) seems to be of Food Vessel or Collared Urn affinities, or both (*e.g.* Gibson 1982, figs MET.1:13, 2:4, 3:1). Food Vessels tend towards the same coarse fabrics and large size as the better-preserved excavated examples (*e.g.* Fig. 104: P381; Gibson 1982, fig. S.F. 3:6).

Other Bronze Age Pottery (Fig. 71, Appendix 31 (microfiche)). The even more uneven distribution of this material must also be due in part to its fabrics, accentuated by its plainness.

Small, weathered fragments certainly or probably of Biconical Urn, like that of the main collections, have been been found in the fields to the west, sometimes with Beaker, sometimes alone (Fig. 103: P366–375). A further rim sherd from the same area (Fig. 104: P382) is of uncertain affinities. A handled pot dug from a depth of 8 feet (2.4m) at an unknown site in Hockwold Fen in the 1930s (Fig. 102: P363) is comparable with vessels from 'site 4' and Site 5373 (22) in the Hockwold fields (Fig. 76: P52, Fig. 86: P155). A minority of the sherds dredged from the river Wissey at Stoke Ferry resemble better-preserved excavated Biconical Urn material (*e.g.* Gibson 1982, fig. S.F. 1:15).

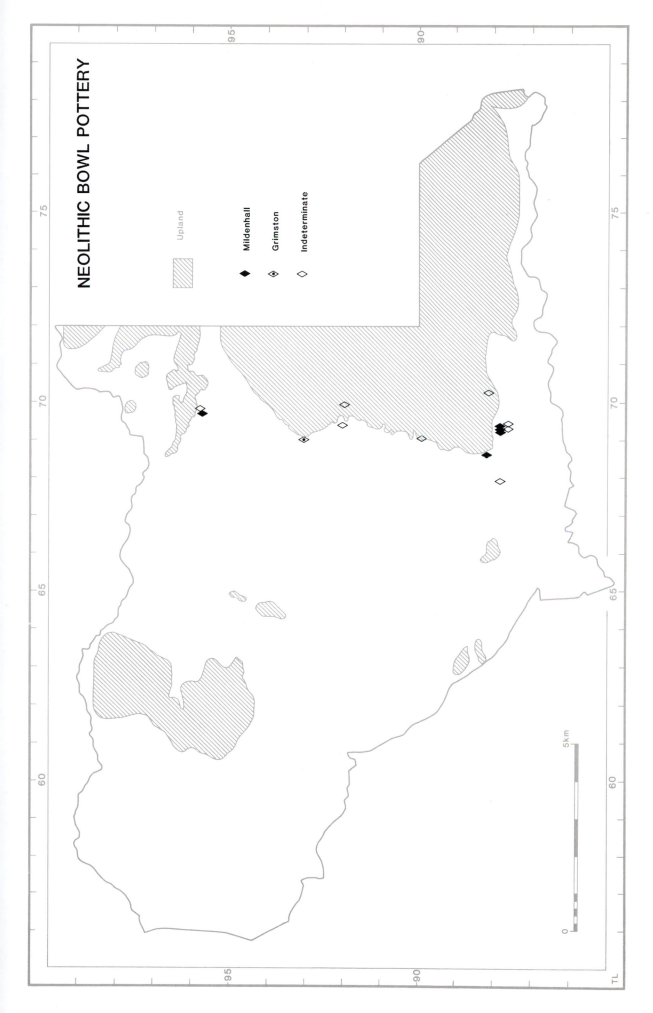

Figure 67 Distribution of Neolithic Bowl pottery, listed in Appendix 27 (microfiche). Scale 1:100,000

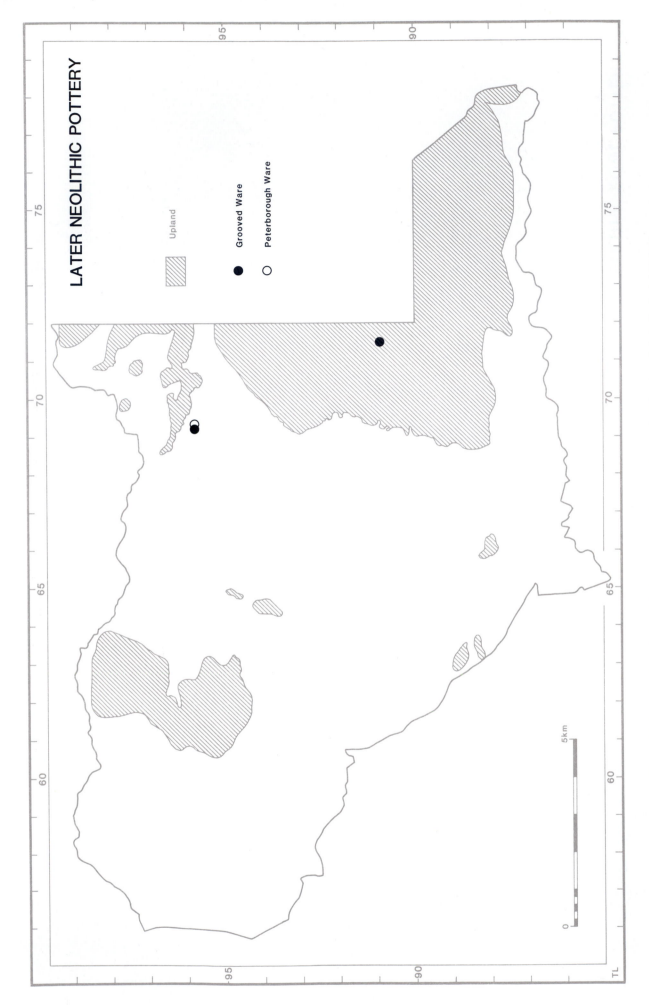

Figure 68 Distribution of Later Neolithic pottery, listed in Appendix 28 (microfiche). Scale 1:100,000

LATER NEOLITHIC POTTERY

Upland

Grooved Ware

Peterborough Ware

5km

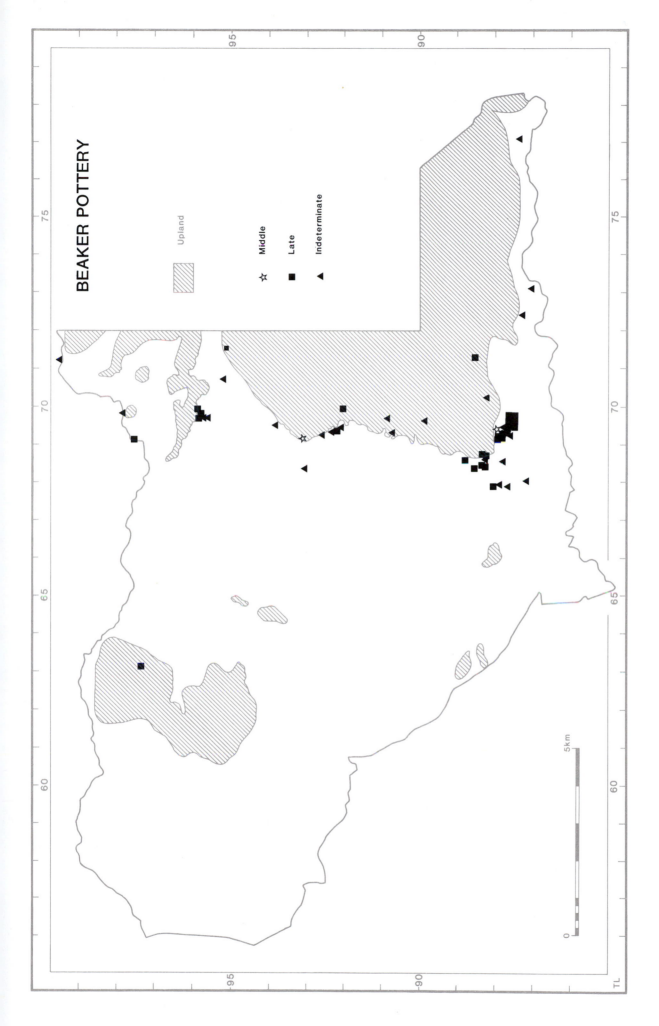

Figure 69 Distribution of Beaker pottery, listed in Appendix 29 (microfiche). Scale 1:100,000

Figure 70 Distribution of Food Vessel and Collared Urn, listed in Appendix 30 (microfiche). Scale 1:100,000

110

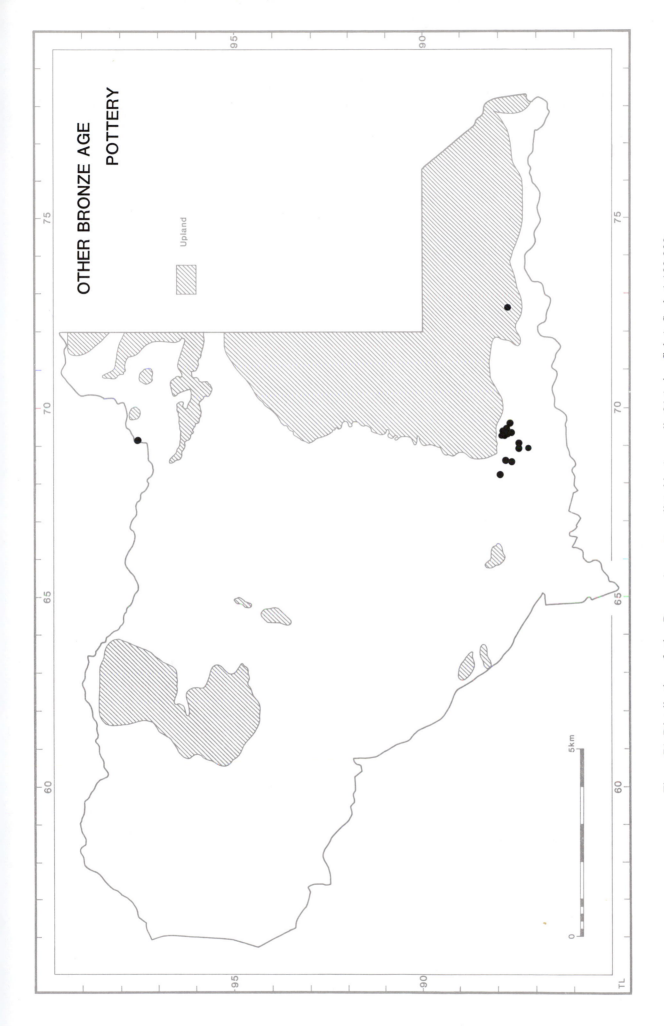

OTHER BRONZE AGE
POTTERY

Upland

Figure 71 Distribution of other Bronze Age pottery, listed in Appendix 31 (microfiche). Scale 1:100,000

111

III.3. Discussion

Chronology
Table 13 summarises the chronology of the main Neolithic and Bronze Age pottery styles in Britain as a whole and assembles the main dating evidence from East Anglia.

The British Museum's programme of radiocarbon determinations on skeletal remains associated with Beakers (Kinnes *et al.* 1991) has confirmed the lack of correspondence between stylistic divisions and the growing body of radiocarbon measurements associated with the ceramic.

Dating evidence for Biconical Urn within East Anglia is slight. The single radiocarbon determination of 3090 ± 60 BP (BM–208; 1430–1310 cal. BC) from Witton (Site 6938/c9; Lawson 1983, 112–4) is younger than the three determinations relating to the style from Shaugh Moor, Devon (Tomalin 1982, 228) and the more plausible of those from unit 6 at Brean Down, Somerset (Bell 1990, 34). Dates from these two sites together suggest a span of *c.* 3500–3000 BP (*c.* 1800–1300 cal. BC). There are other indications that the style was established relatively early. Clarke's suggestion (1970, 236–7, 271–2) of continuity between Final Southern Beakers and the Biconical Urn tradition rested partly on the incised, geometric decoration of a few pots from Mildenhall Fen (Clark 1936, fig. 8), now matched by one sherd from Hockwold (Fig. 95: P271).

At the other end of the style's time range, Biconical Urn and Deverel-Rimbury forms grade imperceptibly into each other (Tomalin 1982, 235). Concurrency is evidenced by radiocarbon determinations and suggested by the occasional presence of Biconical Urns in predominantly Deverel-Rimbury cremation cemeteries, as at Bromfield, Shropshire (Stanford 1982, figs 16–17). At Fison Way, Thetford, some 17km to the east of the Hockwold fields, a Biconical Urn and a Deverel-Rimbury Urn were found in adjacent pits in an otherwise dispersed group of Bronze Age cremations (Site 5853; Healy 1992). There is, however, little sign of relation between the mass of the Hockwold or Mildenhall Biconical Urn and the large assemblage of Deverel-Rimbury pottery used by the Bronze Age occupants of Grime's Graves (Site 5460; Longworth 1981; Longworth, Ellison and Rigby 1988). The closed, shouldered forms of the fen edge assemblages are in strong contrast to the unshouldered, bucket- and barrel-shaped forms of the Breckland one.

Hockwold cum Wilton OS 466, 613, 614 and 616

Change and Decay
The transition within the same fields from the predominantly Bronze Age collections of 1959–62 to the predominantly or solely Beaker ones of the mid-1960s is most easily interpreted as reflecting the progressive exposure of lower ridges and hillocks, which would have gone out of occupation earlier than higher ones (Ch. 3.III). The same process can be seen within pottery styles as well as between them. Beaker in the collections excavated in the later 1960s from Sites 5308/ c4 (61/68), 5333 (95/97) and 5308/c5 (96) has predominantly non-plastic, fingernail-impressed rustication, while that from collections made earlier in the has decade is dominated by plastic, finger-pinched or finger-tipped rustication (Figs 64–5). Whatever its chronological implications, this observation echoes the prevalence of plastic rustication in

Late style Beaker assemblages and of non-plastic rustication in Middle style Beaker ones (Clarke 1970, 258–9; Bamford 1982, 60–64). The minimum of 447 sherds per ha collected and excavated from the fields between 1959 and 1967 gives some indication of what must have been ploughed up elsewhere in the same period.

Composition of Domestic Assemblages
Among the Beaker pottery, Clarke's division into fine, everyday and heavy duty wares (1976, 462) is a matter of gradation rather than of sharp division (III.1). It is unclear how far the Beaker and Early Bronze Age Wares of the mixed groups were used successively and how far contemporaneously. The fact that all the determinable Food Vessel diameters are large (Fig. 62) suggests that they may have served as the heavy duty wares of more diverse assemblages. This seems particularly likely in the collection from Site 5308/c4 (61/68), where a high frequency of Food Vessel coincides with a low frequency of Rusticated Beaker (Fig. 61)

The same division into fine, everyday and heavy duty wares is present in the larger Bronze Age collections, where they roughly correspond to peaks in rim diameter (Fig. 62). These are close to those more clearly seen in the large collection of Deverel-Rimbury pottery from Grime's Graves (Ellison 1988, figs 21–22). Biconical Urns used for burial, such as the Norfolk examples illustrated by Lawson (1980a, fig. 3), Lukis (1843), Tomalin (1986, fig. 96) and Wymer (1990, fig. 1), seem to have been selected from among the larger and more elaborate vessels of contemporary domestic assemblages.

The Character of Occupation
The slightly different stylistic affinities of the Beaker assemblages from Sites 5324 (93) and 5333 (95/97), one Late to Final Southern, the other Primary to Developed Southern, suggests that they represent distinct episodes of occupation. A similar impression is conveyed by the comb-impressed and incised Beaker of the stylistically mixed collections from Sites 5308/c4 (61/68) and 5308/c5 (96), each of which has its own decorative and, to some extent, morphological characteristics (Figs 63, 64, 65, 66). The dispersal of sherds from single pots, some found at opposite extremes of excavated areas (Figs 7, 11, 14), also suggests that some, if not most, of each collection may have resulted from a single occupation.

The Bronze Age wares similarly show clear differences in fabric and form between the two single-site collections, from Sites 5373 (22) and 5332 (66), as well as between them and the larger collections of less well-located material (Fig. 63). Tomalin considers the Site 5373 (22) material, designated by him 'site A', as texturally and formally distinct from the other groups and perhaps of later date (1983, 359). There is the general impression of a succession of discrete, perhaps short-lived, episodes of occupation.

The Survey Area and Beyond

Assemblage compositon
The presence of another distinctive Beaker assemblage is suggested by the record of 'many sherds of handled Beakers' from Site 5317/c3 (23), the location of which is shown in Figure 3.

Style	Approximate currency BP	BC	Selected radiocarbon determinations, stratigraphic relationships and associations from within East Anglia	Sources
Grimston Ware	5200–4400	4000–2900	Broome Heath, Ditchingham (Site 10602) 4579 ± 65 BP (BM-757) 4523 ± 67 BP (BM-756) Charcoal from lower layers of pits containing Grimston Ware	Wainwright 1972, 6–7, 19
			Padholm Road, Fengate, Cambridgeshire 4960 ± 64 BP (GaK-4196) 4395 ± 50 BP (GaK-4197) Wood from foundation trench and possible corner post of Earlier Neolithic 'house'	Pryor 1974, 38
			Peacock's Farm, Shippea Hill, Cambridgeshire 4940 ± 120 BP (Q-527/8) 4860 ± 120 BP (Q-525/6) Charcoal from 'Neolithic layer' in lower peat, equated with the level from which Grimston Ware sherds were recovered in 1934	Clark and Godwin 1962, 19
Mildenhall Ware	5100–4300	3900–2900	Eaton Heath, Norwich (Site 9544) 5095 ± 49 BP (BM-770) Charcoal from pits containing Mildenhall Ware	Wainwright 1973, 9
			Spong Hill, North Elmham (Site 1012) 4950 ± 120 BP (BM-1534) 4650 ± 80 BP (BM-1533) Charcoal from features containing Mildenhall Ware	Healy 1988, 104
			Orsett causewayed enclosure, Essex All associated with Mildenhall Ware: 4741 ± 113 BP (BM-1213) Charcoal from post-hole central to palisade entrance 4585 ± 92 BP (BM-1215) Charcoal from primary silts of inner ditch 4533 ± 112 BP (BM-1214) Charcoal from primary silts of middle ditch	Hedges and Buckley 1978, 295
			The Stumble, Essex 4780 ± 70 BP (OxA-2298) Charred hazelnut shell from pit containing Mildenhall Ware	Information from the Archaeology Section, Essex County Council
			Etton, Haddenham and Great Wilbraham causewayed enclosures, Cambridgeshire Mildenhall Ware in primary contexts	Pryor, French and Taylor 1985, 295–7; Evans 1988, 130; Kinnes 1979, 123
			Haddenham long barrow, Cambridgeshire Mildenhall Ware contemporary with use of monument	Hodder and Shand 1988, 352
Developed Peterborough Ware	4600–3800?	3400–2200?	Haddenham causewayed enclosure, Cambridgeshire Ebbsfleet and Mortlake Ware in late recuts of some ditch segments	Evans 1988, 136
Grooved Ware (Southern substyles)	4300–3700	3000–2100	Barholm, Lincolnshire 4305 ± 130 BP (UB-457) 4255 ± 135 BP (UB-458) Charcoal and bone collagen from pits containing Grooved Ware	Simpson 1993
			Redgate Hill, Hunstanton (Site 1396) 4170 ± 90 BP (OxA-2311) 4005 ± 90 BP (OxA-2310) Animal bone from pits containing Grooved Ware	Healy, Cleal and Kinnes 1993
			Springfield Cursus, Essex 4120 ± 80 BP (HAR-6271) 3990 ± 89 BP (HAR-6266) 3960 ± 80 BP (HAR-6268) Charcoal from deposit including Grooved Ware in upper fill of cursus ditch	Information from the Archaeology Section, Essex County Council

Style	Approximate currency BP	cal. BC	Selected radiocarbon determinations, stratigraphic relationships and associations from within East Anglia	Sources
			Storey's Bar Road, Fengate, Cambridgeshire 6 determinations, from 3980 ± 100 BP (HAR-397) to 3810 ± 150 BP (HAR-409) Charcoal from features containing Grooved Ware	Pryor 1978, 226–7
			Grime's Graves, Weeting with Broomhill (Site 5640) 52 determinations indicating span of *c.* 4050–3750 BP Charcoal and antler from mining contexts in deep, galleried shafts, worked mainly by users of Grooved Ware	Burleigh *et al.* 1979, 43–6
Beaker	4000–3500	2600–1800	*Beeston with Bittering (Site 15995)* 3960 ± 80 BP (HAR-4637) 3540 ± 70 BP (HAR-4635) Charcoal from pits containing Late style (?S4) Beaker sherds	Wymer and Healy forthcoming
			Longham (Site 7239) 3890 ± 70 BP (HAR-8520) Charcoal from feature containing Middle style (EA/BW) Beaker sherds	Wymer and Healy forthcoming
			Jaywick 1, Clacton, Essex 3830 ± 90 BP (HAR-8154) AOC Beaker	Case 1993, 264; Wilkinson and Murphy 1986, fig. 5: 10
			Trowse (Site 9592) 3810 ± 80 BP (HAR-3269) Charred timbers from upper fill of grave containing Late style (S2) Beaker	Healy 1982a, 12
			Fifty Farm, Mildenhall, Suffolk 3800 ± 150 BP (BM-133) Charcoal from fen edge occupation site with Late style (S3–4) Beaker	Leaf 1934
			Barrow 5, Chippenham, Cambridgeshire 3800 ± 150 BP (BM-152) Charcoal from hearth associated with Late style (S2) Beaker	Leaf 1940
			Lion Point, Clacton, Essex, site 114, area 2 3750 ± 150 BP (BM-172) Charcoal from pit containing Middle style (BW) Beaker	Smith 1955; Couchman 1980, 40
			Risby, Suffolk 3660 ± 50 BP (BM-2522) Human bone collagen from burial with FN rusticated Beaker	Vatcher, F. de M. and Vatcher, H. L., 1976; Vatcher, H. L., 1976; Ambers, Matthews and Bowman 1991, 53
			Barnack, Cambridgeshire 3570 ± 80 BP (HAR-1645) Charcoal from grave containing Middle style (W/MR) Beaker	Donaldson 1977, 228
			Bowthorpe, Norwich (Site 11431) 3530 ± 70 BP (HAR-3630) Charcoal from grave containing Late style (S1) Beaker	Lawson 1986, 29–30
			Wattisfield, Suffolk 3520 ± 150 BP (BM-77) Charcoal associated with Late style (S4) Beaker	Smedley 1957
			Waterhall Farm, Chippenham, Cambridgeshire 3520 ± 70 BP (HAR-3880) Human bone from grave containing sherds of a Late style (S2/3) Beaker	Martin 1976a

Style	Approximate currency BP	cal. BC	Selected radiocarbon determinations, stratigraphic relationships and associations from within East Anglia	Sources
			Plantation Farm, Shippea Hill, Cambridgeshire Middle style (BW, E) Beaker, Late style (S2, S4) Beaker and Food Vessel sherds in occupation deposit part of which extended into upper peat, some 50–150 mm above fen clay	Clark 1933
Food Vessel	3700–3200 see also Plantation Farm above	2100–1500	*Harford Farm, (Site 9794)* 3840 ± 70 BP (GU-5191) Charcoal from fill of grave containing a vase Food Vessel	Ashwin in prep.
			Spong Hill (Site 1012) 3810 ± 70 BP (BM-1532) Charcoal and nutshell from pit containing a Food Vessel Urn and a miniature vessel	Healy 1988, 104
			Pilsgate, Cambridgeshire 3522 ± 38 BP (BM-868) 3296 ± 50 BP (BM-869) Charcoal associated with Food Vessel and Middle or Late Collared Urn	Pryor 1981
Collared Urn	3600–3100 see also Pilsgate above	2000–1400	*Bixley (Site 9585)* 3740 ± 80 BP (GU-5187) Charcoal from cremation associated with Late Collared Urn	Ashwin in prep.
			Brightwell Heath, Suffolk 3720 ± 90 BP (NPL-133) Contents of Middle or Late Collared Urn	Gilyard-Beer 1984, 254
			Risby, Suffolk 3495 ± 30 BP (GrN-11358) Human bone from grave containing Early Collared Urn	Martin 1976b
			Eriswell, Suffolk 3470 ± 155 BP (BM-316) Wooden object burnt on top of grave containing Early Collared Urn	Dymond 1973, 6–7
			Spong Hill, North Elmham (Site 1012) 3440 ± 90 BP (HAR-2901) Charcoal from pit containing Collared Urn fragments, including rim of Early or Middle form	Healy 1988, 104
			Storey's Bar Road, Fengate, Cambridgeshire 3410 ± 120 BP (HAR-400) Contents of Collared Urn	Pryor 1978, 226
			Weasenham Lyngs (Site 3659) 3339 ± 56 BP (BM-877) Charcoal from Late Collared Urn	Petersen and Healy 1986, 73
			West Row Fen, Mildenhall, Suffolk 8 determinations from 3520 ± 60 BP (HAR-9269) to 3190 ± 70 BP (HAR-4629) Charcoal and organic fills relating to occupation by users of Collared Urn	Martin 1984, Martin and Murphy 1988
Biconical Urn	3500–3000	1800–1300	*Witton (Site 6938/c9)* 3090 ± 60 BP (BM-208) Charcoal from pit containing sherds of plain, grogged biconical vessels and smaller sherds of (?residual) Beaker	Lawson 1983, 112–4
			Great Bircham (Site 1705/c4) Gold foil-covered beads of Wessex II affinities with cremation contained in Biconical Urn	Lukis 1843, Tomalin 1986

| Style | Approximate currency | | Selected radiocarbon determinations, stratigraphic | Sources |
	BP	cal. BC	relationships and associations from within East Anglia	
			Semer, Suffolk 2 faience beads in cremation contained in Biconical Urn	Smedley and Owles 1964, 192–3
Deverel-Rimbury	3200–2800	1500–900	*Grime's Graves, Weeting with Broomhill (Site 5640)* 13 determinations, indicating span of *c.* 3000– 2800 BP for occupation by users of local Deverel-Rimbury pottery	Burleigh *et al.* 1979
			Rook Hall, Essex 2970 ± 90 BP (HAR-6397) Charcoal from well containing Deverel-Rimbury pottery and cylindrical loom-weights	Adkins *et al.* 1985
Post Deverel-Rimbury	2900–2600	1100–800	*Springfield Lyons, Essex* 2830 ± 70 BP (HAR-6622) Charcoal from post-hole of central roundhouse of enclosure with post Deverel-Rimbury pottery and Ewart Park phase metalworking debris	Buckley and Hedges 1987
			Newark Road, Fengate, Cambridgeshire 2740 ± 80 BP (HAR-773) Charcoal from post-hole containing post Deverel-Rimbury pottery, cut into ditch silts described below	Pryor 1980b, 247
			North Ring, Mucking, Essex 2700 ± 80 BP (HAR-2911) 2630 ± 110 BP (HAR-2893) Charcoal from ditch silts containing post Deverel-Rimbury pottery	Barrett and Bond 1988, 36
			South Rings, Mucking, Essex 2810 ± 70 BP (HAR-1708) 2790 ± 90 BP (HAR-1630) 2770 ± 110 BP (HAR-1634) Charcoal from ditch silts containing post Deverel-Rimbury pottery	Barrett and Bond 1988, 36
			Barham, Suffolk 2640 ± 70 BP (HAR-3160) Charcoal from oven containing post Deverel-Rimbury pottery	Martin 1993
			Beeston Regis (Site 15534) Hoard of Ewart Park phase metalwork found in post Deverel-Rimbury bowl	Lawson 1980b
Determinations not attributable to particular styles			*Newark Road, Fengate, Cambridgeshire* 3980 ± 100 BP (HAR-774) Charcoal associated with rusticated sherds of uncertain affinities (?Beaker)	Pryor 1980b, 103
			Newark Road, Fengate, Cambridgeshire 14 determinations, from 3850 ± 120 BP (HAR-780) to 2890 ± 60 BP (HAR-785) Charcoal and wood from ditch silts and related features containing sherds of Food Vessel, Collared Urn, ?Deverel-Rimbury and indeterminate Bronze Age plain wares	Pryor 1980b, 102–4, 247–9

Based in part on Burgess (1986, 350–1), Ellison (1988, 47–8), Herne (1988), Kinnes *et al.* (1991), Smith (1974a, 106–120), Tomalin (1988)

Table 13 Approximate Chronology of Neolithic and Bronze Age Pottery Styles in East Anglia

The consistently large size of Food Vessels throughout the survey area is compatible with the specialised function suggested for them above. As far as it is possible to tell from the literature, Food Vessel pottery from domestic contexts elsewhere along the south-eastern fen edge also tends to be large and coarse. Examples include Plantation Farm and Peacock's Farm, Shippea Hill, Cambridgeshire (Clark 1933, pl. XLV; Clark et al. 1935, fig. 9), Fifty Farm, Mildenhall, Suffolk (Leaf 1935, 122–125) and Wilde Street, also in Mildenhall (Kelly 1967, 51–52). Food Vessels, as distinct from Food Vessel Urns, from the same zone are from burials, as in the case of the vessel from Hill Close, Feltwell (Fig. 102: P360, or from possible burials, as in the case of a vessel approximately 120mm in diameter found in peat close to unidentified bones at Shippea Hill Farm, Cambridgeshire (Fell and Briscoe 1951).

The domestic use of Food Vessel Urn is one aspect of the general prevalence in local settlements of pottery styles, principally Food Vessel Urn, Collared Urn and Biconical Urn, more often found in funerary contexts. Collared Urn and Food Vessel were also used at Newark Road, Fengate, Cambridgeshire, on the western edge of the fens (Pryor 1980b, 87–104). Settlements whose occupants used these ceramics are rare elsewhere in Britain, and often distant. Longworth lists twenty-two occupation sites with Collared Urn, six of them on the south-eastern fen edge (1984, 76), in contrast to many hundreds of funerary finds. Beyond the Fenland basin, the principal examples of settlements with Food Vessel are Risby Warren, South Humberside (Riley, 1957, 44, fig. 3:9) and Killelen, Islay, Argyllshire (Burgess 1975), while the principal examples of settlements with Biconical Urn are Shaugh Moor, Devon (Tomalin 1982) and Brean Down, Somerset (Woodward 1990, 123–126).

Local or Imported?
Pots may have been among the items brought into the area, alongside more obviously exotic objects of stone and metal. Clarke eloquently demonstrated (1976) that a fine, highly ornamented Beaker could be made only where good quality clay was available, and called for the input of four to six hours of skilled labour, only slightly less than it would take to polish an axe of Great Langdale tuff (Bradley and Edmonds 1993, table 5.4). The long-distance exchange of Beakers which Clarke posited is not evidenced by any obviously foreign tempers among the vessels from the survey area, although thin sectioning might provide evidence to the contrary. Neither do Beakers elsewhere seem to have been transported between regions (Case 1993, 265). Transport within the region may, however, be reflected in the diversity of texture and of temper combinations which distinguish the Beaker in the collections from other styles. Tomalin considers certain minority fabrics among the Biconical Urn to represent imported vessels (1983, 372). The plaited cord decoration of one pot (Fig. 85: P148) suggests the influence of the Trevisker tradition of the south-west, although the grog- and sand-tempered fabric is likely to be a local one.

Relation to the South-eastern Fen Edge as a Whole
The overall composition of the pottery from the survey area is broadly similar to that of contemporary pottery from the rest of the south-eastern fen edge, but differs in some details. The rarity of Grimston Ware among Earlier Neolithic pottery contrasts with its exclusive presence in the lower peat at Peacock's Farm, Shippea Hill, Cambridgeshire (Clark et al. 1935, 301–303). The scarcity of Peterborough Ware and Grooved Ware, both, like Grimston Ware, confined to Methwold, is common to the whole south-eastern fen edge (Cleal 1984, figs 9.1–9.4). Among Beaker pottery the near-absence of all-over-cord decoration is echoed along the fen edge and throughout East Anglia (Clarke 1970, map 1). The relative scarcity of Middle style Beaker of Clarke's East Anglian and Barbed Wire groups and abundance of Late style Beaker of his Southern tradition are usual for the fen edge as a whole.

This emphasises the stylistic foci already apparent in East Anglia: Clarke's Southern tradition (equivalent to Case's southern Group B) is concentrated on the south-eastern fen edge, while his East Anglian and Barbed Wire groups (equivalent to Case's Group E) are concentrated on the Sandlings of the Colchester-Ipswich area (Clarke 1970, maps 4, 7–10; Case 1993, fig. 3).

The preponderance of Food Vessel over Collared Urn contrasts with the presence of domestic Collared Urn assemblages at West Row Fen, Mildenhall, Suffolk, some 12km to the south (Martin and Murphy 1988); while the Biconical Urn assemblages from Hockwold recall that excavated in the same area by Clark (1936).

III. 4. Catalogue of Illustrated Pottery
Entries are ordered as follows: style, filler(s), texture, hardness, colour, decorative technique(s), context, serial number allotted by Tomalin in the course of his fabric analysis of some of the Hockwold material (1983), other bibliographical references, comment.

Some surface colours may have been modified by peat-staining.

Hockwold cum Wilton OS 466 + 616. Site 24866 ('site 8')
Centre TL 6954 8765. NCM accession no. 121.960 (Ch. 3.I.1 Figs 72–75)

P1   **Beaker.** Grog with some sand. Medium. Medium. *Ext.* orange-brown. *core* buff, *int.* buff. Incision.

P2   **Beaker.** Grog with some flint. Fine. Hard. *Ext.* buff, *core* grey, *int.* grey-buff. Incision.

P3   **Rusticated Beaker.** Grog with very little flint. Medium. Medium. *Ext.* buff, *core* grey, *int.* buff-grey. FP.

P4   **Food Vessel.** Grog with very little sand. Coarse. Soft. *Ext.* buff, *core* buff-grey, *int.* buff. Twisted cord impression. Tomalin 83.

P5   **Food Vessel.** Grog. Coarse. Soft. *Ext.* grey-buff, *core* dark grey, *int.* grey-buff. Tomalin 61. Diameter approx. 240 mm.

P6   **Food Vessel.** Grog. Coarse. Soft. *Ext.* buff, *core* dark grey, *int.* grey-buff. Whipped cord impression. Tomalin 93. Single surviving stop ridge on shoulder. Very faint whipped cord impression inside rim bevel.

P7   **Food Vessel.** Grog. Coarse. Soft. *Ext.* buff, *core* grey, *int.* buff. Crescentic (twisted?) cord impressions. Tomalin 79. Diameter approx. 260 mm.

P8   **Food Vessel.** Grog. Coarse. Soft. *Ext.* orange, *core* dark grey, *int.* grey-buff. Incision. Tomalin 91, 92. ?Organic residue on interior.

P9   **Collared Urn.** Grog with a little sand. Coarse. Medium. *Ext.* buff, *core* grey, *int.* buff. Twisted cord impression. Tomalin 63. Longworth 1984, corpus no. 940.

P10   **Collared Urn.** Grog with a little sand. Medium. Medium. *Ext.* buff-grey, *core* dark grey, *int.* buff-grey. Incision, impression. Tomalin 64. Longworth 1984, corpus no. 944.

P11   **Biconical Urn.** Grog with a little sand. Coarse. Soft. *Ext.* buff, *core* dark grey, *int.* buff-grey. Tomalin 446. Applied lug.

P12   **Biconical Urn.** Sand with grog. Medium. Hard. *Ext.* buff, *core* orange, *int.* buff. Tomalin 465. Diameter approx. 50 mm.

P13   **Biconical Urn.** Grog with sand. medium. Hard. *Ext.* grey-buff, *core* dark grey, *int.* grey-buff. Tomalin 450.

P14 **Indet. Bronze Age.** Grog with a little sand. Coarse. Soft. *Ext.* grey-buff, *core* grey, *int.* buff. Incision. Tomalin 475. Sherd of same pot in 'field 79' collection in KLM (accession no. A307).

P15 **Biconical Urn.** Grog with a little flint. Coarse. Medium. *Ext.* buff, *core* dark grey, *int.* buff. (?FN) impression. Tomalin 410. Organic residue on interior.

P16 **Biconical Urn.** Grog with sand and a little flint. Medium. Hard. *Ext.* orange-buff, *core* orange, *int.* orange-buff. Appliqué, comb-impression, FN. Tomalin 733.

P17 **Biconical Urn.** Grog with sand. Medium. Medium. *Ext.* buff, *core* grey, *int.* grey. Round-toothed comb impression. Tomalin 538.

P18 **Biconical Urn.** Grog with some sand. Medium. Medium. *Ext.* orange-buff, *core* dark grey, *int.* orange-buff. Tomalin 463.

P19 **Biconical Urn.** Grog with some sand and flint. Medium. Medium. *Ext.* buff, *core* dark grey, *int.* buff. Tomalin 411.

P20 **Biconical Urn.** Grog with some sand. Medium. Hard. *Ext.* grey-buff, *core* grey, *int.* buff. FT impression. Tomalin 938.

P21 **Biconical Urn.** Grog and sand with a little flint. Medium. Hard. *Ext.* grey, *core* grey *int.* grey-buff. FT impression. Tomalin 434.

P22 **Indet. Bronze Age (? Food Vessel).** Grog with a little sand. Coarse. Soft. *Ext.* buff, *core* grey, *int.* buff.

P23 **Biconical Urn.** Grog. Coarse. Medium. *Ext.* buff, *core* dark grey, *int.* buff-grey. Twisted cord impression. Tomalin 431.

P24 **Indet. Bronze Age (? Food Vessel).** Grog. Coarse. Soft. *Ext.* orange-buff, *core* buff, *int.* orange-buff. FT impression. Tomalin 547.

P25 **Indet. Bronze Age (? Biconical Urn).** Grog with a little sand. Medium. Hard. *Ext.* grey-buff, *core*, grey *int.* buff.

P26 **Biconical Urn.** Grog with sand and a little flint. Medium. Hard. *Ext.* grey-buff, *core* grey, *int.* buff. Tomalin 596.

P27 **Biconical Urn.** Grog with some sand. Medium. hard. *Ext.* buff-grey, *core* dark grey, *int.* buff. FT impression. Tomalin 442. Pitch uncertain.

P28 **Biconical Urn.** Grog with some sand. Coarse. Medium. *Ext.* grey-buff, *core* dark grey, *int.* grey-buff. Appliqué, FT impression. Tomalin 440.

P29 **Biconical Urn.** Grog with some sand. Coarse. Medium. *Ext.* buff, *core* grey, *int.* buff.

P30 **Biconical Urn.** Grog with some sand and a little flint. Medium. Hard. *Ext.* grey-buff, *core*, grey *int.* grey-buff. Tomalin 409.

P31 **Biconical Urn.** Grog with some sand. Medium. Hard. *Ext.* buff, *core* grey, *int.* grey. Tomalin 426.

P32 **Biconical Urn.** Grog. Coarse. Medium. *Ext.* buff, *core* dark grey, *int.* buff. Appliqué, FT impression. Tomalin 432. Pitch uncertain.

P33 **Biconical Urn.** Grog with some sand. Coarse. Medium. *Ext.* grey-buff, *core* dark grey, *int.* buff. Appliqué, FT impression. Tomalin 444. Pitch uncertain.

P34 **Biconical Urn.** Grog with sand and a little flint. Medium. Hard. *Ext.* grey-buff, *core* grey, *int.* buff. Tomalin 435.

P35 **Biconical Urn.** Grog with sand. Medium. Hard. *Ext.* buff, *core* dark grey, *int.* grey. Appliqué. Tomalin 501. ?Organic residue on interior.

P36 **Indet. Bronze Age.** Grog with sand. Medium. Medium. *Ext.* buff, *core* dark grey, *int.* grey. Cordon apparently pinched-up.

P37 **Biconical Urn.** Grog with some sand. Coarse. Medium. *Ext.* buff-grey, *core* dark grey, *int.* grey-buff. FT impression. Tomalin 491

P38 **Probably Biconical Urn.** Grog. Coarse. Medium. *Ext.* buff, *core* dark grey, *int.* buff. Appliqué. Tomalin 432A. Shoulder fragment.

P39 **Biconical Urn.** Grog with some sand. Coarse. Medium. *Ext.* buff, *core* dark grey, *int.* buff-grey. Tomalin 476.

P40 **Biconical Urn.** Grog with sand and a little flint. Coarse. Medium. *Ext.* buff, *core* dark grey, *int.* grey-buff. Appliqué. Tomalin 477.

P41 **Biconical Urn.** Grog with sand. Coarse. Hard. *Ext.* orange-buff, *core* grey, *int.* orange-buff. FN. Tomalin 495.

P42 **Biconical Urn.** Grog with sand. Medium. Hard. *Ext.* grey-buff, *core* grey, *int.* grey. Twisted cord impression, FN. Tomalin 505.

P43 **Indet. Bronze Age.** Grog. Coarse. Soft. *Ext.* buff, *core* dark grey, *int.* grey-buff. Fabric suggests Food Vessel or Collared Urn.

P44 **Indet. Bronze Age.** Grog with sand. Coarse. Medium. *Ext.* buff-orange, *core* dark grey, *int.* grey. Fabric suggests Biconical Urn.

P45 **Indet. Bronze Age.** Grog with some sand. Coarse. Soft. *Ext.* buff, *core* dark grey, *int.* buff. Incision. Fabric suggests Food Vessel or Collared Urn.

P46 **Indet. Bronze Age.** Grog with a little sand. Coarse. Soft. *Ext.* buff, *core* dark grey, *int.* grey-buff. Fabric suggests Food Vessel or Collared Urn.

P47 **Indet. Bronze Age.** Sand with grog. Medium. Hard. *Ext.* buff-grey, *core* grey, *int.* buff-grey. Fabric suggests Biconical Urn.

P48 **?Biconical Urn.** Grog. Coarse. Soft. *Ext.* buff, *core* grey. Tomalin 472. Lid.

P49 **?Biconical Urn.** Grog with sand. Coarse. Medium. *Ext.* buff, *core* grey. Tomalin 784. Lid.

Hockwold cum Wilton OS 466 + 614 + 616. 'Field 79'. Site 14662
Centre TL 6945 8765. KLM A307 (Ch. 3.I.1 Fig. 76)

P50 **Neolithic Bowl.** Flint. Coarse. Hard. Dark grey to black throughout. Impression, incision.

P51 **Beaker.** Flint with some grog. Fine. Hard. *Ext.* buff, *core* dark grey, *int.* grey. Comb impression. Clarke 1970, corpus no. 532F (S3(E)), published as from Feltwell.

Hockwold cum Wilton OS 616. 'Site 4'. ? = Site 5309 (48)
Curtis collection (Ch.3.I.1 Fig. 76)

P52 **Bronze Age, ?Biconical Urn.** Grog. Coarse, friable. Soft. *Ext.* buff, *core* dark grey, *int.* buff. Three lugs survive, apparently perforated after application; pot distorted to oval, diameter approx. 110–130 mm; sketched in S of OS 616 in Plate IV.

Hockwold cum Wilton OS 616. Site 5439 (44)
TL 6942 8762. NCM accession no. 674.964 (Ch. 3.I.1 Fig. 77)

P53 **Beaker.** Grog with sand and some flint. Medium. Hard. *Ext.* orange-buff, *core* grey, *int.* grey-buff. Comb impression, FP. Uncertain whether part of a bowl or of a large Beaker-shaped vessel.

Hockwold cum Wilton OS 616. Site 5309 (48)
TL 6945 8755. NCM accession no. 675.964 (Ch. 3.I.1 Figs 77–78)

P54 **Beaker.** Flint with grog and sand. Fine. Hard. *Ext.* buff-grey, *core* grey, *int.* buff-grey. Comb impression.

P55 **Beaker.** Grog with sand. Medium. Hard. *Ext.* orange-brown, *core* grey, *int.* buff. Comb-impression.

P56 **Beaker.** Grog with some sand. Medium. Medium. *Ext.* orange-buff, *core* grey, *int.* buff. Indet. impression. Possibly of bowl-like profile.

P57 **Beaker.** Grog with some sand. Medium. Hard. *Ext.* buff-grey, *core* dark grey, *int.* buff-grey. Comb impression, FN.

P58 **Beaker.** Grog with some flint and sand. Medium. hard. *Ext.* buff-grey, *core* dark grey, *int.* buff-grey. Comb impression.

P59 **Beaker.** Grog with some sand. Medium. Medium. *Ext.* orange-buff, *core* dark grey, *int.* buff-grey. Comb impression.

P60 **Beaker.** Grog with sand. Fine. Hard. *Ext.* orange, *core* dark grey, *int.* grey-buff. Comb-impression.

P61 **Beaker.** Grog with sand. Fine. Hard. *Ext.* buff-grey, *core* dark grey, *int.* buff-grey. Incision.

Hockwold cum Wilton OS 616. Site 5310 (49)
TL 6950 8755. NCM accession no. 676.964 (Ch. 3.I.1 Fig. 78)

P62 **Rusticated Beaker.** Sand with some flint. Fine. Hard. *Ext.* orange-buff, *core* dark grey, *int.* orange-buff. FN.

P63 **Rusticated Beaker.** Grog with some sand. Coarse. Medium. *Ext.* brown, *core* orange-brown, *int.* grey-brown. FN, appliqué. Distinctive fabric, with large, light-coloured grog particles in dark matrix, makes it almost certain that base and upper fragments come from same vessel. Rim cordon, rounded form and well-defined base suggest affinities with Middle style Beakers of Clarke's East Anglian and Barbed Wire groups.

P64 **Beaker.** Grog with sand and odd flecks of ?haematite. Medium. medium. *Ext.* orange-buff, *core* dark grey, *int.* orange-buff. Incision, FN.

P65 **Beaker.** Grog with sand. Fine. Hard. *Ext.* buff, *core* dark grey, *int.* buff. Incision.

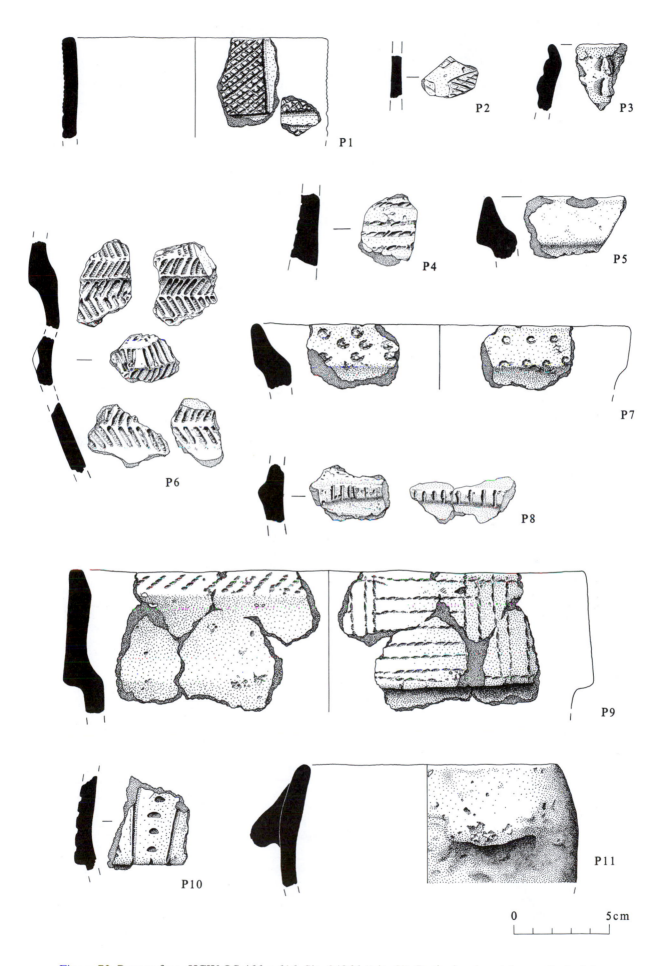

Figure 72 Pottery from HCW OS 466 + 616, Site 24866 ('site 8'). Particulars in catalogue. Scale 1:2

P1

P2

P3

P4

P5

P6

P7

P8

P9

P10

P11

0   5 cm

119

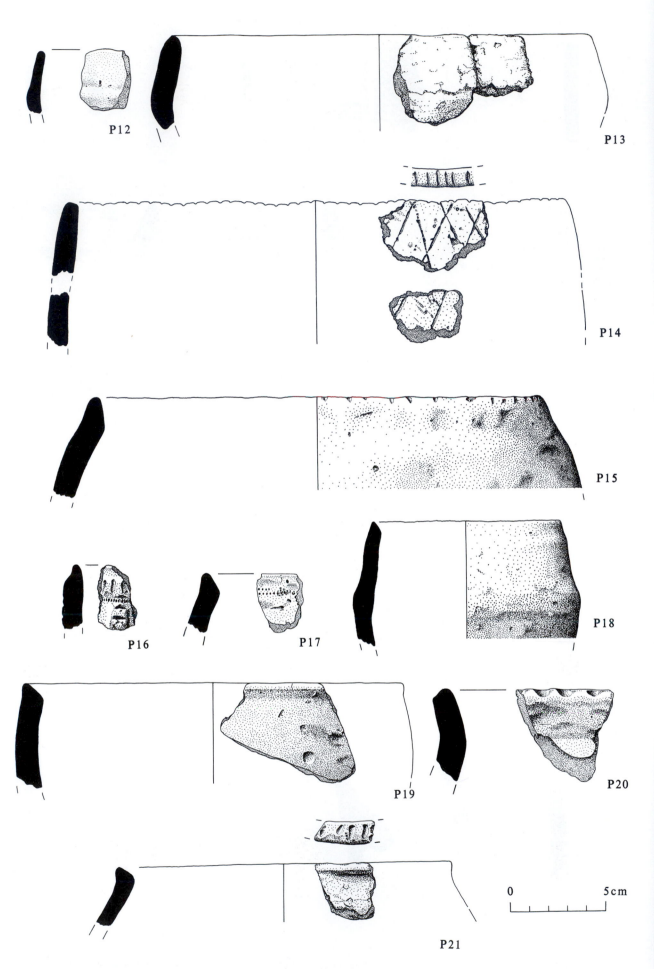

Figure 73 Pottery from HCW OS 466 + 616, Site 24866 ('site 8'). Particulars in catalogue. Scale 1:2

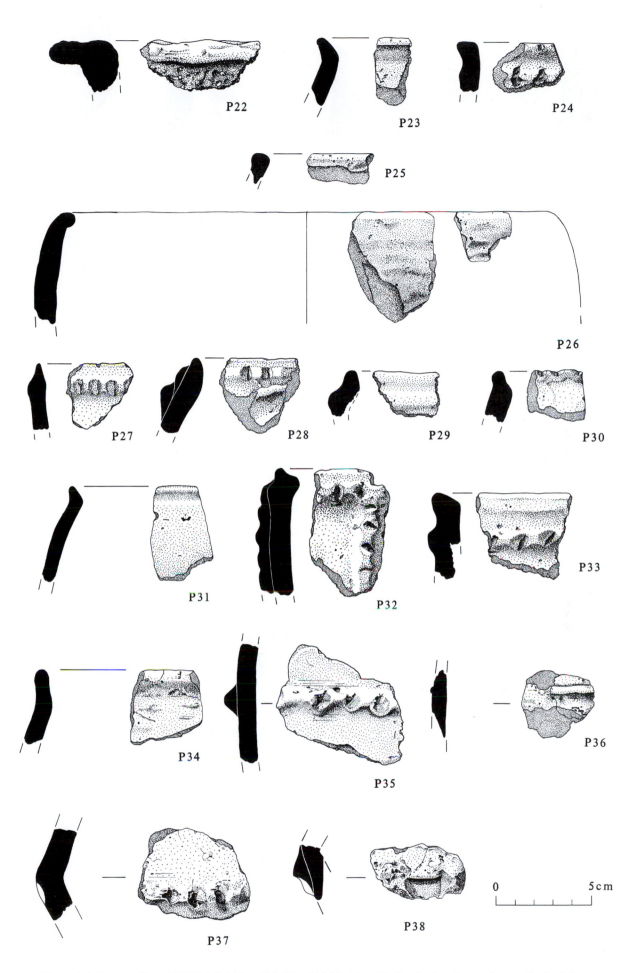

P22

P23

P24

P25

P26

P27

P28

P29

P30

P31

P32

P33

P34

P35

P36

P37

P38

0   5 cm

Figure 74 Pottery from HCW OS 466 + 616, Site 24866 ('site 8'). Particulars in catalogue. Scale 1:2

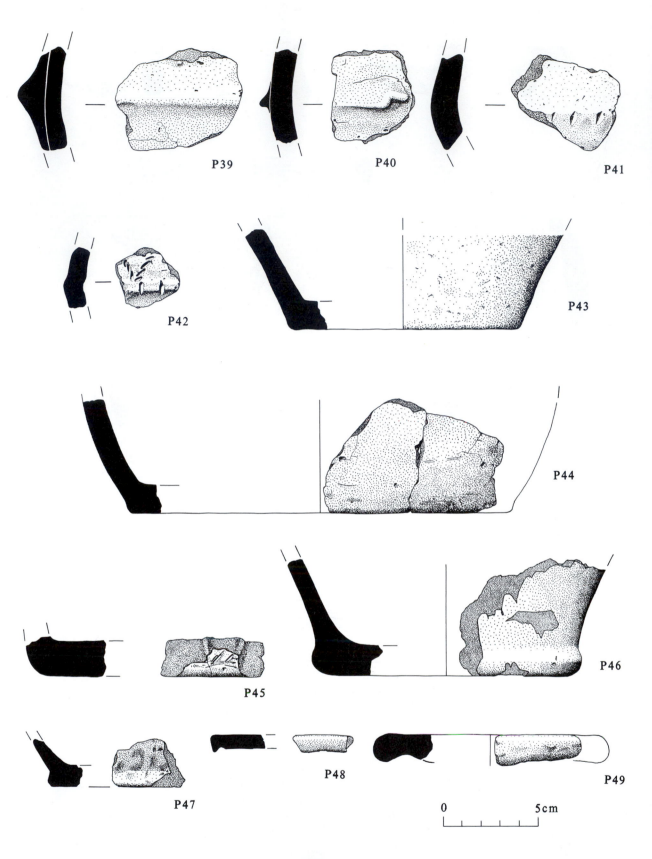

P39

P40

P41

P42

P43

P44

P45

P46

P47

P48

P49

0   5cm

Figure 75 Pottery from HCW OS 466 + 616, Site 24866 ('site 8'). Particulars in catalogue. Scale 1:2

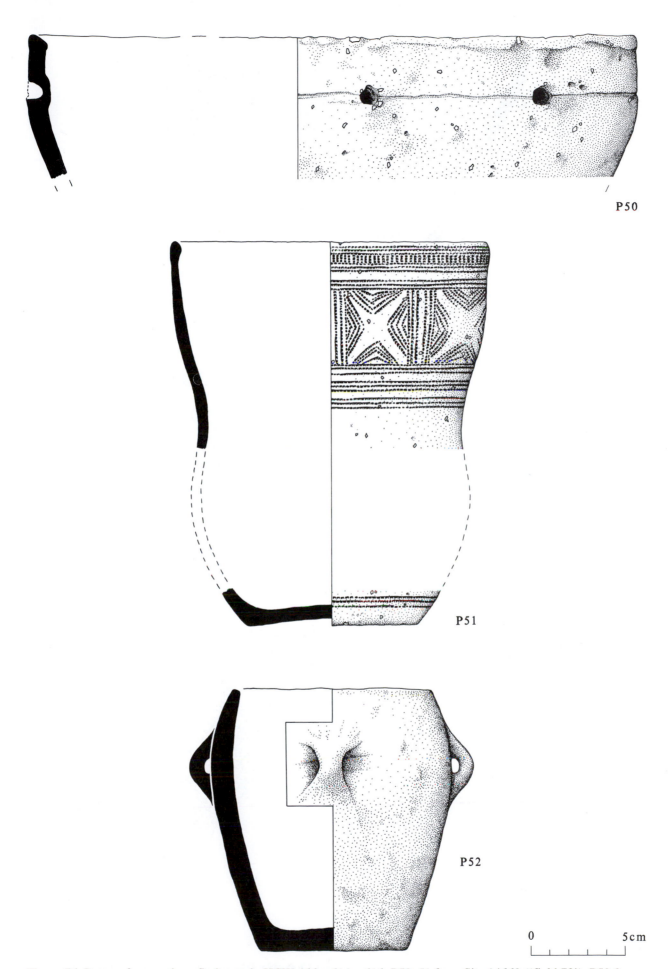

P50

P51

P52

0   5 cm

Figure 76 Pottery from various findspots in HCW 466 + 614 + 616: P50–51 from Site 14662 ('field 79'), P52 from Frank Curtis' 'site 4', ? = Site 5309 (48). Particulars in catalogue. Scale 1:2

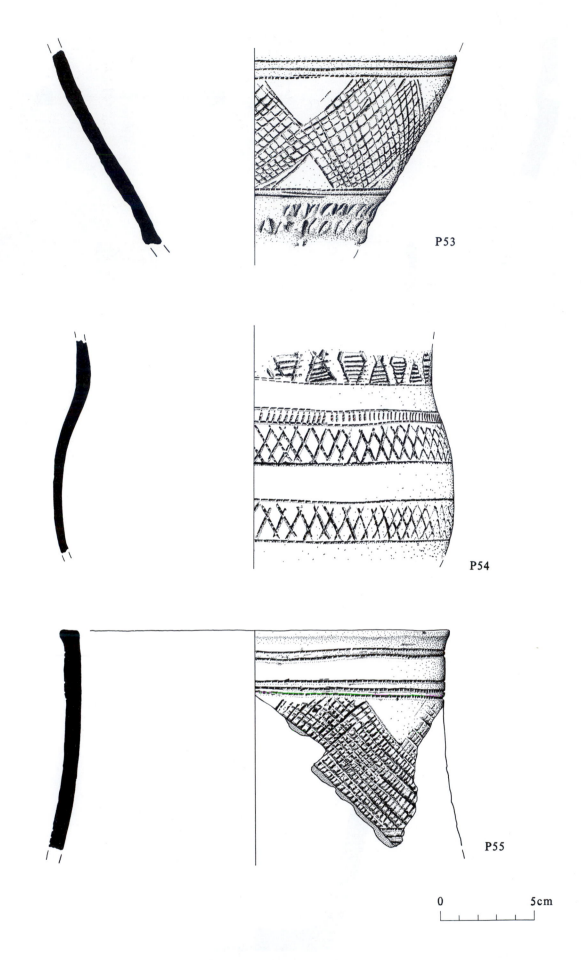

P53

P54

P55

0   5cm

Figure 77 Pottery from HCW OS 616, Sites 5439 (44) and 5309 (48): P53 from Site 5439 (44); P54–5 from Site 5309 (48). Particulars in catalogue. Scale 1:2

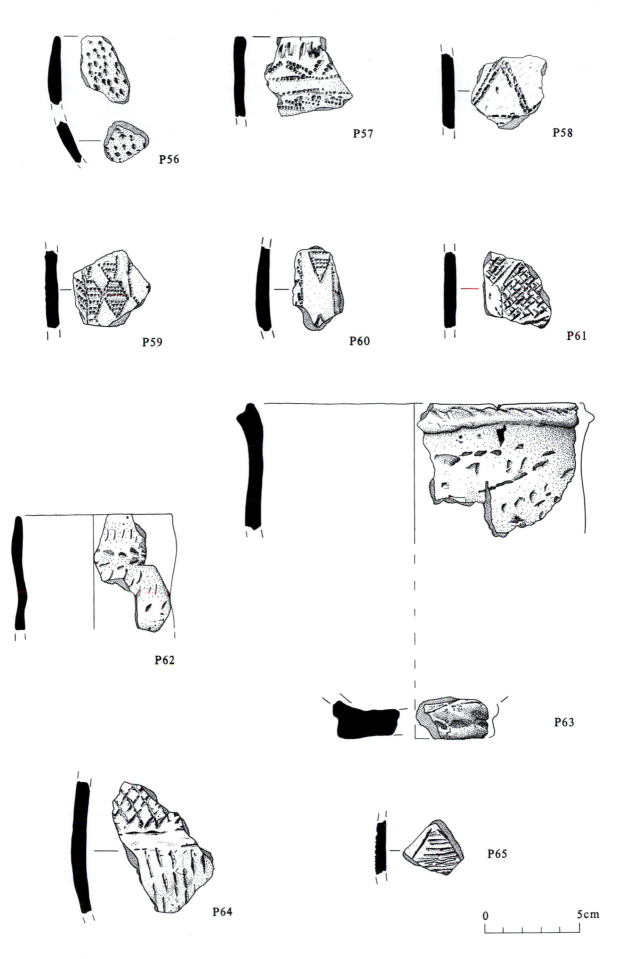

P56

P57

P58

P59

P60

P61

P62

P63

P64

P65

0   5cm

Figure 78 Pottery from HCW OS 616: P56–61 from Site 5309 (48); P62–65 from Site 5310 (49).
Particulars in catalogue. Scale 1:2

125

Hockwold cum Wilton OS 466, 616. Sites 5311 (50) + 5312 (51)

TL 6951 8759 and 6963 8776. NCM accession no. 660.965 (Ch. 3.I.1 Figs 79–85)

P66   **Neolithic Bowl**. Flint with sand. Medium. Hard. *Ext.* grey-brown, *core* brown-grey, *int.* grey. Tomalin 315.

P67   **Beaker.** Flint with sand. Fine. Hard. *Ext.* orange, *core* grey, *int.* orange-grey. Comb-impression. Tomalin 7.

P68   **Beaker.** Sand with some flint. Fine. Hard. *Ext.* buff-grey, *core* grey, *int.* buff-grey. Comb impression, FN. Tomalin 1.

P69   **Beaker.** Grog with sand. Medium. Hard. *Ext.* buff-orange, *core* buff-orange, *int.* buff-orange. Incision. Tomalin 11.

P70   **Beaker.** Grog with sand. Fine. Medium. *Ext.* buff, *core* grey, *int.* buff. Comb impression. Tomalin 8.

P71   **Beaker.** Grog with some sand and flint. Medium. *Ext.* buff-orange, *core* orange, *int.* buff-grey. Comb impression, incision. Tomalin 15.

P72   **Beaker.** Sand with grog. Fine. Hard. *Ext.* grey-buff, *core* dark grey, *int.* grey-buff. Comb impression. Tomalin 2.

P73   **Beaker.** Grog with flint and sand. Medium. Medium. *Ext.* orange-buff, *core* orange-brown, *int.* buff. Comb impression. Tomalin 9.

P74   **Beaker.** Grog with sand and some flint. Medium. Medium. *Ext.* orange-buff, *core* grey, *int.* grey-buff. Incision. Tomalin 19.

P75   **Beaker.** Flint with sand. Medium. Hard. *Ext.* buff, *core* grey, *int.* buff-grey. Comb impression.

P76   **Beaker.** Sand with flint. Medium. Hard. *Ext.* orange-grey, *core* grey, *int.* grey-buff. Comb impression.

P77   **Beaker.** Flint with sand. Medium. Hard. *Ext.* buff-orange, *core* orange, *int.* grey-buff. Comb impression. Tomalin 3.

P78   **Beaker.** Grog with flint. Medium. Medium. *Ext.* grey-buff, *core* grey, *int.* buff. Incision. Exterior much abraded.

P79   **Rusticated Beaker.** Grog with sand and some flint. Medium. Medium. *Ext.* buff, *core* orange, *int.* buff. Subsquare impressions.

P80   **Beaker.** Grog with a little sand and flint. Medium. Medium. *Ext.* buff-orange, *core* grey, *int.* buff-grey. Incision. Tomalin 13.

P81   **Beaker.** Grog with sand. Medium. Medium. *Ext.* buff, *core* grey, *int.* buff-grey. Comb impression, FP.

P82   **Rusticated Beaker.** Sand with grog. Fine. Hard. *Ext.* orange-buff, *core* grey, *int.* grey-buff. FP. Tomalin 1.

P83   **Rusticated Beaker.** Flint with sand. Medium. Hard. *Ext.* brown, *core* dark grey, *int.* grey. FP. Tomalin 2.

P84   **Rusticated Beaker.** Grog. Medium. Medium. *Ext.* orange-buff, *core* grey, *int.* grey-buff. FP. Tomalin 3.

P85   **Rusticated Beaker.** Grog with some sand. Coarse. Medium. *Ext.* buff, *core* buff, *int.* buff-grey. FP. Tomalin 9. Pitch uncertain; possibly of bowl-like profile.

P86   **Rusticated Beaker.** Grog with some sand. Coarse. Medium. *Ext.* buff, *core* buff-grey, *int.* buff. FP, FT. Tomalin 13.

P87   **Rusticated Beaker.** Flint with grog and sand. Coarse. Hard. *Ext.* brown-orange, *core* dark grey, *int.* dark grey. FP. Tomalin 6.

P88   **Rusticated Beaker.** Grog with sand and some flint. Medium. Medium. *Ext.* brown, *core* dark grey, *int.* brown-grey. FP. Tomalin 7.

P89   **Rusticated Beaker.** Grog with sand and some flint. Medium. Medium. *Ext.* buff-grey, *core* grey, *int.* grey. FP.

P90   **Rusticated Beaker.** Flint with sand and grog. Medium. Hard. *Ext.* buff-orange, *core* dark grey, *int.* grey. Indeterminate impressions.

P91   **Rusticated Beaker.** Sand with grog and a little flint. Fine. Hard. *Ext.* orange, *core* orange-grey, *int.* orange-grey. FN.

P92   **Rusticated Beaker.** Sand with some grog and flint and a little ?haematite. Fine. Hard. *Ext.* buff, *core* grey, *int.* grey. FN.

P93   **Beaker.** Flint with grog and sand. Coarse. Hard. *Ext.* buff-orange, *core* grey, *int.* grey. Grooving.

P94   **Food Vessel.** Grog. Coarse. Soft, friable. *Ext.* buff, *core* dark grey, *int.* grey-buff. Incision. Tomalin 67, 68.

P95   **Food Vessel.** Grog. Coarse. Soft. *Ext.* buff, *core* grey, *int.* buff. Twisted and whipped cord impression. Tomalin 59. Diameter approx. 300 mm.

P96   **Food Vessel.** Grog. Coarse. Soft. *Ext.* buff-orange, *core* grey, *int.* buff-orange. Twisted cord impression. Tomalin 66.

P97   **Food Vessel.** Grog. Coarse. Soft. *Ext.* buff, *core* grey, *int.* grey-buff. Whipped cord impression. Tomalin 62, 70.

P98   **Indet. Bronze Age.** Grog with a little flint. Medium. Medium. Buff throughout. Indeterminate (? 'barbed wire' impression). Tomalin 14. Decoration extends over rim bevel and interior as well as exterior.

P99   **Collared Urn.** Grog with sand. Medium. Hard. Orange-buff throughout. Twisted cord and other impression.

P100   **Collared Urn.** Grog. Medium. Medium. Buff throughout. Twisted cord impression. Gibson 1982, fig. H. c W. 10: 11.

P101   **Biconical Urn.** Grog with same. Coarse. Hard. *Ext.* grey-buff, *core* grey, *int.* grey-buff. Tomalin 266.

P102   **Biconical Urn.** Grog with sand. Coarse. Medium. *Ext.* grey-buff, *core* dark grey, *int.* grey-buff. FT impression. Tomalin 237.

P103   **Indet. Bronze Age, ?Biconical Urn.** Grog. Coarse. Soft. *Ext.* buff, *core* dark grey, *int.* grey-buff. Tomalin 256, 313.

P104   **Biconical Urn.** Grog with sand. Coarse. Medium. *Ext.* buff, *core* dark grey, *int.* buff. Tomalin 320.

P105   **?Biconical Urn.** Grog with sand. Medium. Medium. *Ext.* grey-buff, *core* grey, *int.* grey-buff. Depression in rim top suggests all-round deckled effect, as on P108.

P106   **Biconical Urn.** Grog with sand. Medium. Medium. *Ext.* buff-grey, *core* Dark grey, *int.* grey-buff. FN impression. Tomalin 253.

P107   **Biconical Urn.** Grog with sand and a little flint. Coarse. Medium. *Ext.* buff, *core* dark grey, *int.* buff. FT impression. Tomalin 312. Gibson 1982, fig. H. c W.7: 14.

P108   **Biconical Urn.** Grog with sand. Medium. Hard. *Ext.* buff, *core* dark grey, *int.* grey-buff. FT impression. Tomalin 236.

P109   **Biconical Urn.** Grog with sand and a little flint. Medium. Hard. *Ext.* grey-buff, *core* dark grey, *int.* grey-buff. Tomalin 238.

P110   **Biconical Urn.** Grog with sand. Coarse. Hard. *Ext.* grey-buff, *core* grey, *int.* buff. Tomalin 247.

P111   **Biconical Urn.** Grog with sand. Coarse. Soft. Buff throughout. Appliqué, FT impression. Tomalin 235. Pitch uncertain.

P112   **Biconical Urn.** Grog with sand. Medium. Hard. *Ext.* orange, *core* buff, *int.* orange-buff.

P113   **Biconical Urn.** Grog with sand. Medium. Hard. *Ext.* buff-orange, *core* grey, *int.* grey-buff. Tomalin 276.

P114   **Biconical Urn.** Grog with sand and a little flint. Coarse. Medium. Buff throughout. Whipped cord impression. Tomalin 519.

P115   **Biconical Urn.** Grog with sand. Medium. Medium. *Ext.* buff-grey, *core* grey, *int.* buff. Tomalin 275.

P116   **Biconical Urn.** Grog with a little sand. Medium. Medium. Orange-buff throughout. Tomalin 272.

P117   **Biconical Urn.** Grog with sand. Coarse. Medium. *Ext.* grey, *core* grey, *int.* buff. FT impression. Tomalin 274.

P118   **Biconical Urn.** Grog with sand. Medium. Hard. *Ext.* buff, *core* dark grey, *int.* buff. Tomalin 277.

P119   **Biconical Urn?.** Grog with sand. Medium. Medium. *Ext.* buff-grey, *core* grey, *int.* grey-buff. FT impression. Tomalin 348.

P120   **Biconical Urn.** Grog with sand. Coarse. Medium. *Ext.* buff, *core* dark grey, *int.* grey-buff. FP, FT impression. Tomalin 270.

P121   **Biconical Urn.** Grog with sand. Coarse. Hard. *Ext.* grey-brown, *core* dark grey, *int.* grey-buff. FP, FT impression. Tomalin 528.

P122   **Indet. Bronze Age.** Grog with a little sand. Medium. Soft. *Ext.* buff, *core* buff-grey, *int.* buff-grey. Tomalin 250.

P123   **Biconical Urn.** Grog with sand. Coarse. Soft. *Ext.* buff, *core* dark grey, *int.* grey-buff. FT impression. Tomalin 268, 271, 371.

P124   **?Biconical Urn.** Sand with some flint. Fine. Hard. *Ext.* grey-buff, *core* dark grey, *int.* grey-buff. Twisted cord impression on rim. Tomalin 355.

P125   **Biconical Urn.** Grog with sand. Coarse. Medium. *Ext.* buff, *core* dark grey, *int.* buff. FN impression. Tomalin 343.

P126   **?Biconical Urn.** Grog with sand. Coarse. Soft. *Ext.* buff, *core* dark grey, *int.* buff. Tomalin 258.

P127   **Biconical Urn.** Sand with grog and a little flint. Medium. Hard. *Ext.* buff, *core* dark grey, *int.* buff-grey. FN impression. Tomalin 264.

P128   **?Biconical Urn.** Grog with sand and a little flint. Coarse. Medium. *Ext.* buff-grey, *core* dark grey, *int.* buff. Appliqué. Tomalin 246.

P129   **?Biconical Urn.** Grog with sand. Coarse. Medium. *Ext.* grey-buff, *core* dark grey, *int.* grey-buff. Appliqué, FT impression. Tomalin 242.

P130   **Biconical Urn.** Grog with sand. Coarse. Medium. *Ext.* buff, *core* dark grey, *int.* grey. FT impression. Tomalin 241.

P131   **Biconical Urn.** Grog with sand. Medium. Medium. *Ext.* grey-buff, *core* dark grey, *int.* grey-buff. Appliqué, FT impression. Tomalin 251.x

P132   **Biconical Urn.** Sand with grog and a little flint. Coarse. Hard. Buff throughout. FT impression. Tomalin 375.

P133   **Biconical Urn.** Grog with sand. Coarse. Medium. *Ext.* buff-grey, *core* dark grey, *int.* grey-buff. FT impression. Tomalin 373.

P134   **Biconical Urn.** Grog. Coarse. Medium. *Ext.* grey-buff, *core* grey, *int.* grey-buff. Appliqué. Tomalin 260.

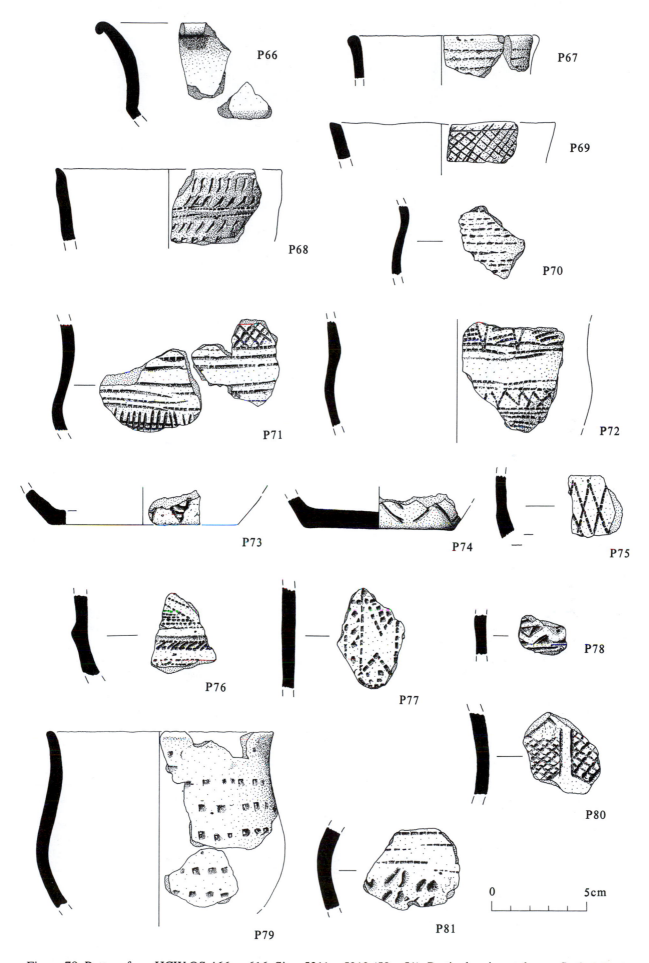

Figure 79 Pottery from HCW OS 466 or 616, Sites 5311 + 5312 (50 + 51). Particulars in catalogue. Scale 1:2

P66
P67
P69
P68
P70
P71
P72
P73
P74
P75
P76
P77
P78
P79
P80
P81

0   5cm

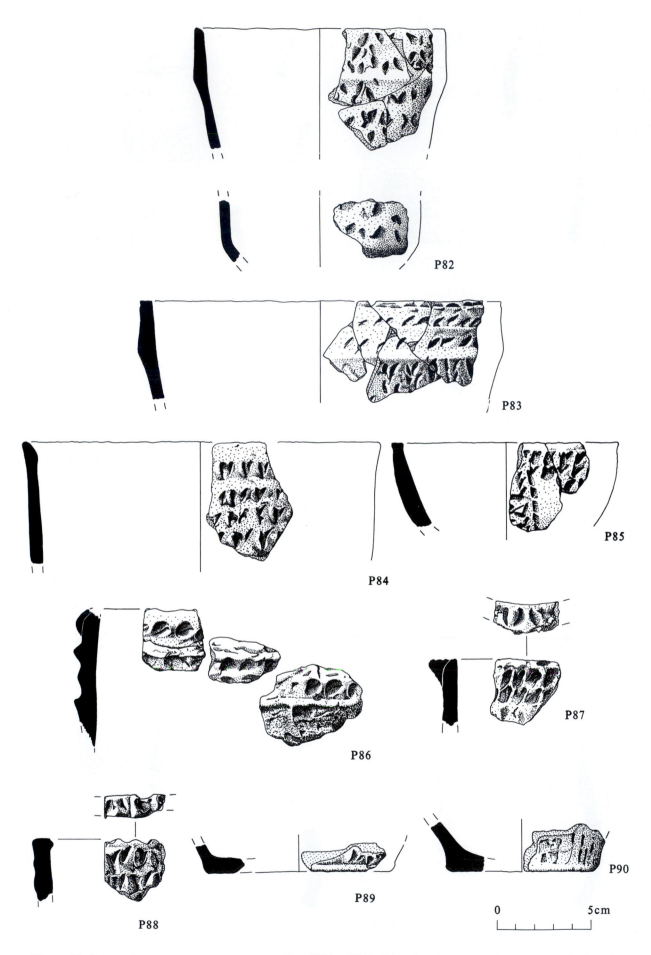

Figure 80 Pottery from HCW OS 466 or 616, Sites 5311 + 5312 (50 + 51). Particulars in catalogue. Scale 1:2

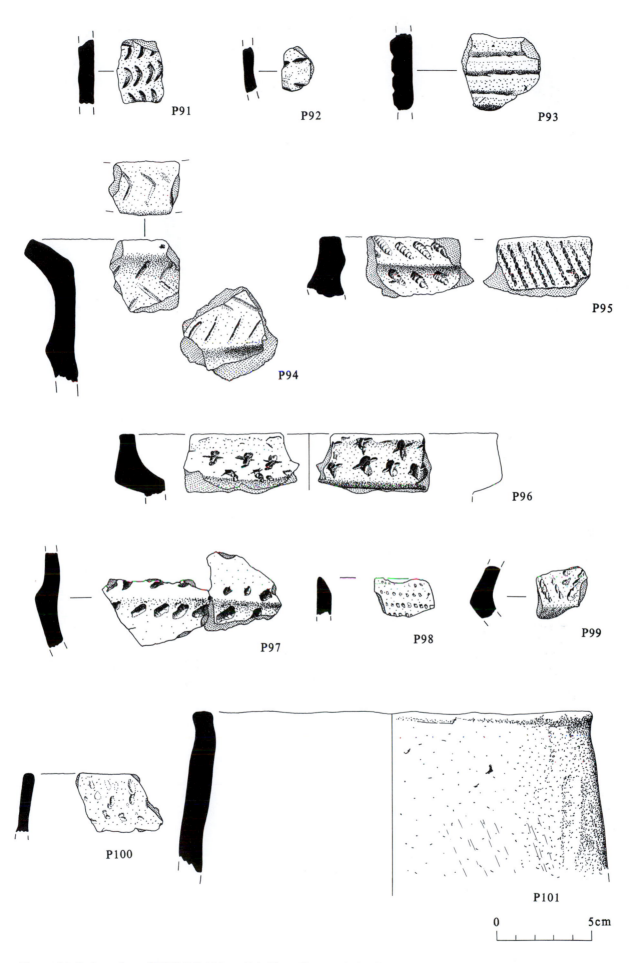

P91

P92

P93

P94

P95

P96

P97

P98

P99

P100

P101

0   5cm

Figure 81 Pottery from HCW OS 466 or 616, Sites 5311 + 5312 (50 +51). Particulars in catalogue. Scale 1:2

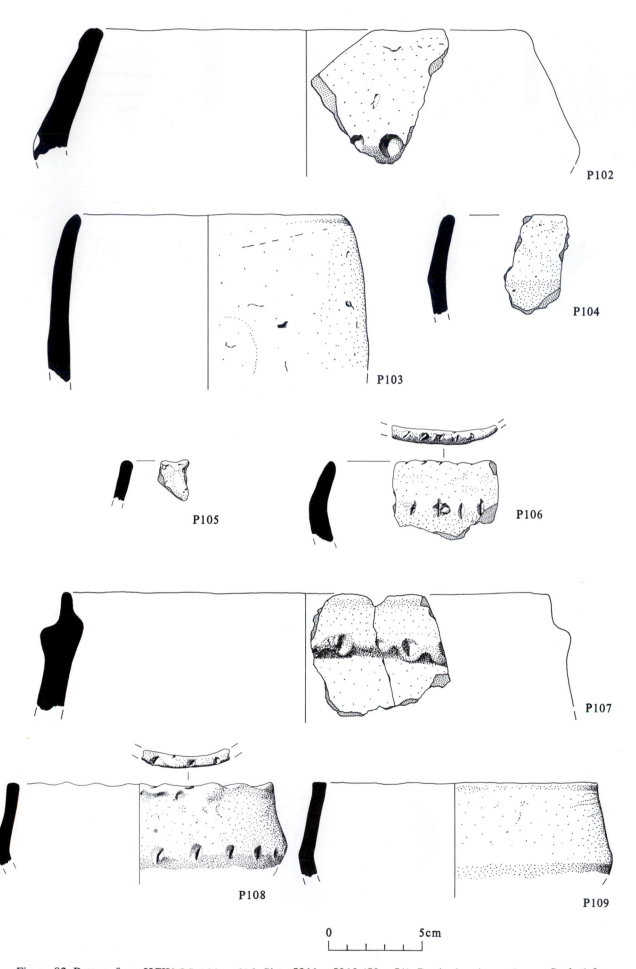

P102

P104

P103

P105

P106

P107

P108

P109

0   5cm

Figure 82 Pottery from HCW OS 466 or 616, Sites 5311 + 5312 (50 + 51). Particulars in catalogue. Scale 1:2

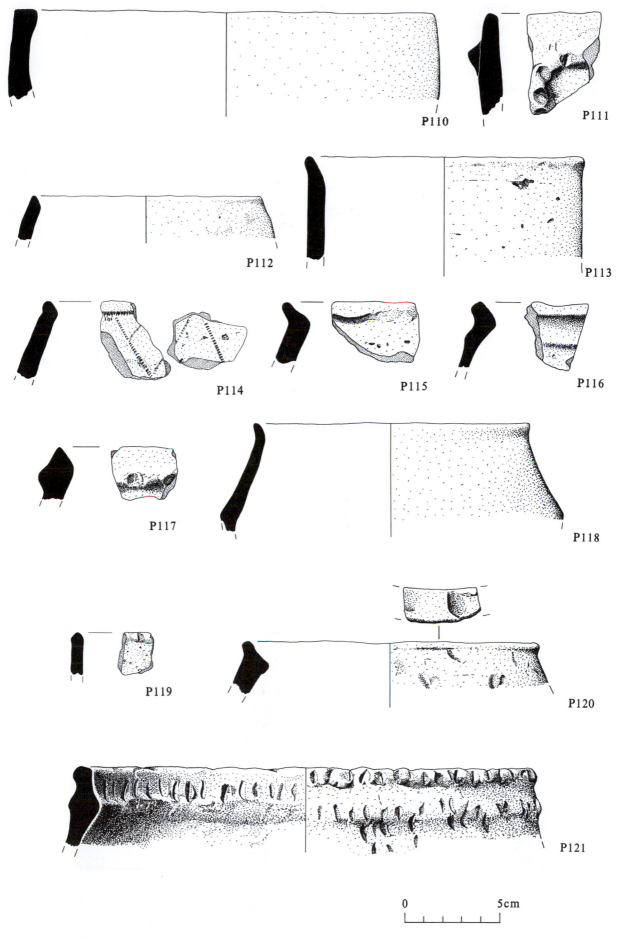

P110

P111

P112

P113

P114

P115

P116

P117

P118

P119

P120

P121

0   5cm

Figure 83 Pottery from HCW OS 466 or 616, Sites 5311 + 5312 (50 + 51). Particulars in catalogue. Scale 1:2

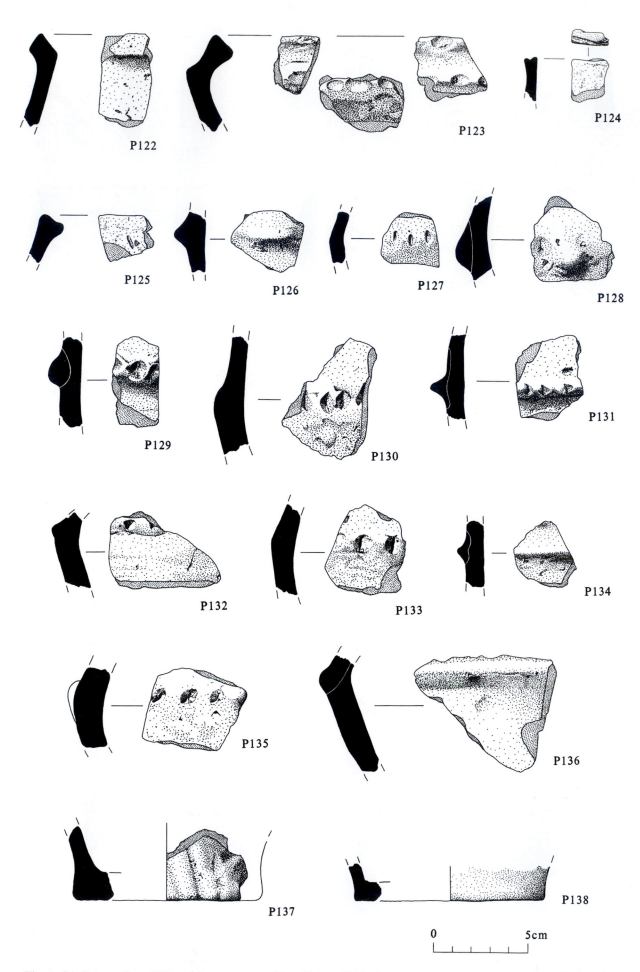

Figure 84 Pottery from HCW OS 466 or 616, Sites 5311 + 5312 (50 + 51). Particulars in catalogue. Scale 1:2

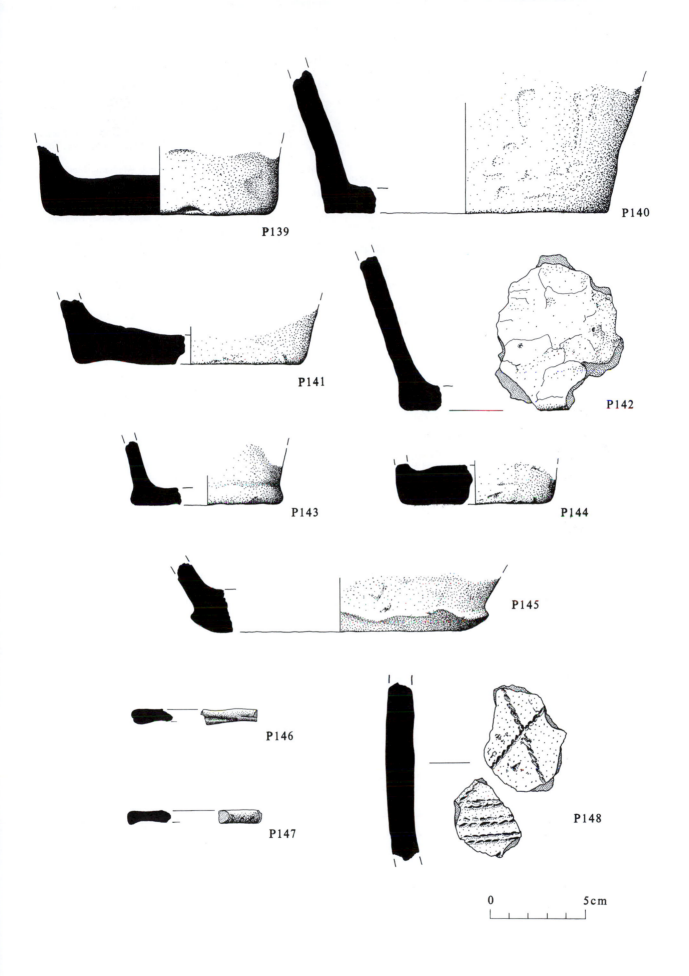

P139

P140

P141

P142

P143

P144

P145

P146

P147

P148

0   5cm

Figure 85 Pottery from HCW OS 466 or 616, Sites 5311 + 5312 (50 + 51). Particulars in catalogue. Scale 1:2

P135 **Biconical Urn.** Sand with grog and a little flint. Coarse. Hard. *Ext.* buff, *core* grey, *int.* grey-buff. FT impression, appliqué. Tomalin 245. Part of applied boss at right-hand end of sherd.

P136 **Biconical Urn.** Grog with sand and a fleck of ?haematite. Coarse. Hard. *Ext.* buff-grey, *core* grey, *int.* grey-buff. Tomalin 257.

P137 **Indet. Bronze Age.** Grog with sand. Coarse. Medium. *Ext.* orange-buff, *core* grey, *int.* grey-orange. Fabric suggests Biconical Urn.

P138 **Indet. Bronze Age.** Sand with grog. Medium. Hard. *Ext.* buff-grey, *core* dark grey, *int.* grey-buff. Fabric suggests Biconical Urn.

P139 **Indet. Bronze Age.** Grog with sand and a little flint and chalk. Coarse. Medium. *Ext.* buff-orange, *core* grey, *int.* grey-buff.

P140 **Indet. Bronze Age.** Grog with sand. Coarse. Soft. *Ext.* buff, *core* grey, *int.* grey-buff.

P141 **Indet. Bronze Age.** Grog with flint. Coarse. Medium. *Ext.* buff, *core* dark grey, *int.* grey-buff. Tomalin 55.

P142 **Indet. Bronze Age.** Grog with a little sand. Coarse. Soft. *Ext.* buff, *core* grey, *int.* grey-buff. Fabric suggests Food vessel or Collared Urn.

P143 **Indet. Bronze Age.** Grog with sand. Medium. Medium. *Ext.* grey-buff, *core* dark grey, *int.* grey-buff. Fabric suggests Biconical Urn.

P144 **Indet. Bronze Age.** Grog with sand. Coarse. Hard. *Ext.* grey-buff, *core* dark grey, *int.* grey-buff. Fabric suggests Biconical Urn.

P145 **Indet. Bronze Age.** Grog with some sand. Coarse. Medium. *Ext.* buff, *core* grey, *int.* grey.

P146 **?Biconical Urn.** Grog with sand. Medium. Medium. *Ext.* buff-grey, *core* grey. Incision. Tomalin 337. Lid.

P147 **?Biconical Urn.** Grog with sand. Medium. Medium. Buff-grey throughout. Tomalin 350. Lid.

P148 **?Biconical Urn.** Grog with sand. Coarse. Medium. *Ext.* buff-grey, *core* dark grey, *int.* grey. Twisted and plaited cord impression. Tomalin 254, 255.

Hockwold cum Wilton OS 614. Site 5373 (22)
TL 6930 8760 (Ch. 3.I.2)
A. NCM accession no. 477.961 (Figs 86–87)

P149 **Biconical Urn.** Grog with sand. Medium. Hard. *Ext.* grey-buff, *core* dark grey, *int.* grey-buff. Tomalin 575.

P150 **Biconical Urn.** Grog with sand. Medium. Medium. *Ext.* buff-grey, *core* dark grey, *int.* grey-buff. FT impression. Tomalin 556. ?Organic residue n interior.

P151 **Biconical Urn.** Grog with sand. Coarse. medium. *Ext.* grey-buff, *core* dark grey, *int.* grey. FT impression. Tomalin 555.

P152 **Indet. Bronze Age.** Grog with sand. Medium. Hard. *Ext.* orange-buff, *core* orange, *int.* grey-buff. Tomalin 579. Fabric suggests Biconical Urn.

P153 **Biconical Urn.** Grog with sand. Coarse. Medium. *Ext.* grey-buff, *core* grey, *int.* grey-buff. FT impression. Tomalin 564.

P154 **?Biconical Urn.** Grog with sand. Medium. Hard. *Ext.* buff-grey, *core* grey-buff, *int.* grey buff. Tomalin 554.

P155 **Indet. Bronze Age.** Sand with grog. Medium. Hard. *Ext.* buff-orange, *core* buff-orange, *int.* buff-grey. Appliqué. Tomalin 562. Approximately a quarter of circumference survives: there may have been more than the one applied lug; fabric compatible with Biconical Urn; ?organic residue on interior towards base.

P156 **Biconical Urn.** Grog with sand. Coarse. Medium. *Ext.* grey-buff, *core* grey, *int.* grey-buff.

P157 **Biconical Urn.** Grog with sand. Coarse. Soft. *Ext.* buff, *core* grey, *int.* buff.

P158 **Biconical Urn.** Grog with a little sand and a fleck of ?haematite. Coarse. Medium. *Ext.* buff-orange, *core* buff-grey, *int.* buff-orange. Appliqué. Tomalin 581.

P159 **Biconical Urn.** Grog with sand. Coarse. Medium. Grey-buff throughout. FN and FT impression. Tomalin 563.

P160 **?Biconical Urn.** Grog with sand. Medium. Medium. *Ext.* buff-orange, *core* grey, *int.* buff-orange. Tomalin 583.

P161 **Indet. Bronze Age.** Grog with a little sand. Coarse. Soft. *Ext.* buff-grey, *core* grey, *int.* buff-grey.

P162 **Biconical Urn.** Grog with sand. Coarse. Medium. *Ext.* grey-buff, *core* grey, *int.* grey-buff. FT impression. Tomalin 592.

P163 **Biconical Urn.** Grog with sand. Coarse. Medium. *Ext.* buff, *core* grey, *int.* grey-buff. FT impression. Tomalin 591.

P164 **Biconical Urn.** Grog. Coarse. Soft. *Ext.* buff-grey, *core* buff, *int.* buff-grey. FT impression. Tomalin 599.

P165 **Biconical Urn.** Sand with grog and flint. Medium. hard. *Ext.* grey-buff, *core* orange, *int.* grey-buff. FT impression. Tomalin 595.

P166 **Biconical Urn.** Grog with sand. Medium. Medium. *Ext.* grey-buff, *core* dark grey, *int.* grey-buff. Tomalin 584.

P167 **Biconical Urn.** Grog with a little sand. Coarse. Soft. *Ext.* buff, *core* buff-orange, *int.* buff. Appliqué. Tomalin 590.

P168 **Indet. Bronze Age.** Grog with sand. Coarse. Medium. *Ext.* buff-grey, *core* dark grey, *int.* grey.

P169 **Indet. Bronze Age.** Grog with sand. Medium. Medium. *Ext.* buff-grey, *core* dark grey, *int.* buff-grey. Fabric suggests Biconical Urn.

P170 **Indet. Bronze Age.** Grog with sand. Coarse. Medium. *Ext.* grey-buff, *core* dark grey, *int.* dark grey. Fabric suggests Biconical Urn; ?organic residue on interior.

P171 **Indet. Bronze Age.** Grog with sand and a fleck of ?haematite. Coarse. Medium. *Ext.* buff-grey, *core* dark grey, *int.* grey-buff. Base with internal finger-tipping.

B. NCM accession no. 673.964 (Figs 87–88)

P172 **Beaker.** Grog with sand and a little flint. Fine. Medium. *Ext.* buff-grey, *core* buff, *int.* buff-grey. Comb impression.

P173 **?Indet. Bronze Age.** Sand with grog. Fine. Hard. *Ext.* buff, *core* grey, *int.* buff.

P174 **Rusticated Beaker.** Sand with grog and flint. Medium. Hard. Grey throughout. FP

P175 **Beaker.** Grog with sand. Medium. Medium. *Ext.* buff, *core* grey, *int.* grey-buff. Incision.

P176 **Beaker.** Grog with sand and flint. Medium. Medium. Buff throughout. Incision, FN impression.

P177 **Biconical Urn.** Grog with sand. Coarse. Soft. Buff throughout.

P178 **Biconical Urn.** Grog. Coarse. Soft. *Ext.* buff, *core* grey, *int.* buff.

P179 **Rusticated Beaker.** Grog with sand. Fine. Medium. Medium. *Ext.* buff, *core* grey, *int.* grey-buff. FP. Tomalin 18.

P180 **Beaker.** Grog with sand. Fine. Medium. Buff-orange throughout. Comb-impression. White filler remains in impressions.

P181 **Rusticated Beaker.** Grog with sand and flint. Medium. Hard. *Ext.* buff, *core* dark grey, *int.* dark grey. FP. Tomalin 20. Minimum diameter 220mm; ?organic residue on interior.

P182 **?Biconical Urn.** Grog. Coarse. Soft. *Ext.* buff, *core* grey, *int.* buff.

P183 **?Biconical Urn.** Grog with sand and flint. Coarse. Medium. *Ext.* grey-buff, *core* dark grey, *int.* buff. FN impression. Tomalin 21. ? Beginning of boss or lug at base of sherd.

P184 **Beaker.** Grog with a fleck of ?haematite. Medium. Medium. *Ext.* orange-buff, *core* grey, *int.* buff. Incision, FP.

P185 **Beaker.** Sand with grog. Medium. Hard. *Ext.* buff-brown, *core* grey, *int.* buff-brown. Incision.

P186 **Beaker.** Sand with grog. Fine. Hard. *Ext.* buff-grey, *core* dark grey, *int.*, grey-buff. Comb-impression.

P187 **Beaker.** Flint with sand. Fine. Hard. *Ext.* buff-grey, *core* buff-orange, *int.* buff-grey. Comb impression.

P188 **Beaker.** Grog with flint. Medium. Medium. *Ext.* buff-orange, *core* buff-orange, *int.* buff. Comb impression.

P189 **Beaker.** Grog with sand. Medium. Medium. *Ext.* buff orange, *core* buff-orange, *int.* grey-buff. Comb-impression.

P190 **Rusticated Beaker.** Grog with sand. Medium. Hard. *Ext.* orange, *core* grey, *int.* grey-orange. FP.

P191 **Rusticated Beaker.** Grog with sand. Medium. Medium. *Ext.* buff, *core* grey, *int.* buff-grey. FN impression.

P192 **Rusticated Beaker.** Sand with grog and flint. Medium. Medium. *Ext.* buff, *core* grey, *int.* buff-grey. FP.

P193 **Rusticated Beaker.** Sand with flint. Medium. Hard. *Ext.* buff-grey, *core* dark grey, *int.* dark grey. Sub-triangular impressions.

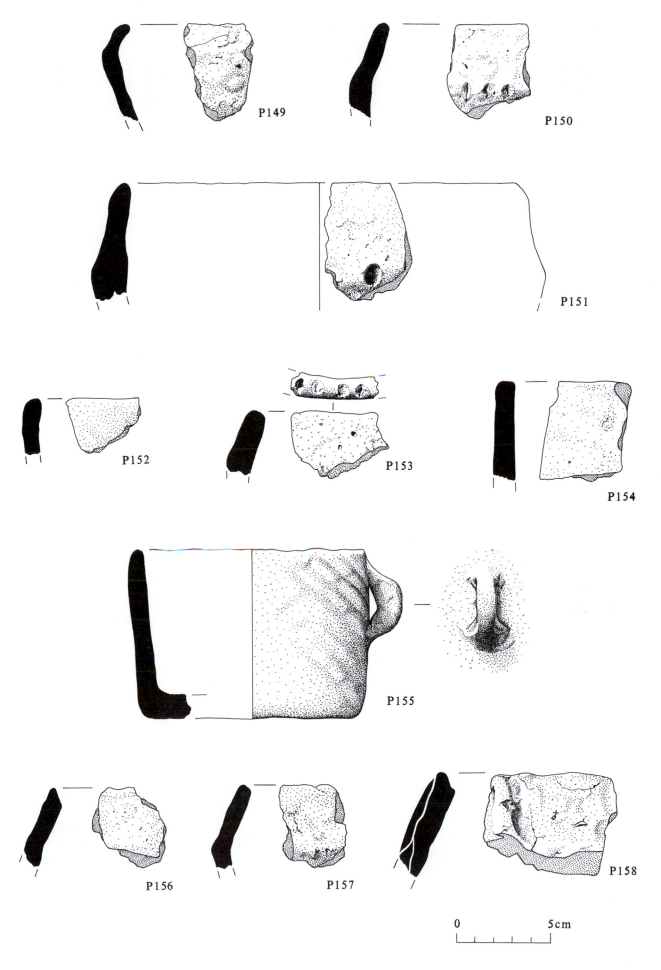

P149

P150

P151

P152

P153

P154

P155

P156

P157

P158

0   5cm

Figure 86 Pottery from HCW OS 614, Site 5373 (22). Particulars in catalogue. Scale 1:2

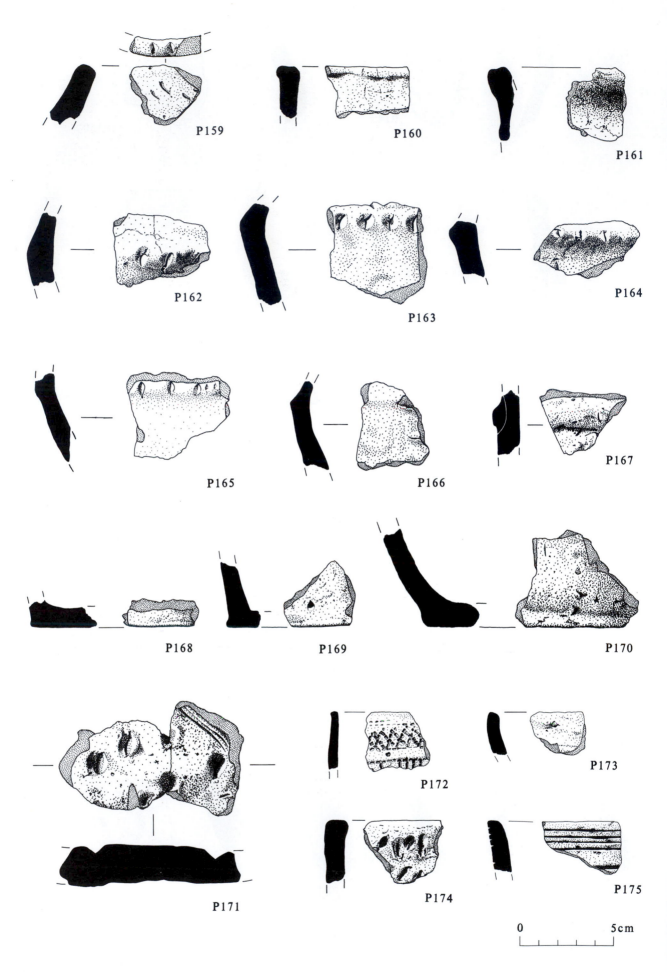

P159

P160

P161

P162

P163

P164

P165

P166

P167

P168

P169

P170

P171

P172

P173

P174

P175

0   5cm

Figure 87 Pottery from HCW OS 614, Site 5373 (22). Particulars in catalogue. Scale 1:2

136

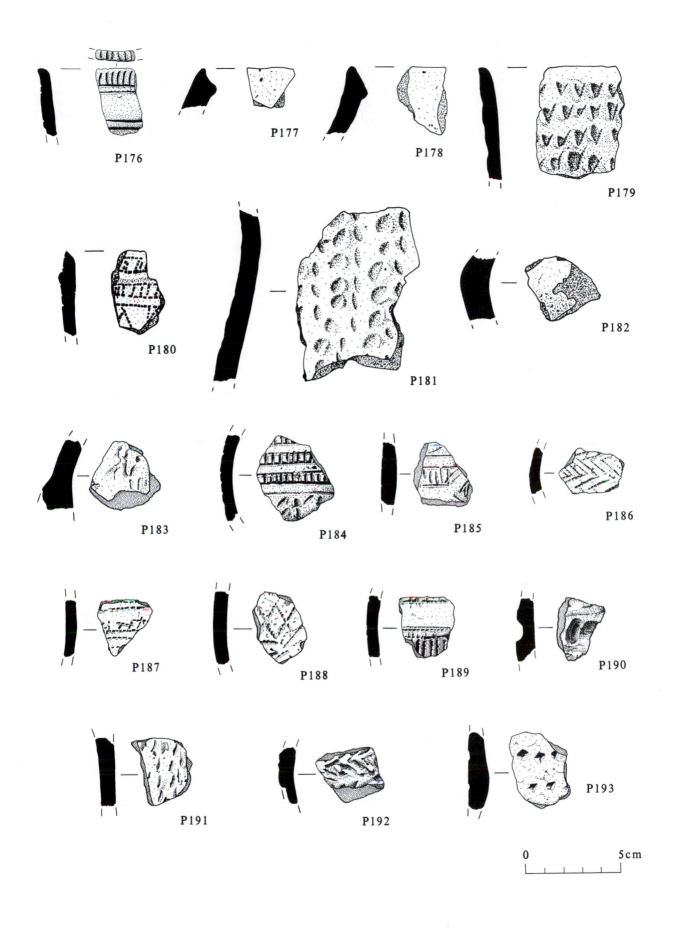

Figure 88 Pottery from HCW OS 614, Site 5373 (22). Particulars in catalogue. Scale 1:2

Hockwold cum Wilton OS 613 + 614. Dykeside. Site 5308/c4 (61/68)

TL 6932 8778. NCM accession no. 511.964, 205.965
(Ch.3.I.6 Figs 89–94)

Notes: Where no context is given, pottery is from site 61, the ungridded, western part of the site in Hockwold cum Wilton 613 excavated in 1964 (Ch. 3.I.5).

Nine Beakers illustrated by Bamford (1982) from Sites 5308/c1 and c3 (63 and 69) include sherds from this site (fig. 14: P63.022, P69.023; fig. 15: P63.048; fig. 16: P63.089, P63.092; fig. 17: P63.100; fig. 20: P63.114; fig. 21: P63.126, P63.140). A further sherd illustrated by her for comparative purposes (fig. 24: A) is also from here.

P194 **Neolithic Bowl (Mildenhall Ware).** Sand and flint. Fine. Hard. *Ext.* black-brown, *core* brown, *int.* black-brown. Channelling. Abraded, ? once burnished.

P195 **Neolithic Bowl.** Flint with sand. Medium. Hard. *Ext.* black-brown, *core* brown, *int.* black-brown.

P196 **Beaker.** Grog with sand. Medium. Medium. *Ext.* orange, *core* buff, *int.* orange-buff. Incision.

P197 **Beaker.** Grog with sand and flint. Medium. Medium. *Ext.* orange-buff, *core* grey, *int.* buff. Comb impression.

P198 **Beaker.** Sand with grog and flint. Fine. Hard. *Ext.* buff-grey, *core* dark grey, *int.* buff-grey. Comb impression. Site 61 and area *5*.

P199 **Beaker.** Grog with sand and flint. Medium. Medium. *Ext.* buff, *core* dark grey, *int.* buff. Comb impression. Abraded.

P200 **Beaker.** Grog with sand. Medium. Medium. *Ext.* orange-buff, *core* dark grey, *int.* grey-buff. Incision.

P201 **Beaker.** Grog with sand and flint. Medium. Hard. *Ext.* buff, *core* grey, *int.* buff. Comb impression.

P202 **Beaker.** Grog with sand. Medium. Hard. *Ext.* brown, *core* grey, *int.* orange-brown. Comb impression.

P203 **Beaker.** Sand with flint. Fine. Hard. *Ext.* orange, *core* grey, *int.* grey-orange. Comb impression.

P204 **?Beaker.** Sand with flint. Medium. Hard. *Ext.* orange-buff, *core* grey, *int.* grey.

P205 **Rusticated Beaker.** Sand with grog. Medium. Hard. *Ext.* brown, *core* grey, *int.* brown. FN.

P206 **Rusticated Beaker.** Sand with flint. Medium. Hard. *Ext.* buff-brown, *core* grey, *int.* buff-grey. FT impression, FP. Site 61 and area *8*. Gibson 1982, fig. H. c W. 5: 35.

P207 **Food Vessel.** Grog with a little sand. Coarse. Soft. *Ext.* buff, *core* grey, *int.* buff. Whipped cord impression.

P208 **Indet. Bronze Age.** Grog with sand and flint. Coarse. Medium. *Ext.* buff, *core* dark grey, *int.* buff. Twisted cord impression.

P209 **Biconical Urn.** Grog with sand. Medium. Medium. *Ext.* grey-buff, *core* dark grey, *int.* grey-buff. Comb impression. Pitch uncertain.

P210 **Indet. Bronze Age.** Grog with a little sand. Medium. Medium. *Ext.* grey-buff, *core* grey, *int.* grey-buff. Appliqué.

P211 **Indet. Bronze Age.** Grog. Coarse. Soft. *Ext.* buff, *core* grey, *int.* grey-buff. Twisted cord impression.

P212 **Indet. Bronze Age.** Grog with a little flint. Coarse. Soft. Buff throughout. Deckled rim.

P213 **?Biconical Urn.** Grog with sand. Medium. Medium. *Ext.* buff, *core* grey, *int.* buff-grey. Pitch uncertain.

P214 **Indet.** Flint with grog. Fine. Hard. *Ext.* grey-buff, *core* grey, *int.* grey.

P215 **Indet. Bronze Age.** Grog. Coarse. Soft. *Ext.* buff, *core* dark grey, *int.* grey-buff.

P216 **Food Vessel.** Grog. Coarse. Soft. *Ext.* buff, *core* dark grey, *int.* buff. Subsquare impressions. Areas *1, 2, 8* and Site 5308/c3 (69) area *11*. Tomalin 95. Gibson 1982, fig. H. c W. 9: 18, 24, 26; Bamford 1982, fig. 28: k.

P217 **Beaker.** Sand with flint. Fine. Hard. *Ext.* buff, *core* grey, *int.* buff. Comb impression. Areas *1, 3*.

P218 **Beaker.** Sand with flint. Fine. Hard. *Ext.* orange-buff, *core* grey, *int.* grey-buff. Comb and other impression. Area *3*.

P219 **Beaker.** Grog with sand and flint. Medium. Medium. Buff-orange throughout. Incision. Area *3*.

P220 **Rusticated Beaker.** Flint with sand. Medium. Hard. *Ext.* brown, *core* dark grey, *int.* grey-brown. FP. Area *3*.

P221 Rusticated Beaker. Flint with sand. Medium. Hard. *Ext.* brown, *core* dark grey, *int.* brown. FT impression. Area *3*.

P222 **?Food Vessel.** Grog. Medium. Medium. *Ext.* buff-orange, *core* dark grey, *int.* buff-orange. Incision. Area *3*. Abraded; pitch uncertain.

P223 **Beaker.** Sand with flint. Medium. Hard. *Ext.* buff-orange, *core* grey, *int.* buff. Comb impression. Area *7*. Gibson 1982, fig. H. c W. 9: 6.

P224 **?Food Vessel.** Grog with sand. Medium. Medium. *Ext.* buff-grey, *core* dark grey, *int.* grey-buff. Twisted cord impression. Area *8*. Pitch uncertain.

P225 **Beaker.** Sand with grog and a little flint. Medium. Hard. Buff-orange throughout. Incision. Area *8*. Handle.

P226 **Indet. Bronze Age.** Grog with sand and a little flint. Medium. Medium. *Ext.* orange-buff, *core* grey, *int.* buff. Area *8*.

P227 **Beaker.** Sand with a little flint. Medium. Hard. Buff throughout. Comb and FN impression. Area *1, 1967*.

P228 **Beaker.** Flint with sand. Medium. Hard. *Ext.* pink-buff, *core* grey, *int.* grey-buff. Comb impression. Area *1*.

P229 **Food Vessel.** Grog with sand. Coarse. Soft. *Ext.* buff, *core* grey, *int.* grey-buff. Twisted cord impression. Area *1, 1967*. Gibson 1982, fig. H. c W. 10: 2.

P230 **Indet. Bronze Age.** Grog with a little sand. Medium. Medium. *Ext.* buff, *core* buff-grey, *int.* buff. Site 61 and area *1*.

P231 Indet. Bronze Age. Grog. Coarse. Soft. *Ext.* buff, *core* grey, *int.* buff-grey. Area *1*.

P232 **Beaker.** Grog with flint. Medium. Medium. *Ext.* buff, *core* grey, *int.* grey-buff. Incision. Site 61 and area *3*.

P233 **Beaker.** Grog with flint. Medium. Medium. *Ext.* buff, *core* grey, *int.* buff-grey. Incision, 'barbed wire' impression, (cockle?) shell impression. Site 61, area *3*.

P234 **Beaker.** Sand with a little flint and a fleck of ?haematite. Fine. Hard. *Ext.* orange, *core* dark grey, *int.* grey-buff. Comb and other impression.

P235 **Indet. Bronze Age.** Sand with grog. Coarse. Hard. *Ext.* buff, *core* grey, *int.* grey-buff. Incision, (?cord) impression. Abraded.

P236 **Beaker.** Sand with grog, flint and a fleck of ?haematite. Medium. hard. *Ext.* buff-orange, *core* grey, *int.* grey-buff. Incision., 'barbed wire' impression. Areas *2, 5, 7*.

P237 **Indet. Bronze Age.** Grog with flint. Coarse. Soft. *Ext.* buff, *core* grey, *int.* buff. Grooving. Area *2*. Unillustrated joining sherd from site 61; ?from rim bevel of large Food Vessel.

P238 **Rusticated Beaker.** Sand with flint. Medium. Hard. *Ext.* buff-orange, *core* grey, *int.* buff-orange. FP. Area *4*.

P239 **Rusticated Beaker.** Flint with sand and grog. Coarse. Hard. *Ext.* buff, *core* grey, *int.* grey. FP.

P240 **Rusticated Beaker.** Grog with sand and flint. Medium. Medium. *Ext.* orange-buff, *core* grey, *int.* grey-buff. FN impression. Abraded.

P241 **Rusticated Beaker.** Grog with sand and flint. Medium. Medium. *Ext.* buff, *core* dark grey, *int.* buff. FN impression.

P242 **Rusticated Beaker.** Sand with flint. Medium. Hard. *Ext.* orange-buff, *core* dark brown, *int.* buff. FN impression.

P243 **Food Vessel.** Grog with sand. Medium. Medium. *Ext.* buff-orange, *core* buff, *int.* buff-orange. Impression. Area *2*. Tomalin 96. Gibson 1982, fig. H. c W. 9: 17.

P244 **Food Vessel.** Grog with sand. Coarse. Soft. *Ext.* buff, *core* grey, *int.* grey-buff. Twisted cord and other impression. Tomalin 41.

P245 **Food Vessel.** Grog with sand. Coarse. Soft. *Ext.* buff, *core* dark grey, *int.* dark grey. Impression. Tomalin 38.

P246 **Food Vessel.** Grog with sand. Coarse. Soft. *Ext.* buff, *core* grey, *int.* buff-grey. Twisted cord impression. Tomalin 48. Gibson 1982, fig. H. c W. 10: 1.

P247 **Food Vessel.** Grog with sand. Medium. Medium. *Ext.* buff-grey, *core* dark grey, *int.* buff-grey. Impression. Tomalin 36.

P248 **Food Vessel.** Grog with sand. Coarse. Medium. *Ext.* buff-grey, *core* grey, *int.* buff-grey. Impression. Tomalin 40.

P249 **Food Vessel.** Grog with flint. Coarse. Medium. *Ext.* buff, *core* grey, *int.* buff. Twisted cord and other impression. Site 61 and Site 5308/c3 (69) area *11*. Tomalin 42, 53.

P250 **Food Vessel.** Grog with sand. Coarse. Soft. *Ext.* orange-buff, *core* dark grey, *int.* buff-grey. Tomalin 35.

P251 **Food Vessel.** Grog with sand. Coarse, friable. *Ext.* buff, *core* dark grey, *int.* grey-buff. Twisted cord impression. Tomalin 39.

P252 **Food Vessel.** Grog with sand. Medium. Medium. *Ext.* buff, *core* grey, *int.* grey-buff. Twisted cord and other impression. Tomalin 46.

P253 **Food Vessel.** Grog. Coarse. Soft. *Ext.* buff, *core* buff-grey, *int.* buff. twisted cord impression. Tomalin 47.

P254 **Food Vessel.** Grog. Coarse. Soft. Buff throughout. Twisted cord and other impression. Tomalin 49. Gibson 1982, fig. H. c W. 10: 10.

P255 **Food Vessel.** Grog with sand. Coarse. Medium. Buff-grey throughout. Twisted cord impression. Tomalin 45. Gibson 1982, fig. H. c W. 10: 8.

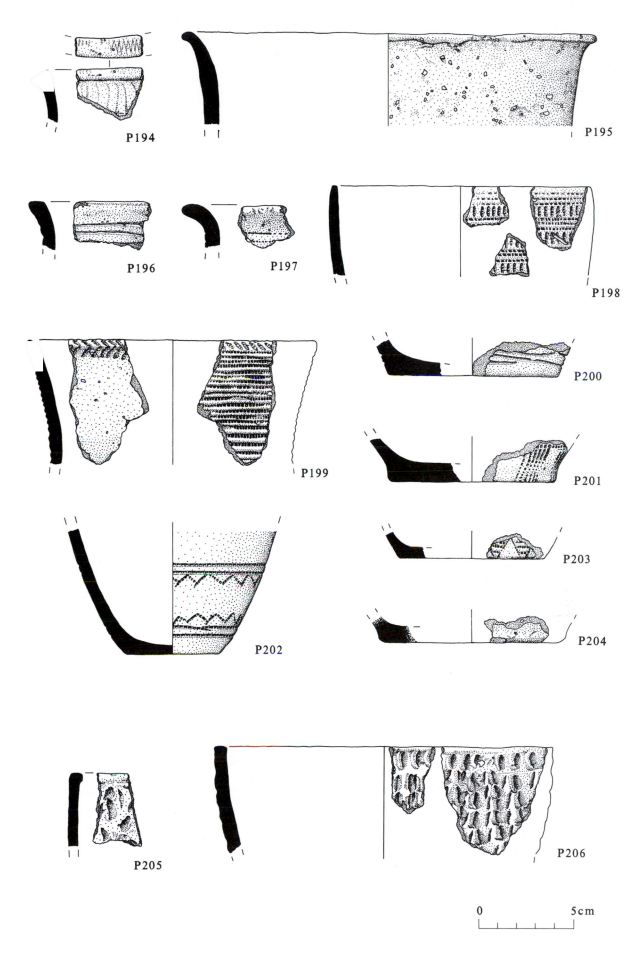

P194

P195

P196

P197

P198

P199

P200

P201

P202

P203

P204

P205

P206

0   5cm

Figure 89 Pottery from HCW OS 613 + 614, Site 5308/c4 (61/68). Particulars in catalogue. Scale 1:2

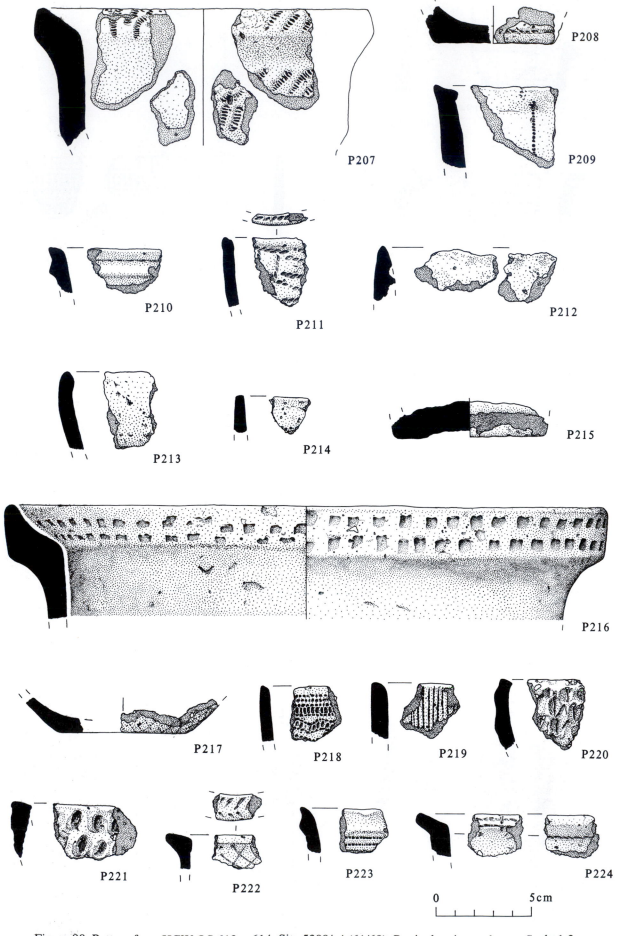

Figure 90 Pottery from HCW OS 613 + 614, Site 5308/c4 (61/68). Particulars in catalogue. Scale 1:2

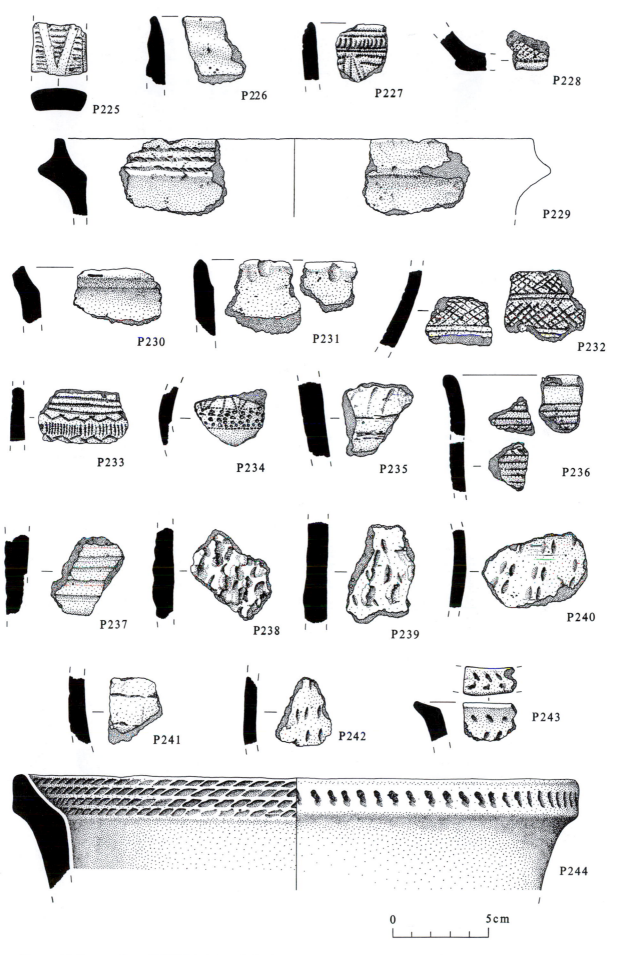

P225

P226

P227

P228

P229

P230

P231

P232

P233

P234

P235

P236

P237

P238

P239

P240

P241

P242

P243

P244

0   5cm

Figure 91 Pottery from HCW OS 613 + 614, Site 5308/c4 (61/68). Particulars in catalogue. Scale 1:2

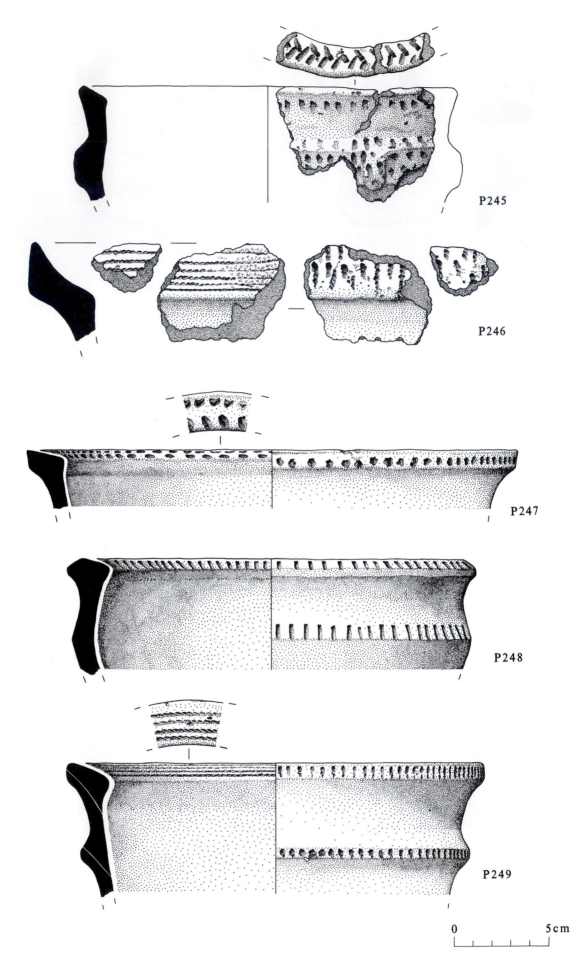

P245

P246

P247

P248

P249

0   5 cm

Figure 92 Pottery from HCW OS 613 + 614, Site 5308/c4 (61/68). Particulars in catalogue. Scale 1:2

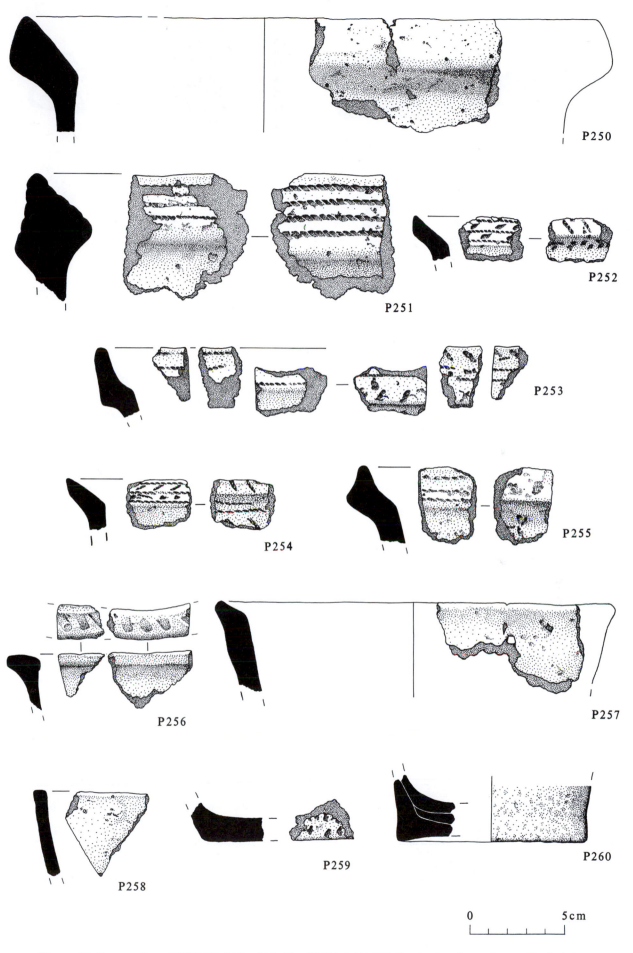

Figure 93 Pottery from HCW OS 613 + 614, Site 5308/c4 (61/68). Particulars in catalogue. Scale 1:2

143

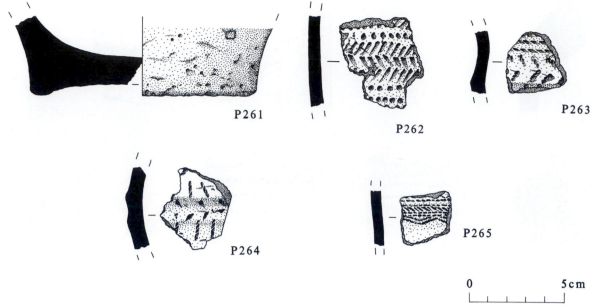

P261

P262

P263

P264

P265

0   5cm

Figure 94 Pottery from HCW OS 613 + 614, Site 5308/c4 (61/68). Particulars in catalogue. Scale 1:2

P256 **?Food Vessel.** Grog with sand. Medium. Medium. *Ext.* pink-buff, *core* dark grey, *int.* buff. Indeterminate impression. Tomalin 37, 43.

P257 **Indet. Bronze Age.** Sand with grog and a little flint. Medium. Hard. *Ext.* buff-orange, *core* grey, *int.* grey-buff. Tomalin 44.

P258 **Indet. Bronze Age.** Sand with grog. Fine. Hard. *Ext.* buff-grey, *core* dark grey, *int.* buff-grey.

P259 **Indet. Bronze Age.** Grog with sand. Coarse. Soft. *Ext.* grey-buff, *core* dark grey, *int.* buff. Indet. impression.

P260 **Indet. Bronze Age.** Grog. Coarse. Soft. *Ext.* buff-grey, *core* grey, *int.* buff.

P261 **Indet. Bronze Age.** Grog with sand. Coarse. Soft. *Ext.* buff, *core* dark grey, *int.* buff-grey. Tomalin 55.

P262 **Indet. Bronze Age, ?Food vessel.** Grog with sand. Coarse. Medium. *Ext.* buff-grey, *core* dark grey, *int.* grey. Indet. impressions. Tomalin 57. Gibson 1982, fig. H. c W. 3: 12.

P263 **Indet. Bronze Age. ?Food Vessel.** Grog with sand. Coarse. Medium. *Ext.* buff-grey, *core* dark grey, *int.* grey. Twisted cord impression. Gibson 1982, fig. H. c W. 11: 5.

P264 **Indet. Bronze Age, ?Food Vessel.** Grog with sand. Coarse. Medium. *Ext.* buff, *core* dark grey, *int.* buff. Twisted cord and other impression. Gibson 1982, fig. H. c W. 11: 3.

P265 **Beaker.** Sand. Fine. Hard. *Ext.* buff, *core* dark grey, *int.* buff. Comb and other impression.

Hockwold cum Wilton OS 614. Site 5332 (66)
TL 6934 8771. NCM accession no. 334.967 (Ch. 3.I.7 Fig. 95)

P266 **Biconical Urn.** Grog with sand. Medium. Medium. *Ext.* buff-grey, *core* dark grey, *int.* grey. ?Single FT impression, ?accidental damage. Tomalin 793.

P267 **Biconical Urn.** Sand and grog. Medium. Hard. *Ext.* orange-buff, *core* dark grey, *int.* buff. Tomalin 792.

P268 **Biconical Urn.** Grog with sand. Coarse. Medium. *Ext.* buff, *core* grey, *int.* buff. Tomalin 794.

P269 **Biconical Urn.** Grog with sand and a little flint. Medium. Hard. *Ext.* buff-grey, *core* dark grey, *int.* grey-buff. Tomalin 790.

P270 **Biconical Urn.** Grog with sand and a little flint. Coarse. Hard. *Ext.* buff, *core* grey, *int.* buff. FT impression. Tomalin 789.

P271 **Biconical Urn.** Grog with some sand. Fine. Hard. *Ext.* buff, *core* dark grey, *int.* grey-buff. Incision, FN impression. Tomalin 789. 'Mildenhall Ware' as defined by Clark (1936, 40–41).

P272 **Biconical Urn.** Grog with sand. Medium. Hard. *Ext.* grey-buff, *core* dark grey, *int.* dark grey. Slight ?burnish on neck, if it is not sand polish. Tomalin 791.

P273 **Biconical Urn.** Grog with sand and flint. Hard. *Ext.* grey-buff, *core* dark grey, *int.* buff. Tomalin 785.

P274 **Biconical Urn.** Grog with sand. Medium. Hard. *Ext.* grey, *core* dark grey, *int.* grey-buff. Tomalin 787. Rim apparently deckled.

P275 **Biconical Urn.** Grog with sand. Medium. Medium. *Ext.* buff-grey, *core* grey, *int.* grey-buff. ?Single FT impression, ?accidental damage. Tomalin 796.

P276 **?Biconical Urn.** Grog with sand and a little flint. Coarse. Hard. *Ext.* grey-buff, *core* dark grey, *int.* dark grey. Indet. impression.

P277 **Biconical Urn.** Grog with sand and a little flint. FT impression. Tomalin 798.

P278 **Biconical Urn.** Grog and sand. Medium. Hard. *Ext.* buff, *core* dark grey, *int.* dark grey. Tomalin 799.

P279 **Biconical Urn.** Grog and sand. Medium. Hard. *Ext.* buff, *core* dark grey, *int.* dark grey. Tomalin 801.

P280 **Indet. Bronze Age.** Grog with sand. Coarse. Soft. *Ext.* buff, *core* dark grey, *int.* dark grey. Of coarser, softer, more friable fabric than most of pottery from site.

P281 **Beaker.** Sand with flint. Fine. hard. *Ext.* orange-brown, *core* buff, *int.* buff. Comb impression.

P282 **Beaker.** Sand with flint. Fine. Hard. *Ext.* buff, *core* buff, *int.* grey. Comb impression.

Hockwold cum Wilton OS 614. Site 5333 (95/97)
TL 6934 8771. NCM accession no. 334.967 (Ch. 3.I.9 Figs 96–98)

Note: Where no context is given, pottery is from site 95, an initial discovery in the ploughsoil which led to the subsequent excavation of site 97, an area divided into 4ft squares (Ch. 3.I.9).

P283 **Rusticated Beaker.** Grog with a little sand. Medium. Medium. *Ext.* buff, *core* grey, *int.* grey-buff. FP. Site 95 and squares *2, 3, 5, 6, 8.* Gibson 1982, fig. H. c W. 3: 8.

P284 **Beaker.** Sand with flint. Fine. Hard. *Ext.* buff, *core* dark grey, *int.* grey-buff. Comb impression.

P285 **Beaker.** Sand with flint. Fine. Hard. *Ext.* grey-buff, *core* dark grey, *int.* grey-buff. FN and other impression.

P286 **Beaker.** Sand with flint. Fine. Hard. *Ext.* grey-buff, *core* dark grey, *int.* grey. Comb and FN impression.

P287 **Beaker.** Sand with grog and flint. Medium. Hard. Buff-grey throughout. Comb and FN impression.

P288 **Rusticated Beaker.** Sand. Medium. Hard. *Ext.* buff, *core* grey, *int.* buff-grey. FN impression.

P289 **Beaker.** Grog with sand. Medium. Medium. *Ext.* buff-orange, *core* grey, *int.* buff. Incision.

P290 **Beaker.** Sand with grog. Fine. Hard. *Ext.* buff, *core* dark grey, *int.* buff-grey. Comb and FN impression. Square *1.*

P291 **Rusticated Beaker.** Grog with sand. Medium. Medium. *Ext.* buff, *core* grey, *int.* grey-buff. FN impression. Squares *1, 3.* Gibson 1982, fig. H. c W. 4: 4. 2 joining sherds.

P292 **Rusticated Beaker.** Sand with flint. Medium. Hard. Buff throughout. FN impression. Square *1.*

144

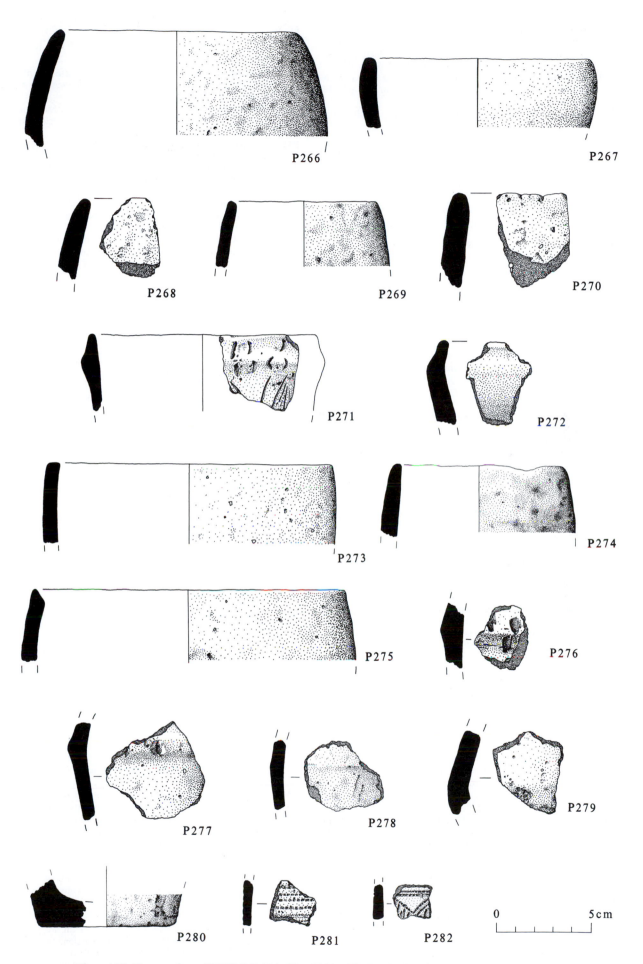

P266

P267

P268

P269

P270

P271

P272

P273

P274

P275

P276

P277

P278

P279

P280

P281

P282

0   5 cm

Figure 95 Pottery from HCW OS 614, Site 5332 (66). Particulars in catalogue. Scale 1:2

P293 **Beaker.** Sand with flint and grog. Medium. Hard. Buff throughout. Incision. Square *2*.

P294 **Beaker.** Grog with flint and sand. Medium. Medium. *Ext.* buff, *core* grey, *int.* grey-buff. Incision. Squares *2, 3, 6*.

P295 **Rusticated Beaker.** Sand with grog and a fleck of ?haematite. Medium. Hard. *Ext.* buff-grey, *core* dark grey, *int.* buff-grey. FP. Square *2*. Gibson 1982, fig. H. c W. 4: 2.

P296 **Beaker.** Grog with sand. Medium. Medium. *Ext.* buff-orange, *core* grey, *int.* buff. Incision. Squares *2, 4, 5, 7*. Gibson 1982, fig. H. c W. 8: 4, 5, 24.

P297 **Beaker.** Grog with sand. Coarse. Soft. *Ext.* buff, *core* grey, *int.* buff. Incision. Square *3*.

P298 Beaker. Sand with grog. Fine. Hard. *Ext.* buff-pink, *core* dark grey, *int.* grey. Incision, indet. impression. Squares *3, 5, 6, 8*. Gibson 1982, fig. H. c W. 9: 12.

P299 **Rusticated Beaker.** Flint with sand. Coarse. Hard. *Ext.* orange-buff, *core* grey, *int.* grey-buff. Grooving, FP. Squares *5, 6*.

P300 **Rusticated Beaker.** Sand with grog and a little flint. Medium. Hard *Ext.* buff-orange, *core* grey, *int.* grey. FN. Square *5*.

P301 **Rusticated Beaker.** Flint with sand. Coarse. Hard. *Ext.* buff, *core* dark grey, *int.* buff. FT impression. Square *6*. Gibson 1982, fig. H. c W. 6: 25.

P302 **Beaker.** Flint with sand. Medium. Hard. *Ext.* buff, *core* grey, *int.* buff-grey. Incision. Squares *7, 8*.

P303 **Beaker.** Sand with grog and a little flint. Medium. Hard. Orange-buff throughout. Square *7*. Gibson 1982, fig. H. c W. 2: 7.

P304 **Beaker.** Grog with sand. Medium. Medium. *Ext.* buff, *core* grey, *int.* buff. Incision. Square *7*.

P305 **Food Vessel.** Grog with sand. Coarse. Soft. *Ext.* buff, *core* dark grey, *int.* buff-grey. Square *8*.

P306 Beaker. Grog with sand. Medium. Medium. *Ext.* buff, *core* grey, *int.* buff. Incision. Square *8*.

P307 **Rusticated Beaker.** Sand with flint. Coarse. Hard. *Ext.* buff-orange, *core* dark grey, *int.* buff-orange. FN and FT impression. Square *8*.

P308 **Beaker.** Sand with grog and flint. Medium. Hard. *Ext.* buff, *core* grey, *int.* buff-grey. Comb and FN impression. Square *6*.

P309 **?Beaker.** Grog with sand and flint. Medium. Medium. *Ext.* buff, *core* dark grey, *int.* buff. Twisted cord impression.

P310 **Beaker.** Sand with grog and flint. Medium. Medium. *Ext.* buff-brown, *core* dark grey, *int.* buff-grey. Incision.

P311 **Beaker.** Sand with flint. Fine. Hard. *Ext.* brown, *core* dark grey, *int.* brown. Comb impression.

P312 **Beaker.** Grog with sand and flint. Medium. Medium. *Ext.* buff, *core* dark grey, *int.* grey. Incision, FP.

P313 **Beaker.** Grog with sand. Medium. Medium. *Ext.* orange-brown, *core* dark grey, *int.* buff. Incision, impression with hollow circular stamp. Trace of white filler remaining in incisions.

P314 **Beaker.** Flint with sand. Medium. Hard. *Ext.* buff-orange, *core* dark grey, *int.* buff-brown. ?'Barbed wire' impression. Square *1*. Much abraded.

P315 **Rusticated Beaker.** Grog with sand. Fine. Medium. *Ext.* buff, *core* dark grey, *int.* grey. ?FN impression. Square *2*. Gibson 1982, fig. H. c W. 4: 35.

P316 **Beaker.** Grog with flint. Fine. Medium. *Ext.* buff-grey, *core* grey, *int.* buff-grey. Impression with hollow, penannular stamp. Square *2*.

P317 **Beaker.** Flint with sand. Medium. Hard. *Ext.* orange-buff, *core* dark grey, *int.* buff-grey. Incision. Square *4*.

P318 **Rusticated Beaker.** Flint with sand. Coarse. Hard. *Ext.* brown-buff, *core* dark grey, *int.* dark grey. FN impression. Square *5*.

P319 **Beaker.** Grog. Medium. Medium. Buff throughout. Incision. *6*.

P320 **Beaker.** Sand with grog and flint. Medium. Hard. *Ext.* buff, *core* grey, *int.* grey-buff. Comb impression, FN impression. Square *7*.

P321 Beaker. Grog with sand. Medium. Medium. *Ext.* orange-buff, *core* dark grey, *int.* buff-orange. Incision. Square *7*.

P322 **Rusticated Beaker.** Grog with flint and sand. Medium. Medium. *Ext.* buff, *core* dark grey, *int.* buff-grey. ?FN impression. Square *8*. Gibson 1982, fig. H. c W. 4: 13.

P323 **Rusticated Beaker.** Sand with grog and a little flint. Medium. Hard. *Ext.* buff, *core* grey, *int.* grey. FN impression. Square *8*. Gibson 1982, fig. H. c W. 5: 23.

Hockwold cum Wilton OS 613. Site 5308/c5 (96)
TL 6928 8767. NCM accession no. 209.967 (Ch. 3.I.10 Figs 99–101)

P324 **Rusticated Beaker.** Flint with sand. Coarse. Hard. *Ext.* grey-buff, *core* dark grey, *int.* dark grey. FT impression. Area *1*. Gibson 1982, fig. H. c W. 7: 3.

P325 **Rusticated Beaker.** Grog with sand. Medium. Medium. *Ext.* brown, *core* dark grey, *int.* grey-buff. FN impression. Area *1*. Gibson 1982, fig. H. c W. 4: 3.

P326 **Beaker.** Flint with grog and sand. Fine. Medium. *Ext.* pink-buff, *core* grey, *int.* buff-grey. Comb impression. Areas *3, 5, 6, 7, 8*.

P327 **Beaker.** Grog with sand and flint. Medium. Medium. *Ext.* grey-buff, *core* dark grey, *int.* grey. Comb impression, grooving. Areas *3, 9*. Gibson 1982, fig. H. c W. 9: 5.

P328 **Rusticated Beaker.** Sand with grog. Medium. hard. *Ext.* buff-grey, *core* grey, *int.* grey-buff. FN impression. Area *3*. Gibson 1982, fig. H. c W. 4: 8.

P329 **Indet. Bronze Age.** Sand with flint and grog. Coarse. Hard. *Ext.* buff-grey, *core* dark grey, *int.* grey-buff. Areas *4, 5, 6*.

P330 **Beaker.** Sand with grog. Medium. Hard. *Ext.* buff-grey, *core* dark grey, *int.* grey. Incision. Areas *5, 6*. Gibson 1982, fig. H. c W. 8: 5, 22.

P331 **Indet. Bronze Age.** Sand with grog. Coarse. Hard. *Ext.* grey-buff, *core* grey, *int.* grey-buff. FT impression. Area *6*. Gibson 1982, fig, H. c W. 3: 28.

P332 Beaker. Sand with grog and flint. Fine. Medium. *Ext.* buff, *core* grey, *int.* buff. Comb impression. *3, 4, 5, 6, 7, 8, 9*

P333 **Beaker.** Grog with sand. Medium. Medium. *Ext.* buff, *core* buff, *int.* buff-grey. Comb and ?bird bone impression. *3, 7*

P334 **Beaker.** Sand with some grog. Fine. Hard. *Ext.* orange-buff, *core* dark grey, *int.* grey-buff. Comb impression. Area *7*. Upper part of strap handle.

P335 **Indet. Bronze Age.** Flint with sand and grog. Coarse. Hard. *Ext.* orange-buff, *core* grey, *int.* buff. ?Applied cordon below rim, shallow grooving or fluting on body. Areas *7, 8*. Reconstruction tentative; fabric and general 'feel' recall larger, coarser rusticated Beakers.

P336 **Rusticated Beaker.** Grog with sand. Medium. Medium. *Ext.* buff, *core* grey, *int.* buff. FN impression. Areas *3, 4, 7*. Gibson 1982, fig. H. c W. 6: 24.

P337 **Rusticated Beaker.** Flint with sand. Coarse. Hard. *Ext.* brown, *core* grey, *int.* grey-brown. FN impression. Area *8*. Gibson 1982, fig. H. c W. 4: 10.

P338 **Indet. Bronze Age.** Grog. Coarse. Soft. *Ext.* buff-orange, *core* dark grey, *int.* grey-buff. FT impression. Area *8*.

P339 Beaker. Sand with grog and flint. Fine. hard. *Ext.* buff-grey, *core* dark grey, *int.* buff-grey. Comb impression. Area *9*.

P340 **Beaker.** Sand with grog. Fine, laminated . Hard. *Ext.* orange-buff, *core* buff-grey, *int.* buff. Comb impression. Area *4*.

P341 **Indet. Bronze Age.** Grog with flint. Coarse. Soft. Buff throughout. FN impression. Area *4*. Gibson 1982, fig. H. c W. 2: 5.

P342 **Indet. Bronze Age.** Grog. Coarse. Soft. Buff throughout. Appliqué, FT impression. Area *4*.

P343 **Beaker.** Flint with grog and sand. Fine. Medium. *Ext.* buff-grey, *core* grey, *int.* buff-grey. Comb impression. *7*. Possibly the rim of P326.

P344 **Beaker.** Sand with flint. Fine. Hard. *Ext.* orange-buff, *core* dark grey, *int.* grey. Comb impression, incision. Area *8*.

P345 **Beaker.** Grog with sand and flint. Coarse. Soft. *Ext.* buff, *core* grey, *int.* buff-grey. Comb and FN impression. Area *5*.

P346 **Beaker.** Grog with sand. Medium. Medium. *Ext.* buff, *core* grey, *int.* grey-buff. Comb impression. Area *2*.

P347 **Beaker.** Grog with sand. Medium. Medium. *Ext.* buff, *core* grey, *int.* buff-grey. Comb impression, incision. Area *8*.

P348 **Beaker.** Grog with flint and sand. Medium. Medium. *Ext.* buff-grey, *core* grey, *int.* buff-grey. Comb impression. Area *5* .

P349 **Rusticated Beaker.** Sand with grog. Medium. Medium. *Ext.* buff-grey, *core* grey, *int.* grey-buff. Comb impression, FP. *8*. Gibson 1982, fig. H. c W. 7: 27.

P350 **Rusticated Beaker.** Sand with grog. Medium. Medium. *Ext.* buff-orange, *core* buff, *int.* buff. FP. Area *6*. Gibson 1982, fig. H. c W. 8: 36. Much abraded.

P351 **Beaker.** Flint with sand. Coarse. Hard. *Ext.* brown-grey, *core* brown. Comb impression. Area *6*.

P352 Rusticated Beaker. Grog with sand. Medium. Soft. *Ext.* buff, *core* grey, *int.* grey-buff. FN impression. Area *7*.

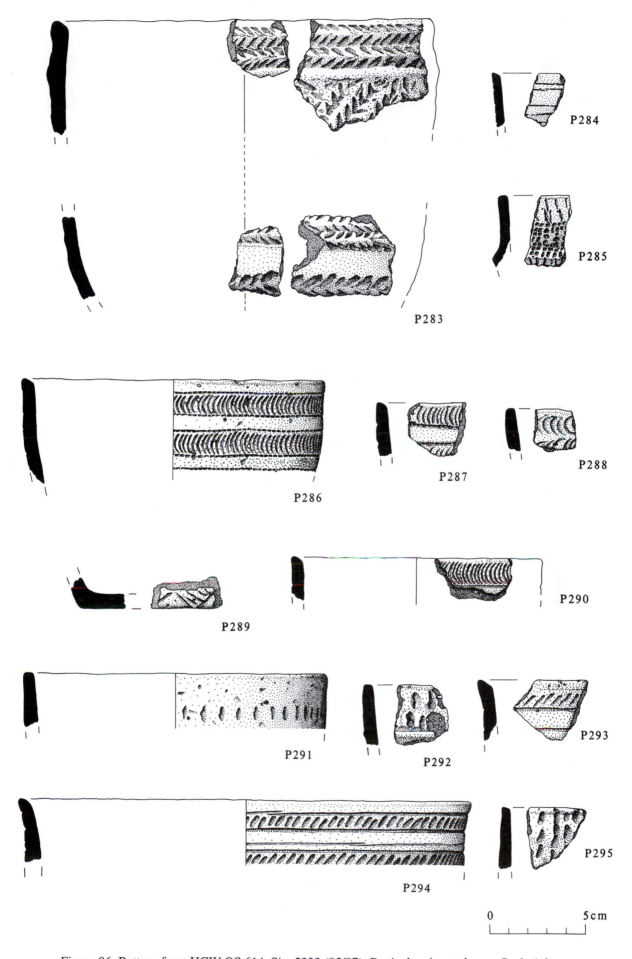

Figure 96 Pottery from HCW OS 614, Site 5333 (95/97). Particulars in catalogue. Scale 1:2

147

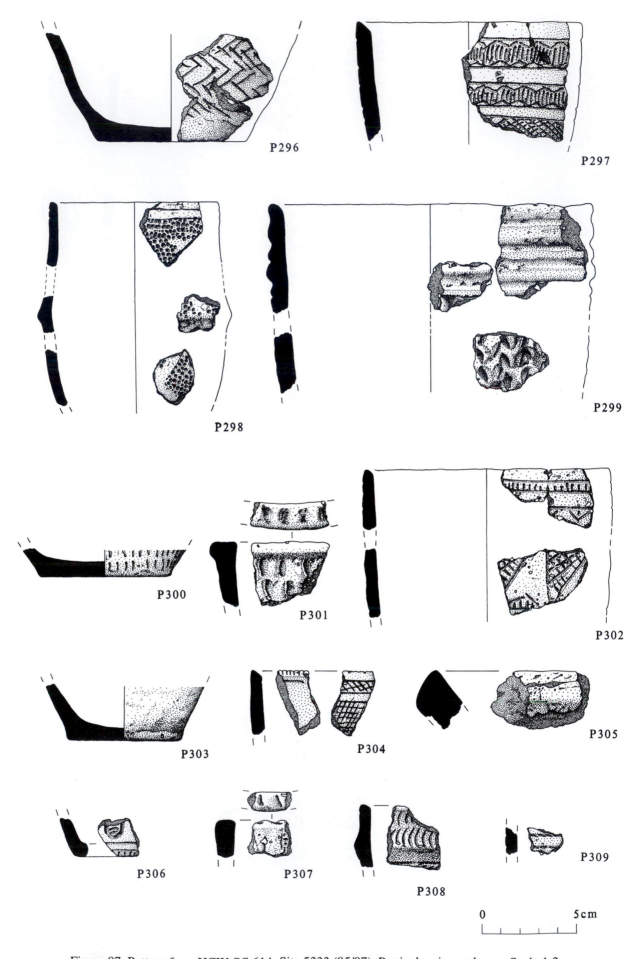

P296

P297

P298

P299

P300

P301

P302

P303

P304

P305

P306

P307

P308

P309

0   5cm

Figure 97 Pottery from HCW OS 614, Site 5333 (95/97). Particulars in catalogue. Scale 1:2

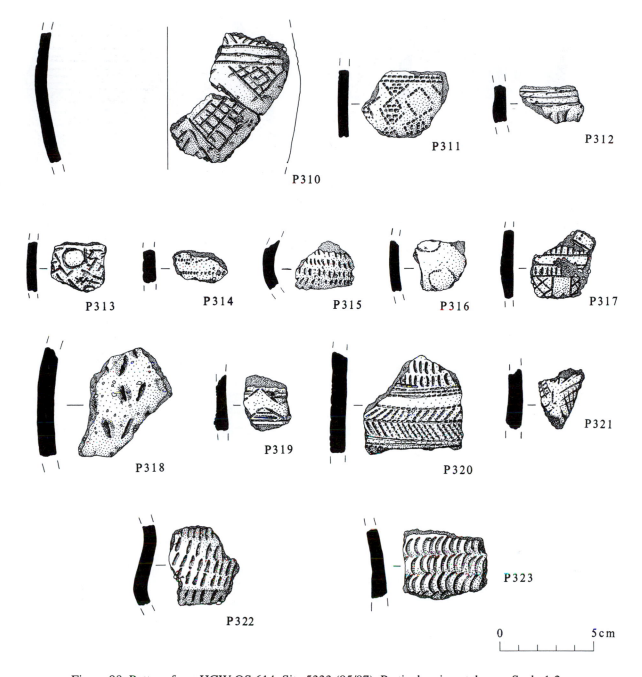

P310 · P311 · P312 · P313 · P314 · P315 · P316 · P317 · P318 · P319 · P320 · P321 · P322 · P323

0   5 cm

Figure 98 Pottery from HCW OS 614, Site 5333 (95/97). Particulars in catalogue. Scale 1:2

P353 **Rusticated Beaker.** Grog with sand and flint. Coarse. Medium. *Ext.* buff, *core* dark grey, *int.* grey-buff. FN impression. Area *3*. Gibson 1982, fig. H. c W. 4: 14.

P354 **Rusticated Beaker.** Sand with grog. Medium. Hard. *Ext.* buff-grey, *core* dark grey, *int.* buff-grey. FP. Area *3*.

P355 Beaker. Sand with flint. Fine. Hard. *Ext.* grey-buff, *core* dark grey, *int.* grey. Comb impression. Area *6*.

P356 **Beaker.** Sand with grog. Medium. Hard. *Ext.* buff-grey, *core* dark grey, *int.* dark grey. Incision. Area *6*.

P357 Beaker. Grog with sand and flint. Medium. Medium. *Ext.* buff, *core* grey, *int.* grey-buff. Comb impression. Area *8*.

Hockwold cum Wilton OS 614. Site 5364 (75)
TL 6940 8771. NCM accession no. 431.965 (Fig. 101)

P358 **Collared Urn.** Grog with sand. Medium. Medium. *Ext.* buff, *core* grey, *int.* grey-buff. Twisted cord impression. Isolated surface find. Longworth 1984, corpus no. 942. External diameter at collar base approx. 220 mm.

Feltwell OS 264. Glebe Farm. Site 4921/c1
TL 7148 9090. NCM accession no. 275.965 (Ch. 3.II. 9 Fig. 102)

P359 **Grooved Ware (Woodlands substyle).** Shell. Medium. Soft. *Ext.* orange-brown, *core* dark grey, *int.* dark grey. Grooving, appliqué.

Feltwell OS 283. Hill Close. Site 5188/c1
TL 6966 9080. NCM accession no. 487.967 (Ch. 4. I.3 Fig. 102)

P360 **Food Vessel.** ?Grog. Coarse. Soft. *Ext.* brown, *core* dark grey, *int.* brown. Twisted cord and other impression. Close to a group of burials (Fig. 19:*3A*). Lawson 1981, 33. Distorted to oval shape; found upside-down, with base removed by plough; restoration with plaster of Paris (white in illustration) makes temper difficult to determine.

P361 **Indet. Bronze Age.** Sand with flint. Coarse. Medium. *Ext.* brown, *core* dark grey, *int.* brown. Appliqué. From north of excavated area, some distance from any burial (Fig. 19:*5*).

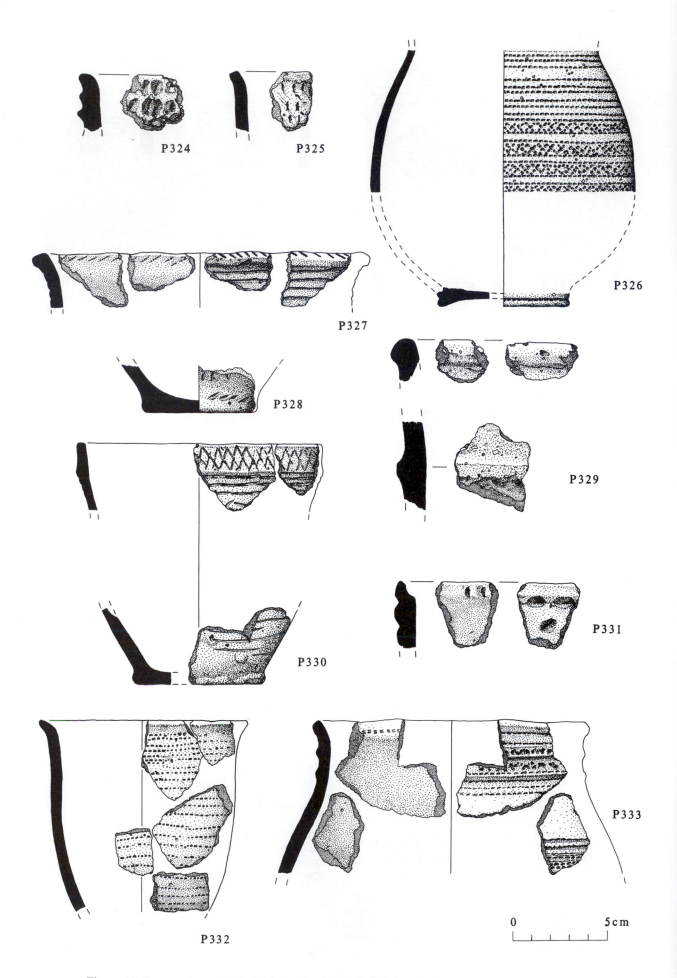

P324

P325

P326

P327

P328

P329

P330

P331

P332

P333

0   5 cm

Figure 99 Pottery from HCW OS 613, Site 5308/c5 (96). Particulars in catalogue. Scale 1:2

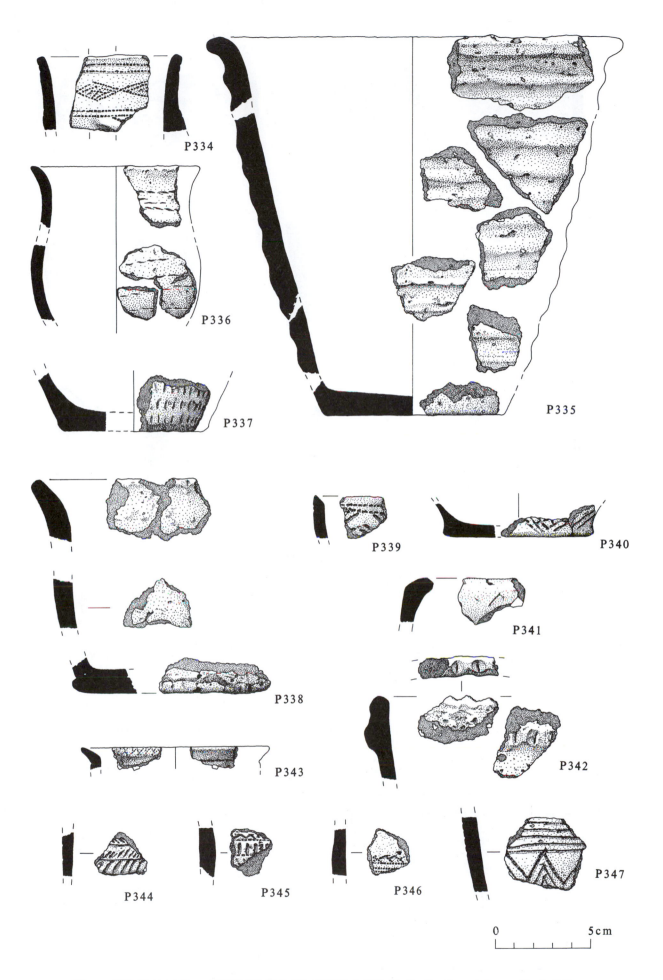

P334

P336

P337

P335

P339

P340

P341

P338

P342

P343

P344 P345 P346 P347

0　　　　　5cm

Figure 100 Pottery from HCW OS 613, Site 5308/c5 (96). Particulars in catalogue. Scale 1:2

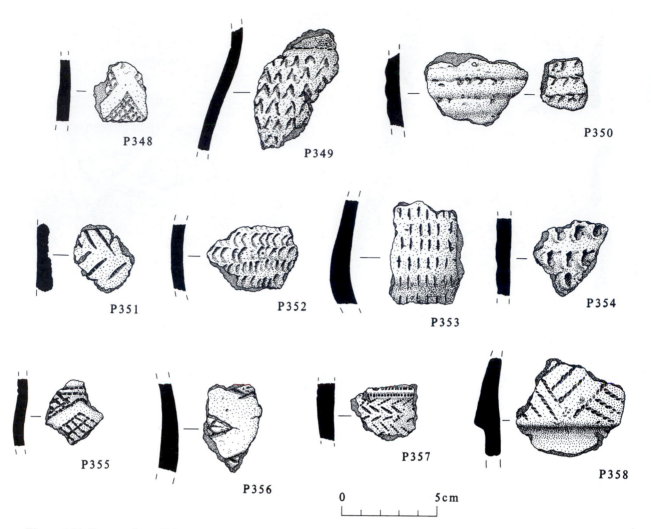

Figure 101 Pottery from HCW OS 613, Site 5308/c5 (96: P348–357) and HCW OS 614, Site 5364 (75: P358).
Particulars in catalogue. Scale 1:2

P362 **Beaker.** Sand with grog. Medium. Soft. *Ext.* buff, *core* dark grey, *int.* buff. Incision. Burial *19* (Fig. 19).

Hockwold Fen. Site 12434
Unlocated. NCM accession no. 43.953 (Fig. 102)
P363 **Indet. Bronze Age.** Sand with grog and flint. Coarse. Hard. *Ext.* orange-brown, *core* brown, *int.* buff. Handle applied. Found 'a few years before 1939...at depth of 8' [2.4m]...while digging with spade'. Restored, but apparently almost complete.

Hockwold cum Wilton OS 48. Site 14734/c2 (77)
TL 6856 8877. NCM accession no. 572.965 (Fig. 103)
P364 **Beaker.** Sand with grog. Fine. Medium. *Ext.* buff, *core* grey, *int.* grey. Incision. Surface find with 2 rusticated Beaker sherds.

Hockwold cum Wilton OS 48. Site 5423 (9)
TL 6841 8844. NCM accession no. 95.960 (Ch. 3.II.2 Fig. 103)
P365 **Beaker.** Sand with flint. Fine. Hard. *Ext.* brown-orange, *core* dark grey, *int.* dark grey. Comb impression. From excavation of 'fireplace'. Base angle fragment.

Hockwold cum Wilton OS 594. Site 5375 (113)
TL 690 874. NCM accession no. 201.961 (Fig. 103)
P366 **?Biconical Urn.** Grog with sand. Coarse. Soft. *Ext.* buff, *core* buff-brown, *int.* buff-grey. FT impression. Surface find with 6 other Bronze Age sherds and a trimmed sandstone disc. Weathered.
P367 **?Biconical Urn.** Grog with sand. Coarse. Soft. *Ext.* buff-orange, *core* grey, *int.* buff-orange. Incision, FT impression. Context and condition as P366.

P368 **?Biconical Urn.** Grog with sand. Coarse. Soft. Buff-orange throughout. ?FT impression. Context and condition as P366.

Hockwold cum Wilton OS 597. Site 5365 (67)
TL 6890 8714. NCM accession no. 198.965 (Fig. 103)
P369 **?Beaker,** ?Bronze Age. Grog with flint. Medium. Medium. *Ext.* buff, *core* grey, *int.* buff-grey. Impression with hollow circular stamp. Surface find with 13 sherds of Bronze Age pottery.
P370 **?Biconical Urn.** Grog with sand. Medium. Medium. *Ext.* brown-grey, *core* grey, *int.* grey-buff. Context as P369.
P371 **?Biconical Urn.** Grog with sand. Coarse. Hard. *Ext.* orange-buff, *core* grey, *int.* buff-grey. Context as P369.

Hockwold cum Wilton OS 607. 'Hill 1'. Site 5321/c2 (71)
TL 6857 8775. NCM accession no. 428.965 (Fig. 103)
P372 **Beaker.** Flint with sand. Medium. Hard. *Ext.* brown-buff, *core* buff, *int.* buff. Comb impression. Surface find with 3 other Beaker sherds, 24 Bronze Age sherds, 2 fragments fired clay, flint flake and 2 scrapers. Some of pottery weathered.
P373 **?Biconical Urn.** Sand with grog. Medium. Hard. *Ext.* buff, *core* buff-grey, *int.* grey. Context as P372.
P374 **?Biconical Urn.** Grog with sand. Coarse. Soft. *Ext.* buff-grey, *core* dark grey, *int.* buff. Appliqué, FT impression. Context as P372.

Hockwold cum Wilton OS 607. 'Hill 2'. Site 5321/c4 (72)
TL 6851 8762. NCM accession no. 429.965 (Fig. 103)
P375 **?Biconical Urn.** Grog with sand. Medium. Medium. *Ext.* buff, *core* dark grey, *int.* grey. FT impressions. Surface find with 9 other Bronze Age sherds, 2 fragments fired clay, 3 flint flakes, 2 'thumbnail' scrapers. Weathered, as are other sherds.

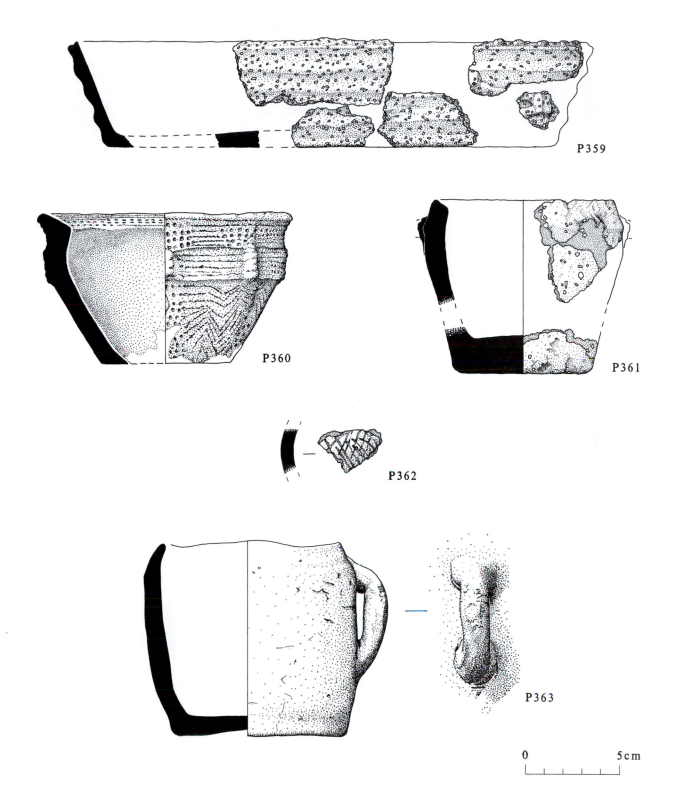

Figure 102 Pottery: P359 from Glebe Farm, Feltwell (Site 4921/c1); P360–362 from Hill Close, Feltwell (Site 5188/c1); P363 from unknown location in Hockwold Fen (Site 12434). Particulars in catalogue. Scale 1:2

Hockwold cum Wilton OS 644. Corner Ground. Site 5317
TL 686 882. NCM accession no. 120.960 (Figs 103–104)

P376 **Neolithic Bowl.** Flint with sand. Medium. Hard. *Ext.* brown-orange, *core* grey, *int.* orange. Traces of ?slip or burnish on weathered outer surface. Surface find with 8 other Bowl sherds. 1 Beaker sherd, 2 Food Vessel sherds, flint blade, animal bone. Gibson 1982, fig. H. c W. 1: 12. Diameter Approx. 250 mm.

P377 **Neolithic Bowl.** Sand with flint. Fine. Hard. *Ext.* grey-orange, *core* grey, *int.* orange-buff. Context as P376. Gibson 1982, fig. H. c W. 2: 3. Weathered; diameter approx. 100 mm.

P378 **Neolithic Bowl.** Flint with sand. Medium. Hard. *Ext.* buff-grey, *core* grey, *int.* grey. Context as P376. Weathered.

P379 **Neolithic Bowl** (Mildenhall Ware). Fine. Hard. *Ext.* grey-orange, *core* grey, *int.* grey-brown. Channelling. Context as P376. Gibson 1982, fig. H. c W. 2: 4. Heavily weathered, little of original surface left.

P380 **Beaker.** Sand with flint. Medium. Hard. *Ext.* buff-grey, *core* grey, *int.* grey-buff. Incision, FN impression. Context as P376. Less weathered than Bowl sherds from same find.

P381 **Food Vessel.** Grog with sand. Coarse. Soft. *Ext.* buff-grey, *core* dark grey, *int.* grey-buff. Whipped cord impressions. Context as P376. Gibson 1982, fig. H. c W. 10: 3.

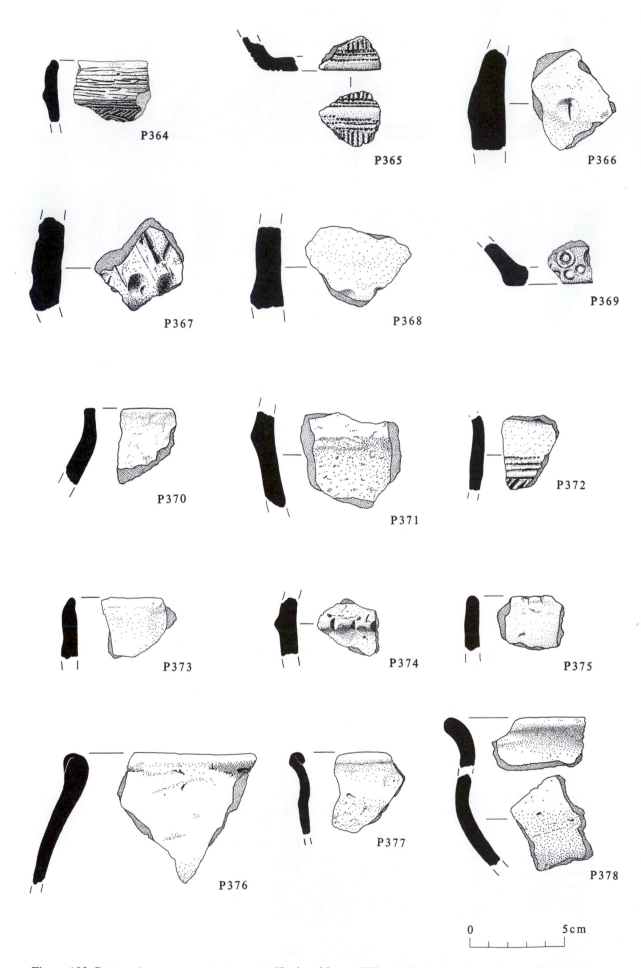

P364

P365

P366

P367

P368

P369

P370

P371

P372

P373

P374

P375

P376

P377

P378

0   5cm

Figure 103 Pottery from various findspots in Hockwold cum Wilton. Particulars in catalogue. Scale 1:2

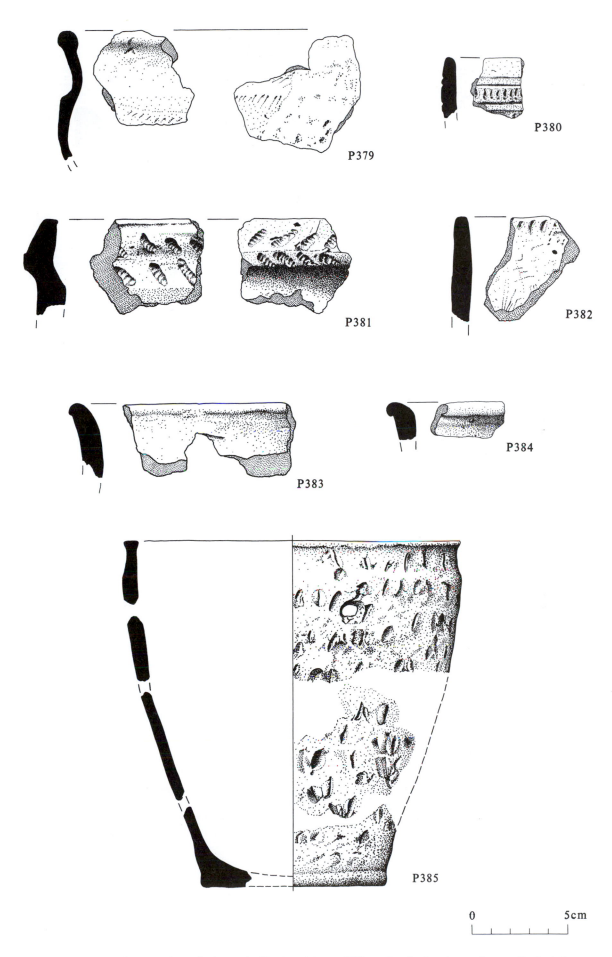

P379

P380

P381

P382

P383

P384

P385

0   5cm

Figure 104 Pottery from various findspots in Hockwold cum Wilton. Particulars in catalogue. Scale 1:2

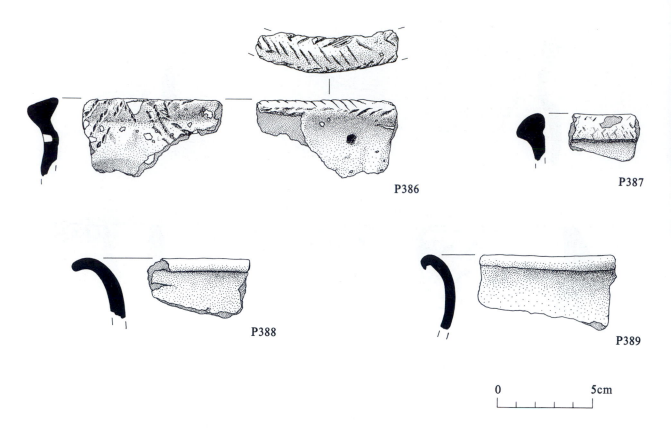

P386

P387

P388

P389

0   5cm

Figure 105 Pottery from various findspots in Methwold. Particulars in catalogue. Scale 1:2

Hockwold cum Wilton 648. Site 5377 (16)
TL 682 879. NCM accession no. 231.960 (Fig. 104)

P382   **Indet. Bronze Age.** Grog. Coarse. Soft. *Ext.* grey-buff, *core* grey, *int.* grey-buff. FN impression. Surface find with triangular arrowhead. Weathered.

Hockwold cum Wilton OS 649. Site 5230/c1 (70)
TL 6795 8785. NCM accession no. 278.965 (Fig. 104)

P383   **Neolithic Bowl.** Sand with flint. Medium. Hard. *Ext.* brown-grey, *core* buff-grey, *int.* brown-grey. Surface find with 13 other Bowl sherds, 1 rusticated Beaker sherd, leaf arrowhead fragment, 5 scrapers, 1 misc. retouched. 2 joining sherds, weathered.

P384   **Neolithic Bowl.** Sand with flint. Medium. Hard. *Ext.* orange-buff, *core* grey-buff, *int.* buff. Context as P383. Much weathered.

Hockwold cum Wilton 650. Site 5318 (14)
TL 6789 8762. NCM accession no. 848.967 (Fig. 104)

P385   **Rusticated Beaker.** Grog. Medium. Medium. *Ext.* brown, *core* brown-grey, *int.* buff-grey. FP. Circumstances of discovery unknown. Gibson 1982, fig. H. c W. 2: 20; Cleal 1988, 144. Sherds form almost entire vessel; single perforation made after firing, probably from both sides; no associations.

Methwold OS 242. '12 ft'. Site 2531
Centre TL 6970 9575. J.D. Wortley coll. (Fig. 105)

P386   **Peterborough Ware (Mortlake).** Shell and sand. Coarse. Hard. *Ext.* dark brown, *core* black, Int. buff. Incision, impression with rounded implement, twisted cord impression. Surface find from field which has produced large collection of predominantly Beaker and Early Bronze Age pottery, some of it illustrated by Gibson (1982, figs MET. 1–3).

Methwold OS 242. '12 ft'. Site 3531
Centre TL 6970 9575
or
Methwold OS 568-70 + 625-6. Whiteplot. Site 5235
Centre TL 6900 9310. J. D. Wortley coll.

P387   **Neolithic Bowl** (Mildenhall Ware). Flint with some sand. Medium, laminated. Hard. *Ext.* & *core* brown, Int. buff. Channelling. Surface find. Abraded.

Methwold OS 568-70 + 625-6. Whiteplot. Site 5325
Centre TL 6900 9310. J.D. Wortley coll. (Fig. 105)

P388   **Neolithic Bowl** (Grimston Ware). Flint with some sand. Medium. Hard. *Ext.* & *int.* brown-grey, *core* dark grey. Surface find.

P389   **Neolithic Bowl** (Grimston Ware). Sand with some flint. Fine. Hard. *Ext.* & *int.* mottled brown-orange, *core* grey. Surface find. ?Once slipped or burnished.

IV. Worked Bone and Antler

(Figs 106–108; Appendix 33 (microfiche))

IV.1. Hockwold cum Wilton OS 466, 613, 614 and 616

The commonest bone artefacts from these fields are simple bone points (*e.g.* Fig. 106: B9, Fig. 107: B10). There is, however, a wide range of artefacts, especially in association with Bronze Age, rather than Beaker, pottery. Most noteworthy are a perforated eagle claw (Fig. 106: B1) from Site 24866 ('site 8') and a finely worked and highly polished blade (Fig. 107: B15) from Site 5332 (66). An antler tine worn to a polish (Fig. 106: B4) seems to have been cut from the beam by a metal implement. Two unillustrated antler fragments with cut marks from Site 5332 (66) suggest on-site antler working.

IV.2. The Survey Area as a Whole

The range of artefacts from the remainder of the area is yet wider. Ornaments are represented by three beads from Feltwell Fen (Plate IX). Numerous pins and points include one (Fig. 108: B20) found in a pit with a Grooved Ware dish (Fig. 102: P359) at Glebe Farm, Feltwell and another (Fig. 108: B21) found with three skeletons close to the Methwold-Southery border.

Five perforated antler implements with bevelled 'cutting' edges include two axe-like forms (with perforation and cutting edge in the same plane) and two adze-like forms (with perforation and cutting edge at right-angles to each other), the latter including B23 (Fig. 108). All are made from antler bases rather than from sections of beam alone. There are at least two antler picks and one bone wristguard (Fig. 108: B22). Red deer antlers generally seem to have been larger than those of modern specimens B14 (Fig. 107), for example, came from a very substantial antler beam. This corresponds to the larger-than-modern size of the red deer antlers from which antler picks were made at Grime's Graves in the Later Neolithic (Clutton-Brock 1984, fig. 5).

IV.3. Discussion

The dating of some of the stray finds is uncertain, since simple, functional bone implements such as points and spatulae were made and used over millennia. This is particularly true of a spatula and three points from the relatively elevated location of Hill Close, Feltwell (Sites 5188, 5261, OS 283–4), which may derive from the Iron Age occupation described by Shand (1985). Most of the material, however, comes from lower-lying fields which saw little post-Bronze Age activity, and is thus likely to be of Bronze Age or earlier date.

Perforated antler 'axes', 'adzes' or 'mattocks' (*e.g.* Fig. 108: B23) have long been considered Mesolithic. Radiocarbon determinations have shown that some British examples are indeed of this date, but that comparable forms continued to be made well into the Bronze Age (Hedges *et al.* 1988, 159–160; 1990, 105; 1993, 311). Dated examples include two from the survey area, one from Feltwell (Site 20979/c3, OS 973) and one from Methwold (Site 29346), with respective ages of 3000 ± 75 BP (OxA–3741; 1400–1130 cal. BC) and 3460 ± 70 BP (OxA–3745; 1890–1690 cal. BC). Within the south-eastern Fens, two have been found in a pit with Middle style Beaker pottery in Burnt Fen, Cambridgeshire (Edwardson 1966).

Some of the artefacts are bone or antler versions of forms which have more often survived in stone. The Feltwell Fen

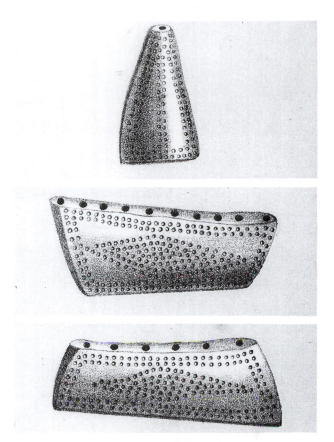

Plate IX Feltwell Fen (Site 5296): bone beads found 1876, 'in clay soil, about five feet below surface, and just above a bed of sand'. Illustration published by Manning (1879). Photo: David Wicks

beads (Pl. IX), as Manning pointed out (1879, 320–325), match the more familiar jet spacer plates of necklaces found in Early Bronze Age burials, as at Snailwell, Cambridgeshire (Lethbridge 1950, 35, pl. VIII) or Risby, Suffolk (Martin 1976b, 48–53, pl. I). The same is true of a set of undecorated bone spacer beads from the Beacon Hill barrow at Barton Mills in the Suffolk Breckland (Cawdor and Fox 1925, fig. 4). A bone wristguard (Fig. 108: B22) echoes the form of more familiar stone examples, such as that from HCW OS 616, Site 5336 (Clough and Green 1972, fig. 14). A perforated strip of antler (Fig. 107: B11) similarly recalls the form of pendant whetstones such as that from the primary cremation in a barrow at Milston, Wiltshire (Annable and Simpson 1964, 362).

Others are closely matched in local Bronze Age contexts. A perforated disc (Fig. 106: B2) has its counterpart in the Middle Bronze Age occupation deposits of Grime's Graves (Site 5640; Mercer 1981, fig. 42: B34). Needles (*e.g.* Fig. 106, B3, B6) also occurred there (Legge 1992, fig. 26). Further needles, together with tubes like B18 and B19 (Fig. 107), were found with a cremation contained in a Collared Urn at Snailwell, Cambridgeshire (Lethbridge 1950, fig. 11). A worn antler tine with a cleanly-cut base (Fig. 106: B4) is identical to an antler tine from Mildenhall Fen in its worn end and cleanly-cut base (Clark 1936, pl. VIII: 11). Further highly polished tines occurred at Grime's Graves, but here they were either perforated or hollowed-out at the base (Legge 1992, figs 28–9). A socketed point with two countersunk lateral loops near the base from Hockwold (Site 15087, OS 24; Lawson 1979b) may be compared with one from Mildenhall Fen which had two or three basal perforations (Clark 1936, fig.

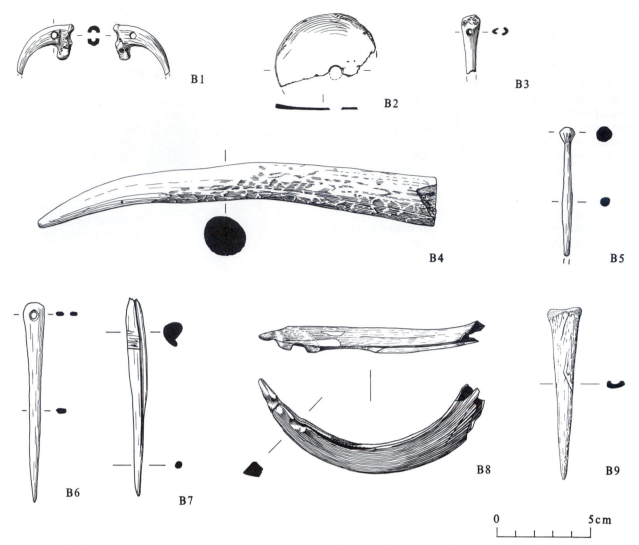

Figure 106 Worked bone and antler from various sites in HCW OS 466 + 614 + 616: B1–3 from Site 24866 ('site 8'); B4 from Site 14662 ('field 79'); B5–B7 from Frank Curtis' 'site 1' (? = Site 5310 (49)); B8–B9 from Site 5373 (22). Particulars in catalogue. Scale 1:2

12) and another from Wilde Street, Mildenhall, with a single, incomplete basal perforation (Kelly 1967, pl. VI: 1).

The perforated eagle claw and antler strip (Fig. 106: B1 and Fig. 107: B11) seem more likely to have been pendants than implements. The use of most of the apparently functional objects remains elusive. Smith suggests that perforated antler implements like B23 were digging tools, on the evidence of the wear patterns on some examples (1989, 282–283). Microwear analysis by Dr Sandra Olsen of bone tools from West Row Fen, Mildenhall, may prove informative for previously recovered material. At present it is simply clear that a wide range of bone and antler implements was used on Early and Middle Bronze Age living sites. The diversity itself calls for explanation. Neolithic assemblages, even from the chalk where bone is well-preserved, have nothing approaching the wealth of forms found at Mildenhall Fen or Grime's Graves. More frequent use of pins and needles may have accompanied the adoption of textiles. But this does not account for the contemporary plethora of other bone and antler artefacts.

IV.4. Catalogue of Illustrated Worked Bone and Antler

Except for B1, which was identified by Enid Allison, Environmental Archaeology Unit, University of York, identifications are by Peter Lawrance, formerly of the Natural History Department, Norwich Castle Museum or John Goldsmith, still of that Department.

Entries are ordered as follows: identification, description, context, comment.

HCW OS 466 + 616. Site 24866 ('site 8')
Centre TL 6954 8765. NCM 121.960 (Ch. 3.I.1 Fig. 106)

B1 Phalange, probably of white-tailed eagle (*Haliaëtus albicella*). Near-cylindrical perforation slightly wider at one end than at other; two cut-marks close to articulation, one illustrated, the other on underside of claw. Pendant?

B2 From scapula or pelvis of large animal such as horse or cow. Fragmentary, perforated ?disc, with trimmed, smoothed or ground edge. Thinness, lightness and eccentric perforation make it unlikely to have been a spindle whorl.

B3 Bird tibia or fibula. Perforated at surviving articular end and ground. Needle? Sketched by Frank Curtis alongside B6 and B7.

HCW OS 466 + 616 + 616. 'Field 79'
Centre TL 6945 8765, NCM unreg.(Fig. 106)

B4 Red deer antler tine. Cut from beam by sawing action, probably with metal implement; tip worn or ground to a smooth, shiny finish.

HCW OS 616. 'Site 1'. ? = Site 5310 (49)
Curtis collection. Ch. 3.I.1 (Fig. 106)

B5 Unidentified. Ground. Pin.

B6 Unidentified. Ground. Needle; sketched by Frank Curtis alongside B3 and B7.

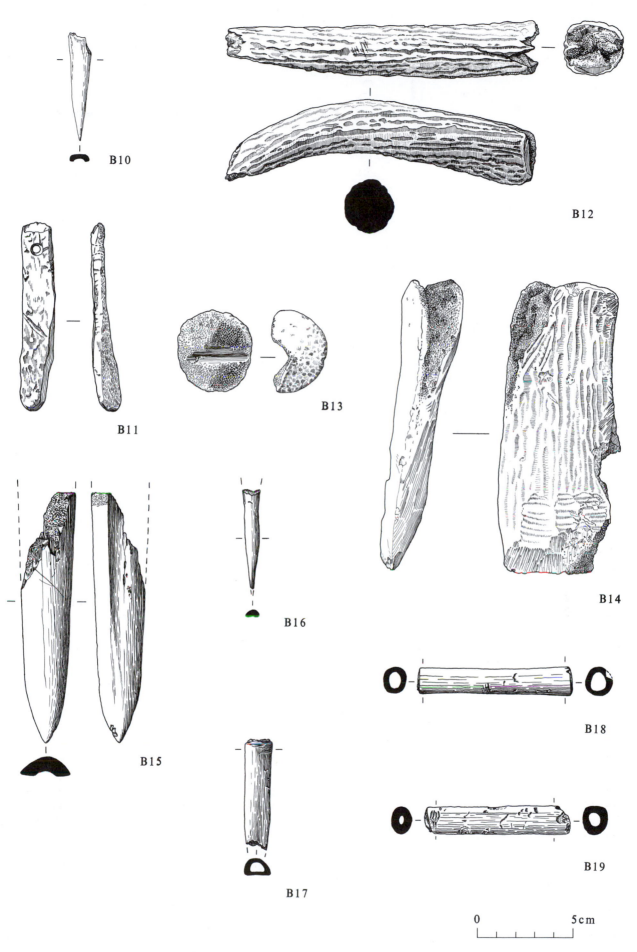

B10

B12

B11

B13

B14

B15

B16

B17

B18

B19

0   5cm

Figure 107 Worked bone and antler from various sites in HCW OS 613 + 614: B10–14 from Site 5308/c4 (61/68); B15–17 from Site 5332 (66); B18–19 from Site 5333 (95/97). Particulars in catalogue. Scale 1:2

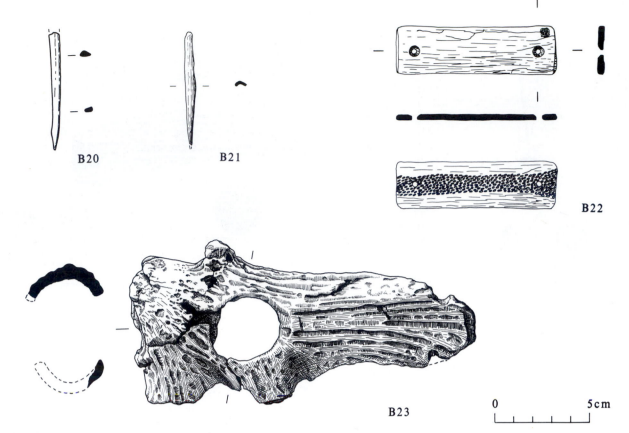

Figure 108 Worked bone and antler form various sites in Feltwell and Methwold: B20 from pit at Glebe Farm, Feltwell (Site 4921/c1); B21 from burial at Site 2585 in Methwold; B22 from Site 20981/c4 in Feltwell; B23 from Site 17531 in Feltwell. Particulars in catalogue. Scale 1:2

B7 Unidentified. Ground, with band of scratched or incised lines. Point; sketched by Frank Curtis alongside B3 and B6.

HCW OS 614. Site 5373 (22)
TL 6930 8760, NCM 673.964 (Ch. 3.I.2 (Fig. 106)
B8 Pig tush. Two bilaterally worked notches towards tip.
B9 Head of fused tibia and fibula of bird, *cf.* heron. Ground. Point.

HCW OS 613 + 614. Dykeside. Site 5308/c4 (61/68)
TL 6932 8778. NCM 511.964, 205.965 (Ch. 3.I.6 Fig. 107)
B10 Unidentified. Ground. Area *1*. Point.
B11 (Red?) deer antler. Ground edges and hour-glass perforation. Area *2* or area *6*. Pendant?
B12 Red deer brow or bez tine. Two grooves at proximal end; double bevel at distal end. Area *2* or area *6*; unclear whether this or B14 equates with 'antler axe' plotted on Figure 5.
B13 Head of cattle femur. Split in half and grooved; base of V-shaped groove distinctly scored. Area *7*.
B14 Large red deer antler beam fragment. Squared and bevelled at one end; recent damage (from pick or fork?) to right edge. Area *2* or area *8*; unclear whether this or B12 equates with 'antler axe' plotted on Figure 6.

HCW OS 614. Site 5332 (66)
TL 6933 8775. NCM 116.965 (Ch. 3.I.7 Fig. 107)
B15 Horse cannon bone. Split; ground to a high shine; longitudinal striations on both faces; sharp point and edges; some recent damage to underside of tip. Knife or dagger?
B16 ?Pig fibula. Ground. Point.
B17 Ovicaprid metapodial. Ground; distal end cut off. Point?

HCW OS Site 5333 (95/97)
TL 6934 8771. NCM 334.967 (Ch. 3.I.9 Fig. 107)
B18 Femur or tibia of large bird (?goose). Both ends cut and ground smooth.
B19 Femur or tibia of large bird (?goose). Cut irregularly at one end; roughly hacked at other; cut-marks on shaft.

FWL OS 264. Glebe Farm. Site 4921/c1
TL 7148 9090. NCM 275.965 (Ch. 3.II.9 Fig.108)
B20 Unidentified. Ground. Point. From pit containing Grooved Ware, struck flint and animal bone.

MTW OS 1231. Site 2585
TL 631 941. KLM (Ch. 4.I.2 Fig. 108)
B21 Unidentified. Ground. Point. Found with three skeletons.

FWL OS 411. Site 20981/c4
TL 6928 9154. Younge collection (Fig. 108)
B22 Long bone of large animal. Both faces ground. Wristguard.

FWL OS 499. Site 17531
Centre TL 6925 9205. Secker collection (Fig. 108)
B23 Large red deer antler beam. Cut off obliquely; perforated at right-angles to brow and bez tines, which are also cut off; one of lateral notches near tip is recent. Adze-like implement.

V. Wood

Wooden artefacts recovered from the survey area up to the 1990s have been few and generally poorly-preserved. A wooden setting beneath a skeleton at Hemplands Farm, Methwold Hythe (Pl. VIII, Fig. 20) disintegrated during excavation; while the surviving tips of the stakes surrounding Site 5324 (93) in Hockwold (Bamford 1982, 11, text fig. 3) are severely shrunken. Portable wooden objects consist almost entirely of rare haft fragments, such as the oak in the shaft-hole of an axe-hammer probably dredged from a drainage ditch in Feltwell (Site 24735, OS 762) and in the socket of a decorated copper alloy axe found in the 'Corner Ground' in Hockwold (Site 5317, OS 644), or the unidentified wood in the socket of the flesh-hook found inside the Feltwell cauldron (Ch. 5.I.3; Site 5191, OS 283).

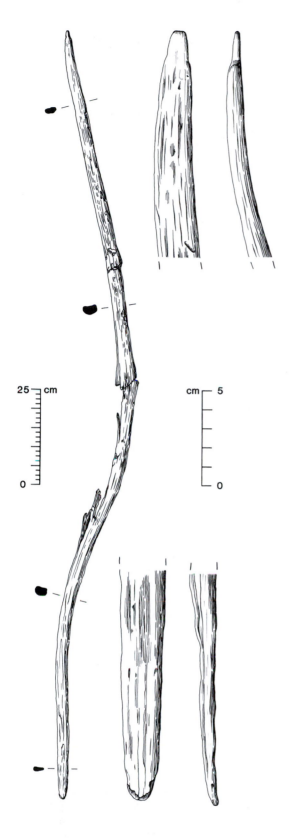

Figure 109 The Methwold bow (MTW OS 990, Site 4460). Scale 1:10 (complete view), 1:2 (details)

A wooden trough in the form of a hollowed half-log with a transom board at each end, excavated in 1992 from a 'pot boiler' site at Feltwell Anchor, stands out as an exceptional find (Site 23650; Hall and Coles 1994, fig. 58). In these circumstances, the recovery of a well-preserved bow is noteworthy.

V.1. The Methwold Bow, MTW OS 990, Site 4460, TL 6492 9558

(Fig. 109)

The discovery is described in a letter written by Frank Curtis to Barbara Green (Keeper of Archaeology, Norwich Castle Museum) in April 1971:

> I believe I have a surprise for you. Last Friday evening, I had a visitor from Southery... He came in and showed me a bronze axe, (a palstave, rather a large one)...

> After about an hour he had to go, I walked with him to his car, and casually he said, "You know, a few years ago, while my uncle and Earnie Fletcher were cuting a new dyke across our land, he saw the end of a bow, sticking out of the side, but before he could stop Earnie he had cut in halves with his hodding spade, but he pulled the other half out of the peat, (Gawd help us) and so got the complete bow" ...After examining it [he] tied it up in a large paper sack... All this happened *15 years ago*...

> Saturday morning I got my son to take me over to see Phillip (the uncle)... We eventually found him. He told us how the bow had been found and, what was the most astonishing thing, that he had rolled it up in the paper sack, tied a string round it, hung it on a nail in his barn, and had never looked at it since, but he believed it was still alright... He...said that he would bring it over to me in the afternoon. He mentioned that it was yew (fen people know the different woods in the peat), that it was beautifully made and smooth as glass, and the notches at the ends were still plain to see, and that it was at least 5' [1.5m] long...

> In the evening, away he came, swinging the two halves in his hand...the only damage was that a few pieces had splintered off, but are with it, and it has warped badly, otherwise it is as dry as a bone and the wood is in good condition, apart from a bad cut or two from the spade and superficial cracks...

> this was found in a new dyke, in undisturbed peat, at a depth of six feet [1.8m], lying on clay...

The findspot was investigated in the summer of 1971 by Gale Sieveking, then of the British Museum, and by Richard Sims, then of the Cambridge Botany School, who visited the site with the finder. The horizon from which it had come was identified as 0.38m above the upper peat/fen clay transition, not on the fen clay as the letter suggests, while analysis of a small sample of pollen from deposits adhering to the bow itself might place it lower down the section, only 0.14m above the transition. Either horizon would would be compatible with an Early Bronze Age date. The finder's identification of the wood as yew was confirmed (Ch. 6.IV.2)

The bow (Fig. 109) is badly warped towards the centre. Both nocks are still visible, and the better-preserved areas are smooth and shiny. There are no visible tool marks.

Its D-shaped section is matched in all of the few known Neolithic and Bronze Age longbows from Britain (Clark 1963; Switsur 1974; Glover 1979; Sheridan 1992). It is closest, geographically and morphologically, to one 'found deep down in the peat near Cambridge in 1885' (Clark 1963, 90, figs 8 and 12, pl. III:5), dated to the Early Bronze Age by a radiocarbon determination of 3680 ± 110 BP (Q–684; 2270–1920 cal. BC). Both are characterised by shouldered nocks of Clark's (1963, 53) class B1 and by the absence of a constricted central handgrip.

6. People, Animals and Vegetation

I. Human Skeletal Remains
by Jacqueline I. McKinley
Written in 1988

I.1. Introduction

The human bone examined was primarily from Site 2585 in Methwold, Hill Close, Feltwell (Site 5188/c1, c4), Hemplands Farm, Methwold (Site 2550) and Methwold Severalls (Sites 2542/c1, c2), all radiocarbon-dated to the Early Bronze Age, with a possible continuation into the Middle Bronze Age for Hill Close (Table 1). In addition, undated individual skeletons from Sites 2534, 2549, and 21967, all in Methwold, were also examined. The details of these findspots are to be found in Appendix 3 (microfiche).

Excavation records exist only for Hill Close, Hemplands Farm, and Methwold Severalls (Ch. 4. I). Some confusion and mixing of the bones of different individuals occurred in both the Hill Close and Methwold Severalls collections (Appendix 34 (microfiche)).

When the study was undertaken, before radiocarbon determinations were available for some of the skeletons, it was felt that apparent disarticulation and the presence of leaf arrowheads at Hill Close might suggest a period of use extending back to the Neolithic. One aim when examining the bone was to detect any morphological variations which might indicate the presence of two populations (Neolithic and Early Bronze Age), as well as to record the usual demographic and palaeopathological observations.

I.2. Method

Each collection was examined for age and sex, any pathology and morphological variations being noted. Where the bones of individuals had become mixed an attempt was made to ascertain the origins of the various bones, this was not always possible in the Hill Close collection due to the number of individuals represented, the incompleteness of most of them, and the disturbed state of parts of the site, especially 'group 3' (burials *10–17*).

The cremated bone was passed through a series of three sieves, of 10mm, 5mm and 2mm mesh size, to obtain percentage fragmentation by weight. The maximum fragment size for skull and long bone was also recorded. Identifiable bone was separated out for further analysis in four skeletal categories of skull, axial skeleton, upper limb and lower limb. Any variation in colour from the usual buff/white was noted.

The *age* of immature individuals was assessed from the stage of tooth development and eruption (van Beek 1983) and the stage of epiphyseal fusion (McMinn and Hutchings 1985; Gray 1977 edition). The age of adults was assessed from the degree of epiphyseal fusion (McMinn and Hutchings 1985); pattern of degenerative changes in the pubic symphyses (Brooks 1955); tooth wear patterns (Brothwell 1972); and the general degree of cranial suture fusion and degenerative changes to the bone.

Age categories, rather than age in years, are used in view of the difficulties surrounding the accurate assessment of age for adult individuals over 25/30 years (that is following final epiphyseal fusion). Tooth wear patterns and the degree of degenerative changes in the bone may vary considerably dependent on the individual and/or the group. The categories used are:

foetus/neonate
infant — 0–5 years
juvenile — 5–12 years
subadult — 13–18 years
young adult — 18–25 years
mature adult — 26–40 years
(younger mature 25–30, older mature 31–40)
older adult — 40 years+

It was occasionally possible to subdivide the categories if adequate evidence survived. It was more often necessary to combine them when incomplete skeletons provided reduced evidence of age

The *sex* of the adults was assessed from the sexually dimorphic traits of the skeleton (Brothwell 1972). Three levels of reliability have been used: certain, ? for probable and ?? for possible. These levels are necessary because of the paucity of information in some cases.

Cranial index was calculated where possible, these and other measurements were taken according to Brothwell (1972).

Stature was estimated where possible, using the regression equations of Trotter and Gleser (1952; 1958).

I.3. Results

(for details see Appendix 34 (microfiche)).

Methwold. Site 2585

1   **Adult: older mature/older. ??Female.** Represented by elements from all skeletal areas.
Pathology/morphological variations
1) Left mandible showed absence of third molar and socket, probably congenital.
2) Dental hypoplasia — few strong lines in remaining teeth.
3) Several carious lesions
Mandibular left second premolar: small cervical lesion in distal portion.
Mandibular left first molar: very large cervical lesion in mesial portion adjacent to that in the premolar crown; lesion extends from cervical portion of root up the crown and into both mesial cusps, resulting in destruction of the entire mesial portion of the crown. A smaller cervical lesion was also noted buccally.
Estimated stature
1.55m (5ft 1in) if female. 1.60 (5ft 3in) if male.

2   **Juvenile: older (c. 8–10 years). ?? Male.** Represented by most of skull and fragments from all other skeletal areas.
Pathology/morphological variations
1) Morphological variations:
Mandibular, left first permanent molar: large crown with small disto-lingual accessory cusp.
Maxillary left first permanent molar: large crown with two small mesial accessory cusps. Unfused frontal suture — metopism (Pl. XI).
2) Dental hypoplasia:— maxillary left first permanent crown has strong line in cervical region.

3) Either this individual or *3* (some elements of both skeletons difficult to distinguish), had gross pitting of the right orbital vault — *cribra orbitalia* (Pl. XI).

3 **Juvenile: older (*c.* 9–11 years). ??Female.** Represented by most of skull and fragments from all other skeletal areas.
Pathology/morphological variations
1) Morphological variation: Unfused frontal suture — metopism (Pl. XI).
2) see note with *2* on *cribra orbitalia*.

Feltwell. Site 5188/c1. Hill Close

i. Ploughed up 1961

Adult: older. ??Male. Represented by skull and elements of axial skeleton, upper and lower limb.
Cranial Index
68.0— Dolichocranic
Pathology/morphological variations
Atlas has slight osteophytosis on inferior margins of anterior facet. Thoracic/lumbar body with gross osteophytosis on anterior lateral margins of one surface, creating flange *c.* 6mm.

ii. Excavated 1965

Note: Bones of more than one individual were often lifted and stored under a single number, especially in the south-east of the excavated area, where a confused mass of bones, originally recorded as 'group 3' was eventually more-or-less resolved into burials *10–17*.

1 **Adult: ??Female.** Represented by fragments of skull, axial skeleton, upper and lower limb. The bones recorded as burial *29* form part of this skeleton.
Pathology/morphological variations
Morphological variation: Two wormian bones either side of lambdoid suture of skull.
Juvenile: 11–12 years. Represented by skull, upper limb and lower limb. Not shown on plan (Fig. 18).
Also present
Fragments burnt animal long bone.

2 **Adult: older mature/older. Male.** Represented by almost entire skeleton.
Cranial Index
72.5— Dolichocranic
Pathology/morphological variations
1) Wear to teeth on left considerably heavier than to those on the right, showing a difference in wear equivalent to *c.* 25 years in terms of assessment of age on patterns of tooth wear. This variation in tooth wear was doubtless as a result of the carious lesion which led to the complete destruction of the right mandibular third molar crown. The lesion probably developed soon after the eruption of the tooth and must have been a problem for many years. No lesions were noted in the surrounding alveolus.
2) Very slight calculus deposits in bucco-lingual and bucco-palatial areas all teeth.
3) Dental hypoplasia was noted on crown of maxillary, right first molar.
4) Morphological variations:
Left mandibular third molar showed a six cusp variation
A minimum of two wormian bones situated in the superior half of the right lambdoid suture Mental protuberance of mandible very squared and prominent.
X-rays showed no Harris lines on long bones.
Also present
Frag. second mandible. = *28*.
33.9 g poorly-cremated adult. ?= *24*
Cow/horse molar fragment.

4 **Adult. ?Female.** Represented by skull and upper limb.
Also present
Skull fragments from one of the infants boxed as *6* and *15*.
Cow/horse scapula.

6/15 There is some confusion here. *6* was recorded as 'child's skull near no. *8*, remainder too friable to move, lying on area of cremated bones and black soil'. *15* was recorded as 'a very small child...only a very paper thin skull and a brown wet smudge' in the south-east of the excavated area (Fig. 18). The bones of four individuals, were stored in a box marked *6* and *15*. Only two of them were numbered. Those numbered *6* comprise fragments of adult cranial vault, and cannot correspond to Frank Curtis' description of *6*. Those numbered *15* appear to tally more closely

with *6* than with his description of *15*. The other two individuals do not figure in his records. All four are described here under the number *6/15*.
Infant: young (10+2 months). Represented by skull. ? = *6*
Also present
0.9g cremated bone from a juvenile individual, ? = *24*
Neonate (almost if not full term). Represented by almost entire skeleton.
Older infant/young juvenile (4 years + 9 months). Represented by skull and a few long bone fragments. ? = *15*.
Fragments of **adult** vault ? = *4/31*?

7 **Adult: younger mature. Female.** Represented by almost entire skeleton.
It is not entirely clear whether the individual was prone or supine. Due to the shortness of the grave, the upper portion of the body was semi-upright and the legs partly flexed at the knees. The arms were bent up toward the head and the head turned sharply to the right. According to drawings and descriptions, the head was facing west out of the grave and the pelvis was somewhat higher than would be likely if the body were laid on its back (Fig. 19).
Cranial Index
84.2—Brachycranic
Pathology/morphological variations
1) *Ante mortem* loss of mandibular teeth — left second premolar, both first molars and right second molar with resorption of sockets, possibly as a result of gross carious destruction of crowns. The spaces left as a result of tooth loss were small (Pl. X), the remaining teeth apparently 'filling in' to a certain extent.
2) Gross dental caries in several teeth.
Mandibular:
Right, second premolar, small lesion in disto-buccal portion of crown.
Left, second molar, large lesion in meso-distal occlusal and cervical regions.
Left, third molar, large lesion had destroyed most of occlusal surface except mesially, with destruction of disto-buccal cervical region.
Right, third molar, small lesion in distal cervical region.
Maxillary:
Left, second premolar, 5.0 x 3.0mm lesion in disto-buccal cervical region. Left, first molar, large cervical lesion mesially.
Left, second molar, a large cervical lesion in mesially portion had destroyed most of crown at neck, also a small 'pin-hole' lesion was present in the centre-edge of the meso-palatial cusp in the occlusal surface
Left, third molar, medium cervical lesion in distal portion. Right, third molar, medium cervical lesion in mesial portion.
Such gross carious lesions, especially in an individual of this age, were fairly unusual in prehistory and may reflect some enamel defect which made the individual susceptible to carious destruction on this scale (Pl. X).
3) Dental hypoplasia in several tooth crowns; all anterior mandibular teeth showed a minimum of four hypoplastic lines in the lower halves of the crowns. All of the recovered maxillary teeth showed two to three hypoplastic lines in the cervical halves of the crowns.
4) Mild calculus deposits on both mandibular and maxillary anterior teeth.
5) Morphological variations:
Prominent mental protuberance to mandible, squared but with sharp point.
Mandibular, right second premolar at ninety degrees to normal, buccal cusp mesially placed and lingual cusp distally placed.
Several variations in tooth form with accessory cusps in maxillary second molar crowns and 'squashing' and skewing of maxillary third molar crowns.
Comment
Post mortem damage to the medial portion of the left supra-orbit made interpretation difficult but there were numerous marks on the lateral portion of the supra-orbit which may be gnaw marks left by a dog chewing at the orbit (Julie Bond, pers. comm.).
Also present
Fragment gracile femur mid-shaft, ?from *4*
Horse ulna

8 **Adult: younger mature. Female.** Represented by most of skeleton.
Cranial Index
70.9 —Dolichocranic
Estimated stature

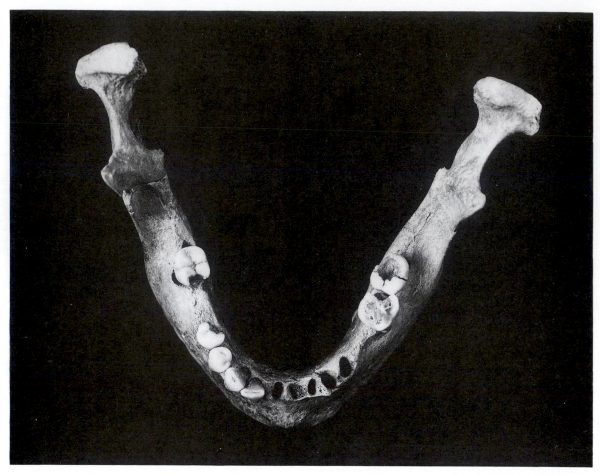

Plate X Hill Close, Feltwell (FWL OS 283, Site 5188/c1), burial *7*. Mandible of younger mature adult female, showing gross cervical and occlusal caries in several tooth crowns, together with spaces left in alveolus from tooth loss, probably as a result of similar lesions. Photo: David Wicks

1.65m (5ft 5in)
Pathology/morphological variations
1) X-rays of right tibia showed the presence of over twenty Harris' lines at both proximal and distal ends of the shaft, covering *c.* 100mm length of shaft from the epiphyses. These lines are indicative of repeated periods of growth arrest during the years prior to epiphyseal fusion.
2) Very slight buccal calculus deposits on maxillary teeth.
3) Morphological variations:
Prominent, squared mental protuberance.
Cusp forms of mandibular left second molar (disto-buccal accessory cusp), maxillary right second molar (mid-distal accessory cusp) and right third molar ('squashed' with accessory grooves).
Metopic suture.
Wormian bones in left portion of lambdoid suture, immediately adjacent to left of sagittal junction, one large — 23 x 18mm (now missing) and one smaller 9 x 4mm.

9 **Adult: mature. ?Male.** Represented by skull, superior portions of axial skeleton and upper limb and femur fragments.
Cranial Index
83.5—Brachycranic

10 **Adult. ?Female.** Represented by fragments from all body areas.
Adult. ?Male. Represented by fragments of ?skull, upper and lower limb. ?Fragments of this individual also in *12*.
Also present
Fragments older juvenile/young subadult upper and lower limb, ? = subadult in *12*.

11 ? = *17*.

12 **Adult: younger mature. Female.** Represented by all skeletal areas.
Pathology/morphological variations
1) Dental hypoplasia in all crowns especially the anterior ones, with a maximum of eight lines spaced across the canine crown. Average of five to seven.

2) Heavy calculus deposits on molar crowns, especially lingually.
3) Large cyst, 7mm diameter and 10mm deep, on edge of left acetabular notch.
4) Morphological variations:
Small wormian bone, 5 x 5mm, in left half of lambdoid suture, 40 mm from sagittal junction.
Subadult *c.* 15 years. ??Male. Represented by fragments skull and limb bones.
Pathology/morphological variations
Mild/medium calculus deposits on molar crowns.
Third molar crown with many accessory cusps.
Also present : Femur, probably from adult male in *10*

13 **Juvenile *c.* 7–8 years. ??Male.** Represented by skull and fragments upper limb.

14 **Adult: older (45 years+). ?Male.** Represented by skull, axis, upper and lower limb.
Pathology/morphological variations
1) *Ante mortem* loss of anterior mandibular teeth and resorption of sockets, possibly as a result of trauma. Excessive wear tends to lead to the loss of the posterior teeth before/as well as the anterior and a blow to the face could lead to the loss of the anterior teeth alone.
2) Medium/heavy calculus deposits on all crowns.

15 See *6/15*.

16 **Adult: older ?.** Represented by fragments from all skeletal areas.

17 ? = *11* **Adult: ??Female.** Represented by a few fragments skull vault, upper and lower limb.
Also present
Two fragments immature vault = *13*.
18.8g poorly cremated lower limb ? = *25*.

18 **Adult. ?Male,** represented by skull (flattened)

19 **Subadult: young.** Represented by skull, fragments innominates, upper and lower limb.
Pathology/morphological variations
1) Dental hypoplasia in both mandibular third molar crowns.

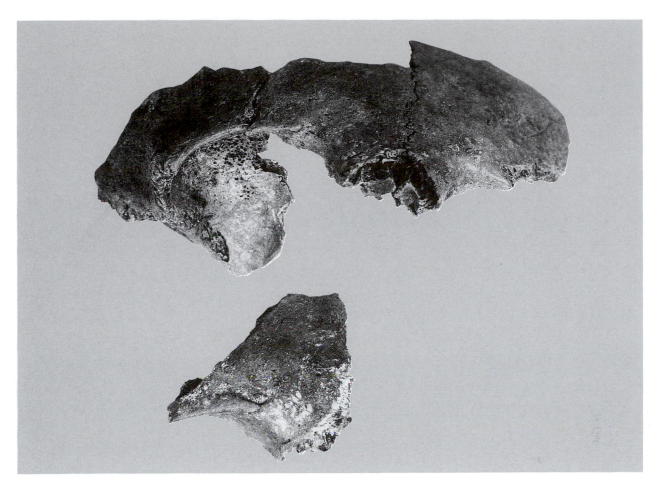

Plate XI Methwold (OS 1231, Site 2585). Frontal vaults of two juveniles, showing the occurrence of a metopic (unfused frontal) suture in both individuals and cribra orbitalia (pitting of the orbital vault) in one.
Photo: David Wicks

2) Morphological variations:
Bipartite root to both mandibular canines. Mandibular third molars have many accessory grooves.
Maxillary third molar has variation in cusp size.

20 **Adult: older mature/older. Female.** Represented by almost entire skeleton.
Pathology/morphological variations
1) Slight calculus deposits on all crowns.
2) Dental hypoplasia in maxillary left first incisor and third molar crowns, and right second premolar and second molar crowns.
3) Large carious lesion in distal cervical region of maxillary left first molar crown and in mesial cervical position of second molar crown, *i.e.* the two lesions were adjacent. Small lesion in distal cervical region of right maxillary second molar crown.
4) Slight osteophytosis of margins of vertebral facet of one of right ribs — osteoarthritis.

21 **Adult.** Represented by upper limb fragments.

22 **Adult: older mature/older. ?Female.** Represented by skull, some upper limb and femur.
Pathology/morphological variations
Heavy deposits of calculus on all remaining teeth.

23 **Adult.** Represented by skull and humerus.
Pathology/morphological variations
Destructive lesion with proliferative new bone on lateral margin of second right mandibular molar socket. Some bone resorption. Possible dental abscess.

24 Area, *c.* 1m diameter and 60mm deep, comprising cremation deposit with cremated bone, burnt flint and charcoal, the last two probably pyre debris.
300.6g total weight of bone.
86.0% in 10mm sieve. 13.7% in 5mm sieve. 0.4% in 2mm.
Max. frag. sizes: skull 52mm, long bone 71mm.
Adult. 53.2% identifiable bone. 17.5% skull. 31.9% upper limb. 50.6% lower limb.

Bone very poorly cremated with much black/grey bone, especially the spongy components, indicating incomplete oxidation. The remains were also poorly fragmented.
Also present
Several fragments unburnt bone from *4* and *6*.

25 Area of dark soil and charcoal, *c.* 1m in diameter and *c.* 50mm deep. A few fragments of cremated bone were recorded on site but none remained for examination. 18.8g cremated subadult/adult bone in *17* may perhaps be from here.

26 **Juvenile: young.** Represented by skull. Bone very friable.
Pathology/morphological variations
1) Dental hypoplasia, left first mandibular permanent molar crown with four hypoplastic lines in lower half of crown.
2) Morphological variation: Left, mandibular first molar has four cusp variation and bulbous, lingually inclined buccal surface.

27 Fragments of cranial vault. ? = *10* or *12*.

28 **Adult.** Represented by skull, upper and lower limb fragments. *2* includes a mandible probably from this individual.

29 = *1, q.v.*

30 **Adult: older.** Represented by skull and upper limb fragments.
Pathology/morphological variations
Ante mortem loss of right mandibular second premolar and second molar with resorption of sockets, probably as a result of excessive wear (all other sockets very shallow).

31 **Subadult. ?female.** Represented by fragments all skeletal elements.
Pathology/morphological variations
Destructive lesion on posterior lateral surface of tibia immediately below neck. 4.5mm diameter lesion with smooth margins, no signs of thickening or pitting of surrounding area.

33 **Adult: older (50 years+). ?Female.** Represented by elements skull, upper and lower limb.
Pathology/morphological variations
Proliferative new bone in alveolus around right mandibular second and third molar resorbed sockets, teeth lost *ante mortem* probably as result excessive wear. Periodontal disease?

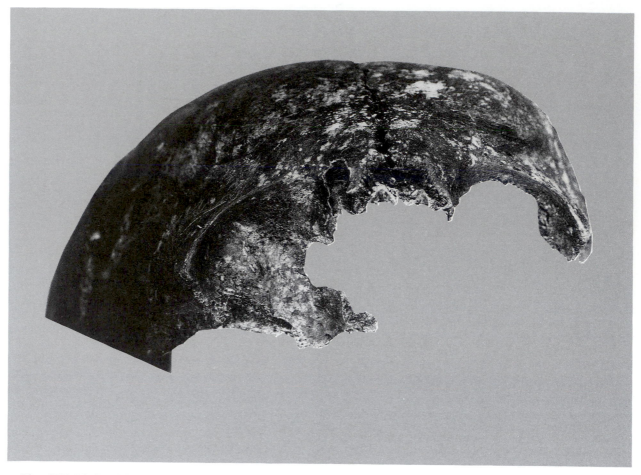

Plate XII Methwold Severalls (MTW OS 1012, Site 2542), burial *5*. Juvenile vault showing the occurrence of a metopic (unfused frontal) suture and cribra orbitalia (pitting of the orbital vault). Photo: David Wicks

Methwold. Site 2550. Hemplands Farm
> **Adult: mature/older. Female.** Represented by elements from all skeletal areas.

Methwold. Site 2542. Methwold Severalls

i. 1967 surface find
> **Adult. ??Female.** Represented by a femur.

ii. Excavated 1968 (2542/c1)
1 **Adult: mature. Female.** Represented by almost entire skeleton.
Cranial Index
77.8 —Mesocranic
Estimated stature
1.65m (5ft 5in).
Pathology/morphological variations
1) Dental hypoplasia:
Mandibular right first incisor two lines on crown. Maxillary left first and second incisors, two strong lines on each.
Maxillary first molars, one line *c.* half-way on each.
Maxillary second molars, one line *c.* half-way on each.
2) Dental caries:
Small carious lesion in buccal fissure of mandibular right second molar occlusal surface.
Medium-large occlusal lesion in buccal fissure of mandibular right third molar — 3 x 4mm, 2mm deep.
3) Schmorl's nodes in second lumbar vertebra.
4) Medium/heavy osteophytosis on margins of fifth lumbar vertebral body.
5) X-rays showed many faint Harris' lines at proximal ends of tibiae.
6) Patella has slight exostoses on superior margin of anterior tendon insertion.
7) Morphological variations:

Overcrowding of teeth, mandibular left second incisor set slightly behind first incisor and skewed mesially from labial.
Pronounced cervical bulge on both distal cusps of left mandibular third molar crowns.
Minimum of one wormian bone each side of sagittal suture in the lambdoid.
Both scapulae have non-fusion of acromion epiphyses.
Possible squatting facet noted on left tibia.

2 **Adult: Female.** Represented by fragments from all skeletal areas. Some confusion surrounds the identification of nos *2* and *3*. See note in Appendix 34 (microfiche).

3 **Adult: mature. Male.** Represented by fragments from all skeletal elements, although shown as skull only in Figure 21. Some confusion surrounds the identification of nos *2* and *3*. See note in Appendix 34 (microfiche).

4 **Juvenile (*c.* 7–8 years).** Represented by almost entire skeleton.
Pathology/morphological variations
Morphological variation: Two small wormian bones in left half of lambdoid suture, superior portion, possibly one to two more further down.
Also present
Fragments from *5* and one of adults.

5 **Juvenile: older.** Represented by most of skeleton.
Pathology/morphological variations
1) Pitting in both orbital vaults — *cribra orbitalia*.
2) Morphological variation:
Maxillary right first permanent molar has small distal accessory cusp.
Non-fusion of frontal suture — metopism (Pl. XII)
Non-fusion of anterior arch of atlas vertebra (usually fused by *c.* fourth year).
Also present
Fragments from *4*.

6 **Young infant — 6 months/2 years?** Represented by fragment of undeveloped tooth crown. Does not correspond to the apparently adult long bones represented in Figure 21.

iii. Excavated 1971 (2542/c2)

7   **Adult: older mature/older. ??Male.** Represented by skull and fragments upper and lower limbs.
Pathology/morphological variations
1) Head of right mandibular condyle flattened and pitted — temporo-mandibular arthritis.
2) Calculus deposits on mandibular canine.
3) Dental caries: small occlusal lesion in left mandibular third molar crown and two small lesions in right mandibular third molar crown.
4) Morphological variations: Left mandibular second incisor slightly twisted in socket, lingual side distally placed.
Mandibular third molars, five cusp variation. Minimum one wormian bone in left side of lambdoid suture just below sagittal junction.

8   **Juvenile: younger (*c.* 6–7 years).** Represented by fragments skull, axial skeleton, upper and lower limbs.

9   **Juvenile: younger (*c.* 5–6 years). ??Male.** Represented by elements of skull, axial skeleton, upper and lower limb.
Also present
Fragments from *8*.

Undated finds
(Appendix 3 (microfiche))

Methwold. Site 2549. Old OS field 181
Found in side of ditch.

    Adult: young. Male. Represented by skull and upper limb.
    Cranial Index
    71.0—Dolichocranic
    Pathology/morphological variations
    1) Morphological variations: Two wormian bones in left half of lambdoid suture immediately adjacent to sagittal junction. Minimum one wormian in right half of lambdoid, *c.* half-way.

Methwold. Site 2534. Old OS field 974
Found with animal bone while trenching in peat.

    Adult: mature/older. Male. Represented by skull and some axial skeleton fragments.
    Cranial Index
    81.06—Brachycranic
    Pathology/morphological variations
    1) Destructive lesions in articular processes of cervical vertebrae indicative of osteoarthritis.
    2) Morphological variation: two wormian bones in each side of lambdoid suture, *c.* half-way.

Methwold. Site 21967. Old OS field 1140
Dug up by farm machinery.

    Adult: younger mature. Male. Represented by skull (minus mandible).
    Cranial Index
    83.2—Brachycranic
    Pathology/morphological variations
    1) Slight calculus deposits on left canine.
    2) Slight dental hypoplasia, one line each, on right canine and first premolar.
    3) Morphological variation:
    Congenital absence of third molars.
    Right maxillary second premolar misaligned, buccal cusp 45° angle to normal, up against first premolar.

I.4. Discussion
It was noted that the tooth wear patterns (Brothwell 1972), which are only to be treated as a guide anyway, were indicating a younger age for the adults than that suggested by epiphyseal fusion in the 'young adult' age category, the discrepancy being about five years. Adjustments to the estimated age were therefore made for all adults in the collections.

81.0% of the adults from Hill Close, Feltwell, and all adults from the Methwold sites were sexed (Table 14).

It would be usual to find a higher number of infants in a population — the occurrence of at least three at Hill Close, including one neonate, would suggest that infants were treated no differently from the other members of society. Although fragile infant bone is often subject to preferential destruction in burial conditions, the skeleton of the Feltwell neonate is particularly well-preserved and almost complete. On other parts of the site, however, where juveniles were recovered, Frank Curtis commented on the poor preservation of the fragile bone and how it was impossible to lift. The *6/15* neonate may have been fortunate in its positioning and hence survived exceptionally well. Alternatively, given its absence from the records, it may have been excavated from another site and subsequently confused with the Hill Close material.

The obvious disturbances of the sites, both ancient and modern, would have aided preferential destruction of young bone. This may account for the low number of infants recorded.

The average age of death for adults appears to have been thirty to forty years, though the lack of any identified young adults in the Hill Close collection and the presence of only one from Methwold is rather unusual, as is the high proportion of females to males at Hill Close. In this case at least, young adult males may have been buried elsewhere, whether deliberately or fortuitously, for example if males were spending much time away from the group. Fairly equal proportions of males and females seem to have survived to older adulthood (*c.* 40 years+), older adults forming a relatively high proportion: 38% of adults at Hill Close and 30% in the combined Methwold collections (Table 14).

It must be born in mind, however, that the small size of the total sample may make it unrepresentative of the population from which it was drawn.

Hill Close, Feltwell (Site 5188/c1)
The burials were all fairly shallow, generally within *c.* 0.30–0.40 m of the modern surface (Pl. VII). A number of the inhumations appeared to have disturbed earlier burials, in several cases the plan shows some bones of a single skeleton still articulated and others scattered (Fig. 18: *9, 21, 28*). Dependent on the soil and burial conditions, it may only take a few years for a body to skeletalize, though ligaments may hold the skeleton together for much longer. It would be difficult to determine how long there was between the interments. Disturbance of earlier burials may only reflect the lack of grave markers and therefore cover a fairly short space of time.

Although Frank Curtis thought that some of the burials had been disarticulated at the time of deposition, it would seem more likely that originally articulated burials were disturbed due to subsequent interments disregarding earlier ones and the shallowness of the graves.

Methwold Severalls (Site 2542)
The plan (Fig. 21) here presents an even bigger jumble and one more difficult to interpret. It is possible that some of the remains were disarticulated at the time of deposition, however the disturbed nature of the site precludes any definite comment on this point. At least some of the bones illustrated on the plan (Fig. 21) appear to have been articulated, and post-depositional disturbance, possibly both ancient and modern, would seem as likely as original disarticulation.

1. Hill Close, Feltwell (Site 5188)

		Totals
Adult	4f, 2m, 3?	9
Adult: young (18–25)		0
Adult: mature (25–40)	4f	4
Adult: older (40+)	3f, 3m, 2?	8
Infant (0–5)	neonate, younger, older	3
Juvenile (5–12)	1m, 2?	2
Subadult (13–18)	2f, 1 younger	3
Total		30

2. Various sites in Methwold

	2585	2542/c1	2542/c2	2550	2549	2534	21967	Totals
Adult		2f						2
Adult: young (18–25)					1m			1
Adult: mature (25–40)		1f, 1m		1f			1m	4
Adult: older (40+)	1f		1m			1m		3
Infant (0–5)		1						1
Juvenile (5–12)	1f, 1m	2?	1m, 1?					6
Subadult (13–18)								0
Totals	3	7	3	1	1	1	1	17

f = female, m = male

Table 14 Summary of age and sex determinations

Morphological Variation
Numerous morphological variations were noted within the collections, some of which may illustrate links between individuals perhaps of a family nature.

Wormian bones (additional small bones situated in the sutures of the skull vault). Between one and five wormians were noted in nine individuals, *i.e.* 19% of the collections. (A not abnormal occurrence according to Brothwell (1973), for both Neolithic and Bronze Age populations).

Metopism (non-fusion of the frontal suture). Four individuals showed this trait, including both juveniles found at Site 2585 in Methwold. In the circumstances this may indicate a family relationship. The 11% occurrence of this trait is again not that unusual according to Brothwell (1973).

Tooth crown variations. Variations in the form of tooth crowns and roots is accepted as one of the more reliable morphological variants for illustrating genetic/family links. The third molar is particularly prone to variation, much more so than the other teeth and is therefore not so useful. A number of variants were noted, perhaps most unusually in burial *19* from Hill Close, where both mandibular canines showed a bipartite root. Variations in the first molar crown were noted in three cases, including two with accessory cusps, *2* from Site 2585 and *5* from Methwold Severalls, both juveniles who also shared the trait of metopism. Accessory cusps in the second molar crown were noted in three instances, including the two extended burials at Hill Close. Variations in the third molar crown were, as mentioned above, most numerous, with accessory cusps and grooves being noted in four cases, plus variations in size and shape. In only one instance was the third molar absent.

Two more unusual variations were noted, both cases of non-fusion. *1* from Methwold Severalls, an adult female, showed bilateral non-fusion of the acromion epiphyses of the scapula. Such a variation has been noted in other collections, most famously the *Mary Rose* 'archers' (Stirland 1984), where it was thought to be the result of occupational stress experienced prior to bone fusion, but it would not be possible to say if that were so in this case.

Even more unusual was the non-fusion of the anterior arch of the atlas vertebra in the Methwold Severalls *5* juvenile.

Cranial index
Only nine skulls were sufficiently complete to enable measurements to be taken. Of those, four fell into the Dolicranic group, four into the Brachycranic and one into the Mesocranic. There was no additional evidence to suggest any links within these groups, and the data was insufficient on which to make any further comment.

Pathology

Caries. As is usual, the most commonly noted lesions were those affecting the teeth. 20% of the adults had carious lesions, mostly older adults but also including some mature adults. Both occlusal and cervical caries were evident — the former, where the lesion develops in consequence of the dentine surfaces being exposed by enamel fracture (Miles 1967), is more unusual in ancient populations, the latter is generally experienced secondary to tooth wear and found in older individuals (Miles 1969). Such a high percentage of dental caries, of whichever form, is rather unusual in prehistory and may reflect some other enamel defect in this particular group making the individuals more susceptible to caries development. *7* from Hill Close, a younger mature adult female, had carious lesions in nine teeth and had lost four others *ante mortem* probably as a result of carious destruction. The teeth were not particularly heavily worn (possibly partly as a result of the great discomfort resulting from the lesions), but gross carious lesions over primarily cervical but also occlusal areas were evident.

Twice as many females were affected as males and the males were both older individuals with occlusal caries.

Dental hypoplasia (defects in the enamel formation of the tooth crown, resulting at the time of development due to some external influence arresting the growth of the crown).

Between one and eight lines, medium-heavy, were noted on one or several crowns of eight individuals. More females were affected than males.

Harris' lines. Three tibiae survived sufficiently intact to enable x-ray for Harris' lines (lines of growth arrest similar in nature to those of hypoplasia in the tooth crowns but at the epiphyseal lines, most obviously in the tibia). Two of those x-rayed were female, both showing the presence of many lines (max. eighteen proximal and distal). The other was male and showed no lines. All three had some dental hypoplasia.

Dental calculus (calcified plaque deposits). These were noted on the teeth of most adults. In no case was the deposit gross, slight/mild deposits were generally noted.

Cribra orbitalia (pitting of the orbital vaults — much argument surrounds the possible cause of this lesion but it is generally thought to be the result of some kind of deficiency disease). Noted in two juveniles, Site 2585 2 or 3 and Methwold Severalls 5.

Degenerative joint lesions. These were noted in only two instances — cervical osteoarthritis in an older adult male (Site 2534) and temporo-mandibular osteoarthritis in an older adult male (Methwold Severalls 7).

On a general level it would appear that females were subject to greater stress during the growing period than males, as illustrated by the greater incidence of hypoplasia and Harris' lines. This may be interpreted as showing that female children were considered of less importance than males and were therefore at the end of the food queue in times of shortage.

Cremated Bone

Three cremation-related contexts were noted at Hill Close, *24, 25* and *32*, the last recorded as an area of dark soil only.

24, an area *c.* 1m in diameter and 60mm deep, contained 300.6g of cremated bone mixed with burnt flint and charcoal. This may represent a pyre site with all pyre debris *in situ*. The bone represents only *c.* 12% by weight of that expected from an adult cremation, but, as it appears that at least one subsequent burial *(8)* cut through the pyre site, much may have been lost as a result of disturbance. Alternatively, a proportion of the remains may have been collected for burial elsewhere.

The bone was not heavily fragmented (86% being over 10mm) and was poorly cremated, mostly black/grey in colour indicative of incomplete oxidation of the bone (McKinley 1989). The lack of any bones from the axial skeleton was probably due to their removal or post-depositional loss and not to their crumbling from complete combustion. Deliberate breakage of the bone after cremation was unlikely.

25 was a similar area of dark soil and charcoal, of the same diameter as *24* and 50mm deep. Fragments of cremated bone were noted at the time of excavation but did not remain for examination (though *c.* 18g of bone recovered with *17* nearby may be from here).

Scatters of cremated bone from elsewhere on the site may have originated from one of the two areas. *24* and *25* may represent pyre sites or dumps of pyre debris.

II. Dietary Reconstruction by Means of Stable Isotope Analysis of Bone
by Rosemary H. Lennon

II.1. Principles
Carbon and nitrogen isotopes are fractionated by various natural processes, and the characteristic fractionation pattern is passed down the food chain to be incorporated into the bodies of the consumers. Bone collagen is composed of amino acids which derive largely from ingested materials. Its slow turnover rate in cortical bone (*c.* thirty years) and its resistance to decay both mean that collagen is an ideal source of past dietary information.

Carbon
Carbon isotopes are fractionated by processes such as photosynthesis and the absorption of carbon dioxide in water. The extent of fractionation is affected by the type of pathway the plant uses to fix carbon dioxide and differs in marine and terrestrial plants.

The small differences in isotopic composition are expressed as the $^{13}C/^{12}C$ ratio with respect to an agreed standard and are quoted in 'per mil' (‰), *i.e.*

$$\sigma^{13}C \ (‰) = \left(\frac{^{13}C/^{12}C \ (sample)}{^{13}C/^{12}C \ (standard)} - 1 \right) \times 1000$$

The standard for carbon is Peedee belemnite marine carbonate from South Carolina (PDB in Table 15), chosen because it is more enriched in ^{13}C than nearly all other natural carbon-based materials. Atmospheric carbon dioxide has a value of *c.* -7‰ with respect to this standard.

Due to kinetic effects, terrestrial plants which follow the normal Calvin (C_3) photosynthetic pathway are depleted in the heavy carbon ^{13}C, giving more negative (*i.e.* lighter) $\delta^{13}C$ values of, for example, *c.* -26.5‰ to -25.5‰ (Ambrose and DeNiro 1986; Chisholm *et al.* 1982). Terrestrial animals feeding on such plants show a similar ^{13}C content, although with a slight shift towards higher ^{13}C content, partly because the respired carbon dioxide may be enriched in the lighter isotope, ^{12}C (*i.e.* $\delta^{13}C$ = -18 to -25‰).

Site	Individual	Sex	Age	$\sigma^{13}C_{PDB}$ (⁰/₀₀)	$\sigma^{15}N_{AIR}$ (⁰/₀₀)
Methwold OS 1231 (Site 2585)	2 or 3	-	juv.	-21.3	9.1
Hill Close, Feltwell (Site 5188/c1)	1	F?	A	-20.8	10.1
	2	M	A	-20.4	9.8
	6/15	-	juv.10 mth.	-20.8	10.8
	7	F	A	-19.7	10.8
	8	F	A	-21.4	11.7
	10	?	A	-21.3	10.7
	11 ?=17	F	A	-20.7	9.4
	12	F	A	-20.7	10.2
	14	M	A	-21.2	11.1
	16	?	A	-20.8	11.3
	19	?	sub–A 12–14 yr.	-20.5	10.2
	20	F	A	-20.5	9.4
	22	F?	A	-20.8	11.5
	28	?	A	-20.2	10.1
	?	?	A	-21.6	11.6
Hemplands Farm, Methwold (Site 2550)	-	F	A	-21.3	10.4
Methwold Severalls (Site 2542)	1	F	A	-21.8	9.0
	5	-	juv.11 yr	-22.0	9.6

Table 15 Sex, age and stable isotope ratios

In areas where Hatch-Slack (C_4) photosynthesis predominates plants are less depleted in ^{13}C and have $\delta^{13}C$ values ranging from *c.* -9 to -16‰, with an average of -12.5‰ (van der Merwe and Vogel 1978; Farnsworth *et al.* 1985). Such plants are prevalent only in arid and sub-tropical regions, the most important cultivated species being maize, sugar cane and millet. In temperate regions such as north America and northern Europe, the influence of indigenous C_4 plants can be excluded, a fact which is especially useful in areas where marine food is available.

Absorption of carbon dioxide in water and the subsequent formation of bicarbonate is governed by kinetic effects and by thermodynamic equilibrium processes which lead to an enrichment in the heavy carbon isotope over air. Where marine bicarbonate is assimilated during photosynthesis of submerged plants, reaction kinetics again result in a depletion in ^{13}C to give values similar to those produced by C_4 photosynthesis (*i.e.* -10 to -19‰; Tauber 1981; Chisholm *et al.* 1982; Ambrose and DeNiro 1986).

Nitrogen

Nitrogen isotope ratios can also distinguish marine from terrestrial plants and, within a terrestrial environment and under good conditions, nitrogen-fixers (primarily legumes) from other plants. Marine vegetation is less depleted in the heavy isotope, ^{15}N, than are plants which use soil nitrogen (Wada, Kadonga and Matsuo 1975; Virginia and Delwiche 1982). This difference in ^{15}N content is carried up food chains, causing marine animals to have heavier (*i.e.* more positive) $\delta^{15}N$ values that those of terrestrial animals. Marine animals have average $\delta^{15}N$ values of *c.* +14.3‰; terrestrial animals average values of *c.* +6.3‰ (Schoeninger *et al.* 1983). Plants which fix their own nitrogen are most depleted and have an isotopic composition very like atmospheric nitrogen (Delwiche *et al.* 1979). AIR is the standard against which all $\delta^{15}N$ values are expressed and its value is defined as 0‰.

There is also an apparent trophic level effect of *c.* 3‰ (Schoeninger and DeNiro 1984) at each stage in the food chain, which means that meat has a more positive $\delta^{15}N$ value than vegetable matter.

Given these fundamental differences in the isotopic composition of food resources and their reflection in animal tissues, it is possible to use the isotopic $\delta^{13}C$ and $\delta^{15}N$ values in temperate north-western Europe (in this case Norfolk) to distinguish broadly between human populations whose diets were based on marine or terrestrial foods and to give an indication of the relative importance of leguminous plants and meat in the diet.

II.2. Methods

Fifteen individuals with intact or partially intact femora, listed in Table 15, were selected for analysis. Samples were cut from the midshaft of each femur in order to eliminate the possibility of inter-individual variation which might confuse the results.

Soil was removed manually from the outer surfaces of the bone, which was then washed in an ultrasonic bath in distilled water. The water was changed several times until no further discoloration occurred. The samples were then oven-dried at 50° C and crushed to a coarse powder which was subsequently decalcified with 1M HCl for twenty minutes at room temperature. Humic contaminants were removed by treatment with 0.125M NaOH for twenty hours at room temperature. After this time the bone was filtered and washed to neutrality and the collagen fraction solubilized by incubation in distilled water (pH 3) at 90° C for ten hours. Finally the bone collagen was filtered and freeze-dried.

10mg aliquots of collagen were weighed into a quartz tube with excess CuO and silver foil. The tube was evacuated, sealed and combusted at 700° C and it was then allowed to cool very slowly to room temperature over a period of ten hours.

The combustion products, carbon dioxide, nitrogen and water vapour, were separated by sequential cryogenic distillation and nitrogen was collected by compressing with a Toepler pump for ten minutes. Volumes of carbon dioxide and nitrogen were respectively measured manometrically and with a vacuum control unit. Isotope ratios of carbon and nitrogen were measured on a Finnigan Mat (model Delta) double inlet, triple collector isotope ratio mass spectrometer.

Results are expressed in Table 15 in the δ notation, as the number of samples is small, ranges rather than standard deviations are quoted. The precision of the measurements, as determined by the analyses of twenty aliquots of a commercial purified gelatine (May and Baker Limited, Dagenham, U.K), was ± 0.2‰ for $\delta^{13}C$ and ± 0.4‰ for $\delta^{15}N$ (1 s.d. in each case). Samples with C/N ratios outside the range of modern collagen (2.9–3.4) were rejected. There were no significant differences between the individuals from Hill Close (Site 5188/c1) and those from various sites in Methwold Fen.

II.3. Discussion

Carbon

Taking the popular value of c. +5.1‰ (van der Merwe and Vogel 1977) as the enrichment factor between diet and human collagen, the values expected for a population living almost exclusively on terrestrial products would be c. -20.0‰ (Chisholm *et al.* 1982; Ambrose 1986).

Schoeninger *et al.* (1983) found that prehistoric European agriculturalists had $\delta^{13}C$ values ranging from c.-18.9 to -21.0‰, and Johansen *et al.* (1986) quote a boundary of -19.9‰ for diets with over 90% terrestrial dependence. All the results in the present study tally with these figures and it would appear therefore that there was a negligible contribution from marine resources in the diet of the individuals sampled.

An indication of the proportion of terrestrial to marine food sources can be gained by assuming that the isotopic composition of collagen is a simple and constant function of diet and is a linear combination of two components:

i) a component depleted in ^{13}C and consisting of a mixture of C_3 plants and the flesh of terrestrial and freshwater animals that themselves fed largely on C_3 plants and
ii) a component enriched in ^{13}C consisting of marine plants and animals which fed exclusively on marine plants and plankton.

The isotopic composition of the collagen of an individual can then be related to the proportion of terrestrial food in the diet by the equation

D = T(x) + M(1−x)

where

D	=	$\delta^{13}C$ of collagen
T	=	assumed value of terrestrial sources (in collagen)
M	=	assumed value of marine sources (in collagen)
x	=	proportion of terrestrial sources
1-x	=	proportion of marine sources

i.e.

T	=	-25.5 + 5.1 = -21.4‰
M	=	-17.5 + 5.1 = 12.4‰

Using the extreme values and considering the maximum error for the sites, the proportion of terrestrial sources ranged from 79% to 100% for the individuals from Hill Close (Site 5188/c1) and from 94% to 100% for individuals from the various sites in Methwold Fen.

Nitrogen

Given that values of marine food sources are generally greater than +11‰, and taking 3‰ as the enrichment factor, the values expected for human collagen derived from a marine diet would would be heavier than + 14‰.

All the results in the present study are less than + 11.7‰ which therefore reinforces the indication from the $\delta^{13}C$ data in suggesting little or no marine input.

Schwarcz *et al.* (1985) quote a value of 12‰ for a 50:50 meat:fish protein diet. Taking the 3%. enrichment into consideration all the Norfolk values are less than the value of 15%. predicted for such a diet, which implies that meat and fish products did not play a large role in the diet. This is in accordance with the results of Schoeninger *et al.* (1983), who found that prehistoric European agriculturalists had $\delta^{15}N$ values of c. +8.0 to +10.2‰. Ambrose (1986) also found that pastoralists depending mainly on animal protein are separated from farmers relying more on domestic plants by their $\delta^{15}N$ values: pastoralists had mean $\delta^{15}N$ greater than or equal to +13.8‰, while farmers had values less than or equal to +10.4‰, the latter figure being very similar to the mean value of +10.3‰. for the individuals studied here.

If leguminous plants are assigned $\delta^{15}N$ values of 0.0‰ (DeNiro and Epstein 1981), there appears to have been no lowering effect, due to such species, on the present results. The results are, in fact, typical of a population existing predominantly on terrestrial plants (other than legumes) as a food supply.

In the case of nitrogen it is not safe to assume that diet is the only source of variation in $\delta^{15}N$ values. Trophic level, soil salinity and the ability of the animal to retain water all play a part, and it is correspondingly difficult to quantify the sources of nitrogen. Nonetheless, significant patterns can be discerned.

II.4. Conclusions

It appears from the isotopic evidence that the individuals buried in Hill Close on the upland and those found in Methwold Fen all relied very heavily on terrestrial resources, to the virtual exclusion of seafood. This conforms with their Early Bronze Age date, since at this time the marine transgression represented by the fen clay had subsided and freshwater conditions were restored (Ch. 2.II.2). The diet probably consisted of cultivated cereals supplemented by a little meat. This accords with the heavy occlusal tooth wear and exposed dentine of the skeletons (Ch. 6.I), indicative of a diet of much stone-ground cereal. There is no evidence, although numbers are small, for a difference in diet between males and females, or, indeed, between adults and children.

It has been suggested recently (Kreuger and Sullivan 1984) that the $\delta^{13}C$ values of collagen reflect predominantly the meat portion of the diet, isotopes from vegetable carbohydrates being incorporated into the mineral part of the bone. Whether this is true or not, the nitrogen figures indicate that meat was not heavily relied upon and the carbon results imply that what meat was eaten had come from animals which had fed on terrestrial resources.

With the natural scatter of the $\delta^{13}C$ and $\delta^{15}N$ values, estimates of the relative proportions of dietary components are necessarily rather unreliable. The isotopic enrichment patterns do, however, give an indication of the orders of magnitude involved and the method provides a valuable means of supporting and extending the conclusions drawn from archaeological evidence.

III. Animal Bone

III.1. Hockwold cum Wilton. Site 24866 ('site 8') and other sites investigated in 1959–62
(Ch. 3.I.1)
by Chris Balyuzi, Marion Chapman, Wendy McIsaacs, Graham Jones and Diana Pert with A.J. Legge

Site 24866 ('site 8')

The 'site 8' material is an uncontrolled sample, given the circumstances in which it was collected (Ch.3.I.1). The proportions of the species identified may therefore not be representative of the original economy. 322 bones and 403 teeth have been identified, the identifications being listed in Appendix 35 (microfiche), as are those of small quantities of bones and teeth from two other settlements in Hockwold excavated in the same years, Sites 5373 (22) and 5317 (60). Preservation of the material is fair, though much is very fragmentary. Most teeth are loose, and few remain as even part tooth rows. Consequently few measurements were possible.

The species identified were, in order of frequency, sheep/goat, cattle, pig, dog, red deer, roe deer, beaver, otter, cat, fox, badger, horse and duck. The percentages for the most abundant species can be seen in Table 16 and in Figure 110. It is evident that ovicaprines were the most common species; typically bone survival is relatively worse in the smaller species, but the dense mandibles and teeth survive well. It is common to find the situation where a raw count of identified bones gives emphasis to the larger species, while a crude minimum number calculation form the teeth and mandibles shows quite different proportions.

Sheep/Goat

Both species were represented, but due to poor preservation it was not possible to differentiate between them in most cases. Although one or two of the bone measurements indicate goat, most bones probably come

	Pig	Cattle	Sheep/Goat	Red Deer	Roe Deer	Dog	Beaver	Otter
A. from identified bones	16.1%	35.3%	40.1%	1.9%	0.9%	4.0%	0.6%	0.6%
B. from identified M$_3$ and dp$_4$	13.5%	25.0%	61.5%					

For details of identifications and numbers see Appendix 35 (microfiche)

Table 16 Proportions of species from Site 24866 ('site 8')

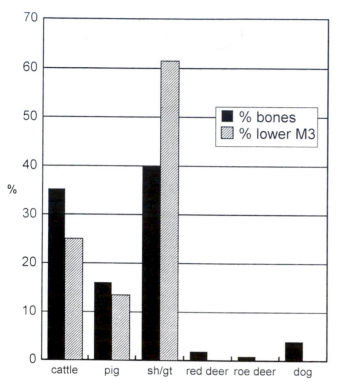

Figure 110 Proportions of main species identified from HCW OS 466 + 616, Site 24866 ('site 8')

from sheep. The two species were represented by 131 post-cranial bones and 246 teeth. Most of the skeleton was represented, as shown in Figure 111, which compares the percentage of survival of different bones from a minimum number of individuals based on fourteen lower right M$_3$s. Three tibias showed evidence of dog-gnawing. Most of the animals were adult, but there were two unfused distal humeri (therefore from animals less than six months old) and ten of the 246 teeth were milk molars.

Cattle
There were 114 post-cranial bones and 97 teeth. Most of the skeleton was again represented, as shown in Figure 112, with the minimum number of individuals based on right M$_3$s. The sample was relatively small and this accounts for the 'stepped' appearance of the chart. Most bones were fully-fused and therefore adult, and out of ninety-seven teeth only four were from juveniles. Due to the poor preservation few measurements were taken. Of the two distal humeri measured one fell within the range of specimens from the Bronze Age occupation of Grime's Graves (Legge 1981, fig. 48; Legge 1992, 72) while the other was very large (BT 80.0mm, HT 48.5mm) and much larger than any specimen from Grime's Graves. It may therefore have come from a Neolithic cow.

Pig
There were forty post-cranial bones and thirty-four teeth, and therefore only a small number of individuals. Three milk molars were found and there was also an unfused metacarpal. An adult metacarpal was dog-gnawed.

Red and Roe Deer
There were only six red deer bones, three roe deer bones and nine roe deer teeth.

Dog
In addition to the evidence of dog-gnawing, at least one dog was represented by twelve bones and six teeth.

Horse
Horse is represented only by one molar.

Discussion
Low proportions of sub-adult cattle among the 'site 8' material are probably a function of both rather harsh burial conditions and the collection method. In general, more cattle bones than sheep would have been expected; the percentages of cattle bones from two excavations in the Middle Bronze Age midden deposits of Grime's Graves, 12km to the east, are 56.5% and 53.2%, with only 34.5% and 39.0% sheep/goat (Site 5640; Legge 1992, table 2). It is, however, difficult to determine whether this is a true reflection of the 'site 8' fauna or a result of the collection method. The figures from this site do, however, seem to resemble more closely the percentages from the Iron Age at Haddenham, 30km to the south-west, where cattle accounted for only 21% of the level V fauna, while sheep were 74%, based on a minimum number of individuals (Evans and Serjeantson 1988). It is quite common for later Bronze Age sites to show such high proportions of sheep. The percentage of pig bones is, however, much higher than from Bronze Age Grime's Graves (Legge 1992, table 2).

The high proportion of sheep/goat in relation to cattle and the low proportion of deer suggests that woodland could be found only at some distance from the site, or, in the case of deer, that hunting was not an important aspect of the economy. The proportion of wild animals is low in the Bronze Age of the region, as again was found at Grime's Graves (Legge 1981, 79–84). It is generally accepted that there was a domestic horse population in Britain by the Bronze Age. The occasional finds of beaver, otter and duck indicate the proximity of the fen.

III.2. Sites excavated in 1964–67
The far smaller faunal assemblages excavated in subsequent years have been identified by Peter Lawrance. His identifications are summarised in Table 17 and are listed at greater length in Appendix 35 (microfiche). Quality of retrieval is, as ever, uncertain. Both red and roe

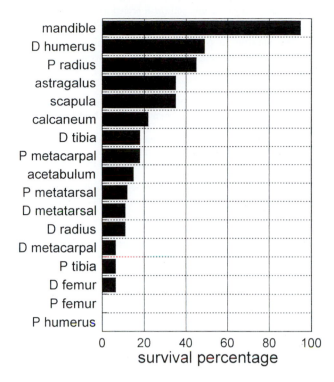

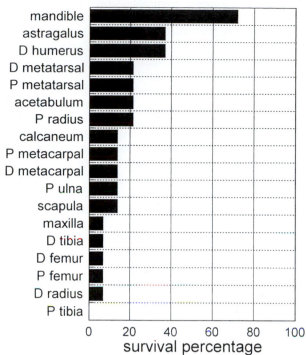

Figure 111 Sheep/goat survival chart for HCW OS 466 + 616, Site 24866 ('site 8')

Figure 112 Cattle bone survival chart for HCW OS 466 + 616, Site 24866 ('site 8')

		Site 5308/c4 (61/68)	Site 5332 (66)	Site 5333 (95/97)	Site 5308/c5 (96)	Site 4921/c1 (Glebe Farm)	Totals	
Cattle	bone	82	10	8	11+	20	131+}	205+
	teeth	40	8	4	22		74 }	
Sheep/Goat	bone	32	20	8		4	64 }	105
	teeth	22	2	14	3		41 }	
Pig	bone	12	1	1		8	22 }	52+
	teeth	25	1	3+		1	30+}	
Horse	bone					2	2 }	3
	teeth	1					1 }	
Deer	bone	2					2 }	
	teeth	1					1 }	18
	antler	11	2	2			15 }	
Cat	bone	2					2 }	4
	teeth	2					2 }	
Bird	bone	5	1	1			7	
Totals		237	45	41+	36+	35	394+	

Uncertain identifications and indeterminate fragments are excluded.

Table 17 Unworked animal bone from sites excavated in 1964–67

173

deer are represented among the antler fragments, two red deer antler fragments from Site 5332 (66) having cut marks. The few bird bones consist almost entirely of limb bone fragments from duck- or goose-sized specimens.

The preponderance of sheep or goat among the 'site 8' material, uncertain as its genesis may be, is matched in the small Bronze Age collection from Site 5332 (66), and echoed in the Late style Beaker-associated fauna of Site 5324 (93) (Bamford 1982, 29). Cattle predominate in the multiperiod collection from Site 5308/c4 (61/68), as at adjoining Site 5308/c1 (63) (Bamford 1982, 29–30). Pig is everywhere scarce, least so in the collection found with a Grooved Ware dish in a pit at Glebe Farm, Feltwell (Site 4921/c1).

IV. Sediments and Miscellaneous Biological Remains from Test Pits dug in Site 5308/c4 (68) in 1981

(Ch. 3.I.11)
by Peter Murphy

IV.1. Introduction

Besides the strictly archaeological objectives of test-pitting, it was hoped that an examination of sediments and biological remains would provide information on local conditions during the prehistoric occupation of the site and on subsequent habitat change. In the event, it was found that drainage had lowered the water-table to such an extent that the peats and subjacent archaeological deposit had become extensively disturbed by moles, rabbits and roots penetrating from nearby elder scrub, and were also being re-worked by an active soil fauna including earthworms and nematodes. These factors have resulted in the destruction of most biological remains originally present, in cross-contamination between layers and in the introduction of modern contaminants. Thus, although the soils and sediments at this site include a high proportion of largely amorphous organic material, preservation conditions proved to be little better than in archaeological deposits at upland sites on sand.

IV.2. The Deposits

Soils in the immediate vicinity are developed on thin Fen Peat (Adventurers' Series, shallow phase; Seale and Hodge 1976, 12 and map). The subdued micro-relief of the area has resulted in the formation of slightly thicker surface peat layers in hollows. Consequently, although ploughing was found to have completely disturbed the surface peats on the crests of hummocks, some less disturbed peat survived at the base of the A_{op} horizon in hollows, overlying the 'occupation layer'. The section in pit 3 (Fig.15: E–F) showed the following sequence:

Mean depths
1. 0–25 cm A_{op} horizon. Black stoneless structureless peaty loam; fibrous and fleshy roots common; merging boundary.
2. 25–35 cm B_0 horizon. Black sandy peat; blocky structure; friable, but hard when dry; some small wood fragments; rare small flint fragments (some heat-shattered); roots; merging boundary.
3. 35–45 cm 'Occupation layer'. Dark greyish-brown structureless humose sand with patches of clean sand and peat-filled root channels; slightly stony, with small flints (some heat-shattered) and very rare small chalk fragments; bone, pottery fragments; roots; sharp boundary.
4. 45–55 cm Greyish-brown structureless sand with peat-filled root channels; rare small chalk fragments and flints; fine roots; merging boundary.

5. 55 cm+ Chalk marl. Greyish-brown to white sandy silt loam to sandy clay loam with yellowish-brown mottles and peat-filled root channels; abundant small-medium chalk lumps.

The section in pit 1, at a slightly higher elevation, showed more extensive plough disturbance (Fig.15: C–D).

Mean depths
1. 0–35 cm A_{op} horizon. Black stoneless structureless peaty loam; fibrous and fleshy roots common; merging boundary.
2. 35–45 cm 'Occupation layer'. Dark greyish-brown to dark grey structureless humose sand with peat-filled root channels and discrete patches of clean sand; slightly stony, with small flints (some heat-shattered); bone, pottery, flint flakes; roots; sharp boundary.
3. 45–50 cm Yellowish-brown sand with peat-filled root channels; small-medium chalk fragments and flints; roots; merging boundary.
4. 50 cm+ Chalk marl.

After washing, the sand component of the 'occupation layer' was indistinguishable from that of the subjacent sandy horizon, consisting predominantly of rounded and subangular quartz grains. Its amorphous organic component must be derived partly from dumped organic refuse and partly from inwashed material. It appears that the 'occupation deposit' is simply a trampled and disturbed sandy palaeosol, incorporating domestic debris.

IV.3. Biological remains

All deposits beneath the A_{op} horizon in pit 3 were sampled and a single sample was taken from the 'occupation layer' (layer 2) in pit 1. The samples (4kg from the 'occupation layer'; 1kg from other deposits) were disaggregated and washed out over a 250 micron mesh sieve. Organic material was separated by water flotation, collecting the flots in a 250 micron mesh and the mineral residues were washed over a 500 micron mesh. The organic fraction was initially sorted in a wet state but when the poor preservation of the material became apparent it was dried to accelerate sorting. The following material was present:

Bone: Mammal bone fragments were recovered from pit 1 (layer *2*), pit 2 (layer *3*) and pit 3 (unstratified) (Appendix 35 (microfiche)). Pit 1 (layer *2*) also produced potentially intrusive small mammal bone including a rodent incisor.

Molluscs: In view of the fact that the sediments above the chalk marl were non-calcareous, the few land molluscs present are presumably recent and intrusive. They comprise *Pupilla muscorum, Vallonia excentrica, Cochlicopa* sp., *Trichia* sp, and *Cepaea* whorl fragments.

Uncharred plant remains: Modern roots were present in all samples, together with a few poorly-preserved seeds of ruderals (*Stellaria media, Silene* sp., *Urtica dioica, Chenopodium* sp, *Polygonum* sp., and *Sambucus nigra*). The latter species is most abundant, and since elder scrub was present just next to the site there can be no doubt that these seeds are contaminants.

Charred plant remains: There was a concentration of charred material, thought to be *in situ*, in the samples from the 'occupation layer'. The charcoal consists of small twiggy fragments, not definitely identified.

The sample from pit 1 (layer *2*) produced a single charred emmer-type wheat grain (*Triticum dicoccum* Schübl).

IV.4. Discussion

The main finding of this investigation is that drainage has resulted in aeration of the sediments with consequent disturbance and humification. How far this is applicable to other sites in the Hockwold area can only be established

174

The Methwold Bow (Site 4460): Pollen Analysis

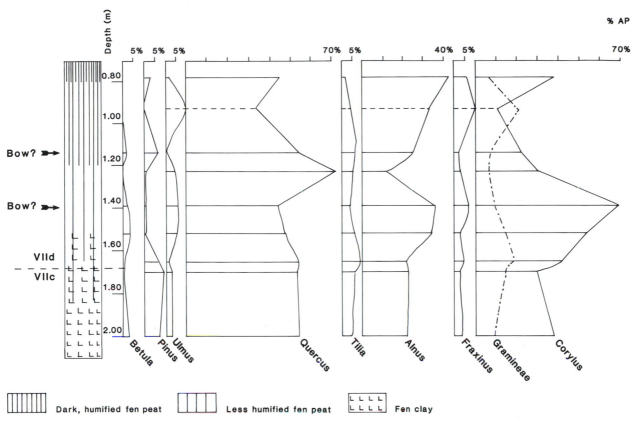

Figure 113 The Methwold bow (MTW OS 990, Site 4460): 1971 pollen analysis showing both horizons from which the bow may have come

by further work, but obviously at this site detailed palaeo-ecological studies comparable to those undertaken at Bronze Age fen edge sites in the Mildenhall area (Martin and Murphy 1988) will not be possible, unless deep pits containing sealed, structured organic deposits are present.

Nevertheless some information has been gained. In stratigraphic terms the site conforms with the sequence known from elsewhere on the fen edge: second millennium BC deposits formed in relatively dry conditions are overlain by peats, reflecting higher local water-table levels. It is unfortunate that the surviving peat at this site was too disturbed for ^{14}C dating to be attempted, and the date of the beginning of peat formation here therefore remains unknown. From an economic point of view the bone recovered in this and earlier excavations has provided at least some information on stock-rearing (Ch. 6.III.2), and the presence of a charred emmer-type grain indicates some reliance on cereal production, though only more extensive sampling will determine the importance of arable farming. It may, however, be of significance that even this very small-scale sampling has produced some evidence of cereal growing.

V. Palynological Evidence

V.1. Site 2542/c1. Methwold Severalls

(Ch. 4.I.5)

Shortly after the excavation of a group of skeletons by Frank Curtis in 1968, Dr F.A. Hibbert, then of the Cambridge Botany School, visited the site with him and collected pollen samples from close to where the skeletons

had been found. Slides and pollen count sheets then prepared are now unfortunately lost. All that remains is Dr Hibbert's preliminary report, part of which is reproduced here. Three of the skeletons are now dated to the Early Bronze Age (Table 1).

> The peat stratigraphy of the site at Methwold shows a phase of fen development followed by the establishment of fen woodland as the water level shallowed. This woodland phase was subsequently over-whelmed and the deposits are more characteristic of wetter conditions: abundant remains of *Phragmites* (reed) and *Cladium* (saw-toothed sedge) are found in the latter. This succession is in accord with the general stratigraphy, so far as it is known, from this part of the fenland. It is from these later-formed, wetter deposits that the bones were recovered.
>
> Preliminary pollen analysis of the deposits shows a marked increase in pollen from those plants normally associated with agricultural activities in those deposits just below the level from which the bones were taken. There is no appreciable fall in the total tree pollen, in particular pollen of elm, which is common in earlier, Neolithic settlements; this, along with the presence of beech, would indicate a later age: Bronze or Iron on the basis of pollen analysis alone.

V.2. The Methwold Bow. Site 4460

(Ch. 5.V)

by Richard Sims

The following is a summary of a report prepared by the author for the British Museum in 1971.

The aims of the palaeobotanical investigation were twofold: to estimate the age of the bow using pollen analysis and to determine the wood from which the bow was made.

The site of the bow was located by the finder to within 1m laterally and 100mm in depth. This placed the bow at 1.15 ± 0.05m below the present surface of the peat, just at

175

the junction of light and dark fen peats, 0.38 ± 0.05m above the fen peat/fen clay transition (Fig. 113).

Stratigraphy
0.00–1.20 m. Dark, humified fen peat
1.20–1.53 m. Light, less humified fen peats
1.53–1.67 m. Fen peat/fen clay transition
1.67–2.10 m. Fen clay to bottom of section

Dating of the bow
The results portrayed in the pollen diagram indicate, using the criteria of Godwin (1940), that a boundary between two pollen zones can be drawn at 1.68m. This is the VIIc/VIId boundary and is based on the *Ulmus* pollen minimum, *Tilia* pollen maximum and the general trends shown in the curves for *Alnus* and *Quercus* pollen frequencies.

Stratigraphically the lithology would support his correlation as Godwin's VIIc and VIId pollen zones were in the fen clay and fen peat respectively.

Pollen from a sample of mud taken from the bow itself was composed as follows:

Species	% Arboreal Pollen
Betula	9%
Pinus	7%
Ulmus	7%
Quercus	32%
Tilia	9%
Alnus	35%
Corylus	74%
Gramineae	25%

This would place the bow at approximately 1.39m from the surface in less humified fen peat, rather than at the 1.15 ± 0.05m in dark, humified peat indicated by the finder. The analysis is, however, based on only forty-three arboreal pollen grains and may in addition have been affected by differential destruction of pollen in the fifteen years during which the bow was exposed to the air.

The bow itself was made form the wood of yew (*Taxus baccata*).

7. The Story So Far...

I. Record and Reality

I.1. Archaeological Visibility

The balance of pottery styles recovered from fields 466, 613, 614 and 616 in Hockwold cum Wilton changed in the course of the 1960s. Bronze Age wares gave way to Beaker as the dominant style, and some features of the Beaker itself, notably the frequency of non-plastic as opposed to plastic rustication, altered as the decade progressed (Figs 61, 64, 65). Earlier occupation, represented by small quantities of Mesolithic and Earlier Neolithic material in the collections of the 1960s, had become many times more visible by the 1980s, when numerous Mesolithic and Earlier Neolithic sites were located in the course of the Fenland Project (Silvester 1991, figs 45–46).

The implicit rate of erosion is of the order of a hundred years of settlement per annum. The full picture of local prehistoric occupation may therefore be built up only over time, since the archaeology visible in an eroding landscape in any year or few years is volatile. The survival of occupation deposits formed towards the end of the Early Bronze Age at West Row, Mildenhall, Suffolk (Martin and Murphy 1988) may represent favourable local preservation conditions.

I.2. Settlement History?

In these circumstances, it is difficult to tell whether apparent gaps or troughs in the local settlement record are real. The two most obvious fall in the Later Neolithic and in the Middle and Late Bronze Age.

Later Neolithic

Within the survey area, Grooved Ware and Peterborough Ware are confined to two sites, one of them on the upland (Fig. 68). Confidently-identified finds of Neolithic Bowl, Grooved Ware and Peterborough Ware (together), and Beaker occur in the proportions 8:1:34 (Figs 67–69; Appendices 27–29 (microfiche)), in contrast to proportions of 2:1:7 for Norfolk as a whole (Healy 1984, figs 5.1, 5.6, 5.11). In the Fenland Project collections of the 1980s, Grooved Ware and Peterborough Ware remained scarce and of restricted distribution and flint scatters of Later Neolithic character were relatively few, although the frequency of Neolithic Bowl greatly increased (Healy 1991a). The zone contrasts with the Breckland to the east, where there is a regional concentration of Grooved Ware (Cleal 1984, fig. 9.4; Healy, Cleal and Kinnes 1993, fig. 2), a lesser concentration of developed Peterborough Ware (Cleal 1984, figs 9.2, 9.3), and abundant contemporary flint scatters. There, Later Neolithic assemblages with little or no Beaker component are frequent, as at Honington, Suffolk (Fell 1951), or Middle Harling, Norfolk (Site 6033; Healy 1995).

The low representation of Later Neolithic pottery styles and the high representation of Beaker may owe something to stylistic or cultural preference. But physical conditions are important too. The currencies of Peterborough Ware and Grooved Ware and the earlier part of the currency of Beaker coincide with the local maximum of the fen clay transgression (Ch.2.II.2; Table 13). Beyond the limits of the transgression itself (Fig. 2), wetter and more saline conditions may have made the fringes of the basin inhospitable to a population whose habits and skills were geared to different resources. The later part of the currency of Beaker, on the other hand, coincides with the post-transgression environment of falling water levels, extensive freshwater peat, and developing fen woodland, which may have been far more attractive to the occupants of the surrounding areas. The apparently low level of Later Neolithic activity along the fen edge is likely to have been a real one. Most of the occupation represented by Beaker pottery in the zone probably took place after the floruit of Grooved Ware, a conclusion compatible with the possibly concurrent use of Beaker and Food Vessel Urn (Ch. 5.III.3).

Middle style Beaker is also relatively scarce on the fen edge (Cleal 1984, fig. 9.6). The most distinctive and numerous local variants, Clarke's Barbed Wire and East Anglian styles, equivalent to Case's (1993) Group E, have their regional focus on the Sandlings of the Colchester-Ipswich area (Clarke 1970, map 4), while Late style Beakers, especially of his Southern series, equivalent to Case's southern Group B, are massively concentrated on the south-eastern fen edge (Cleal 1984, fig. 9.7; Clarke 1970, maps 7–10).

Middle and Late Bronze Age

Disparities between adjoining regions and the survey area are as great for Bronze Age pottery styles as for Neolithic ones. Collared Urn, almost absent from the survey area, outnumbers Food Vessel and Biconical Urn in finds from Norfolk barrows (Lawson, Martin and Priddy 1981, 40). Deverel-Rimbury pottery, present, if at all, in small quantities in the survey area, outnumbers Biconical Urn in all contexts in the county (Lawson 1980a, 287–289, fig. 1).

Here too the dating of the pottery styles suggests a relationship to increasing wetness. If the end of a period of intensive occupation is marked by the Biconical Urn pottery illustrated here, then it fell in the late second millennium cal. BC (Table 13). This would correspond to the renewed onset of wetness seen in the transition from fen carr to sedge fen at Welney Washes and Redmere (Ch.2.II.2) and to the progressive abandonment of the ditched enclosure system of Fengate, Cambridgeshire, on the western fen edge after a thousand or more years of use (Pryor 1992, 520).

The case is strong but it is less convincing than that for diminished occupation in the Later Neolithic for two main reasons:

(i) A Middle and Late Bronze Age presence is evidenced by numerous finds of contemporary metalwork (Figs 24–25), and the record is beginning to be filled out by radiocarbon determinations on artefacts of other materials, like an antler 'axe' from Feltwell (Site 20979/c3) now dated to *c*. 1400–1130 cal. BC (Hedges *et al.* 1993, 311).

(ii) The progressive destruction of archaeological deposits seen in the collections recovered from the Hockwold fields over the last thirty years may have had a longer history. If the last Biconical Urn assemblage was ploughed up in 1965, did the last Deverel-Rimbury assemblage meet the same fate in 1930 and the last post-Deverel-Rimbury assemblage in 1900? In times of more extensive pasture and more traditional methods of cultivation destruction would not have proceeded as rapidly as in the 1960s. Nonetheless, centuries of drainage, peat wastage, peat cutting and cultivation may have taken a selective toll of living sites at higher levels than those described here.

There is little trace of Middle or Late Bronze Age settlement on the slightly more elevated land abutting the zone so densely occupied in the preceding thousand years. Preservation here is bad, but finds from the area should still give some indication of its prehistoric occupation. On the very edge of the upland, a single radiocarbon measurement suggests that burials continued to be inserted into a natural hillock in Hill Close, Feltwell, down to *c*. 1440–1270 cal. BC (Table 1; Fig. 17: Site 5188). A small amount of Late Bronze/Early Iron Age pottery was found on the upland edge of the Little Ouse valley at Salway's site 7088 (Fig. 3: Site 5316/c7). There is also a record of one West Harling-like Late Bronze/Early Iron Age sherd from the edge of the large island of Southery and Hilgay (Site 17103), echoing the island location of Late Bronze Age occupation at Stonea in the Cambridgeshire Fens to the west (Potter and Jackson 1984–5, 9–10). Contemporary settlement is particularly well represented at Lingwood Farm, Cottenham, Cambridgeshire, close to the findspot of the Wilburton Fen hoard (Evans 1993).

The overwhelming majority of the pre-Iron Age material from the immediate upland dates, however, from the Early Bronze Age or before, like the artefacts from the fen edge. The recognition of Iron Age occupation at Salway's sites 7088 and 7188 (Sites 5316/c7 and 5316/c2; Salway 1967, 44, 49) and in Hill Close (Site 5188; Shand 1985), as well as of numerous Romano-British sites, suggests that Middle and Late Bronze Age settlements would have been found too if they were present, especially as the area is favoured by collectors and metal-detector users.

It seems more likely that contemporary local settlement was again focused in the Breckland, where living sites have been located, despite equally poor preservation. The Middle Bronze Age presence is clearest in the post-mining occupation of Grime's Graves (Site 5640; Mercer 1981; Longworth, Ellison and Rigby 1988; Longworth *et al.* 1991; Legge 1992). It is also represented by urned cremations at Fison Way, Thetford (Site 5853; Healy 1992). Within the same area, Late Bronze Age settlement is known at Brettenham (Site 5955; Shand 1985), and the Late Bronze/Early Iron Age site of Micklemoor Hill, West Harling, is nearby (Site 6019; Clark and Fell 1953).

II. Settlement Character

II.1. Pre-Fen Clay

Widespread wastage of the Upper Peat has now opened up this phase of settlement to investigation. The work of Smith *et al.* (1989) demonstrates the potential of the data.

Within the survey area the distribution of both Mesolithic material and leaf arrowheads shows a slight concentration on the fen margin in Feltwell, between northings 9000 and 9300 (Figs 34–35). This has become more marked in the Fenland Project collections (Healy 1991a, figs 70–71), and suggests that soils formed on the chalky deposits of the basin floor in this area may have been more attractive to contemporary populations than those formed on sands and gravels farther south.

Grimston Ware is consistently rare and Mildenhall Ware relatively frequent among the Neolithic Bowl pottery. If Herne (1988) is correct in seeing Grimston bowls as marking an early Neolithic horizon, perhaps *c*. 4900–3600 cal. BC, then the predominantly Mildenhall style pottery of the survey area may date from rather later, when peat had already begun to form on the basin floor. In this case it could represent occupation of the then fen edge analogous to that which succeeded the fen clay transgression. It is possible to visualise a picture similar to that sketched by French and Pryor (1993, 101) for the contemporary settlement of small islands surrounded by the growing basal peat in the North Bedford Level: one of intermittent, perhaps brief, episodes of use accompanied by small-scale reduction of woodland cover and considerable disturbance of the soil.

Any or many of the numerous flint and stone axes from the area may date from this phase.

II.2. Post Fen Clay

Material of this phase, recovered in quantity in the 1930s and 1960s, remains by far the most abundantly represented in the lithics collected during the Fenland Survey, although most contemporary pottery has long since disintegrated after years in the ploughsoil (Healy 1991a). The place of Beaker and Early Bronze Age settlement in local landscape history is classically represented by the stratigraphy of Plantation Farm, Shippea Hill, where a lens of debris derived from occupation by users of Beaker and Food Vessel Urn was preserved in the upper peat 50–150 mm above the fen clay (Clark 1933, pl. XLIII).

Ten years before, Fox had described contemporary settlement to the south of the survey area (1923, 68):

> The distribution of finds and remains of the Bronze Age in the Cambridge Region shows that settlement was mainly confined to the eastern borders of the fens and the valleys of the Cam and Lark; while the number of finds within the fens themselves points to the increasing use of inland waterways. Numerous round barrows — dating, it is probable, mainly in the II millennium — are disposed along the open hill country bordering the settlements. Poverty in associated objects and variety of funeral customs are outstanding features of these burials. The beaker-folk were buried for the most part not in barrows on the hills, but by fen and riverside, and even in the fens.

Almost every word remains true. The pattern can, furthermore, be extended northward from the Lark to the

Wissey. New information enhances Fox's picture rather than alters it.

'Pot-boiler' Sites

A persistently mystifying aspect of contemporary settlement is the presence of numerous 'pot-boiler' sites. They figure only occasionally in the records drawn on here, mainly because they are so common in the survey area that its residents have taken little note of them. A few have produced prehistoric artefacts, including a flake of Group VI rock and struck flint from Site 5183 and Beaker sherds and struck flint from Site 5159/c2, both in Feltwell. Their density became apparent only in the course of the Fenland Project, when over 300 were recorded in the Norfolk peat fen, many in areas not occupied after the Bronze Age (Silvester 1991, 85–87, fig. 49). Radiocarbon determinations place two Suffolk examples in the Early Bronze Age, while excavation of animal bones and a withy- and wood-lined trough within another at Swale's Fen, Mildenhall, suggests that at least some were used for cooking (Martin 1988). A wooden trough was also found beside a 'pot-boiler' site in Feltwell, where a burial beneath the mound adds a further dimension to the use of such accumulations (Site 23650; Hall and Coles 1994, 88).

Living Sites

Fen edge settlements of this phase have often been interpreted as representing temporary, seasonal encampments, occupied by herders exploiting the summer pasture of the fen. This has stemmed mainly from the documented medieval use of the fen as summer pasture (Darby 1974, 61–82), and partly from the scarcity of structures or subsoil features on the sites themselves. Evans (1987) points out that settlement features are sometimes present, as at West Row Fen, Mildenhall (Martin and Murphy 1988, fig. 1). They were also present on some of the sites described in this volume (Ch.3.III). He makes the important point that midden-like accumulations of artefacts, especially sherds of fragile and sometimes large pots, are scarcely the mark of a mobile population. In the relatively dry local conditions of the second millennium, probably with extensive flood-free pasture, he sees a localised land use pattern which, while using seasonally available grazing, involved more permanent settlement than previously thought.

The accumulations themselves differ from contemporary upland settlements only in their better preservation. Many, even most, Beaker and early Bronze Age settlements on the upland consist of spreads of rubbish with few or no structural or subsoil features. Some are relatively well-preserved under barrows, as at Bowthorpe, Norwich (Site 11431; Lawson 1986, 33) or Weasenham Lyngs (Site 3660; Petersen and Healy 1986), but those not so protected are reduced to a mass of plough-damaged struck flint with or without a handful of small, abraded sherds, as on Spong Hill, North Elmham (Site 1012; Healy 1988, 107, 109).

The impression of a series of distinct, relatively short-lived, episodes of occupation given by the pottery from the Hockwold sites (Ch. 5.III.3) similarly mirrors the upland picture, where extensively excavated areas tend to show repeated, small-scale occupation over hundreds of years, as on Spong Hill, North Elmham (Site 1012; Healy 1988, 73) or Redgate Hill, Hunstanton (Site 1396; Healy, Cleal and Kinnes 1993). This in turn accords with Edmonds' interpretation of extensive Later Neolithic to Early Bronze Age flint scatters as the result of frequent relocation of living sites within a relatively restricted area (1987, 174).

Economy

None of the animal bone collections from the survey area is satisfactory, whether in size, completeness, method of collection or contextual integrity. Within their limitations, however, they present a consistent picture (Ch. 6.III) of the herding of cattle and sheep and/or goats, with little dependence on game of any sort, including wetland species, although these were available (Ch.2.III). Cattle may have been the most numerous in the centuries following the transgression, with ovicaprines dominant later on. Scanty and imperfect as this picture is, it accords with preliminary results from West Row Fen (Martin and Murphy 1988, 356) and with brief accounts of animal bone excavated from Cambridgeshire and Suffolk sites in the 1930s (e.g. Jackson 1933, 1935, 1936). These assemblages are compatible with the use of fenland summer pasture traditionally ascribed to fen edge sites. It is impossible to tell how far the emphasis on milk — rather than meat — production seen by Legge (1981, 1992) in Middle Bronze Age animal husbandry at Grime's Graves may have obtained in this different environment at an earlier date.

Cereal processing is evidenced by numerous finds of saddle querns (Fig. 43) and rubbers (Appendix 25 (microfiche)) throughout the occupied zone. While these are inherently undateable, there some grounds for linking them to an established phase of the post-fen clay occupation. At Methwold Severalls, there was an upsurge in the frequency of pollen of plants associated with agriculture immediately below a group of skeletons radiocarbon-dated to c. 2190–1780 cal. BC (Ch. 6.V.1; Table 1). The only reworked flint saddle quern fragments recorded in this volume form part of collections dominated by Biconical Urn pottery (Ch. 5.II.2), corresponding to others found with Biconical Urn at Mildenhall Fen (Clark 1936, 44–5), with Collared Urn in the nearby West Row Fen industry (Healy in prep.), and in Bronze Age collections made during the Fenland Project (Healy 1991a, 124). The scarcity of earlier instances suggests that the main local use of saddle querns may have begun towards the end of the Early Bronze Age. Several fragments occur in the Middle Bronze Age industry of Grime's Graves to the east (Herne 1992, figs 31–2).

Cereals themselves are represented only by a single charred grain of emmer wheat found during test-pitting at Site 5308/c4 (Ch. 6.IV.3). Its recovery from such limited sampling may, as Peter Murphy points out, be significant. Cereal impressions were not searched for in the pottery published here, although a few were noted on sherds in the assemblages published by Bamford (1982, 19). Rosemary Lennon's stable isotope analysis of Early Bronze Age skeletons from the survey area (Ch. 6.II) points to a diet of cultivated cereals supplemented by a little meat.

These threads of evidence all suggest that cereals were important in the diet, as they seem to have been elsewhere in the south-eastern fens. At West Row Fen, emmer wheat, with smaller quantities of spelt and hulled barley, has been recovered and quern fragments and rubbers were abundant. It is unclear, however, whether the cereals were grown at the site or brought from farther away (Martin and

Murphy 1988, 356–357). The pollen record of the upper peat correspondingly indicates clearance and cultivation of dry land forest at this time (Waller 1994, 154).

The concentration of settlement on the south-eastern fen edge, between the rivers Cam and Wissey, is relevant. Here the fen abuts mainly on chalk or on chalky deposits; north of the Wissey, where occupation drops off abruptly (Cleal 1984, fig. 9.7), it abuts mainly on Greensand. Preference for more fertile and resilient chalk soils over acidic and easily impoverished Greensand ones by inhabitants of the fen edge would be consistent with cultivation of the immediate upland. Use of upland resources is seen in the chalk flint which forms a substantial part of contemporary fen edge industries (Table 3).

It is possible to visualise year-round occupation of the sites described here on the lines suggested by Evans (1987). Location at the boundary of fen and upland would have permitted the complementary use of both from a single base, the balance between the two varying with the seasons. This would be compatible with contemporary burial both in the fen and in barrows on the upland (Fig. 17). Botanical evidence from West Row Fen, in a similar location, points to occupation in spring, summer, and perhaps autumn, with nothing to preclude a year-round presence (Martin and Murphy 1988, 357). The stylistic features of pottery from living sites could suggest shifts of location within the boundary area at intervals of years or decades.

Relation to the Western Fen Edge
Investigation of contemporary settlement on the other side of the basin, at Fengate, Cambridgeshire, has produced economic and organisational evidence of a quality unmatched here. Common features include the importance of fenland pasture and an emphasis on herding (Pryor 1984, 206), and small, relatively short-lived dwelling sites shifting within the occupied zone (Pryor 1980b, 185).

But the differences were substantial. Fengate had a regular, extensive system of ditched paddocks and droveways, maintained through a thousand years of use. The system was, furthermore, initiated by users of Grooved Ware in the Later Neolithic, one of the apparent troughs in the settlement record of the south-eastern fen edge, where the few early field systems so far identified seem to date from the full Bronze Age (Hunn et al. 1993; Evans 1993). Its development is interpreted as an intensification of land use in response to a reduction of usable land area by the fen clay transgression (Pryor 1984, 206–207). Fengate has produced no querns, rubbers or grain impressions, with the implication that cereal cultivation and processing were unimportant there (Pryor 1980b, 180–181).

III. The Contents of Stores, Drawers, Garden Sheds and Display Cases

III.1. Fine Flint and Stone Objects
Another major distinction between the south-eastern and the western fen edges is the former's concentration of fine flint and stone objects. The south-eastern fen edge is one of several focal areas, most of them already apparent in the distribution plots of Clark (1928, 1932b) and Grimes (1931), in which exotic stone implements and the more elaborate flint artefacts of the Later Neolithic and Early Bronze Age are particularly abundant (Ch. 5.II.4). Each, as Bradley (1984b) emphasises, has its own genesis, character, and internal development. Many seem to have initially centred on Neolithic monuments, whether the Rudston complex of east Yorkshire (Manby 1974, figs 35, 38, 40, 41; Pierpoint 1980, 271–275), the Arbor Low henge in Derbyshire (Bradley and Hart 1983, 182–186), the Windmill Hill-Avebury area in Wiltshire (Thomas 1984, 173), or the Dorset cursus and its related monuments (Gardiner 1991, 64–69). The long currency of flint and stone axes suggests that this phenomenon may have had its origins in the Earlier Neolithic. The vast numbers of arrowheads from the survey area (Green 1980, fig. 52) are surely to be seen in this context and perhaps in that of human conflict, rather than as the residue of hunting for which evidence is consistently slight.

Whilst some smaller concentrations of exotic and fine implements, such as those centred on Christchurch, Dorset, or the downs above Eastbourne, Sussex have no apparent monumental focus (Gardiner 1984, figs 3.10, 3.11), the lack of major monuments in a massive concentration like that of the south-eastern fen edge is exceptional. The nearest known foci are Stonea to the west and Haddenham to the south-west, both 25–30km away in Cambridgeshire (Fig. 0) or Fornham All Saints in the Suffolk Breckland, some 20km to the south-east (Palmer 1976, fig. 20:40).

This reflects the general scarcity of causewayed enclosures, henges and related sites in Norfolk and all but the extreme south-east of Suffolk. To the east of the fens, counterparts to the communal monuments of Maxey, Haddenham and Stonea are persistently scarce, although an already high total of ring-ditches increases with every season of aerial photography. Convincing equivalents to the Fengate enclosure system also remain elusive. There is a case for a regional habit of social organisation in which small, even family-sized, units were more autonomous than elsewhere, with less effective co-ordinating authority. In these circumstances the symbolic value of fine, scarce and exotic artefacts might have been particularly high and long-lived.

The concentration perhaps finds its closest echo on and in the lower Thames from Kingston eastwards, well downstream of the obvious local ceremonial centre formed by a causewayed enclosure at Staines and a cursus and related monuments at Stanwell (Needham and Trott 1987, 481–482). Here, a major concentration of stone axes (Cummins 1979, fig. 1; Field and Cotton 1987, fig. 4.7), which amount to approximately a third of the axes from the river (Adkins and Jackson 1978, 9), is accompanied by concentrations of all the elaborate lithic artefacts for which data have been published. Among them are discoidal knives (Clark 1928; Cotton 1984, fig. 2), flint daggers (Grimes 1931, fig. 12; Needham 1987, fig. 5.4), maceheads (Roe 1979, fig. 11), battle-axes (Roe 1979, fig. 4) and axe-hammers (Needham 1987, 101).

In these and other cases wealth and ostentation are easy to see and impossible to comprehend. The social complexities which may underlie the abandonment of an object on a settlement site, let alone its more purposeful deposition, are spelt out by Barrett and Needham (1988).

III.2. Beakers
The use of intricately-decorated, finely-made Beakers may also have extra-functional connotations (Ch.5.III.3).

While the bulk of the Beaker pottery from the survey area was found as sherds in accumulations of settlement debris, a few vessels have been found, complete or near-complete, apart from the flint industries and animal bone which characterise living sites. They include a complete Late style Beaker 'found in June 1857 in Hilgay Fen nr. Wood Hall at a depth of 10 ft. by clay diggers' (Site 4450; Lethbridge and O'Reilly 1937, 75, pl. IIa; Clarke 1970, corpus no. 50, fig. 980) and a complete rusticated Beaker found on the borders of Feltwell and Methwold before 1885 (Site 4856; Abercromby 1912, pl. IX, fig. 80; Fox 1923, 322; Clarke 1970, corpus no. 569, fig. 439). Accompanying burials may, of course, have gone unrecognised. This was not so in the case of a semi-complete rusticated vessel (Fig. 104: P385) found by Frank Curtis some 1.5km to the west (fenward) of the prolific Hockwold fields, in an area where living sites had not yet emerged by the time of the Fenland Project (Site 5318, at TL/6789 8762). There was also certainly no burial with a complete Late style Beaker found in a small pit on Salway's site 7188 on the chalk upland (Site 5316/c2; Salway 1967, 52, fig. 12: F1; Clarke 1970, corpus no. 559, fig. 752).

These finds recall some of the characteristics of 'special deposits'. East Anglian examples identified by Cleal (1984) include a pit containing sherds of elaborately decorated Middle style Beaker and two perforated antler implements, one adze-like, found in Burnt Fen, Cambridgeshire (Edwardson 1966). There is a strong echo of Pryor's view (1992b) that 'The people who used Beaker pottery have ... much to answer for in the later Bronze Age ... we ought to be searching for Beaker ritual activity in those areas that later saw extensive deposition of Bronze Age metalwork.'

III.3. Metalwork

The metalwork itself poses yet more questions. The area's tally of bronzes is, like its accumulation of fine flint and stone implements, comparable with that of the lower Thames. Most is of Middle and Late Bronze Age date, and hence without obvious settlement context. In this it contrasts with the fine and exotic lithics, most of which were found within the zone of dense settlement and in some cases on settlement sites themselves.

Much of the metalwork was found in deep peat or in or near water-courses, a particularly high proportion of dirks, rapiers and swords coming from findspots of this kind (Table 2). Deliberate deposition away from settlements is arguable for much of it. The evidence would accommodate Bradley's scenario of the deliberate removal from circulation of classes of object endowed with extra-functional significance, in a context of conspicuous consumption, ritual conflict, or funerary rite (Bradley 1984a, 96–127; 1990, 97–154).

III.4. Human Remains

The human remains from the fen of the survey area are exceptional in that the dated individuals all lived towards the end of the Early Bronze Age (Table 1), as did 'Shippea Hill Man' (Ch. 4.III.3). They correspond to the peak of local post-fen clay occupation but are unusually early for bog or river burials in Britain. They seem to presage practices which became more widespread in later centuries.

It has recently become clear that the deposition of human bodies or bones in rivers and other wet places was contemporary, even simultaneous, with that of metalwork (Bradley and Gordon 1988; Bradley 1990, 107–109). The two are linked most dramatically at Fengate/Flag Fen (Pryor 1991), where at least one human skeleton and disarticulated bones of others were deposited with animal bone, pottery, and a wealth of metalwork, most of it of the Late Bronze Age, along an alignment of vertical timbers established in the Middle Bronze Age and maintained over at least four hundred years (Neve 1992). Significant here are the alignment's earlier origins, seen in its relation to the ultimately late Neolithic ditched enclosure system of the adjacent fen edge and in the location of pits containing Beaker pottery at its junction with dry land (Pryor 1992a). The alignment and the practices that went with it and the deposition of bodies and artefacts in the south-eastern fens can be seen as parallel developments within existing traditions. The contrast between the highly visible focus of Fengate/Flag Fen and the inconspicuous, diffuse deposits of the south-eastern fens perpetuates a pre-existing distinction between a society which created numerous communal monuments and works and a perhaps differently organised society which generated very few.

Bibliography

Abercromby, J., 1912 — *The Bronze Age Pottery of Great Britain and Ireland and its Associated Grave-Goods* (Oxford, Clarendon Press)

Adkins, R. and Jackson, R., 1978 — *Neolithic Stone and Flint Axes from the River Thames*, Brit. Mus. Occas. Pap. 1 (London)

Adkins, P., Brown, N., Murphy, P. and Priddy, D., 1985 — 'Rook Hall', in Priddy, D., (ed.), 'Work of the Essex County Council Archaeology Section 1983–84, *Essex Archaeol. Hist.* 16, 82–122

Ambers, J., Matthews, K. and Bowman, S., 1991 — 'British Museum Natural Radiocarbon Measurements XXII', *Radiocarbon* 33(1), 51–68

Ambrose, S.H., 1986 — 'Stable carbon and nitrogen analysis of human and animal diet in Africa', *J. Hum. Evol.* 15, 717–731

Ambrose, S.H. and DeNiro, M.J., 1986 — 'Reconstruction of African human diet using bone collagen carbon and nitrogen isotope ratios', *Nature* 319, 321–323

Annable, F.K. and Simpson, D.D.A., 1964 — *Guide Catalogue of the Neolithic and Bronze Age Collections in Devizes Museum* (Devizes, Wiltshire Archaeological and Natural History Society)

Ashwin, T., in prep. — *The Norwich Southern Bypass,* E. Anglian Archaeol.

Bamford, H.M., 1982 — *Beaker Domestic Sites in the Fen Edge and East Anglia,* E. Anglian Archaeol. 16

Barrett, J.C., 1980 — 'The pottery of the later Bronze Age in lowland England', *Proc. Prehist. Soc.* 46, 297–319

Barrett, J.C., 1986 — 'The pottery', in Pryor, F., Taylor, M. and French, C., 'Flag Fen, Peterborough I: discovery, reconnaissance and initial excavation', *Proc. Prehist. Soc.* 52, 12

Barrett, J.C. and Bond, D., 1988 — 'The pottery', in Bond, D., *Excavation at the North Ring, Mucking, Essex: a Late Bronze Age Enclosure,* E. Anglian Archaeol. 43, 25–37

Barrett, J.C. and Needham, S.P., 1988 — 'Production, circulation and exchange: problems in the interpretation of Bronze Age metalwork', in Barrett, J.C. and Kinnes, I.A., (eds), *The Archaeology of Context in the Neolithic and Bronze Age, Recent Trends* (Sheffield, Department of Archaeology and Prehistory), 127–143

Barrett, W.H., 1961 — 'Fenland folklore: in the steps of the Romans at Hockwold', *Eastern Daily Press* 28 August

Bell, M., 1990 — *Brean Down Excavations 1983–1987,* English Heritage Archaeol. Rep. 15 (London)

Bennett, K.D., 1983 — 'Devensian Late-Glacial and Flandrian vegetational history at Hockham Mere, Norfolk, England', *New Phytol.* 95, 457–487

Bradley, R., 1984 a — *The Social Foundations of Prehistoric Britain* (Harlow, Longman)

Bradley, R., 1984 b — 'Regional systems in Neolithic Britain', in Bradley, R. and Gardiner, J., (eds), *Neolithic Studies: a Review of Some Current Research,* Brit. Archaeol. Rep. 133 (Oxford), 5–14

Bradley, R., 1987 — 'Flint technology and the character of Neolithic settlement', in Brown, A.G. and Edmonds, M., (eds), *Lithic Analysis and Later British Prehistory,* Brit. Archaeol. Rep. 162 (Oxford), 181–186

Bradley, R., 1990 — *The Passage of Arms. An Archaeological Analysis of Prehistoric Hoards and Votive Deposits* (Cambridge, University Press)

Bradley, R. and Hart, C., 1983 — 'Prehistoric settlement in the Peak District during the third and second millennia bc: a preliminary analysis in the light of recent fieldwork', *Proc. Prehist. Soc.* 49, 177–193

Bradley, R., Cleal, R., Gardiner, J. and Green, M., with Bowden, M., 1984 — 'The Neolithic sequence in Cranborne Chase', in Bradley, R. and Gardiner, J., (eds.), *Neolithic Studies: a Review of Some Current Research,* Brit. Archaeol. Rep. 133 (Oxford), 87–106

Bradley, R. and Gordon, K., 1988 — 'Human skulls from the river Thames, their dating and significance', *Antiquity* 62(236), 503–509

Bradley, R. and Edmonds, M., 1993 — *Interpreting the Axe Trade. Production and Exchange in Neolithic Britain* (Cambridge, University Press)

Brothwell, D.R., 1972 — *Digging up Bones* (London, British Museum (Natural History))

Brothwell, D.R., 1973 — 'The human biology of the Neolithic population of Britain', in 'Die Anfänge des Neolithikums vom Orient bis Nordeuropa', teil 8a 'Anthropologie', 280–299, *Fundamenta* Reihe B, Band 3 (Cologne, Böhlau Verlag)

Brown, M.A., 1982 — 'Swords and sequence in the British Bronze Age', *Archaeologia* 107, 1–42

Buckley, D.G. and Hedges, J.D., 1987 — *The Bronze Age and Saxon Settlements at Springfield Lyons, Essex,* Essex County Council Occas. Pap. 5

Burgess, C., 1975 — 'An Early Bronze Age settlement at Kilellan Farm, Islay, Argyll', in Burgess, C. and Miket, R.,(eds), *Settlement and Economy in the Third and Second Millennia B.C.,* Brit. Archaeol. Rep. 33 (Oxford), 181–208

Burgess, C., 1980 — *The Age of Stonehenge* (London)

Burgess, C., 1986 — ' "Urnes of no small variety": Collared Urns reviewed', *Proc. Prehist. Soc.* 52, 339–351

Burgess, C.B. and Gerloff, S., 1981 — 'The dirks and rapiers of Great Britain and Ireland' *Praehistorishe Bronzefunde* 4, Bd. 7 (Munich, C.H. Beck)

Burleigh, R., Hewson, A., Meeks, N., Sieveking, G. and Longworth, I., 1979 — 'British Museum natural radiocarbon measurements X', *Radiocarbon* 21 (1), 41–47

Burleigh, R., Matthews, K. and Ambers, J., 1982 — 'British Museum natural radiocarbon measurements XIV', *Radiocarbon* 24(3), 229–261

Campbell Smith, W., 1963 — 'Jade axes from sites in the British Isles', *Proc. Prehist. Soc.* 29, 133–172

Care, V., 1982 — 'The collection and distribution of lithic materials during the Mesolithic and Neolithic periods in southern England', *Oxford J. Archaeol* 1 (3), 269–285

Case, H., 1977 · 'The Beaker culture in Britain and Ireland', in Mercer, R.J., (ed.), *Beakers in Britain and Europe,* Brit. Archaeol. Rep. S26 (Oxford), 71–101

Case, H., 1993 · 'Beakers: deconstruction and after', *Proc. Prehist. Soc.* 59, 241–68

Cawdor, the Earl, and Fox, C., 1925 · 'The Beacon Hill barrow, Barton Mills, Suffolk', *Proc. Cambridge Antiq. Soc.* 26, 19–57

Chappell, S., 1987 · *Stone Axe Morphology and Distribution in Neolithic Britain,* Brit. Archaeol. Rep. 177 (Oxford)

Chisholm, B.S., Nelson, D.E. and Schwarcz, H.P., 1982 · 'Stable carbon isotope ratios as a measure of marine versus terrestrial protein in ancient diets', *Science* 216, 1131–1132

Clark, J.G.D., 1928 · 'Discoidal polished flint knives — their typology and distribution', *Proc. Prehist. Soc. E. Anglia* 6, 40–54

Clark, J.G.D., 1932a · 'The date of the plano-convex flint-knife in England and Wales', *Antiq. J.* 12 (2), 158–162

Clark, J.G.D., 1932b · 'The curved flint sickle blades of Britain', *Proc. Prehist. Soc. E. Anglia* 7 (1), 67–81

Clark, J.G.D., 1933 · 'Report on an Early Bronze Age site in the south-eastern fens', *Antiq. J.* 13, 266–296

Clark, J.G.D., 1934 · 'Derivative forms of the *petit tranchet* in Britain', *Archaeol. J.* 91, 32–58

Clark, J.G.D., 1936 · 'Report on a Late Bronze Age site in Mildenhall Fen, West Suffolk', *Antiq. J.* 6, 29–50

Clark, J.G.D., 1960 · 'Excavations at the Neolithic site at Hurst Fen, Mildenhall, Suffolk (1954, 1957 and 1958)', *Proc. Prehist. Soc.* 26, 202–245

Clark, J.G.D., 1963 · 'Neolithic bows from Somerset, England, and the prehistory of archery in north-western Europe', *Proc. Prehist. Soc.* 29, 50–98

Clark, J.G.D., Godwin, H. and M.E. and Clifford, M.H., 1935 · 'Report on recent excavations at Peacock's Farm, Shippea Hill, Cambridgeshire', *Antiq. J.* 15, 284–319

Clark, J.G. D. and Fell, C.I., 1953 · 'The Early Iron Age site of Micklemoor Hill, West Harling, Norfolk, and its pottery', *Proc. Prehist. Soc.* 29, 1–40

Clark, J.G.D. and Higgs, E.S., 1960 · 'Flint industry', in Clark, J.G.D., 'Excavations at the Neolithic site at Hurst Fen, Mildenhall, Suffolk (1954, 1957 and 1958)', *Proc. Prehist. Soc.* 26, 214–226

Clark, J.G.D. and Godwin, H., 1962 · 'The Neolithic in the Cambridgeshire Fens', *Antiquity* 36, 10–23

Clarke, D.L., 1970 · *Beaker Pottery of Great Britain and Ireland* (Cambridge, University Press)

Clarke, D.L., 1976 · 'The Beaker network — social and economic models', in Lanting, J.N. and van der Waals, J.D. (eds), *Glockenbecher Symposion Oberried 1974* (Bussum/Haarlem, Fibula-van Dishoek), 459–477

Clarke, R.R., 1957 · 'Archaeological discoveries in Norfolk, 1949–54', *Norfolk Archaeol.* 31 (4), 395–416

Clarke, W.G., 1913 · 'Norfolk barrows', *The Antiquary* 49, 416–423

Clarke, W.G. (ed.), 1915 · *Report on the Excavations at Grime's Graves, Weeting, Norfolk: 1914* (London, Prehistoric Society of East Anglia)

Cleal, R., 1984 · 'The Later Neolithic in eastern England, in Bradley, R. and Gardiner, J., (eds), *Neolithic Studies, a Review of Some Current Research,* Brit. Archaeol. Rep. 133 (Oxford), 135–58

Cleal, R., 1988 · 'The occurrence of drilled holes in Later Neolithic pottery', *Oxford J. Archaeol.* 7, 139–145.

Clough, T.H. McK. and Green, B., 1972 · 'The petrological identification of stone implements from East Anglia', *Proc. Prehist. Soc.* 38, 108–155

Clough, T. H. McK. and Cummins, W.A., (eds), 1988 · *Stone Axe Studies Volume 2,* Counc. Brit. Archaeol. Res. Rep. 67

Clutton-Brock, J., 1984 · 'Neolithic antler picks from Grime's Graves, Norfolk, and Durrington Walls, Wiltshire: a biometrical analysis', *Excavations at Grime's Graves, Norfolk, 1972–1976* Fascicule 1 (London, British Museum Publications)

Colquhoun, I. and Burgess, C.B., 1988 · *The Swords of Britain,* Praehistorishe Bronzefunde 4, Bd. 5 (Munich, C. H. Beck)

Coombs, D., 1992 · 'Flag Fen platform and Fengate Power Station post alignment — the metalwork', *Antiquity* 66(251), 504–17

Corbett, W. M., 1973 · *Breckland Forest Soils* (Harpenden, Soil Survey of England and Wales, Special Survey 7)

Cotton, J., 1984 · 'Three Later Neolithic discoidal knives from north-east Surrey, with a note on similar examples from the county', *Surrey Archaeol. Collect.* 75, 225–233

Couchman, C., 1980 · 'The Bronze Age in Essex', in Buckley, D. (ed.), *Archaeology in Essex to AD 1500,* Counc. Brit. Archaeol. Res. Rep. 34, 40–46

Cowie, T. G., 1978 · *Bronze Age Food Vessel Urns in Northern Britain,* Brit. Archaeol. Rep. 55 (Oxford)

Craddock, P.T., Cowell, M.R., Leese, M.N. and Hughes, M.J., 1983 · 'The trace element composition of polished flint axes as an indicator of source', *Archaeometry* 25, 135–163

Cummins, W. A., 1979 · 'Neolithic stone axes: distribution and trade', in Clough, T.H.McK. and Cummins, W.A. (eds.), *Stone Axe Studies,* Counc. Brit. Archaeol. Res. Rep. 23, 5–12

Darby, H.C., 1974 · *The Medieval Fenland* (Newton Abbot, David & Charles)

Darby, H.C., 1983 · *The Changing Fenland* (Cambridge, University Press)

Delwiche, C.C., Zinke, P.J., Johnson, C.M. and Virginia, R.A., 1979 · 'Nitrogen isotope distribution as a presumptive indicator of nitrogen fixation', *Bot. Gaz.* 140, S65–S69 (suppl.)

DeNiro, M.J. and Epstein, S., 1981 · 'Influence of diet on the distribution of nitrogen isotopes in animals', *Geochim. Cosmochim. Acta* 45, 341–351

Donaldson, P., 1977 · 'The excavation of a multiple round barrow at Barnack, Cambridgeshire', *Antiq. J.* 57, 197–231

Downes, J., 1993 · 'Distribution and significance of Bronze Age metalwork in the North Level', in French, C.A.I. and Pryor, F.M.M., *The South-west Fen Dyke*

Survey Project 1982–6, E. Anglian Archaeol. 59, 21–30

Dymond, D.P., 1973   'The excavation of a prehistoric site at Upper Chamberlain's Farm, Eriswell', *Proc. Suffolk Inst. Archaeol. Hist.* 27, 1–18

Edmonds, M., 1987   'Rocks and risk: problems with lithic procurement strategies', in Brown, A.G. and Edmonds, M., (eds), *Lithic Analysis and Later British Prehistory,* Brit. Archaeol. Rep. 162 (Oxford), 155–179

Edwardson, A.R., 1966   'Beaker and rusticated sherds associated with red deer antler sockets', *Proc. Cambridge Antiq. Soc.* 59, 135–139

Ellison, A., 1988   'Discussion', in, Longworth, I., Ellison, A. and Rigby, V., 1988 'The Neolithic, Bronze Age and Later Pottery', *Excavations at Grimes Graves Norfolk 1972–1976* Fascicule 2 (London, British Museum Publications), 36–50

Evans, C., 1987   'Nomads in "Waterland"? Prehistoric trans-humance and fenland archaeology', *Proc. Cambridge Antiq. Soc.* 76, 27–39

Evans, C., 1988   'Excavations at Haddenham, Cambridgeshire: a "planned" enclosure and its regional affinities', in Burgess, C., Topping, P., Mordant, C. and Maddison, M., (eds), *Enclosures and Defences in the Neolithic of Western Europe,* Brit. Archaeol. Rep. S403 (Oxford), 127–148

Evans, C., 1993   'Sampling settlements: investigations at Lingwood Farm, Cottenham and Eye Hill Farm, Soham', *Fenland Research* 8, 26–30

Evans, C. and Serjeantson, D., 1988   'The backwater economy of a fen-edge community in the Iron Age; the upper Delphs, Haddenham', *Antiquity* 62, 360–370

Evans, J., 1881   *The Ancient Bronze Implements, Weapons, and Ornaments, of Great Britain and Ireland* (London, Longmans, Green & Co.)

Evans, J., 1897   *The Ancient Stone Implements, Weapons, and Ornaments, of Great Britain* (London, Longmans, Green & Co., 2nd. edition).

Evans, J.G., 1981   'Subfossil land-snail faunas from Grimes Graves and other Neolithic flint mines', in Mercer, R.J., *Grimes Graves, Norfolk, Excavations 1971–72: Volume I,* Department of the Environment Archaeol. Rep. 11, (London), 104–111

Farnsworth, P., Brady, J.E., DeNiro, M.J. and MacNeich, R.S., 1985   'A re-evaluation of the isotopic and archaeological reconstructions of diet in the Tehuacan valley', *Am. Antiquity* 50, 102–116

Fasham, P.J. and Ross, J.M., 1978   'A Bronze Age flint industry from a barrow site in Micheldever Wood, Hampshire', *Proc. Prehist. Soc.* 44, 47–67

Fell, C.I., 1951   'A Late Bronze Age urnfield and Grooved Ware occupation at Honington, Suffolk', *Proc. Cambridge Antiq. Soc.* 45, 30–43

Fell, C.I. and Briscoe, G., 1951   'An Early Bronze Age Food-Vessel from Shippea Hill Farm', *Proc. Cambridge Antiq. Soc.* 45, 63

Field, D. and Cotton, J., 1987   'Neolithic Surrey: a survey of the evidence', in Bird, J. and D.G. (eds.), *The Archaeology of Surrey to 1540* (Guildford, Surrey Archaeological Society), 71–96

Ford, S., Bradley, R., Hawkes, J. and Fisher, P., 1984,   'Flint-working in the metal age', *Oxford J. Archaeol.* 3(2), 157–173

Fox, C., 1923   *The Archaeology of the Cambridge Region* (Cambridge, University Press)

French, C., 1992   'Fengate to Flag Fen: summary of the soil and sediment analyses', *Antiquity* 66, 458–61

French, C.A.I. and Pryor, F.M.M., 1993   *The South-west Fen Dyke Survey Project 1982–86,* E. Anglian Archaeol. 59

Gallois, R.W., 1988   *Geology of the Country around Ely* (London, HMSO)

Gardiner, J., 1984   'Lithic distributions and Neolithic settlement patterns in central southern England' in Bradley, R. and Gardiner, J., (eds.), *Neolithic Studies: a Review of Some Current Research,* Brit. Archaeol. Rep. 133 (Oxford), 15–40

Gardiner, J., 1987   'Tales of the unexpected: approaches to the assessment and interpretation of museum flint collections', in Brown, A.G. and Edmonds, M.R., (eds.), *Lithic Analysis and Later British Prehistory,* Brit. Archaeol. Rep. 162 (Oxford), 49–66

Gardiner, J., 1991   'The flint industries of the study area', in Barrett, J.C., Bradley, R. and Green, M., *Landscape, Monuments and Society. The Prehistory of Cranborne Chase* (Cambridge, University Press), 59–69

Gerloff, S., 1975   *The Early Bronze Age Daggers in Great Britain and a Reconsideration of the Date of the Wessex Culture,* Praehistorishe Bronzefunde 6, Bd. 2 (Munich, C. H. Beck)

Gerloff, S., 1986   'Bronze Age class A cauldrons: typology, origins and chronology', *J. Roy. Soc. Antiq. Ireland* 116, 84–115

Gibson, A. M., 1982   *Beaker Domestic Sites, a Study of the Domestic Pottery of the Late Third and Early Second Millennium BC in the British Isles,* Brit. Archaeol. Rep. 107 (Oxford)

Gilyard-Beer, R., 1984   'The Devil's Ring, Brightwell Heath', *Proc. Suffolk Inst. Archaeol. Hist* 35, 247–278

Glover, W., 1979   'A prehistoric bow fragment from Drumwhinny Bog, Kesh, Co. Fermanagh', *Proc. Prehist. Soc.* 45, 323–327

Godwin, H., 1940   'Studies of the post-glacial history of British vegetation. III. Fenland pollen diagrams. IV. Post-glacial changes of the relative land- and sea-level in the English Fenland', *Phil. Trans. Roy. Soc. London* B230, 239–303

Godwin, H., 1978   Fenland: its Ancient Past and Uncertain Future (Cambridge, University Press)

Godwin, H. and Godwin, M.E., 1933   'Pollen-analysis of peats from Plantation Farm', in Clark, G., 'Report on an Early Bronze Age site in the south-eastern fens', *Antiq. J.* 13, 281–289

Godwin, H., Godwin, M.E., Clark, J.G.D. and Clifford, M.H., 1934   'A Bronze Age spearhead found in Methwold Fen, Norfolk', *Proc. Prehist. Soc. E. Anglia* 7(3), 395–398

Godwin, H., Godwin, M.E. and Clifford, M.H., 1935   'Analysis of peats', in Clark, J.G.D., Godwin, H., Godwin, M.E. and Clifford, M.H., 'Report on recent excavations at Peacock's Farm, Shippea Hill, Cambridgeshire', *Antiq. J.* 15, 307–316

184

Godwin, H., Godwin, M.E. and Clifford, M.H., 1936 'Plant remains in the peat', in Clark, J.G.D., 'Report on a Late Bronze Age site in Mildenhall Fen, West Suffolk', *Antiq. J.* 6, 34–36

Godwin, H. and Willis, E.H., 1961 'Cambridge University natural radiocarbon measurements', *Radiocarbon* 3, 60–76

Gray, H., 1977 *Anatomy, Descriptive and Surgical,* edited by T.P.Pick and R. Howden (New York, Bounty)

Green, B., 1988 'The petrological identification of stone implements from East Anglia: second report', in Clough, T.H. McK. and Cummins, W.A., (eds.), *Stone Axe Studies Volume II,* Counc. Brit. Archaeol. Res. Rep. 67 (London), 36–40

Green, H.S., 1980 *The Flint Arrowheads of the British Isles,* Brit. Archaeol. Rep. 75 (Oxford)

Green, H.S., Houlder, C.H. and Keeley, L.H., 1982 'A flint dagger from Ffair Rhos, Ceredigion, Dyfed, Wales', *Proc. Prehist. Soc.* 48, 492–501

Gregory, T., 1978 'A Mesolithic barbed bone point from Feltwell', *Norfolk Archaeol.* 37(1), 130

Gregory, T., 1992 *Excavations in Thetford, 1980–1982, Fison Way,* E. Anglian Archaeol. 53

Grimes, W.F., 1931 'The Early Bronze Age flint dagger in England and Wales', *Proc. Prehist. Soc. E. Anglia* 6, 340–355

Hall, D., 1987 *Fenland Project 2: Fenland Landscapes and Settlement between Peterborough and March,* E. Anglian Archaeol. 35

Hall, D., 1988 'Survey results in the Cambridgeshire fenland', *Antiquity* 62 (235), 311–314

Hall, D. and Coles, J., 1994 *Fenland Survey. An Essay in Landscape and Persistence,* English Heritage Archaeol. Rep. 1, London

Harmer, F.W., 1928 'The distribution of erratics and Drift', *Proc. Yorkshire Geol. Soc.* 21 (2), 79–150

Hawkes, C.F.C., 1954 *The Stoke Ferry Hoard,* Inventaria Archaeologica GB.8 2

Healy, F., 1980 'The Neolithic in Norfolk', (unpubl. Ph D thesis, Univ. of London)

Healy, F., 1982a 'A round barrow at Trowse: Early Bronze Age burials and medieval occupation', in *Trowse, Horning, Deserted Medieval Villages, King's Lynn,* E. Anglian Archaeol. 14, 1–34

Healy, F., 1982b 'A chalk object from Feltwell', *Norfolk Archaeol.* 38 (2), 204–206

Healy, F., 1984, 'Farming and field monuments: the Neolithic in Norfolk', in Barringer, C., (ed.), *Aspects of East Anglian Pre-history (twenty years after Rainbird Clarke)* (Norwich, Geo Books), 77–140

Healy, F., 1985 'The struck flint' in Shennan, S.J., Healy, F. and Smith, I.F., 'The excavation of a ring-ditch at Tye Field, Lawford, Essex', *Archaeol. J.* 142, 177–207

Healy, F., 1986 'Struck flint', in Petersen, F.F. and Healy, F., 'The excavation of two round barrows and a ditched enclosure on Weasenham Lyngs, 1972', in Lawson, A.J., *Barrow Excavations in Norfolk,* E. Anglian Archaeol. 29, 80–89

Healy, F., 1988 *The Anglo-Saxon Cemetery at Spong Hill, North Elmham, part VI: Occupation During the Seventh to Second Millennia BC,* E. Anglian Archaeol. 39

Healy, F., 1991a 'Appendix 1: lithics and pre-Iron Age pottery', in Silvester, R.J., *Fenland Project 4: The Wissey Embayment and the Fen Causeway, Norfolk,* E. Anglian Archaeol. 52, 116–139

Healy, F., 1991b 'The hunting of the floorstone', in Schofield, A.J., (ed.) *Interpreting Artefact Scatters: Contributions to Ploughzone Archaeology,* Oxbow Monograph 4 (Oxford), 29–37

Healy, F., 1992 'Lithic material', 'Pre-Iron Age pottery' and 'Pre-Iron Age activity' in Gregory, T., *Excavations in Thetford, 1980–1982, Fison Way,* E. Anglian Archaeol. 53, 143–147, 148–154, 188

Healy, F., 1993 'Appendix III: the lithics', in Lane, T. and Hayes, P., *Fenland Project 8: Lincolnshire Survey, the Northern Fen-edge,* E. Anglian Archaeol. 66, 98–106

Healy, F., 1995 'Prehistoric material', in Rogerson, A., *A Late Neolithic, Saxon and Medieval Site at Middle Harling, Norfolk,* E. Anglian Archaeol. 74, 32–46

Healy, F., forthcoming 'Lithic material', in Gregory, T., *A Romano-British farmyard at Weeting, Norfolk,* E. Anglian Archaeol.

Healy, F., in prep. 'Lithics', in Martin, E., *West Row Fen, Mildenhall,* E. Anglian Archaeol.

Healy, F. and Silvester, B., 1991 'Appendix 2: The Decoy Farm sandhill, Hockwold' in Silvester, R.J., *Fenland Project 4: The Wissey Embayment and the Fen Causeway, Norfolk,* E. Anglian Archaeol. 52, 141–142

Healy, F., Cleal, R. and Kinnes, I., 1993 'Excavations on Redgate Hill, Hunstanton, 1970-71', in Bradley, R., Chowne, P., Cleal, R.M.J., Healy, F. and Kinnes, I., *Excavations on Redgate Hill, Hunstanton, Norfolk and at Tattershall Thorpe, Lincolnshire,* E. Anglian Archaeol. 57, 1–77

Healy, F. and Housley, R.A., 1992 'Nancy was not alone. Skeletons of the Early Bronze Age from the Norfolk peat fen', *Antiquity* 66(253), 948–955

Hedges, J. and Buckley, D., 1978 'Excavations at a Neolithic causewayed enclosure, Orsett, Essex, 1975', *Proc. Prehist. Soc.* 44, 219–308

Hedges, R.E.M., Housley, R.A., Law, I.A. and Perry, C., 1988 'Radiocarbon dates from the Oxford AMS system: *Archaeometry* datelist 7', *Archaeometry* 30(1), 155–164

Hedges, R.E.M., Law, I.A., Bronk, C.R. and Housley, R.A., 1989 'The Oxford accelerator mass spectrometry facility: technical developments in routine dating', *Archaeometry* 31(2), 99–113

Hedges, R.E.M., Housley, R.A., Law, I.A. and Bronk, C.R., 1990 'Radiocarbon dates from the Oxford AMS system: *Archaeometry* datelist 10', *Archaeometry* 32(1), 101–108

Hedges, R.E.M., Housley, R.A., Bronk Ramsey, C. and Van Klinken, G.J., 1993 'Radiocarbon dates from the Oxford AMS system: *Archaeometry* datelist 17', *Archaeometry* 35(2), 305–36

Hedges, R.E.M., Housley, R.A., Bronk Ramsey, C. and Van Klinken, G.J., 1994
'Radiocarbon dates from the Oxford AMS system: *Archaeometry* datelist 18', *Archaeometry* 36(2), 337–74

Herne, A., 1988
'A time and a place for the Grimston bowl', in Barrett, J.C. and Kinnes, I.A., (eds), *The Archaeology of Context in the Neolithic and Bronze Age, Recent Trends* (Sheffield, Department of Archaeology and Prehistory), 9–29

Herne, A., 1991
'The flint assemblage', in Longworth, I., Herne, A., Varndell, G. and Needham, S., 'Shaft X: Bronze Age flint, chalk and metal working', *Excavations at Grimes Graves Norfolk 1972–1976* Fascicule 3, 21–93

Hodder, I. and Shand, P., 1988
'The Haddenham long barrow: an interim statement', *Antiquity* 62, 349–53

Hunn, J.R., Palmer, R. and Evans, C., 1993
'The Block Fen field system', *Fenland Research* 8, 10–16

Jackson, W., 1933
'Animal remains', in Clark, G., 'Report on an Early Bronze Age site in the south-eastern fens', *Antiq. J.* 13, 278

Jackson, W., 1935
'Animal remains', in Clark, J.G.D., Godwin, H. and M.E. and Clifford, M.H., 'Report on recent excavations at Peacock's Farm, Shippea Hill, Cambridgeshire', *Antiq. J.* 15, 306

Jackson, J. W., 1936
'Report on the animal remains', in Clark, J.G.D., 'Report on a Late Bronze Age site in Mildenhall Fen, West Suffolk' *Antiq. J.* 6, 33

Jacobi, R., 1978
'The Mesolithic of Sussex', in Drewett, P.L. (ed.), *Archaeology in Sussex to AD 1500,* Counc. Brit. Archaeol. Res. Rep. 29 (London), 15–22

Johansen, O.S., Gulliksen, S. and Nydal, R., 1986
'δ^{13}C and diet: analysis of Norwegian human skeletons', *Radiocarbon* 28, 754–761

Jones, V., Bishop, A.C. and Woolley, A.R., 1977
'Third supplement of the catalogue of jade axes from sites in the British Isles', *Proc. Prehist. Soc.* 43, 287–293

Kelly, T.C., 1967
'A series of Late Middle Bronze Age sites, Wilde Street, Mildenhall', *Proc. Suffolk Inst. Archaeol. Hist.* 31 (1), 47–56

Kinnes, I., 1979
Round Barrows and Ring-ditches in the British Neolithic, Brit. Mus. Occas. Pap. 7 (London, British Museum Publications)

Kinnes, I., Gibson, A., Ambers, J., Bowman, S., Leese, M. and Boast, R., 1991
'Radiocarbon dating and British Beakers: the British Museum programme', *Scottish Archaeol. Review* 8, 35–78

Kreuger, H.W. and Sullivan, C.H., 1984
'Models for carbon isotope fractionation between diet and bone', in Turnland, J.E. and Johnson, P.E., (eds), *Stable Isotopes in Nutrition* (Am. Chem. Soc.), 205–220

Lanting, J.N. and van der Waals, J.D., 1972
'British Beakers as seen from the continent', *Helinium* 13, 368–58

Larwood, G.P., 1970
'The Lower Cretaceous deposits of Norfolk' in Larwood, G.P. and Funnell, B.M., (eds), *The Geology of Norfolk* (Norwich, Geological Society of Norfolk), 280–292

Lawson, A.J., 1979a
'A Late Middle Bronze Age hoard from Hunstanton, Norfolk', in Burgess, C. and Coombs, D. (eds), *Bronze Age Hoards Some Finds Old and New,* Brit. Archaeol. Rep. 67 (Oxford), 43–92

Lawson, A.J., 1979b
'A bone point from Hockwold-cum-Wilton', *Norfolk Archaeol.* 37, 216–217

Lawson, A.J., 1980a
'The evidence for Later Bronze Age settlement and burial in Norfolk', in Barrett, J. and Bradley, R., (eds), *Settlement and Society in the British Later Bronze Age,* Brit. Archaeol. Rep. 83 (Oxford), 271–294

Lawson, A.J., 1980b
'A Late Bronze Age hoard from Beeston Regis, Norfolk', *Antiquity* 56, 217–219

Lawson, A.J., 1981
'The barrows of Norfolk', in Lawson, A.J., Martin, E.A. and Priddy, D., *The Barrows of East Anglia,* E. Anglian Archaeol. 12, 32–63

Lawson, A.J., 1983
The Archaeology of Witton, near North Walsham, E. Anglian Archaeol. 18

Lawson, A.J., 1984
'The Bronze Age in East Anglia with particular reference to Norfolk', in Barringer, C., (ed.), *Aspects of East Anglian Pre-history (twenty years after Rainbird Clarke)* (Norwich, Geo Books), 141–178

Lawson, A.J., 1986
'The excavation of a ring-ditch at Bowthorpe, Norwich', in Lawson, A.J., *Barrow Excavations in Norfolk, 1950–82,* E. Anglian Archaeol. 29, 20–49

Lawson, A.J. and Ashley, S.J., 1980
'The Hilgay hoard', *Norfolk Archaeol.* 37 (3), 328–333

Lawson, A.J., Martin, E.A. and Priddy, D., 1981
The Barrows of East Anglia, E. Anglian Archaeol. 12

Leaf, C.S., 1934
'Report on the excavation of two sites in Mildenhall Fen', *Proc. Cambridge Antiq. Soc.* 35, 106–127

Leaf, C.S., 1940
'Further excavations in Bronze Age barrows at Chippenham, Cambs.', *Proc. Cambridge Antiq. Soc.* 39, 33–68

Leah, M., forthcoming
'The Fenland Management Project: Norfolk', *Fenland Research* 8

Leahy, K., 1986
'A dated stone axe-hammer from Cleethorpes, South Humberside', *Proc. Prehist. Soc.* 52, 143–152

Legge, A.J., 1981
'The agricultural economy' in Mercer, R., *Grimes Graves, Norfolk, Excavations 1971–72: Volume I,* Department of the Environment Archaeol. Rep. 11, (London), 79–118

Legge, A.J., 1992
'Animals, environment and the Bronze Age economy', *Excavations at Grime's Graves, Norfolk, 1972–1976* Fascicule 4 (London, British Museum Publications)

Lethbridge, T.C., 1950
'Excavation of the Snailwell group of Bronze Age barrows', *Proc. Cambridge Antiq. Soc.* 43, 30–49

Lethbridge, T.C., Fowler, G. and Sayce, R.U., 1931
'A skeleton of the Early Bronze Age found in the Fens', *Proc. Prehist. Soc. E. Anglia* 6, 362–364

Lethbridge, T.C. and O'Reilly, M.A., 1937
'Archaeological notes', *Proc. Cambridge Antiq. Soc.* 37, 74–75

Longworth, I.H., 1960
'Pottery', in Clark, J.G.D., 'Excavations at the Neolithic site at Hurst Fen, Mildenhall, Suffolk

(1954, 1957 and 1958)', *Proc. Prehist. Soc.* 26, 228–240

Longworth, I.H., 1979
'The Neolithic and Bronze Age pottery', in Wainwright, G.J., *Mount Pleasant, Dorset: Excavations 1970–1971,* Rep. Res. Comm. Soc. Antiq. London 37 (London), 75–124

Longworth, I.H., 1981
'Neolithic and Bronze Age pottery', in Mercer, R.J., *Grimes Graves, Norfolk, Excavations 1971–72: Volume I,* Department of the Environment Archaeol. Rep. 11, (London), 39–59

Longworth, I.H., 1984
Collared Urns of the Bronze Age in Great Britain and Ireland (Cambridge, University Press)

Longworth, I., Ellison, A. and Rigby, V., 1988
'The Neolithic, Bronze Age and later pottery', *Excavations at Grimes Graves Norfolk 1972–1976,* Fascicule 2, (London, British Museum Publications)

Lukis, F.C., 1843
A Brief Account of Barrows near Bircham Magna (Guernsey, priv. pub.)

Manby, T.G., 1970
'Long barrows of northern England; structural and dating evidence', *Scot. Archaeol. Forum* 17, 1–25

Manby, T.G., 1974
Grooved Ware Sites in Yorkshire and the North of England, Brit. Archaeol. Rep. 9 (Oxford)

Manning, C.R., 1879
'Bone ornaments, forming part of a necklace of the British period, found in Feltwell Fen, 1876', *Norfolk Archaeol.* 8, 319–325

Martin, E.A., 1976a
'The excavation of two tumuli on Waterhall Farm, Chippenham, Cambridgeshire, 1973', *Proc. Cambridge Antiq. Soc.* 66, 1–14

Martin, E.A., 1976b
The excavation of a tumulus at Barrow Bottom, Risby, 1975, E. Anglian Archaeol. 3, 43–62

Martin, E.A., 1980
'A Late Bronze Age sword from Brandon', *Proc. Suffolk Inst. Archaeol. Hist.* 34(4), 281–282

Martin, E.A., 1984
'West Row Fen, Mildenhall', *Fenland Research* 1, 40–43

Martin, E.A., 1988
'Swale's Fen, Suffolk: a Bronze Age cooking pit?', *Antiquity* 62, 358–359

Martin, E.A., 1993
Settlements on Hill-tops: Seven Prehistoric Sites in Suffolk, E. Anglian Archaeol. 65

Martin, E.A. and Denston, C.B., 1986
'A Bronze Age multiple burial at Exning', *Proc. Suffolk Inst. Archaeol. Hist.* 36(2), 131–134

Martin, E.A. and Murphy, P., 1988
'West Row Fen, Suffolk: a Bronze Age fen-edge settlement site', *Antiquity* 62 (235), 353–358

Mathews, M., 1988
'A Bronze Age sword from Fordham, Norfolk', *Fenland Research* 5, 20–22

Megaw, J.V.S. and Simpson, D.D.A., 1979
Introduction to British Prehistory (Leicester, University Press)

Mercer, R.J., 1981
Grimes Graves, Norfolk, Excavations 1971–72: Volume I Department of the Environment Archaeol. Rep. 11, (London)

Miles, A.E.W., 1967
'The dentition of the Anglo-Saxons', *Proc. Roy. Soc. Medicine* 62 (12), 881–886

Miller, S.H. and Skertchly, S.B.J., 1878
The Fenland Past and Present (London, Longmans, Green and Co.; Wisbech, Leach and Son)

Murphy, P., 1984a
'Prehistoric environments and economies', in Barringer, C., (ed.), *Aspects of East Anglian Pre-history (twenty years after Rainbird Clarke)* (Norwich, Geo Books), 13–30

Murphy, P., 1984b
'Environmental archaeology in East Anglia', in, Keeley, H.C.M., (ed.), *Environmental Archaeology: a Regional Review,* Directorate of Ancient Monuments and Historic Buildings Occas. Pap. 2 (London, Department of the Environment), 13–42

McKinley, J. I., 1989
'Cremations: expectations, methodologies and realities', in Roberts, C.A., Lee, F. and Bintliff, J., (eds), *Burial Archaeology, Current Research, Methods and Developments,* Brit. Archaeol. Rep 211 (Oxford), 65–76

McMinn, R.M.H. and Hutchings, R.T., 1985
A Colour Atlas of Human Anatomy (London, Wolfe Medical Publications)

Needham, S., 1979
'The extent of foreign influence on Early Bronze Age axe development in southern Britain', in Ryan, M., (ed.) *Proceedings of the Fifth Atlantic Colloquium, Dublin 1979,* 265–93

Needham, S., 1987
'The Bronze Age', in Bird, J. and D.G. (eds.), *The Archaeology of Surrey to 1540* (Guildford, Surrey Archaeological Society), 97–138

Needham, S., 1988
'Selective deposition in the British Early Bronze Age', *World Archaeol.* 20(2), 229–248

Needham, S., 1990
'Middle Bronze Age ceremonial weapons: new finds from Oxborough, Norfolk, and Essex/ Kent', *Antiq. J.* 70, 239–52

Needham, S.P., 1991
'Middle Bronze Age spearhead casting at Grime's Graves' and 'The Grimes Graves metalwork in the context of other Middle Bronze Age Assemblages', in Longworth, I., Herne, A., Varndell, G. and Needham, S., 'Shaft X: Bronze Age flint, chalk and metal working', *Excavations at Grimes Graves Norfolk 1972–1976* Fascicule 3, 154–179

Needham, S.P. and Trott, M.R., 1987
'Structure and sequence in the Neolithic deposits at Runnymede', *Proc. Prehist. Soc.* 53, 479–482

Neve, J., 1992
'An interim report on the dendrochronology of Flag Fen and Fengate', *Antiquity* 66, 470–5

Norfolk Museums Service 1977
Bronze Age Metalwork in Norwich Castle Museum (Norwich, 2nd revised edition)

Northcote, E.M., 1980
'Some Cambridgeshire Neolithic to Bronze Age birds and their presence or absence in England in the Late-glacial and Early Flandrian', *J. Archaeol. Sci.* 7, 379–383

Northover, P., 1988
'Appendix 2. The analysis and metallurgy of British Bronze Age swords', in Colquhoun, I. and Burgess, C.B., *The Swords of Britain,* Praehistorishe Bronzefunde 4, Bd. 5 (Munich, C. H. Beck), 130–146

O'Connor, B., 1980
Cross-channel Relations in the Later Bronze Age, Brit. Archaeol. Rep. S91 (Oxford)

Palmer, R., 1976
'Interrupted ditch enclosures in Britain: the use of aerial photography for comparative studies', *Proc. Prehist. Soc.* 42, 161–186

Peake, N.B. and Hancock, J.M., 1970
'The Upper Cretaceous of Norfolk', in Larwood, G.P. and Funnell, B.M., (eds), *The Geology of Norfolk* (Norwich, Geological Society of Norfolk), 293–339

Petersen, F.F. and Healy, F., 1986
'The excavation of two round barrows and a ditched enclosure on Weasenham Lyngs, 1972',

in Lawson, A.J., *Barrow Excavations in Norfolk 1950–82*, E. Anglian Archaeol. 29, 70–103

Phillips, P., Cummins, W.A. and Keen, L., 1988
'The petrological identification of stone implements from Yorkshire: second report', in Clough, T.H. McK. and Cummins, W.A. (eds.), *Stone Axe Studies Volume II*, Counc. Brit. Archaeol. Res. Rep. 67, 52–59

Pierpoint, S., 1980
Social Patterns in Yorkshire Prehistory, Brit. Archaeol. Rep. 74 (Oxford)

Piggott, S., 1954
The Neolithic Cultures of the British Isles (Cambridge, University Press)

Pitts, M.W., 1978
'Towards an understanding of flint industries in post-glacial England', *Univ. London Inst. Archaeol. Bull.* 15, 179–197

Potter, T.W. and Jackson, R.P.J., 1984–5
'The British Museum Excavations at Stonea', *Fenland Research* 2, 9–15

Prigg, H., 1888
'On the recent discovery of a bronze sword at Chippenham, Cambridgeshire, with notices of similar discoveries in the western district of Suffolk', *Proc. Suffolk Inst. Archaeol. Hist.* 6, 184–94

Pryor, F., 1974
Excavation at Fengate, Peterborough, England: the First Report, (Toronto, Royal Ontario Museum Archaeology Mono. 3)

Pryor, F., 1978
Excavation at Fengate, Peterborough, England: the Second Report (Toronto, Royal Ontario Museum Archaeology Mono. 5)

Pryor, F., 1980a
A Catalogue of British and Irish Prehistoric Bronzes in the Royal Ontario Museum (Toronto)

Pryor, F., 1980b
Excavation at Fengate, Peterborough, England: the Third Report (Northampton, Northamptonshire Archaeol. Soc. Mono. 1; Toronto, Royal Ontario Museum Archaeology Mono. 6)

Pryor, F., 1981
'Two radiocarbon dates from the cremation pit at Pilsgate, near Barnack', *Proc. Cambridge Antiq. Soc.* 81, 73

Pryor, F., 1984
Excavation at Fengate, Peterborough, England: the Fourth Report (Northampton, Northamptonshire Archaeol. Soc. Mono. 2; Toronto, Royal Ontario Museum Archaeology Mono. 7)

Pryor, F., 1988
'Etton, near Maxey, Cambridgeshire: a causewayed enclosure on the fen-edge', in Burgess, C., Topping, P., Mordant, C. and Maddison, M., (eds), *Enclosures and Defences in the Neolithic of Western Europe*, Brit. Archaeol. Rep. S403 (Oxford), 107–126

Pryor, F., 1991
English Heritage Book of Flag Fen Prehistoric Fenland Centre (London, Batsford/English Heritage)

Pryor, F., 1992a
'Introduction to current research at Flag Fen, Peterborough' and 'Discussion: the Fengate/Northey landscape', *Antiquity* 66, 439–57, 518–31

Pryor, F., 1992b
'Late Bronze Age', in Evans, C., (ed), 'Fenland research priorities', *Fenland Research* 7, 6–7

Pryor, F.M.M. and French, C.A.I., 1985
Fenland Project 1: Archaeology and Environment in the Lower Welland Valley, E. Anglian Archaeol. 27

Pryor, F., French, C. and Taylor, M., 1985
'An interim report on excavations at Etton, Maxey, Cambridgeshire, 1982–1984', *Antiq. J.* 65, 275–311

Reynolds, T., 1992
A Buried Prehistoric Landscape at Barnack (Cambridgeshire Archaeology Report 58)

Riley, D., 1957
'Neolithic and Bronze Age pottery from Risby Warren and other sites in north Lincolnshire', *Proc. Prehist. Soc.* 23, 40–65

Roe, F.E.S., 1966
'The battle-axe series in Britain', *Proc. Prehist. Soc.* 32, 199–245

Roe, F.E.S., 1979
'Typology of stone implements with shaftholes', in Clough, T.H.McK. and Cummins, W.A., (eds.) *Stone Axe Studies*, Counc. Brit. Archaeol. Res. Rep. 23, 23–48

Rowlands, M. J., 1976
The Organisation of Middle Bronze Age Metalworking, Brit. Archaeol. Rep. 31 (Oxford)

Sainty, J.E., 1945
'Mesolithic sites in Norfolk', *Norfolk Archaeol.* 28 (4), 234–237

Salway, P., 1967
'Excavations at Hockwold-cum-Wilton, Norfolk, 1961–62', *Proc. Cambridge Antiq. Soc.* 60, 39–80

Saville, A., 1981a
Grimes Graves, Norfolk, Excavations 1971–72: Volume II the Flint Assemblage (London, Department of the Environment Archaeological Reports 11)

Saville, A., 1981b
'The flint and chert artefacts', in Mercer, R.J., 'Excavations at Carn Brea, Illogan, Cornwall, 1970–73 — a Neolithic fortified complex of the third millennium bc', *Cornish Archaeol.* 20, 101–52

Saville, A., 1985
'The flint assemblage', in Field, N., 'A multi-phased barrow and possible henge monument at West Ashby, Lincolnshire', *Proc. Prehist. Soc.* 51, 127–131

Schoeninger, M.J. and DeNiro, M.J., 1984
'Nitrogen and carbon isotopic composition of bone collagen from marine and terrestrial animals', *Geochim. Cosmochim. Acta* 48, 625–639

Schoeninger, M.J., DeNiro, M.J. and Tauber, H., 1983
'$^{15}N/^{14}N$ ratios of bone collagen reflect marine and terrestrial components of prehistoric human diet', *Science* 220, 1381–1383

Schwarcz, H.P., Melbye, J., Katzenburg, M.A. and Knyf, M., 1985
'Stable isotopes in human skeletons of southern Ontario: reconstructing palaeodiet', *J. Archaeol. Sci.* 12, 187–206

Seale, R.S., 1975
Soils of the Ely district [sheet 173], Soil Survey of Great Britain England and Wales (Harpenden, Rothamstead Experimental Station, Lawes Agricultural Trust)

Seale, R.S. and Hodge, C.A.H., 1976
Soils of the Cambridge and Ely district, Soil Survey of Great Britain England and Wales, Special Survey 10, (Harpenden, Rothamsted Experimental Station, Lawes Agricultural Trust)

Shand, P., 1985
'Cauldron Field, Feltwell. Excavations of an Early Iron Age settlement on the Fen edge, 1962' and 'Snarehill Urnfield, Brettenham. Excavations of a Late Bronze Age settlement near Thetford, Norfolk, 1959', (unpubl. B.A. dissertation, Univ. of Reading)

Shawcross, F.W., with Higgs, E.S., 1961
'The excavation of a *Bos primigenius* at Lowe's Farm, Littleport', *Proc. Cambridge Antiq. Soc.* 54, 3–16

Sheridan, A., 1992
'Two Scottish Firsts', *Past* 14, 6–7

Silvester, R.J., 1991
Fenland Project 4: The Wissey Embayment and the Fen Causeway, Norfolk, E. Anglian Archaeol. 52

Simpson, W.G., 1993 'The excavation of a Late Neolithic settlement at Barholm, Lincolnshire.', in Simpson, W.G., Gurney, D., Neve, J. and Pryor, F., *Fenland Project 7: Excavations in Peterborough and the Lower Welland Valley 1960–69*, E. Anglian Archaeol. 61, 7–28

Smedley, N., 1957 'Archaeology in Suffolk 1956' *Proc. Suffolk Inst. Archaeol. Hist.* 27(2), 117

Smedley, N. and Owles, E., 1964 'Pottery of the Early and Middle Bronze Age in Suffolk', *Proc. Suffolk Inst. Archaeol. Hist.* 29, 175–197

Smith, A.G. Whittle, A., Cloutman, E.W. and Morgan, L., 1989 'Mesolithic and Neolithic activity and environmental impact on the south-east fen-edge in Cambridgeshire', *Proc. Prehist. Soc.* 55, 207–249

Smith, C., 1989 'British antler mattocks', in Bonsall, C., (ed.), *The Mesolithic in Europe. Papers Presented at the Third International Symposium Edinburgh 1985*, U.I.S.P.P. Mesolithic Commission (Edinburgh, John Donald), 272–283

Smith, I.F., 1954 'The pottery', in Childe, V.G. and Smith, I., 'Excavation of a Neolithic barrow on Whiteleaf Hill, Bucks', *Proc. Prehist. Soc.* 20, 221–228

Smith, I.F., 1955 'Late Beaker pottery from the Lyonesse surface and the date of the transgression' *Univ. London Inst. Archaeol. Annu. Rep.* 11, 29–42

Smith, I.F., 1965 *Windmill Hill and Avebury* (Oxford, Clarendon Press)

Smith, I.F., 1974a 'The Neolithic', in Renfrew, C., (ed.), *British Prehistory, a New Outline* (London, Duckworth), 100–27

Smith, I.F., 1974b 'The Neolithic pottery from Fengate 1972', in Pryor, F., *Excavation at Fengate, Peterborough, England: the First Report*, Royal Ontario Mus. Archaeol. Mono. 3 (Toronto), 31–3

Smith, I.F., 1979 'The chronology of British stone implements', in Clough, T.H.McK. and Cummins, W.A., (eds.) *Stone Axe Studies*, Counc. Brit. Archaeol. Res. Rep. 23, 13–22

Smith, I.F. and Simpson, D.D.A., 1966 'Excavation of a round barrow on Overton Hill, North Wiltshire', *Proc. Prehist. Soc.* 32, 122–155

Smith, M.A., 1957 *The Feltwell Fen Hoard*, Inventaria Archaeologica GB. 35

Sparks, B.W. and West, R.G., 1972 *The Ice Age in Britain* (London, Methuen)

Stanford, S.C., 1982 'Bromfield, Shropshire — Neolithic, Beaker and Bronze Age sites', *Proc. Prehist. Soc.* 48, 279–320

Stirland, A., 1984 'A possible correlation between os acromiale and occupation in the burials from the *Mary Rose*', *Fifth European Meeting of the Palaeopathology Association*, Sienna 1984, 327–334

Stone, J.F.S., 1936 'An enclosure on Boscombe Down East', *Wiltshire Archaeol. Natur. Hist. Mag.* 47, 466–489

Stone, J.F.S., 1937 'A Late Bronze Age habitation site on Thorny Down, Winterbourne Gunner, Wilts.', *Wiltshire Archaeol. Natur. Hist. Mag.* 47, 640–659

Straw, A., 1960 'The limit of the "last" glaciation in north Norfolk', *Proc. Geologists' Assoc.* 71, 379–390

Stuiver, M. and Kra, R. (eds), 1986 'Proceedings of the twelfth international radiocarbon conference — Trondheim, Norway', *Radiocarbon* 28 (2B)

Stuiver, M. and Rumer, P.J., 1987 *User's Guide to the Programs CALIB and DISPLAY 2.1* (Seattle, Quaternary Istope Laboratory, University of Washington)

Switsur, R., 1974 'The prehistoric longbow from Denny, Scotland', *Antiquity* 48 (189), 56–58

Tauber, H., 1981 '[13]C evidence for dietary habits of prehistoric man in Denmark', *Nature* 292, 332–333

Thomas, J., 1984 'A tale of two polities: kinship, authority and exchange in the Neolithic of south Dorset and north Wiltshire', in Bradley, R. and Gardiner, J., (eds), *Neolithic Studies: a Review of Some Current Research*, Brit. Archaeol. Rep. 133 (Oxford), 161–176

Tixier, J., Inizan, M.-L. and Roche, H., 1980 *Préhistoire de la Pierre Taillée. I. Terminologie et Technologie* (Antibes, Cercle de Recherche et d'Etudes Préhistoriques)

Tomalin, D.J., 1982 'The formal and textural characteristics of the Biconical Urn assemblage from Shaugh Moor enclosure 15, and their implications', in Baalam, N., Smith, K. and Wainwright, G.J., 'The Shaugh Moor project: fourth report — environment, context and conclusion', *Proc. Prehist. Soc.* 48, 228–237

Tomalin, D.J., 1983 'British Biconical Urns: their character and chronology and their relationship with indigenous early Bronze Age ceramics', (unpubl. Ph D thesis, Univ. of Southampton)

Tomalin, D.J., 1986 'Garboldisham, *c.* 1963', in, Lawson, A.J., *Barrow excavations in Norfolk, 1950–1982*, E. Anglian Archaeol. 29, 110–113

Tomalin, D.J., 1988 'Armorican *vases à anses* and their occurrence in southern Britain', *Proc. Prehist. Soc* 54, 203–221

Trotter, M. and Gleser, G.C., 1957 'A re-evaluation of estimation of stature based on measurements of stature taken during life and long bones after death', *American J. Phys. Anth.* 16 (1), 463–514

Trump, B.A.V., 1968 'Fenland rapiers', in Coles, J.M. and Simpson, D.D.A., (eds.) *Studies in Ancient Europe. Essays Presented to Stuart Piggott* (Leicester, University Press), 213–225

van Beek, G.C., 1983 *Dental Morphology*, 2nd edition (Bristol, Wright. PSG)

van der Merwe, N.J. and Vogel, J.C., 1978 '[13]C content of human collagen as a measure of prehistoric diet in woodland North America', *Nature* 276, 815–816

van der Plicht, J. and Mook, W.G., 1989 'Calibration of radiocarbon ages by computer', *Radiocarbon* 31(3), 805–816

Vatcher, F. de M. and Vatcher, H.L., 1976, 'The excavation of a round barrow near Poor's Heath, Risby, Suffolk', *Proc. Prehist. Soc.*, 42, 263–22

Virginia, R.A. and Delwiche, C.C., 1982 'Natural ^{15}N abundance of presumed N_2-fixing and non-N_2-fixing plants from selected ecosystems', *Oecologia (Berl.)* 54, 317–325

Wada, E., Kadonaga, T. and Matsuo, S., 1975 '^{15}N in nitrogen of naturally occurring substances and global assessment of denitrification from an isotopic viewpoint', *Geochem. J.* 9, 139–148

Wainwright, G.J., 1972
'The excavation of a Neolithic settlement on Broome Heath, Ditchingham, Norfolk, England', *Proc. Prehist. Soc.* 38, 1–107

Wainwright, G.J., 1973
'The excavation of prehistoric and Romano-British settlements at Eaton Heath, Norwich', *Archaeol. J.* 130, 1–43

Wainwright, G.J. and Longworth, I.H., 1971
Durrington Walls: Excavations 1966–1968, Rep. Res. Comm. Soc. Antiq. London 29

Waller, M., 1988
'The Fenland Project's environmental programme', *Antiquity* 62, 336–343

Waller, M., 1994
Fenland Project 9: Flandrian Environmental Change in Fenland, E. Anglian Archaeol. 70

Warburton, J.S., 1913
'Some implements of "Cissbury type" found in Norfolk', *Proc. Prehist. Soc. E. Anglia* 1 (4), 420–427

Wheeler, A., 1989
'Flandrian deposits at Wood Fen: a palaeobotanical investigation', *Fenland Research* 6, 34–38

Whitaker, A.W.R. and Jukes-Browne, B.A., 1899
The Geology of the Borders of the Wash Including Boston and Hunstanton (London, Memoirs of the Geological Survey England and Wales 69, Old Series)

Wilkinson, T.J. and Murphy, P., 1986
'Archaeological survey of an intertidal zone: the submerged landscape of the Essex coast, England', *J. Field Archaeol.* 13, 184–94

Woodward, A., 1990
'The Bronze Age pottery', in Bell, M., *Brean Down Excavations 1983–1987,* English Heritage Archaeol. Rep. 15 (London), 121–145

Woolley, A.R., Bishop, A.C., Harrison, R.J. and Kinnes, I.A., 1979
'European Neolithic jade implements: a preliminary mineralogical and typological study', in Clough, T.H.McK. and Cummins, W.A., (eds), *Stone Axe Studies,* Counc. Brit. Archaeol. Res. Rep. 23, 90–96

Wymer, J. J., (ed.) 1977
Gazetteer of Mesolithic Sites in England and Wales, Counc. Brit. Archaeol. Res. Rep. 20

Wymer, J.J., 1985
Palaeolithic Sites of East Anglia (Norwich, Geo Books)

Wymer, J., 1986
'Flints', in Gurney, D., *Settlement, Religion and Industry on the Fen-edge: Three Romano-British Sites in Norfolk,* E. Anglian Archaeol. 31, 22, 72, figs. 17, 45

Wymer, J.J., 1990
'A cremation burial at Alpington', *Norfolk Archaeol.* 41 (1), 71–4

Wymer, J. J. and Healy, F., forthcoming
'Neolithic and Bronze Age activity and settlement at Longham and Beeston with Bittering', in Wymer, J.J., *Barrow Excavations in Norfolk, 1984–88.* E. Anglian Archaeol.

Index

Note: Places are in Norfolk unless otherwise stated. In addition, (C) = Cambridgeshire, (E) = Essex, (S) = Suffolk.

animal husbandry, 175, 179, 180
antler, 17, 27, 157–60 (Figs 106–8), 174
  'adzes', 157, 181
  'axes', 157, 178
  beam, 157
  catalogue, 158–60
  implements, 157, 158, 181
  'mattocks', 157
  picks, 157
  strip, 157, 158
  tines, 157
  see also bone objects
Arbor Low henge, Derbyshire, 180
Avebury, Wiltshire, 180

Bacton Wood Mill Farm, Edingthorpe,
Bacton, 75
Barnack, (C), 41
barrows, 41, 157, 177, 179, 180
Barton Mills, (S): Beacon Hill barrow, 157
bath house, Romano-British (Feltwell), 28
Beacon Hill barrow, Barton Mills, (S), 157
Beacon Hill, Charnwood Forest,
Leicestershire, 51
beads
  bone, 41, 157 (Pl. IX)
  jet/amber, 41, 51, 62, 74
  lead, 37
Beeston with Bittering: pottery, 62
biological evidence, 23, 174–5
Blackdyke Farm *see under* Hockwold cum
Wilton
bodies and burials, 30–42, 178
  Bronze Age, Early, 30–7
  beaker burials, 178
  burial No. 7 (Hill Close), 33, 35 (Fig. 19),
  164 (Pl. X), 169
  cremations, 33, 157
    Deverel-Rimbury, 112
    urned, 178
  from *Mary Rose*, 168
  funerary evidence, 31 (Fig. 17)
  funerary rites, 181
  grave goods, 38, 75, 157, 181
    tradition of object deposition, 48
  inhumations, 33, 167
  lithics, 60, 63
  multiple burial: lithic finds, 60
  'Nancy' ('the Southery Fen female'), 30, 39,
  41, 43, 62
  see also barrows; bone, human
bone, animal, 12, 15, 16, 17, 19, 23, 28, 41,
60, 105, 171–4 (Table 16; Fig. 110), 175, 179
  aurochs, 9
  badger, 171
  beaver, 9, 12, 171, 172
  cat, 171
  cattle, 28, 33, 171, 172, 173 (Fig. 112),
  174, 179
  deer, 9, 171, 172–4
  deposition of, 181
  dog, 171, 172
  fox, 171
  goat, 171–2, 173 (Fig. 111), 174, 179
  horse, 33, 171, 172
  otter, 9, 171, 172
  ovicaprines, 171, 179
  ox, 9, 26
  pig, 26, 28, 41, 171, 172, 174
  sheep, 171–2, 173 (Fig. 111), 174, 179
  teeth, 171, 172
  unworked, 173 (Table 17)
  see also antler

bone, bird, 9, 174
  duck, 171, 172, 174
  eagle claw, 157, 158
  goose, 174
bone, human, 162–9, 175, 181
  Bronze Age, Early, 30–7
  age determination, 162, 167, 168 (Table
  14), 170 (Table 15)
  cranial index, 162, 168
  cremated, 162, 169
  isotope analysis, 169–71 (Table 15), 179
  laid on wood, 36 (Fig. 20), 37 (Pl. VIII),
  39, 160
  metopism, 168
  morphological variation, 168
  'Nancy' ('the Southery Fen female'), 30,
  39, 41, 43, 62
  pathology, 169
  radiocarbon dating, x, 30, 38, 39 (Table 1),
  40 (Fig. 22), 41, 162, 179
  sex determination, 162, 167, 168 (Table
  14), 170 (Table 15)
  stature, 162
  teeth, 162, 164–6 (Pls X–XII)
    crown variations, 168
    dental disease, 33, 39, 169
    tooth wear, 162, 167, 169, 171
  wormian bones, 168
  see also bodies and burials
bone objects, 17, 157–60 (Figs 106–8)
  awls, 11, 17, 30
  beads, 41, 157 (Pl. IX)
  blade, 157
  catalogue, 158–60
  needles, 11, 27, 41, 157
  ornaments, 157
  perforated disc, 157
  points, 28, 60, 105, 157
  spatulae, 157
  spear head, 17
  wristguard, 157
  see also antler
Boscombe Down: Deverel-Rimbury
industries, 63
Bowthorpe, Norwich: burials, 38, 179
Brean Down, Somerset, 112, 117
Breckland
  geology, 7
  lithics, 50, 51, 60, 74
  settlement, 48, 178
  topography, 10
Brettenham: Late Bronze Age settlement, 178
Bromfield, Shropshire, 112
burials *see* bodies and burials
Burnt Fen, (C), 157, 181
Burwell Fen, (C), 41

Cam, River, 1, 74, 75, 180
  valley, 178
Cambridge region: metalworking, 47
Carnaby Top site 12, Yorkshire, 63
Catsholm *see under* Methwold
causewayed enclosures, 180
cereals, 171
  barley, 179
  emmer-type grain, 23, 175, 179
  processing, 179, 180
  see also vegetation
Charnwood Forest, Leicestershire: Beacon
Hill area, 51
Chippenham, (C), 38, 48
Christchurch, Dorset: lithics, 180
Colchester-Ipswich area, pottery, 117, 177

Cottenham, (C): Lingwood Farm, 178
Creeting St Mary, (S): pottery, 63
crop marks, 26
cursus monuments, 180

dating
  of burials, 37–8
  Methwold bow, 161, 176
  radiocarbon
    animal bone, 9
    antler/bone objects, 157
    artefacts, 177–8
    human bone, x, 30, 38, 39 (Table 1), 40
    (Fig. 22), 41, 162, 179
    'pot-boiler' sites, 179
    pottery, 112
    vegetation, 9
Decoy Farm Sandhill, 50
defixio, Roman, 37
demography, 162
Denver sluice, 43
dietary reconstruction, 169–71, 179
Dorset cursus, 180
Dykeside *see* Hockwold cum Wilton (Site
5308/c4)

Eastbourne, Sussex: lithics, 180
Ely, (C), 41
Exning, (S): burials, 41

Feltwell, 1, 3, 5, 41
  fen margin, 178
  lithics, 51, 60, 89–92 (Figs 55–8)
  Glebe Farm (Site 4921/c1), 28
    animal bone, 174
    lithics, 51, 60, 85, 88 (Fig. 54)
    pottery, 105, 106, 149, 153 (Fig. 102)
    worked bone, 157, 160 (Fig. 108)
  Lower Hill Close: lithics, 86
  Site 4904: lithics, 85
  Site 4907: lithics, 85
  Site 5159/c2: lithics, 179
  Site 5162: lithics, 86
  Site 5177: lithics, 87
  Site 5178: lithics, 87
  Site 5179/c2: lithics, 86
  Site 5183: lithics, 179
  Site 5184: lithics, 86
  Site 5185: lithics, 87
  Site 5191
    metalwork, 43
    wooden remains, 160
  Site 5294: lithics, 85
  Site 17193/c2: metalwork, 48
  Site 17483: metalwork, 50
  Site 17531: antler object, 160 (Fig. 108)
  Site 20979/c3: antler, 157, 178
  Site 20981
    lithics, 86
    worked bone, 160 (Fig. 108)
  Site 22311: lithics, 87
  Site 23650 (Feltwell Anchor), 161
  Site 24735
    lithics, 62
    wood remains, 160
  Site 24838: lithics, 87
  see also Hill Close; Shrubhill
Feltwell Common: vegetation, 9
Feltwell Fen, 41, 53
  animal bone, 9
  metalwork hoard, 43, 47, 62
  worked bone, 157 (Pl. IX)
Fengate, (C), 28, 48

burials, 41, 181
economy and organisation, 180
enclosure system, 9, 177, 180
lithics, 62
Newark Road, 62, 117
Fengate Power Station, 37
Fifty Farm, Mildenhall, (S), 28, 41, 117
'fire pit', 17 (Pl. V)
fired clay, 16, 19, 20 (Fig. 7), 22 (Fig. 11), 25 (Fig. 14), 96–7 (Table 12), 105
Fison Way, Thetford, 7, 112, 178
Flag Fen, Peterborough, (C), 48, 105, 181
food: dietary reconstruction, 169–71, 179
Fordham (Site 24114): metalwork, 50
forest see woodland
Fornham All Saints, (S), 180

geology, 7–9 (Fig. 2)
    Flandrian stage, 7, 9, 51
    Pleistocene stage, 7
Glebe Farm see under Feltwell
Grime's Graves, 7, 50, 51
    animal bone, 172
    animal husbandry, 179
    antler objects, 157
    lithics, 63, 74
    metalwork, 48
    Middle Bronze Age settlement, 178
    pottery, 112, 179
    worked bone, 157, 158

Haddenham, (C), 172, 180
Hayland House, Mildenhall, 28
hearths, 15, 16, 17, 27 (Fig. 16), 28, 105
Hemplands Farm, Methwold Hythe (Site 2550), 36 (Fig. 20), 37 (Pl. VIII), 39, 160
    human bone, 162, 166
henges, 180
Herringay Hill, Northwold, 41, 60
Hilgay, 1, 62
    geology, 7
    lithics, 51, 94 (Fig. 60)
    metalwork, 43
    pottery, 106
    and Southery island (Site 17103), 178
Hilgay Fen
    lithics, 61
    Wood Hall, 41, 181
Hill Close, Feltwell
    Site 5188, 30–5 (Pl. VII; Figs 18–19), 38–9, 178
        burials, 178
        dating, 37–8
        dietary reconstruction, 171
        human bone, 162, 163–5 (Pl. X), 167, 168, 169
        lithics, 51, 60, 85, 88 (Fig. 54)
        pottery, 105, 117, 149–52, 153 (Fig. 102)
        worked bone, 157
    Sites 5195/24840: lithics, 74
Hockham Mere: pollen analysis, 7
Hockwold cum Wilton, xi, 3, 9, 13 (Pl. III), 15 (Pl. 4), 16 (Pl. IV), 178
    antler, 157–60 (Figs 106–7)
    Blackdyke Farm (Site 5343), 3, 11–12 (Pls I–II), 87
    Drain Bank Site, 12, 13
    enclosure system excavated, 1
    lithics, 53, 54–5 (Tables 4–7), 60, 62–3, 74, 80 (Fig. 46), 92–3 (Figs 58–9)
    pottery, 95–105 (Table 12; Figs 61–6), 106, 112, 126–34 (Figs 79–84), 154–5 (Figs 103–4), 177, 179
    Wilton Bridge, 7
    worked bone, 157–60 (Figs 106–7)
    Site 5230: pottery, 106, 156
    Site 5307: lithics, 53
    Site 5308, 41
        c1 (63), 4, 5, 15, 16, 17 (Pl. V), 28

animal bone, 174
pottery, 95, 99
c2 (62), 5, 15, 17 (Pl. V)
c3 (69), 5, 15, 16, 17, 19, 28
fired clay, 105
pottery, 95, 99
c4 (61/68): Dykeside, 3–4, 15, 16–17, 18–23 (Figs 5–7), 26 (Fig. 15), 28
animal bone, 174
biological remains, 174–5
cereal remains, 179
lithics, 50, 53, 56–7 (Figs 28–30), 58–9 (Figs 31–3), 63, 74, 81–4 (Figs 48–50)
pottery, 95, 102, 104, 112, 138–44 (Figs 90–4)
worked bone/antler, 159–60 (Fig. 107)
c5 (96), 4, 23–5 (Figs 12–14), 28, 104
fired clay, 105
lithics, 51, 53, 56–7 (Figs 28–30), 58–9 (Figs 31–3), 84–5, 87 (Fig. 53)
pottery, 112, 146–9, 150–2 (Figs 99–101)
South Site, 19
Site 5309 (48)
    lithics, 80 (Fig. 46)
    pottery, 118, 123–5 (Figs 76–8)
Site 5310 (49): pottery, 118, 125 (Fig. 78)
Site 5313: lithics, 88
Site 5314: lithics, 88
Site 5316, 28
    lithics, 88
    pottery, 106
    c1: lithics, 88
    c2/c5/c6 ('site 7188'), 26–7
        Iron Age occupation, 178
        pottery, 181
    c4: metalwork, 43, 47
    c7/c8 ('site 7088'), 7, 27
        pottery, 105, 178
Site 5317 (Corner Ground)
    animal bone, 171
    pottery, 106, 153
    wooden remains, 160
    c2 (25), 28
    c3 (23), 27–8
    pottery, 105, 112
Site 5318: pottery, 156, 181
Site 5321: pottery, 152
Site 5324 (93), 4, 13, 19, 28
    animal bone, 174
    metalwork, 48
    pottery, 43, 95, 112
    wood remains, 160
Site 5332 (66), 3, 17 (Pl. VI), 21 (Fig. 8), 28
    antler, 157, 174
    lithics, 53, 84–5 (Fig. 51)
    pottery, 95, 105, 112, 144, 145 (Fig. 95)
    worked bone, 157, 159–60 (Fig. 107)
Site 5333 (95/97), 4, 19, 21–2 (Figs 9–11), 28
    lithics, 51, 53, 56–7 (Figs 28–30), 58–9 (Figs 31–3), 84, 86 (Fig. 52)
    pottery, 95, 104, 112, 144–6, 147–9 (Figs 96–8)
    worked bone, 159–60 (Fig. 107)
Site 5336: lithics, 157
Site 5339: lithics, 88
Site 5344: lithics, 88
Site 5364: pottery, 149, 152 (Fig. 101)
Site 5365 (67): pottery, 152
Site 5373 (22), 15, 28
    animal bone, 171
    lithics, 53, 80–1 (Fig. 47)
    pottery, 105, 106, 112, 133–7 (Figs 85–8), 139 (Fig. 89)
    worked bone, 158 (Fig. 106), 160
Site 5374 (19), 26
Site 5375 (113): pottery, 152
Site 5377 (16): pottery, 156

Site 5394 (Sluice Drove), 27, 29, 105
Site 5423 (9), 12, 24–6, 152
Site 5439 (44): pottery, 118, 124 (Fig. 77)
Site 14662
    antler, 158 (Fig. 106)
    pottery, 118, 123 (Fig. 76)
Site 14734/c2 (77): pottery, 152
Site 15087: worked bone, 157
Site 16590: metalwork, 50
Site 17541: metalwork, 48
Site 17542 (Hockwold Heath): lithics, 87
Site 24866 ('site 8'), 11–15, 26, 28
    animal bone, 157, 171–4 (Figs 110–12; Table 16)
    lithics, 51, 53, 58–9 (Figs 31–3), 63, 78–9 (Figs 44–5)
    pottery, 104, 105, 117–18, 119–22 (Figs 72–5)
    worked bone, 158 (Fig. 106)
Hockwold Fen
    pottery, 106
    Site 5381: metalwork, 43
    Site 12434: pottery, 152, 153 (Fig. 102)
    Site 24837, 24, 27 (Fig. 16)
Hockwold Heath: lithics, 53, 87
Honington, (S), 177
hunting, 172, 180
Hurst Fen, Mildenhall, 28, 51

Ipswich-Colchester area, pottery, 117, 177
Isleham Fen, (C): metalwork hoard, 47

Kelling Heath, 27
Killelen, Islay, Argyllshire, 117
kilns, 105

Lakenheath Fen, 42
Lark valley, 178
Lawford, (E): pottery, 63
Lingwood Farm, Cottenham, (C), 178
lithics, x, 11, 16–17, 19 (Fig. 6), 22 (Fig. 10), 24 (Fig. 13), 27, 62 (Table 11), 64 (Fig. 34), 72 (Fig. 42), 178, 180
    catalogue, 78–94 (Figs 44–60)
    industries, 181
    terms used, 75–7
    amber, 51, 74
    arrowheads, 51, 61 (Table 8), 75, 180
        barbed and tanged, 60, 63, 68 (Fig. 38), 74
        Ballyclare forms, 60, 63
        chisel, 60, 66 (Fig. 36), 74
        Conygar Hill forms, 60, 63
        Green Low forms, 60, 63
        leaf, 33, 37–8, 60, 65 (Fig. 35), 74, 162, 178
        oblique, 60, 67 (Fig. 37), 74
        petit tranchet, 63
    axe-hammers, 53, 62, 74, 180
    axes, 51, 61–2 (Table 10), 63, 70–1 (Figs 40–1), 74, 75, 180
        flaked, 60, 74
        ground flint, 74
        jadeite, 51
        stone, 17, 28
        tranchet, 60
    battle-axes, 62, 74, 180
    beads, 41, 51, 62, 74, 75
    blade cores, 53, 60
    blades, 53, 60
        long blade industries, 53, 63
        serrated, 60
    borers, 60
    bracelet, 62
    buttons, 51, 62, 74, 75
        stone/jet, 53
    'Cissbury type' implements, 74
    cores, 53, 54 (Table 6), 60, 61, 62, 74
        keeled, 60
    daggers, 60, 63, 74, 75, 180

denticulate, 60
'fabricator', 51, 53
fine and exotic, 180, 181
flake tools, 61
flaked quartzite pebble, 53
flakes, 16, 53, 60, 61, 62–3
   unretouched, 53, 56–7 (Figs 28–30), 63
flint flakes/pebbles, 30
flint scatters, 41, 177
grooved sandstone block, 53
hammerstone, 62
hand-axes, 53
jet, 41, 47, 51, 53, 74, 157
knives, 33, 60, 61 (Table 9), 69 (Fig. 39), 75
   discoidal, 60, 63, 74, 75, 180
   plano-convex, 60, 63, 74, 75
   retouched scale-flaked, 63
   scale-flaked, 51, 60, 75, 81
Levallois-like technique, 53
maceheads, 53, 74, 180
microliths, 60
necklace, jet, 41
ornaments, 51, 62
Parrott collection, 60, 87, 88
pebble-hammers, 60, 74
petrological identifications, 51–2 (Table 3), 61
picks, 74
raw materials, 50–2, 53, 54 (Table 4)
retouched pieces, 55 (Table 7)
saddle querns, 51, 53, 62, 73 (Fig. 43), 74, 179
scrapers, 17, 27, 37, 51, 53, 60, 63
   flake, 58–9 (Figs 31–3)
   'thumbnail', 60, 63
shaft-hole implements, 62, 74, 75
sickles, 74, 75
'sponge-fingers', 74
struck flint, 16, 23, 26, 27, 28, 50, 51, 53, 61, 105, 179
tranchet tools, 74
waisted tools, 60, 74
wristguards, 62, 74, 75, 157
Little Ouse, River, 1, 9
lithics, 50, 51, 75
metalwork finds, 48
Little Ouse valley, 11
geology, 7
lithics, 60
pottery, 178
Littleport, (C), 9, 41–2
longbows, 161

Mary Rose: human bone, 168
Maxey, (C), 180
metalwork, x, 19, 44–6 (Figs 23–5), 181
Middle/Late Bronze Age, 177
catalogue, 48–50 (Fig. 26)
deposition of, 181
modes of discovery, 47 (Table 2)
awls, 30, 37, 43
axes, 48, 160
   flanged, 43
   socketed, 43, 48
cauldrons, 30, 43, 48, 160
chisel, 43
Clouston collection, 43
daggers, 43, 48
dirks, 43, 47, 48, 181
   'ceremonial', 48
Ewart Park phase, 43
Feltwell Fen hoard (Site 5295), 43, 47, 62
flesh-hooks, 30, 43
goldwork, 43
gouges, socketed, 43
halberds, 43, 48
knives, 43
lead beads, 37
ornaments, 47, 48

foil, 43
palstaves, 41, 43, 48
Penard phase, 30, 43
rapiers, 41, 43, 47, 48, 181
razor, 43
sheet lead, 37
spear ferrule, 43
spearheads, 43, 47, 48
   'ceremonial', 48
Stoke Ferry hoard (Site 4725), 43, 48
swords, 43, 48, 50 (Fig. 27), 181
tools, 48
torc, 43, 47
weaponry, deposition of, 47–8
Wilburton phase hoard (Isleham Fen, (C)), 47
Methwold, 1, 3, 41
lithics, 51, 93 (Fig. 59)
pottery, 117, 156 (Fig. 105)
Catsholm
   metalwork, 48
   Site 2534, 41
   human bone, 162, 167
   Site 2537, 47
   Site 2540, 47
Catsholm House, 43, 48
Poppylot, 9
Queen's Ground, 7–9
Whiteplot, 106, 156
Site 2549: human bone, 162, 167
Site 2550 (Hemplands Farm) *see*
Hemplands Farm, Methwold Hythe
Site 2585, 30, 38, 39, 41
   human bone, 162–3, 165 (Pl. XI), 168, 169
   worked bone, 160 (Fig. 108)
Site 2586: 'Nancy' ('the Southery Fen female'), 30, 39, 43, 62
Site 4460: Methwold bow, 161 (Fig. 109), 175–6 (Fig. 113)
Site 4738: lithics, 53
Site 4874: metalwork, 50
Site 5233: lithics, 62
Site 5235/c13–14: pottery, 106
Site 5245/c7: lithics, 88
Site 5307: lithics, 53
Site 21967: human bone, 162, 167
Site 29346: worked antler, 157
Methwold Fen: dietary reconstruction, 171
Methwold Hythe
pottery, 106
Site 2531/c1, 28, 106
Site 4844, lithics, 60
see also Hemplands Farm
Methwold Severalls (Site 2542), 36–7, 38 (Fig. 21), 39, 41
   human bone, 162, 166–7 (Pl. XII), 168, 169
   lithics, 60, 85, 88 (Fig. 54)
   metalwork, 43, 48
   pollen analysis, 175, 179
Micklemoor Hill, West Harling, 178
microwear analysis, 158
Middle Harling, Norfolk, 177
Mildenhall Fen, (S), 28
   animal bone, 9
   antler objects, 157
   pottery, 105, 112, 179
   vegetation, 9
   worked bone, 158
Mildenhall, (S)
   palaeo-ecological studies, 175
   Swale's Fen, 179
   see also Fifty Farm; Hurst Fen; West Row Fen; Wilde Street
Milston, Wiltshire: cremation, 157
molluscs: Later Neolithic/Early Bronze Age evidence, 7
Montelius II, 43
monuments, Neolithic, 180

'Nancy' ('the Southery Fen female') *see*
Methwold (Site 2586)
Newark Road, Fengate, (C), 62, 117
North Elmham: Spong Hill, 63, 179
Northwold, 1, 41, 60

Old Decoy: peat growth, 7
ovens, 27 (Fig. 16), 28, 105
Oxborough Fen, 48

Park Farm, Witton, 75
Peacock's Farm, Shippea Hill, (C), 1, 28
   peat growth, 7
   pottery, 117
   vegetation, 9
peat
   formation, 175
   growth, 7–9, 28
Plantation Farm, Shippea Hill, (C), 1, 28
   animal bone, 9
   lithics, 63
   post-fen clay, 9
   pottery, 117
   stratigraphy, 178
pollen analysis, 37
   Hockham Mere, 7
   Methwold bow, 161, 175–6 (Fig. 113)
   Methwold Severalls, 175, 179
   Methwold (Site 2546), 30
   and peat growth, 7
   upper peat, 180
Poppylot, Methwold, 9
'pot-boilers'
   Feltwell, 28, 41, 61, 161, 179
   Hockwold, 12, 16, 17, 23
   and settlement, 179
pottery, 20 (Fig. 7), 22 (Fig. 11), 25 (Fig. 14), 95–156
   Neolithic
      Early, 117
      Later, 105, 106, 108 (Fig. 68), 177
   Bronze Age, 12, 13, 15, 16, 17, 19, 23, 26, 27, 28, 41, 53, 95, 99, 104–5, 106, 112, 157, 177
      Early, x, 28, 33, 48, 99, 105, 106, 112
      Middle, 177–8
      Late, 7, 27, 105, 177–8
      distribution, 111 (Fig. 71)
      urn styles, 63
   Iron Age, 27
      Early, 7, 27, 105, 178
   Romano-British, 26, 27
   catalogue, 117–56 (Figs 72–105)
   chronology, 112, 113–16 (Table 13)
   composition, 95–8 (Table 12; Fig. 61)
   decorative techniques, 101–3 (Figs 64–6), 104
   flat-based, lugged pot, 33
   grogged, 41
   morphological characteristics, 100 (Fig. 63)
   rim diameters, 99 (Fig. 62)
   styles, 180
   TYPES
      Beaker, x, 6, 11, 12, 17, 23, 27, 28, 29, 41, 63, 95, 102–4 (Fig. 66), 105, 112, 177, 178, 179
      Middle style, 16, 17, 19, 104, 105, 106, 112, 117, 157, 177, 181
      Late style, 15, 16, 17, 19, 26, 28, 33, 38, 41, 43, 48, 62, 63, 95, 104, 105, 106, 112, 117, 174, 177, 181
      All-over-cord decoration, 106, 117
      distribution, 109 (Fig. 69)
      European Bell, 104, 106
      fine and rusticated, 13, 15, 26, 99
      function of, 180–1
      rusticated, 11, 12, 16, 28, 41, 102, 104, 112, 181
      trade in, 117

Biconical Urn, 9, 17, 95, 99, 104, 105, 106, 112, 117, 177, 178, 179
Bowl, plain, 106
Collared Urn, 95, 99, 104, 106, 117, 157, 177, 179
    distribution, 110 (Fig. 70)
Deverel-Rimbury, 105, 112, 177, 178
Food Vessel, 16, 33, 41, 63, 95, 99, 104, 105, 106, 112, 117, 177
    distribution, 110 (Fig. 70)
Food Vessel Urn, 16, 17, 104, 117, 177, 178
Grimston Ware, 106, 117, 178
Grooved Ware, 28, 60, 63, 106, 117, 157, 174, 177, 180
    Durrington Walls substyle, 106
    Woodlands substyle, 105
Mildenhall Ware, 99, 106, 178
Neolithic Bowl, 16, 17, 23, 27, 28, 62, 63, 95, 99, 105, 106, 107 (Fig. 67), 177, 178
Peterborough Ware, 28, 106, 117, 177
Trevisker tradition, 117
Pymore, (C): vegetation, 9

Queen's Ground, Methwold, 7–9

Redgate Hill, Hunstanton, 63, 179
Redmere, (S), 9, 177
ring-ditches, 180
Risby, (S): Early Bronze Age burials, 157
Risby Warren, South Humberside, 117
roddons, 9
round barrows, 41
rubbish/debris from settlements, 179
Rudston monument complex, east Yorkshire, 180

Shaugh Moor, Devon, 112, 117
Shippea Hill, (C)
    pollen spectrum, 30
    'Shippea Hill Man', 41, 181
    see also Peacock's Farm; Plantation Farm
Shippea Hill Farm, Littleport, 41–2, 117
Shrubhill, Feltwell: lithics, 51, 53, 61
Sluice Drove *see* Hockwold cum Wilton (Site 5394)
snail shells, 30

Snailwell, (C): burials, 157
Soham Fen, (C), 41
Southery, 1, 62
    geology, 7
    and Hilgay island (Site 17103): pottery, 178
    lithics, 51
    Site 2567, 41
    Site 13454: lithics, 88
'Southery Fen female' ('Nancy') *see* Methwold (Site 2586)
Spong Hill, North Elmham, 63, 179
Staines: causewayed enclosure, 180
Stanwell: monuments, 180
Stoke Ferry
    Site 2523, pottery, 106
    Site 4725, metalwork hoard, 43, 48
Stoke Ferry Fen, 41
Stonea, (C), 178, 180
Storey's Bar Road, Fengate, (C), 62
Swale's Fen, Mildenhall, 179

textiles, 158
Thames, River, 47, 180, 181
Thetford: Fison Way, 7, 112, 178
Thorny Down, Wiltshire: Deverel-Rimbury industries, 63
topography, 10, 47, 60
turbary, 11
vegetation
    botanical evidence, 180
    brackish conditions, 9
    carr, 9
    charred plant remains, 7
    Feltwell Common, 9
    fen carr, 177
    plant macrofossils, 23
    pollen, 37, 179
    reed, 39
    reedswamp, 9
    sedge, 39
    sedge fen, 9, 177
    see also cereals; woodland

Waterhall Farm, Chippenham, (C), 38
Weasenham All Saints: pottery, 105
Weasenham Lyngs, 179

Weeting with Broomhill, 1
    lithics, 60, 94 (Fig. 60)
    Site 5587 (West Fen): lithics, 88
    Site 5596: lithics, 60
    Site 5599 (Fengate): lithics, 88
    see also Grime's Graves
Welney Washes, (C), 9, 177
West Harling, 178
    Micklemoor Hill, 178
West Row Fen, Mildenhall, 41
    botanical evidence, 180
    cereal remains, 179
    pottery, 117, 179
    settlement, 177, 179
    worked bone, 158
West Water Reservoir, Peeblesshire, 37
Whitedyke Farm *see* Feltwell (Site 5294)
Whiteplot *see under* Methwold
Wilburton Fen hoard, 178
Wilde Street, Mildenhall, 117, 158
Wilton Bridge, Hockwold cum Wilton, 7
Wilton Hill (Site 5303), 53
Windmill Hill-Avebury, Wiltshire, 180
Witton, North Walsham, 112
wood
    longbows, 161
    Methwold bow, 161 (Fig. 109), 175–6 (Fig. 113)
    shaft-hole, 160
    skeleton laid on, 36 (Fig. 20), 37 (Pl. VIII), 39, 160
    trough, 179
    yew, 161, 176
Wood Fen, (C): vegetation, 9
Wood Hall, Hilgay Fen, 41, 181
woodland/forest, 11, 28, 172
    alder carr, 9
    bog 'oaks', 9
    clearance, 7, 180
    conifer, 10
    deciduous, 7
    development of fen, 177
    lime, 7, 9
    oak, 9
    reduction in cover, 178
    transition to wetter conditions, 37
    wood charcoal, 26

Coláiste na hOllscoile Gaillimh

Coláiste na hOllscoile Gaillimh